An Idea Betrayed: Jews, Liberalism, and The American Left

Juliana Geran Pilon

An Idea Betrayed:
Jews, Liberalism, and The American Left

Juliana Geran Pilon

Academica Press
Washington ~ London

Library of Congress Cataloging-in-Publication Data

Names: Pilon, Juliana Geran, author.
Title: An idea betrayed : jews, liberalism, and the american left / Juliana Geran Pilon
Description: Washington : Academica Press, 2023. | Includes bibliographical references and index.
Identifiers: LCCN 2023933051| ISBN 9781680538281 (hardcover) | ISBN 9781680538304 (paperback) | ISBN 9781680538298 (ebook)

By the same author:

Notes from the Other Side of Night

The Bloody Flag: Post-Communist Nationalism in East-Central Europe – Spotlight on Romania

Why America is Such a Hard Sell: Beyond Pride and Prejudice

Soulmates: Resurrecting Eve

The Art of Peace: Engaging a Complex World

The Utopian Conceit and the War on Freedom

Cover photo: Detail from Hanukkah lamp designed by Manfred Anson (1922-2012) to mark the centennial of the Statue of Liberty in 1986. Anson, who escaped Nazi Germany as a teenager, later reunited with family who had immigrated to the United States. The lamp is located in the National Museum of American History.

For my parents Charlotte and Peter Geran of blessed memory, fortunate survivors of the Holocaust in Romania, with gratitude for having defied the Communist regime's prohibition against celebrating Passover; and after seventeen years of waiting for permission to emigrate, finally bringing our family to this great country. They are always with me.

May the same wonder-working Deity, who long since delivering the Hebrews from their Egyptian Oppressors planted them in the promised land—whose providential agency has lately been conspicuous in establishing these United States as an independent nation—still continue to water them with the dews of Heaven and to make the inhabitants of every denomination participate in the temporal and spiritual blessings of that people whose God is Jehovah.

George Washington to the Hebrew Congregation in Savannah, Georgia, June 14, 1790

The Citizens of the United States of America have a right to applaud themselves for having given to mankind examples of an enlarged and liberal policy: a policy worthy of imitation. All possess alike liberty of conscience and immunities of citizenship. It is now no more that toleration is spoken of, as if it was by the indulgence of one class of people, that another enjoyed the exercise of their inherent natural rights.

George Washington to the Hebrew Congregation in Newport, Rhode Island, August 18, 1790

Flash forward to the 1960s, when Jews were both agents and beneficiaries of the civil-rights movement that finally extended the legal promise of America to all its citizens.... American Jews have been no doomsaying Daniels at Belshazzar's feast but equal partners in this great experiment, and we bear our share of responsibility – no more and no less – for the Republic whose benefits we reap. If America fails us, it fails itself, but the failure is equally ours.

Ruth R. Wisse, "Is the Writing on the Wall for America's Jews?"
Mosaic, ***August 8, 2022***

The risk of woke ideology is not, of course, limited to the spread of antisemitism. It is a fundamental threat to the liberal idea in America. ...In my judgment, the role of the Jew is not to join forces with the ideological fads of the day, but to stand up for independent thought and the liberal principles on which the democracies of the world were founded.

Natan Sharansky, Foreword to **Woke Antisemitism** ***(2022)***

Contents

Introduction:

"Not like the brazen giant"

The sevenfold rays of broken glass
Over thy sorrow joyously will pass,
For God called up the slaughter and the spring together,
The slayer slew, the blossom burst, and it was sunny weather!
- Hayyim Nahman Bialik, "The City of Slaughter" (1903)

None of us slept on the way over from Paris. And not just because of the menacing rumblings of the wabbly propeller (actually, not bad for 1962) that could keep awake the deaf, let alone a bunch of Jewish immigrants praying they would be spared forty years in the wilderness - most didn't have that much time left. The majority were from Romania, though others hailed from as far as Morocco, and who knows where else. But all of us, all night, did what Jews do best: worry.

It was the usual Semitic sort of worry, a mixture of hope and fear. Above all, hope: that in this fancy New World, which none of us had ever seen, we might be treated like everyone else, as equals. Fear too: that we would indeed be so treated, despite having next to no assets besides ill-fitting clothes. Our skills were largely obsolete, and most of us could speak no English. Well, so be it; no whining, get with the program.

Sure, we were equal before God. That much we didn't doubt; we were Jews after all, even if our identity came mostly by osmosis, as much culturally-imbibed as visceral. But we had heard that we really would be equally treated by laws that applied to everyone, at least theoretically. OK, maybe; but what about in practice? Would this island-continent prove, in the end, as forbidding to us as a desert? We didn't even have a Moses to assure us that, God willing, it will all work out. Besides, even if God willed it, it was now up to us, which wasn't all that comforting. Anyway, who's worried about forty years when you don't even have forty cents.

Perhaps if we had glimpsed that Statue of Liberty everyone talked about, the Deity of Diaspora, we might have felt a little better. Unfortunately, it was hard to spot from an airplane, especially above the clouds. In any event, could we have believed her promise, inscribed on the plaque at her feet, that all of her homeless, tempest-tossed children would be truly welcome? Ragged as we were?

Maybe it would have helped to know that its words had been penned by a young poet, Emma Lazarus, who had also been Jewish, indeed descended from the very first group of Hebrews to settle where we had landed, albeit three centuries earlier, in 1654. They had been fleeing from Brazil, where they had settled after expulsion from Portugal and, earlier still, from Spain (as it happens, alongside my father's ancestors - who had headed East instead). Those twenty-three peripatetic descendants of Jacob, who had wavered off course into New rather than Old Amsterdam (toward which they had been headed), were eventually, if reluctantly, allowed to stay. A mere two centuries or so later, their Emma would become a famous poet! So if they, equally destitute, had survived and even thrived, why shouldn't we?

Our plane was approaching Manhattan, revealing a surreal skyline against the sunniest June day we had ever seen before or, I daresay, since. Were we awake, alive, sane? Could those obelisk-shaped objects be real buildings, or were we hallucinating? The rumbling grew to an apocalyptic roar, the huge rip of unfolding wheels announcing the jolt of descent - heart-stopping, had our hearts not already stopped, in mid-breath. We remembered to exhale, then emerged, dazed, into the light, a burning bush in the pit of our stomachs. Was it the heartburn of being reborn, absent an umbilical cord?

Reborn we had to be. And so we proved to be, my little family, indeed with astonishing rapidity. It didn't have to take forty years to get used to not being a slave if you had never really been one. Because thanks to my parents' good sense, we had somehow kept our wits about ourselves during all those years under communism.

Though clearly risky if it had been discovered or even suspected, it actually hadn't been that hard to see through the clumsy attempts by the mandarins of the Communist Party to camouflage their naked overfed bellies. Their ill-fitting ideological suits ready-made in Moscow, one-size-fits-all, were too obviously transparent. But even the stupidest little girl knew to keep her trap shut: there was no point in pointing out the imperial nudity so patently manifest. That had been her nursery school lesson number one. (Also numbers two and three.)

The little girl wasn't so stupid as not to notice how her parents used the never-read newspapers only as toilet paper, nor how they listened intently to a barely audible radio broadcast after they thought her asleep. And how they would tell their friends jokes in a whisper, believing she couldn't overhear. True, she didn't get the punchline; but she knew better than to ask questions when there would be no answers.

More puzzling was grandma's Friday night ritual of candle lighting. As she draped her always-neatly combed hair in a gossamer-thin scarf, and whispered some mysterious incantation while circling lovingly above the lights, why did tears fall softly on her face? Was this *her* way of asking questions? Maybe it was her way of getting answers.

Until the answers stopped. A few months after we had arrived in America in June, the children she had not seen in four decades would make it clear it was far too late for her. Then her tears merely accompanied her *kaddish*: for the relatives sent to Auschwitz who were never mentioned, and for the severely paralyzed adult son for whom she had cared for over three decades, who had died in Paris on our way over from Romania. Before long, she would melt into the darkness that long ago claimed all the dreams she barely dared to have.

The Mother of Exiles, as Emma Lazarus called the secular goddess of Liberty, couldn't keep the promise she made to all those who washed up on its shores. In truth, it wasn't really a promise so much as a nod to go ahead and wash up. In my grandmother's case, the tide had already receded by the time she reached us in America, a few weeks after our own arrival; we scooped her up as best we could, but her wings had been torn long ago, even if she didn't know it then. She died a few short years after arriving in the United States, a shadow of herself.

As for the rest of us, we had to be ready as soon as we could, to exercise our newfound "liberty." Whatever that meant; we didn't really know. The main problem with growing up under communism is that you can never take words at face value but have to read between lines, and you couldn't be sure you got it right, since the official lexicon had to be translated by unorthodox, underground, mostly silent methods. To cite but a few examples:

Democracy: everyone must vote. Not-voting, abstaining, and write-ins are treasonous, subject to unimpeachable and (obviously!) unappealable discretion.
Dictatorship of the proletariat: dictatorship.
Equality: inequality.
Equality: nonexistent except under socialism/communism/people's democracy.
Peaceful coexistence: voluntary disarming of non-Communist regimes so militarily superior Communist countries would have an easy time of it when liberating their lucky inhabitants.
Liberation: Communist takeover.
Cosmopolitan: Jewish.
Trotskyite: Jewish.
Jewish: a nationality; not a religion.
Religion: under socialism/communism, none.
Religion: opium of the people.
Fascist: anti-Communist.
Racist: anti-Communist.
Capitalist: anti-Communist.
Truth: what the Party says it is.
Falsehood: what the Party doesn't want to be said.
Enemy of the people: whoever party leaders want to get rid of.
Trial: a spectacle to fool Communist sympathizers in the West into imagining that not all the accused are already known to be guilty.
Trial by jury: a strictly Western charade.
Communist economics: an oxymoron.

I did know that words are no laughing matter. They can do much more than turn reality on its head - they can actually change flesh to ashes. Slippery things, words, if you look at them closely. Take allegories with their deceptive simplicity. For example, when the Mother of Exiles beckons all those "yearning to breathe free," who is she addressing? The nearly choking who want to breathe *anything*, or merely those looking for cleaner air? Some of the former may have only the vaguest idea what oxygen ***is***, let alone how much of it they needed. We weren't quite in that situation, but close enough. And what is she promising? At least she might not turn us away – which is more than Europe's Jews could say when the alternative was crematoria. What did seem clear to me was that the yearning itself is a powerful enough impulse for human beings to risk almost everything.

Not knowing what would await us, our little delegation of freedom-seekers had modest goals: we wanted to live anew, join the near-mythical country that seemed willing to give us a chance, and we would gladly do our best to justify the privilege. We implicitly pledged to link our various histories, habits, and hopes with those of people we would soon call neighbors and compatriots. We would thus effectively become the latest adoptees of the American family, themselves descendants of the self-orphaned.

It was easy for us to be part of a people who had declared the God-given right to liberty as self-evident in what they called a Declaration of Independence. That parchment, signed by men who risked being hanged for treason on its account, represented a covenant (in Hebrew, *brit*) with the Creator, whose protection in turn was conditioned on their own rightful actions. It was, one might say, in our biblically conditioned bones.

But oh, there was so much we didn't know. We didn't realize, for example, to what extent America's Founders had indeed been informed by the Hebrew Bible. Considering themselves to have been chosen to be free, they were determined to keep that freedom, believing themselves to have been entrusted with a sacred responsibility. The Declaration of Independence, either preempted or later echoed by the state constitutions, was ultimately enshrined in the nation's birth certificate, the U.S. Constitution. Which turned out to be both very short and remarkably easy to read even two centuries later. America considered itself at the outset to be a creedal nation in the biblical tradition, with the potential to attempt once again to respect all humans as equally unequal.

That creed, unfortunately, is increasingly under attack. Alongside an increasingly vocal and virulent anti-Americanism the academy and the media, antisemitism has risen as well, hardly by coincidence. Disguised as anti-Zionism, it has found resonance among Jews themselves; so what should we expect from the surrounding culture? Having first landed in this country a lifetime ago – ten decades, to be exact – I am appalled to see many of my friends giving up on America, afraid of escalating antisemitism. I share Ruth Wisse's dismay, as well as her admission that

> [e]verything about the upsurge of anti-Jewish politics in the United States troubles me: the role of universities, media, and cultural elites in abetting anti-Zionism, the successor and incorporator of anti-Semitism; the organization of grievance brigades against the allegedly privileged Jews; the ease with which the Arab and Islamist war against the Jewish people has found a home on the left; the electability of known anti-Semites to government; the lone shooters who choose Jews for their targets; the underreported street attacks on visible Jews; and the timidity and stupidity of some American Jewish spokesmen in response to all this aggression.

And then comes the clincher: "It wasn't the escalation of anti-Jewish activity that surprised me, but the idea that it's therefore time for Jews to give up on America altogether." Not only isn't it time but it would be deeply immoral, given how much we owe this amazing nation. But even more profoundly, it would amount to betraying our very essence as a liberal community. Yes, liberal. Not in the mutated, mendacious sense in which it has been used for nearly a century, but the original, biblical sense: that we are all created equal in God's image. We owe it to ourselves.

Rabbi Meir Soloveichik perfectly captures the role of Jews in helping "to make the case for the exceptional nature of this country for which Jews have always been grateful. The welcome that Jews received in America from the very beginning highlighted America's uniqueness, how its Founders revered the Hebraic tradition, and fused Lockean ideas with the covenantal thought they found in the Hebrew Bible, forging a worldview that saw Americans as endowed with individual rights but also bound in common destiny."[1] It is at bottom common sense - still the best defense against cant, lies, and attacks on simple faith in the goodness of creation.

Aren't most if not all the answers to life's greatest mysteries simple questions? A child knows as much, as did Rabbi Hillel in the first century BCE, who is reputed to have asked: "If I am not for me, who will be for me? And when I am only for myself, what am I? And if not now, then when?"[2] The effective protection of individual liberty, far from excluding empathy, presupposes it. Over the millennia, Jews have paid dearly for this insight. But they exemplify the human condition. "Because the Jewish struggle for freedom is always launched against political despotism," explains Harvard Professor emerita Ruth Wisse, now a distinguished fellow at the Tikvah Fund, "it benefits everyone else who truly clings to freedom."[3] Don't be fooled by words: the liberal idea is no mere ism. It is a way of life, and hope, and compassion.

Bethesda, Maryland, December 2022/5783

Chapter I:

The Liberal Idea in America

Defining "Liberal"

"Originally a liberal man was a man who behaved in a manner becoming a freeman, as distinguished from a slave."

- Leo Strauss, *Liberalism Ancient and Modern* (1968)

October 1962. Our family had celebrated exactly one year since we received the infamous postcard (on Yom Kippur!) stating flatly that, after a mere seventeen-year wait, we had been given permission to leave the Romanian workers' paradise. Also, it was four months since we had safely landed in Detroit, Michigan. We had many reasons for rejoicing. Our social worker - and instant friend - from HIAS, the Hebrew organization that helped immigrants settle in America, Ellen Rackway practiced her German with my father, who relished his first job, as salesman in a hardware store. It bothered him not a bit that his legal and economic education proved quite superfluous, for surely "every job is a blessing." In fact, he was elated: "What amazing gadgets there are here in America, you should see!" My mother meanwhile took up sewing for a delighted Hungarian and Romanian speaking clientele, but also Americans who marveled at her rapid progress in English.

And then, it happened: the Cuban missile crisis. Everyone learned from all the networks and newspapers that late that summer, the USSR had started construction of missile launch facilities on Cuban territory, perilously close to America's shores. What had prompted it? What did we still not know?

Our little family couldn't fathom that it might all end like this, in an Armageddon with no conceivable redemption. Back in the Workers' Paradise, hadn't it been impressed upon us, relentlessly and stridently, that the capitalist bloc led by the United States was constantly threatening the

Socialist world? Sooner or later, the rich and evil West was bound to attack the Paradise which, in turn, could not fail to defend itself.

But since the United States had not attacked, there was nothing to worry about. Unless, that is, American officials had believed Moscow's propaganda, becoming overly confident, and were caught unprepared. It certainly looked like Premier Nikita Khrushchev thought it unlikely that his actions, however bold, would encounter little if any pushback. But did that guarantee anything? Nothing said officially under communism could be trusted, obviously. I was not just worried but mortified, finding it impossible to sleep. My teachers were equally frightened, to say nothing of my fellow students. Each day seemed to us endless; possibly the end itself was nigh.

The United States government took a gamble, categorically refusing to make any concessions. Or so it seemed. Years later, we would learn that President John F. Kennedy's face-saving public bluster had been included in the bargain: behind the scenes, Kennedy had agreed to remove American missiles from Turkey, provided the matter stayed secret for another quarter century.[1] By then, he figured his political future would be safe. We didn't know then how real the danger had been - and thank heavens for that.

The young president may have inadvertently emboldened the Russian elite from the outset with his triumphalist rhetoric. Exhilarated with his unexpected victory over the seasoned Republican politician Richard Nixon, Kennedy had pledged at his inauguration, on January 20, 1961: "Let every nation know, whether it wishes us well or ill, that we shall pay any price, bear any burden, meet any hardship, support any friend, oppose any foe, in order to assure the survival and the success of liberty." The thundering applause confirmed what everyone knew: Americans loved hyperbole. Some, if not most, may have half-believed what was patently impossible: that anything can ever assure such a thing, let alone at "any price." The trouble was that from very high one can fall harder.

After the Cuban missile crisis, the country did fall hard: the care-free Fifties had come to an abrupt end. There would be no return to business as usual. A lingering sense of general insecurity irked this proudly insular country, having interrupted its citizens' pursuit of the happiness to which they assumed to be entitled. Americans were irritated by uncaused outside interference disturbing their highly prized peace of mind. The simplest cure being denial, the national post-traumatic shock disorder following those harrowing October days went largely unrecognized and hence left untreated.

Having just experienced the fright of their lives, they were relieved to have ducked the not-so-metaphorical bullet. The last thing they wanted was an escalation of conflict with an ideological enemy on the other side of the planet. This was particularly true of my contemporaries, whose attitude toward whatever was supposed to be "communism" did not deserve being called a "view," as it never rose beyond a general impression. They seemed to be parroting slogans. In 1963, my high school junior year, I was at a loss how to talk about any political matters.

And then, as I read Alexis de Tocqueville's *Democracy in America* in history class, a sliver of understanding emerged. This great-grandson of a guillotined aristocrat, who had witnessed in his own country the lethal power of crowds and the tyranny of slogans, had warned against the ability of an ideocracy in a democratic state like the United States "to supply a multitude of ready-made opinions for the use of individuals, who are thus relieved from the necessity of forming opinions of their own."[2] Meaning the media, the academy, in general the thought-elite, "ideocracy" is a term that Tocqueville would have welcomed. Political scientists Jaroslav Piekalkiewicz and Alfred Wayne Penn identify two kinds of ideocracy: one characterized by ideological monism, and another by pluralism, which permits the coexistence of multiple belief systems in a social order.[3] The former would seduce the intellectual heirs of the French egalitarians in America as well.

It was a century later, in 1935, when Sidney and Beatrice Webb defined ideocracies, meant to include theocracies, as "organized exponents of particular creeds or philosophical systems [which] have, in effect, ruled communities irrespective of their formal constitutions, merely by keeping the conscience of the influential citizens."[4] The word found an echo in the writings of the Russian philosopher Nicholas Berdyaev (1874-1948), when describing Russian communism, which resembles theocracy in that its idea-mongers are secular clergy, anointed by history. All ideocrats claim special knowledge that gives them authority over their lessers. Witness to the French Revolution and its bloody aftermath, Tocqueville had intimate knowledge of such elites, all too eager to "relieve" the multitudes from "the necessity of forming opinions of their own." The intellectual equivalent of ready-made clothiers, they provide one-size-must-fit-all intellectual straightjackets for the mind. Should anyone dare to dissent, the idea is eviscerated - if possible, even *in utero*.

I was appalled by the common slogans proliferating all around me, eerily reminiscent of my very recent past. Since learning English turned out to be easier than I had feared (thanks in part to the many Latin cognates adopted into this rich language), I was beginning to catch on to the political culture surrounding me. Alarm supplanted my confusion: I had thought that by emigrating we had escaped groupthink – or, more precisely, group*talk*. Perhaps it was only group-nonthink, but the effect was the same.

It saddened me. I knew my colleagues, most of them anyway, were smart - one or two were veritable geniuses. They were also invariably kind to me, friendly beyond expectation (especially in contrast to our experience in Paris, where even my little seven-year-old sister wasn't spared the ostracism reserved for *les etrangers,* notwithstanding her accent-less French learned in under three weeks). Far from xenophobic, Americans struck me as welcoming in the extreme, more intrigued than repelled by our foreignness, especially as most had never heard of our country of origin, as was usually the case with Eastern Europeans. (Even if Bucharest seemed to them vaguely familiar, it sounded far too much like Budapest, a confusion whose combustible pedigree would have been met with utter incomprehension.)

To my consternation, while I grew fonder of my new country with each passing year, my peers were traveling in the other philosophical and political direction. As the Vietnam War escalated, young men were desperately trying to avoid being drafted, often fleeing to Canada, their animus against evil, racist Amerikkka,[5] later abbreviated to Amerika, exponentially increased to the point of hatred. It soon became the prevailing narrative. Denunciations of USA as the great capitalist imperialist warmonger grew in direct proportion to radical sympathy for

Communist guerillas, which spread on campuses nationwide like wildfire. "What's wrong with people choosing communism?" was the question that would stop me in my tracks. How do you explain that while living under communism you had never met anyone, **anyone**, who would have "chosen" it?

My fellow-boomers were passionate and well-meaning, often personally and actively engaged supporters of civil rights for everyone, which struck me as wonderful and long overdue. Those who were old enough to do so traveled South to organize marches and help as best they could in the effort, sometimes at great risk. I appreciated their sincerity, and understood that the same empathy was being extended to the Vietnamese as to southern Blacks, who were perceived as similarly fighting against oppression. America's bombing of helpless peasants seemed too much like the police brutality in segregated Southern states. It was a plausible analogy.

Yet no amount of well-intentioned fervor can replace historical context and international perspective. It should be possible to empathize with suffering wherever it occurs, and seek the most appropriate remedy, without making things much worse, as generally happens when a complex situation is misunderstood. But hatred of America, exacerbated by a torrid love-affair with revolutionary rhetoric and paraphernalia, was increasingly skewing perception and leading to wildly inaccurate assessments of world events. Little did I know then that the cancer would spread, within a mere half century, gradually sapping its gullible host of lifeblood.

Even on my own campus, the University of Chicago of Great-Books-fame, raised fists started to proliferate alongside flower-power signs and peasant dresses. The rowdy youngsters called themselves radical, sported a torn-jeans-&-uncombed-hair look, and were generally high on something. They skipped class and listened to what passed for music that sought to compensate in decibels what it lacked in melody. Basically, I felt I was on the wrong planet.

I therefore did what any red-blooded brand-new-American would do: I repaired to Harper Library and sank my nose inside Plato and his footnotes.[6] Thankfully, most students continued to attend classes, so occasionally we would have those late-night conversations about education, the nature of reality, truth, etc., that had earned U of C the infamous America's Nerdiest College award (and "where fun goes to die"). But the moment the conversation veered to current affairs I would turn mute: I had neither the information nor the detachment needed to engage. Tears came to my eyes; I felt defeated.

Ordinary words were difficult enough to master, but the political culture required me to navigate amidst semantic landmines. What did party labels mean anyway? How could faceless government officials and my spacey colleagues all be Democrats? Many Americans accused others of treason. But weren't we all, in this fine country, on the side of Lady Liberty, which some called liberalism? Was that the right word? I was clueless. Not having the appropriate vocabulary even in my native language, I was equally tongue-tied and brain-tied. It was back to the proverbial drawing board.

Meaning, again, Harper Library. There I found Arthur Schlesinger, Jr.'s fortuitously titled *Liberalism in America* (1956), which proclaimed that "[i]n a sense all of America is liberalism." I had rather thought so. But what did it really mean? He explained:

> With freedom thus a matter of birthright and not of conquest, the American assumes liberalism as one of the presuppositions of life. With no social revolution in his past, the American has no sense of the role of catastrophe in social change. Consequently, he is, by nature, a gradualist; he sees few problems which cannot be solved by reason and debate; and he is confident that nearly all problems can be solved.[7]

Liberalism sounded about right for my money. But gradualism didn't seem overly popular at the time, at least not in my neck of the urban academic woods. Those around me who trumpeted their unquenchable outrage and rejected what they called "the system" were growing daily more numerous. They sought, or said they sought, Revolution, and relished vilifying President Lyndon Johnson along with his administration, with escalating furor. (There were no debating Republicans, assuming there were any around. Perhaps they were hiding somewhere in the stacks or just didn't care for campuses; I certainly never ran into one, as far as I could tell. Not until I met Roger, in graduate school. It was love at first argument: we both won.)

The hard-core radicals were ostentatiously not debating anyone, preferring to march, copulate, smoke, often all of the above, more or less simultaneously. Beer-soused and high, having given up on all parties of a political nature for the ear-drum-busting variety, they rejected what they called the Establishment and warned against trusting anyone over 30. It wasn't clear whether they themselves expected during the next decade to establish Paradise or overdose. If pushed to opt for an ism, they were likely to choose plain new anti-Americanism.

Two decades later, I learned why Schlesinger's definition confused me: my generation, wrote Allen J. Matusov in *The Unraveling of America* (1984), had witnessed "a disillusionment with liberalism."[8] All around me there had been a "great uprising against liberalism... by hippies, new leftists, black nationalists, and the antiwar movement." So I still had no understanding of what "liberal" meant.

Except vaguely, having remembered from my heavily ideologized middle school education some bourgeois political group called the National Liberal Party (NLP) mentioned in the satires of I. L Caragiale, Romania's Moliere. Somewhere I had found that it had been established in 1875 but dissolved after the country's ostensibly joyous so-called liberation by the Soviet Army. In a word, no arcane political factoid from my backwater native land where we all spoke in code would be of much use. No doubt about it: *la lettre* that had lodged uncertainly inside my wash-resisting brain *avant* my arrival to this – mercifully normal – country had to be entirely revisited.

I wasted no time; there was so much catching up to do. Starting with the presumption that "liberal" may describe a political party, had there ever been one in America? A few months after starting high school in Detroit, I learned that parties as such were not even mentioned in the United States Constitution. Called "factions," groups intent on pursuing their special interests were distrusted by the Founders, notably by James Madison, most famously in *Federalist #10.* Following the Baron de Montesquieu, a balance of power among various constituencies would be weaved into the fabric of the new republican experiment, an intricate texture blending local, county, state, and tripartite functional governments at all levels. If less than efficient, the result was superior in political legitimacy.

The Founders' answer to short-sighted pursuit of group special interests, then, was not to abolish them but to disperse their influence, preventing the accumulation of excessive power without denying the right of association. Let them duke it out, pitted against each another, diffusing the impact. No one expected representatives of such varied, multiple constituencies not to disagree, indeed passionately so. Disagreement is necessary for a society to be free, provided it does not lead to dismemberment and dissolution of the body politic itself.

Before long, however, from *pluribus* emerged - thank heavens not, as in dictatorships, *unum*, but second best – *duo.* Majoritarian electoral systems (technically called "first-past-the-post") eventually congeal into roughly two opposing camps. And so too in America two parties emerged almost from the outset: Federalist and Republican. The former stressed the centralizing, unifying forces of government necessary to a fledgling new nation to survive, while the latter worried about preserving local self-government. The two were in many ways complementary rather than contradictory, reflecting the healthy yin-yang of civil society. Fortunately, all tacitly accepted Benjamin Franklin's verdict, expressed upon signing the Declaration, that "we must all hang together, or we shall surely hang separately."

The party names evolved: a few more emerged, only to disappear or be absorbed, redefined, adapted to the times - an ever-changing mélange of interests reshuffled into Manichean conglomerates. Yet the opposing labels tended to denote not so much antithetical goals as different means of allocating government power. They represented different constituencies and political tribes. That everyone seemed to want good things, preferably paid by someone else, was simply how democracy works, or doesn't work, or works as well as may be expected.

Alas, liberalism's centrality to America's very essence notwithstanding, barely concealed under the surface lies a profound complexity. This is so even after setting aside the glaring elephant in the room, slavery. Some truths were less self-evident than they seemed. Schlesinger explains:

> The American political tradition is essentially based on a liberal consensus. Even those Americans who privately reject the liberal tradition - like the Communists of the '30's and '40's or the McCarthyites of the '50's - can succeed only as they profess a relationship to liberalism. They wither and die in a liberal society when their antiliberal purposes are fully exposed and understood. But this invocation of consensus does not perhaps tell the whole story. As historians of the '30's saw the American past too much in terms of conflict, so there is a danger that historians and political scientists today may see the past too much in terms of agreement.

Schlesinger's concluding observation, that "however much Americans have united on fundamentals, there still remain sharp and significant differences," would become an ever-greater understatement. All the more reason to look under the conceptual hood to examine the intellectual pistons powering the seemingly inexhaustible engine of this exceptional country. America was overwhelmingly liberal before it could call itself that; but whether invoking the term is itself proof of allegiance is anything but certain.

Exodus on the Rocks

"The eyes of all people are upon us; so that if we shall deal falsely with our God, we shall be made a story and a by-word through the world."
- John Winthrop, "Dreams of a City on a Hill," Nov. 11, 1630

It all started on November 11, 1630, when a small group of Englishmen, on their way to Plymouth Rock in today's Massachusetts, made the following vow: "[S]olemnly and mutually, in the presence of God, and one of another, [we] covenant and combine our selves together into a civil body politic." This entitled them "to enact, constitute, and frame such just and equal laws, ordinances, acts, constitutions and offices, from time to time, as shall be thought most meet and convenient for the general good of the Colony, unto which we promise all due submission and obedience."[9] It would forthwith define the nation's path: this had been America's Exodus.

In a speech now known as "City on a Hill," Reverend John Winthrop invoked this covenantal image:

> Thus stands the case between God and us: We are entered into a covenant with Him... [and if He] shall please to hear us... then hath He sealed our

> commission… but if we shall neglect the observation of these articles… [and] fall to embrace this present world… seeking great things for ourselves and our posterity, the Lord will surely break out in wrath against us. … [W]e must consider that it shall be as a city upon a hill. The eyes of all people are upon us; so that if we shall deal falsely with our God, we shall be made a story and a by-word through the world.[10]

No wonder the image became canonical. For it captured a genuine and serious commitment that went far beyond the Pilgrims, whose rediscovery of Old Testament language and sentiment was hardly unique. Partly as a result of the recent growth of Hebraic political studies, writes Haifa University Professor Eran Shalev, "we can now better appreciate that many European and Atlantic communities similarly felt themselves to be new Israels in the seventeenth century."[11] Calvinist colonists to North America, who frequently described themselves as the modern equivalent of Jews, outnumbered all other Christian denominations in the early years. The pioneer Pilgrims, writes Shalev, "introduced the 'chosen people' doctrine into the New World and viewed themselves as the successors of the Children of Israel."

A similar ritual would follow eight decades later, in 1701, when Pennsylvania Governor William Penn signed the state's "Charter of Privileges." Its first and principal commitment was to freedom of religion: "[B]ecause no People can be truly happy, though under the greatest Enjoyment of Civil Liberties, if abridged of the Freedom of their Consciences, as to their Religious Profession and Worship."[12] On the Charter's 50th anniversary, in 1751, that state's capital, Philadelphia, would erect a large Liberty Bell, inscribed with a verse that invoked the same biblical event as the Mayflower Compact, the great Exodus across the Sinai. Found in *Leviticus* 25:10, the words attributed to God were: "Proclaim Liberty throughout all the land unto all the inhabitants thereof." The previous phrase, known to all, needed no citation: "And ye shall hallow the fiftieth year…" Those assembled heard God speaking again - this time, directly to them.

The story behind the bell is remarkable, and as Rabbi Meir Soloveitchik observes, "is bound up with the unique story of American freedom, containing a profound lesson for our time." The consummate rabbi-raconteur tells the tale that began in 1701, when Pennsylvania's

Governor William Penn enshrined a Charter of Liberties guaranteeing freedom of conscience in his state. Providentially, Penn's agent in the region was James Logan, later mayor of Philadelphia.

> The historian Edwin Wolf describes how Logan "bought himself Hebrew Bibles and Hebrew prayer-books, and read them and made notes in them. When he was more fluent, he added a *Shulhan Arukh* and the great six-volume edition of the *Mishna* with the Maimonides and Bertinoro commentaries. In fact, Logan gathered together in Philadelphia in the first half of the eighteenth century one of the largest collections of Hebraica which existed in frontier America." Logan, Wolf explains, then taught Hebrew to his daughter Sally, whom he described as a child "reading the 34th Psalm in Hebrew, the letters of which she learned very perfectly in less than 2 hour's time, an experiment I made of her capacity only for my Diversion." Sally, in turn, married Isaac Norris, speaker of the State Assembly. Norris was a Hebraist in his own right...[13]

If this sounds like your uncle's joke that never ends, here's the punchline: "It was from this Hebraic household that the bell emerged. In 1751, Isaac Norris commissioned it from Whitechapel to mark the 50th anniversary of the Charter of Liberties. He chose to emblazon the bell with words from Leviticus, describing how every 50 years, indentured servants are freed..." Meir Soloveitchik concludes with congenital rabbinical eloquence:

> The bell embodies a people who, ever imperfect, ever exceptional, were inspired by the Bible to advance the cause of liberty on its own soil and throughout the world. In 2004, on the 60th anniversary of D-Day, the people of Normandy dedicated a near-exact replica of the bell and rung it over the cliffs of Normandy, with the original sound of the bell echoing over the cliffs of Pointe du Hoc. We cannot fail to see in this a reminder of our obligation to preserve the true tone of the bell, the Hebraic grammar of American liberty...

Though colonists had not literally been released from bondage, they hoped for greater freedom in the New Promised Land. The biblical passage citing the Almighty's vow to the Israelites fleeing Egypt that they would be able to return to their families to have their properties restored implied that the moral universe would be set aright, that life, liberty, and property, prerequisites for the pursuit of happiness, would be respected once again. A short half-century later, their fellow countryman John Locke (1632-1704) would find refuge in Holland to promote the same ideas.

But they harken far into the past: respect for private property is basic to Abrahamic monotheism. In the Jewish tradition specifically, the primary purpose of ownership of property is explained in the context of ethical human dominion over all creation. Man, explains Rabbi Joseph Isaac Lifshitz, "is enjoined to act responsibly in the material realm."[14] Responsibility is central to Jewish law; thus each person should be given an opportunity to exercise it. Generosity, moreover, is the highest virtue. As a result, property is a great good, and "its protection is a recurring theme in the Bible and the Rabbinic teachings. The significance with which the Torah[15] invests the right of ownership is evident in the numerous prohibitions pertaining to the property of others."[16]

Giving, of course, requires having something to give. Otherwise, without the ability to give, how will the soul be nourished?

Thou Shalt Not Covet

> *"If Jews did not glorify poverty, neither did they sanctify the attainment of wealth or value physical labor for its own sake.... The life of mitzvot (commandments) meant a style of life based on discipline, on the conscious planning of action...."*
>
> **- Jerry Z. Muller, *Capitalism and the Jews* (2010)**

Aside from behavioral commandments related to property, prohibiting theft and fraud, the Torah includes a crucial spiritual, imperative not to begrudge another's possessions. "You shall not covet your neighbor's house ... or his ox, or his ass, or anything that belongs to your neighbor," declares the Tenth Commandment (*Exodus* 10:14). The extraordinary power of this law cannot be overstated. It captures simply and profoundly the momentous ethical implications of the idea that every man is created in the Creator's (obviously inexpressible) "image": no one may legitimately take that which belongs to another free and clear. Rabbi Lifshitz continues:

> The Rabbinic tradition, as well, emphasized the gravity of acts that violate another's property, equating them with the destruction of the foundations of society.... The definition of ownership as complete dominion is a fundamental principle of Jewish law, the aim of which is to preserve the individual's dignity and sovereignty and to prevent any encroachment on his dominion over his small portion of the material world. ... Yet Judaism's affirmation of ownership does not end with the protection of property; in many places it also encourages the

accumulation of wealth. Economic success is considered a worthy aim, so long as one achieves it through honest means.[17]

But don't even "honest means" still leave plenty of room for rapacious, selfish, survival-of-the-fittest competition oblivious to the fallout? Not if one takes seriously the most important aspect of property possession acclaimed by the Hebrew Bible: charity.

The term itself did not exist in the Hebrew scriptures, where instead the closely related term *tzedakah* occurs 157 times. Typically used in relation to "righteousness" per se, usually in the singular, but sometimes in the plural, *tzedekot*, it refers to acts of charity. In *Exodus* 23:10-11; *Leviticus* 19:9-10; 23:22; *Deuteronomy* 24: 6-13, all books venerated by Jews and Christians alike, God is said to expect kindness to the defenseless, and display generosity, civility, and fellow-feeling through *tzedeko*t.

Thus the Jewish tradition takes the self as a starting point, both in order to turn it toward God and to encourage civic responsibility. Writes Lifshitz:

> In Judaism, the idea of charity focuses on the donor and his relationship with the poor, not on the recipient. Its aim is to cultivate a sense of responsibility, as a moral and religious obligation. For this reason, the rabbis maintained that the donor should favor his relatives over strangers: "When choosing between your own poor and the poor of the city, your own poor come first."[18] By giving to those for whom he feels a special obligation, the donor expresses his self-understanding as a unique individual who takes responsibility for those around him. This kind of giving also underscores the fact that we are talking not about an act of "justice," of satisfying the just claims of the poor against the wealthy but about an act of personal obligation stemming from his sense of responsibility for those around him. This is borne out by the fact that Jewish legal codes have always placed the laws of charity among religious duties (*isur veheter*), rather than civil law (*dinei mamonot*).[19] Although both categories are equally binding on the Jew, they are two separate worlds within Jewish law.

The commandment to contribute to the care of the poor is a key *religious* obligation in Judaism, both as a philosophy and a cultural-social tradition. In the words of the great twelfth century Jewish philosopher and physician, Rabbi Moses Maimonides: "We have never seen nor heard of a Jewish community that did not have a charity box." Of course, there is considerable difference between religious duties and civil law, which goes beyond the manner and source of coercion.

The purpose of religious charity has little if anything to do with social engineering. Specifically, religious duties not only may but must be fulfilled voluntarily, lest they lose spiritual meaning. This duty does not mean that rabbis could not authorize compelling members of a community to fulfill their (religious) obligations to the poor, lest they be ostracized. Maimonides, for example, has ruled: "He who does not want to give charity, or gives less than is proper, will be forced to do so by the rabbinical court," although Lifshitz explains that this type of coercion is "not restricted to the enforcement of charity." Rather, it "appears in other areas – always as an essentially pedagogical tool meant to bring a wayward individual back to the fold of the righteous."[20]

Admittedly not all pedagogues were equally effective. So too, appealing to divine exhortation was often met with limited pedagogical success, as illustrated by this anecdote: A rabbi was angry about the amount of money his congregants were giving to charity. One day, he prayed that the rich should give more charity to the poor. "And has your prayer been answered?" asked his wife upon his return from the synagogue. "Half of it was," replied the rabbi. "The poor are willing to accept the money." It's a start.

Their congregants' stinginess notwithstanding, rabbis recognized that forced charity is self-contradictory. Ultimately, the practice of giving is "not [seen] as a means of distribution and justice but as a way of enforcing a minimum level of moral and religious rectitude among its citizens. It is a moral corrective, not an economic one."[21] A pedagogical tool cannot act like a guillotine. A religious duty is not designed to limit one person's wealth and adding to another's, but to address a moral deficiency in oneself as well as in the community.

In this sense, a *religious duty* is at once self-oriented and other-directed, implicitly fusing self-interest and community welfare. But an individual's moral myopia constitutes a social disease that can only be cured by spiritual means. While spiritual solutions are far more difficult to implement, they alone can address spiritual problems, for they attend to the soul. By contrast, a *civil obligation* is merely an action required by law, enforced by state institutions. Compliance need be motivated by nothing other than avoidance of sanction - a singularly unpraiseworthy sentiment that reduces humans to fear-driven animals who happen to be speech-endowed.

Unlike a strictly secular means of guiding and enforcing social behavior, the biblical imperative to be charitable presupposes a moral universalism. Based on the premise that all humanity, the healthy and the sick, handsome and homely, talented and mediocre, rich and poor, dwell side by side before their Creator, each person is commended to make all possible efforts to minimize another's suffering. For in Judaism, as in Christianity, what ultimately matters is the quality of every man's spiritual health, whose expression is found in gratitude and sharing.

What Jews and Christians called charity approximated the Romans' *liberalitas*, but only up to a point. Derived from *liber*, meaning both free and generous, and *liberalis*, befitting a free-born person, the Latin noun was designed to denote being free primarily from the arbitrary will of a master, but also from domination by any man. Though it reflected generosity and magnanimity, *liberalitas* was nonetheless considered primarily a civic virtue, justified by its utility rather than on spiritual grounds. Unlike in Judaism, where its function was religious, for the Romans it was quintessentially secular. Though highly praised as a character trait, it was admired mainly for its salutary effects on the polis.

Writes City University of New York Professor Helena Rosenblatt:

> To the ancient Romans, being free required more than a republican constitution; it also required citizens who practice *liberalitas*, which referred to a noble and generous way of thinking and acting toward one's fellow citizens. Its opposite was selfishness, or what the Romans called "slavishness" – a way of thinking and acting that regarded only oneself, one's profits, and one's pleasures. In its broadest sense, *liberalitas* signified the moral and magnanimous attitude that the ancients believed was essential to the cohesion and smooth functioning of a free society.[22]

An eloquent description of *liberalitas* in Cicero's book *De Oficiis* ("On Duties"), written in 44 BCE, greatly impressed the fourth Chief Justice of the United States, John Marshall, who commended it to his grandsons as "among the most valuable treatises in the Latin language, a salutary discourse on the duties and qualities proper to a republican gentleman."[23] Cicero had written:

> [W]e ought to follow nature as a guide, to contribute our part to the common good, and by the interchange of kind offices, both in giving and receiving, alike by skill, by labor, and by the resources at our command, to strengthen the social union of men among men.[24]

Yet Cicero realistically cautioned that "a large number of persons, less from a liberal nature than for the reputation of generosity, do many things that evidently proceed from ostentation rather than from good will."[25] He considered generosity both in conformity with "nature" and indispensable to strengthening "the social union of men among men" – that is, civil society.

At the same time, Cicero, not unlike the Torah, underscored that generosity is fully compatible with a scrupulous respect for private property. "For the chief purpose in the establishment of cities and republics was that each person might have what belongs to him. For, although it was by nature's guidance that men were drawn together into communities, it was in the hope of safeguarding their possessions that they sought the protection of cities" (*On Duties*, 2.21.73)

Though no match for the Divine bestselling Author, Cicero became a pillar of Western civilization long before America's founding. "For nearly two millennia," writes historian Carl J. Richard, "every educated European and American read Cicero. Indeed, Cicero's very character, or rather idealized version of Cicero's character, became the model for future Western statesmen."[26] He certainly did for John Adams (1735-1826) who, in 1774, urged all aspiring politicians to adopt Cicero as their model. What had especially impressed Adams had been the orator's dedication to his country, even at great personal cost. He consciously molded his own career on that of his illustrious classical predecessor.[27]

Adams noted, for example, that in serving Rome, Cicero "did not receive this office as Persons do now a days, as a Gift, or a Farm, but as a public Trust, and considered it as a Theatre, in which the Eyes of the World were upon him."[28] This passage from Cicero's dialogue *De Legibus* ("On the Laws") particularly appealed to Adams: "Law ... is something eternal which rules the whole universe ... in agreement with the primal and most ancient of all things, Nature." (1.9.26; 1.12.34; 2.4.8) His American admirers two millennia later appreciated the pre-eminence accorded to law as "something eternal," and public service a sacred trust, not a benefit incurred through wealth.

Setting up a new political entity in an unwelcome climate, with virtually no resources, would have been impossible without strong commitment, confidence in their own personal abilities, trust in one another, faith in providential guidance, and a large dose of chutzpa. When they first set upon life together, avoiding the extremes of state-of-nature/state-of-war chaos on one side and tyranny on the other was for them no mere theoretical exercise. Unlike the flock that Moses led out of Egypt, the colonists constituted not one but many communities. Even if the Mother Country, or a colonial business enterprise such as the West India Company, did secure them a certain amount of protection, they were still strangers in a new land.

The colonists had had to lead themselves in many ways similar to the circumstances of the Hebrew emigrants. But there was one notable exception: they had no Moses. In fact, they faced a situation rather more akin to that of the Jews in the year 70, after the Romans devastated Jerusalem and sacked their Temple. During the ensuing centuries, the Jewish Diaspora would emerge as nothing short of a political miracle. Ruth Wisse has called it "one of history's boldest political experiments, an experiment as novel as the idea of monotheism itself, and inconceivable without it. … [Yet] Jews did not consciously plan to continue their national life outside the Land of Israel."[29] They were being forced to survive together outside a nation-state, trusting in the Torah and its laws as in biblical times, as God had urged them to do. It might have seemed providential had it not felt like punishment. Being tested by circumstances, they had to protect themselves. So they did.

Beware of Kingly Power

"*[T]he day will come when you cry out because of the king whom you yourselves have chosen; and the Lord will not answer you on that day.*"
- I *Samuel* 8:18

Fortunately, the Hebrews had their lodestar law. Indeed, they had been duly warned by their Father to worry less about not having a state and more about being oppressed by a *tyrannos*. It had been the prophet Samuel who delivered God's admonition to the Jews to dispense with kings, who tend to end up thinking themselves superior to their subjects. When

Samuel, tasked by the Israelites to inform God of their desire to be "like other nations," and allow them to have a king to protect them against enemies, God was sorely disappointed. Bemoaning their weakness, He tells Samuel: "Like everything else they have done ever since I brought them out of Egypt to this day – forsaking Me and worshiping other gods – so they are doing to you. Heed their demand; but warn them solemnly and tell them about the practices of any king who will rule over them." (*I Samuel* 8: 8-9)

According to the story, Samuel does as God instructed, cautioning the Jews against conferring too much power upon a strong ruler. He warns them to beware, for such a man will surely become drunk with power, seize their choice fields, vineyards, and olive groves for use by his courtiers, and do many other bad things just because he can. Without doubt, "the day will come when you cry out because of the king whom you yourselves have chosen; and the Lord will not answer you on that day." (I *Samuel* 8:18) Giving any man too much authority, thus effectively deifying a mortal, is tantamount to idolatry. It constitutes a tragedy for the people and tyrant alike.

The Jewish people's odyssey told in the Torah, at once story and proto-common law, serves as a guide to resolving ethical and moral dilemmas through example and deliberation. The complexity of biblical narratives, whose study became a virtual religious imperative, inevitably had the effect of turning Jews into debaters. Proficiency in comparative analysis, metaphorical and analogous thinking, and dialectic argument led to their achieving remarkable mental dexterity and acquiring unusual legal acumen. While the stories gained universal popularity primarily for their literary brilliance, the Torah's preeminence in Jewish life also brought profoundly practical benefits. The corollary of distrusting hubristic kings is learning and practicing morally sound principles on the part of all who can afford the time and energy.

Is it any wonder that reading and arguing became as natural for Jews as breathing? Writes Wisse: "No doubt Jews sometimes romanticize the importance of legal study in sustaining Diaspora life, yet it *was* the basis of their autonomous civilization.... The democratization of education instilled what we might call a 'constitutional culture' among not only the learned but all those who aspired to learning."[30] True, women came late to the yeshiva, but eventually they did as well; accusing the Torah of outright misogyny is thus to completely misunderstand it.[31]

In brief, parallels between the Hebrew and colonial communities are strikingly numerous. Like the Jews of Exodus and after the fall of Jerusalem, the Pilgrims had been equipped with solid commandments and were determined to survive, convinced of God's protection. Ordinary emigrants to the New World, like the Diaspora Jews far from home, representing a wide range of social and economic groups, displayed great interest in both the Bible and the law – specifically, the history of the English common law and its philosophical underpinnings. Also, just as the Jews sought practical direction in their difficult lives, what animated the colonists were not only ideas but pragmatic guidance and moral support. Above all, they yearned to know how their liberty - to live as they chose and not as others chose for them - which had prompted them to settle in new and alien surroundings, may be protected from the crushing power of men in authority who too easily usurped their office.

No historian has documented in more exquisite detail the "intellectual excitement of the pre-Revolutionary years" than Wisse's great Harvard colleague Professor Bernard Bailyn, particularly in his seminal 1967 book *The Ideological Origins of the American Revolution*. Fortunate son of Jewish parents who conspired to addict him to reading, they in turn "had an expert to advise them. Hartford's [Connecticut, where he was born] biggest and best bookstore, which once had sold books to Mark Twain, was then owned by a friend of theirs, Israel Witkower, an émigré from Vienna,"[32] explains Bailyn in his extraordinary intellectual autobiography, *Illuminating History: A Retrospective of Seven Decades*, published posthumously in 2020.

It is fascinating to learn what Bailyn found most striking as he prepared revisions for Harvard's commemorative 50th-year edition of *The Ideological Origins*: "[O]f all my impressions on re-reading the book, the most vivid by far is the Americans' obsession with Power." Specifically, "their central, overwhelming concern" was "power and its ravages," indeed

> power in its essence, in its nature, whatever its manifestation—as an autonomous entity, a dark, independent, primordial force, pervasive and malign. As such it could be described only in metaphors, similes, and analogies. Power, they wrote, however evoked, "is like the ocean, not easily admitting limits to be fixed in it." It is like "jaws ... always open to devour." It is "like cancer, it eats faster and faster every hour." And it is everywhere in public life, and everywhere it is dominating, grasping, and absorbing. Liberty, its opposite, could not strongly stand before it. For liberty, as John Adams put it, always "skulking about in corners ... hunted and persecuted in all countries by cruel power," was in its nature delicate and sensitive, weak in the presence of power.[33]

This was no Manichean antithesis, light versus darkness. The sensible colonists knew that power, albeit easy to abuse, is necessary in order to forestall chaos. History is replete with instances of power gone awry, power used arbitrarily by men who turned the people's trust into personal power, thereby destroying the very polity they purported to serve. The colonists were fascinated by historical analogues of empires – most shockingly, Rome, home of Cicero, whose once freedom-loving people tragically lost it, having failed to protect it. A similar fate appeared to await Britain, and for many of the same reasons. It was their job to rescue the cause of English – nay, human - liberty beyond the Atlantic. Their leaders looked to past ideas with great interest but not without skepticism, considering the longstanding record of civilizational failure. As the Old World was decaying, it was time to rescue its best values elsewhere.

If many, if not most, colonists were idealistic, some even millenarian, they were anything but starry-eyed utopians. Devotees of ancient wisdom, they valued the highest and rarest virtue: humility. Yet articulating the true nature of their sacred goal, "noble" liberty, proved a formidable task, they readily confessed, "to which no human mind is equal, for neither the sublimest wits of antiquity, nor the brightest geniuses of late or modern time, assisted with all the powers of rhetoric and all the stimulations of poetick fire . . . ever did, or ever could, or ever can, describe . . . sufficiently the beauty of the one [liberty] or the deformity of the other [power]. *Language fails in* [this] . . . *words are too weak.*"[34] So wrote the Radical Whigs in 1722, in their enormously popular pamphlet *Cato's Letters,* articulating the profoundly libertarian commitment of most colonists.

There had to be some sort of common principles enshrined in law, a constitution of sorts. In Britain, the "unwritten constitution" referred to "a loose bundle of statutes, common law, and sanctioned practices, without explicit boundaries."[35] Professor Bailyn explains why, given the highly diverse constituency and the urgency of the task, America's constitution had to evolve beyond that. So it

> emerges in the colonies as an articulated foundational structure of explicit powers and rights, "a thing antecedent to government" superior to and confining any subsequent enactments. "The balance of powers"— traditionally a balance of social orders or estates— emerged as a balance of functioning branches of government— though in some places and in some minds social orders had long been assumed to embody, in some fashion, functions of government, and in others the old concept for a time persisted.[36]

The colonists thus pressed by circumstance, and informed by their readings, managed to distil a centuries-old tradition of Anglo-Saxon practice into a parchment that became the most enduring of its kind in history. An entire web of effective civic associations in synergy with robust political engagement had paved the way. But equally important was the astonishingly sophisticated debate, which took place over the course of eleven months during 1787-88. Gathered into a 2,300-page volume,[37] Professor Bailyn describes the historic deliberation as nothing short of "epochal."

> **That famous debate has no parallel in the history of political thought.** It lasted for eleven months, involved twelve state conventions in which at least 1,500 official delegates participated directly. It reached into every town, county, village, and plantation in the thirteen states, and produced a flood of writings—speeches, pamphlets, correspondence, newspaper columns, and records of a torrent of oratory.[38]

How to create a stable nation in the face of a still dominant fear of government power seemed a daunting task. The main opposition had come from those who - "majorities in some states, vocal minorities in others— could never be satisfied with a document that created power but did not explicitly defend freedom. For 'the very idea of power,' Edward Rutledge declared, 'included a possibility of doing harm.' They demanded, if not a formal Bill of Rights, then its equivalent in enumerated liberties."[39]

Those liberties were understood to belong to all. Just as the most downtrodden Jew felt he could talk to God no less directly than could a rich man, so a humble colonist toiling on his farm refused to be treated with condescension by his own, let alone London's, officials, nor even by the King. Was he not as entitled to have his interests represented in Parliament as any other English subject? It's not as if he and his fellow colonists had not proven themselves capable of self-rule.

No one understood this better than Benjamin Franklin's old friend Edmund Burke, the celebrated foe of the French Revolution. The Irish-born Whig lawmaker and philosopher, impressed by the colonists' demonstrated ability for self-rule and fierce commitment to liberty, argued before his fellow members of Parliament in 1775, in favor of American independence: "In this Character of the Americans, a love of Freedom is the predominating feature which marks and distinguishes the whole: and as an ardent is always a jealous affection, your Colonies become suspicious, restive, and untractable, whenever they see the least attempt to wrest from them by force, or shuffle from them by chicane, what they think the only advantage worth living for."

But the most important determinant of the colonists' extraordinary performance and attitude, in Burke's estimation, was "their education. In no country perhaps in the world is the law so general a study."[40] The colonists were people of the books *par excellence.* Accordingly, they did what book lovers do best: they argued about ideas. As, famously, did the ancient Greeks before them, to say nothing of the Jews. As University of Tulsa Professor Jacob Howland has demonstrated in his captivating study *Plato and the Talmud*, "the dialectical character of rabbinic thought… [is characterized by a] preference for raising questions rather than furnishing answers, and by its open-ended, conversational forms."[41]

Like the Socratic conversations in the Academy founded by Plato in 5th century BCE, the colonists engaged in critical thinking. Yet they knew that, however necessary, reason hardly sufficed. Socrates, for example, citing the Delphi oracle as evidence for his claim of ignorance, implied having been "prepared from the outset to acknowledge the god's authority as a speaker of truth." Not unlike "the concept of the Oral Torah, this communication authorizes [Socrates's] philosophizing guaranteeing that his basic questions have answers, and thus that there is some meaningful truth that can in principle be discovered by inquiry."[42]

The plethora of learned citations peppering writings and speeches from those days, however, concealed their authors' limited acquaintance with the actual sources. Some mistakenly took Plato for a liberty-loving revolutionary, which the Academy's Founder was not quite. Even the erudite John Adams had cited the great Greek, in 1774, as an advocate of equality and self-government, by relying on secondary sources alone. Adams was reputedly so "shocked when he finally studied the philosopher that [he at first assumed] the Republic must have been meant as a satire."[43]

But the colonists did embrace Socratic dialogue. They looked for historical analogies, read their Old and New Testaments, sought guidance in legal discourse ranging from the Romans through the Christian classics, and scoured the English common law. They read as voraciously as men with day jobs could afford to do, with the classics enhancing their own reflections. Except that unlike mere academics, their task was urgent and practical. They could not afford to read uncritically. Explains Bailyn: the great books were "everywhere illustrative, not determinative, of thought. They contributed a vivid vocabulary but not the logic or grammar of thought, a universally respected personification but not the source of political and social beliefs."[44]

An excellent example is provided by the word "power" itself, which represented what they had to avoid, at great personal peril to themselves, their families, their community. Beyond the physical context, as in the power of earthquakes or floods, they worried about governing power: the state. Explains Bailyn: "The theory of politics that emerges from the political literature of the pre-Revolutionary years rests on the belief that what lay behind every political scene, the ultimate explanation of every political controversy, was the disposition of power."[45] Some powers are inevitable. A more precise word was needed to capture the main object of their concern.

For whatever advantages an analogy with the physical world may have provided for understanding human interactions, the intellectual architects of America's experiment sought a specific term that could better capture that which some men wielded over others through various types of force, compulsion, and authority. At last John Adams chose "dominion," and his "whole generation concurred," writes Bailin. "'Power' to them meant the dominion of some men over others, the human control of human life, [above all] its endlessly propulsive tendency to expand itself beyond legitimate boundaries."[46]

Dominion that disregards a person's agency altogether is tantamount to slavery. Which is just what many, if not most, colonists gradually came to feel in relation to the Mother Country. By the eighteenth century, Americans defined slavery as someone's power and control over another's "actions and properties." Far from mere rhetoric, explains Bailyn, the term referred "to a specific political condition, a condition characteristic of the lives of [many across the globe] …. The degradation of chattel slaves… was only the final realization of what the loss of liberty could mean everywhere."[47] The fact that such dominion over slaves imported from Africa by Southern states was not outlawed outright in the Constitution inevitably cast a sinister shadow over that historic document – and the Founders knew it. But at the time, they didn't think they had much choice.

Liberty in Practice: A Jewish Blueprint

"*What had been primarily an ideological expression of a grand theory became a fundament of culture, a shaper of institutions, and a major influence on political and other behavior.*"

- Daniel Elazar, *Covenant and Constitutionalism* (1998)

"*The voluntary nature of Jewish self-government [in exile] contrasted sharply with the largely feudal, autocratic, despotic, or tyrannical political arrangements of the surrounding nations.*"

- Ruth R. Wisse, *Jews and Power* (2007)

Over time, American liberty was defining itself, in practice. Like the Jews, who had demonstrated their communities' ability to regulate their own affairs not just by talking about it but by living it, so too the colonists first established and then managed effectively their budding proto-states: each had its own legislature, governor, and judiciary. In turn, each colony consisted of subunits - counties, townships, and villages.

Second only to Burke, the Englishman who best understood the importance of the Jewish tradition in the practice of liberty was Lord John

Emerich Edward Dalberg Acton (1834–1902). The great defender of individual rights, who declared that "[t]he most certain test by which we judge whether a country is really free is the amount of security enjoyed by minorities,"[48] Lord Acton credits

> the Chosen People [for providing] the first illustrations of a federated government, held together not on physical force, but on a voluntary covenant. The principle was carried out not only in each tribe, but in every group of at least 120 families; and there was neither privilege of rank nor inequality before the law.

From their example, Lord Acton extrapolates that "the parallel lines on which all freedom has been won – the doctrine of national tradition and the doctrine of the higher law; the principle that a constitution grows from a root, by process of development, and not of essential change; and the principle that all political authority must be tested and reformed according to a code which was not made by man."[49]

Those parallel lines similarly existed – and met, in the relativistic topology of real-time politics – within and among the American colonies. A federal system was creating itself, while a civil society grew ever more robust. People were taking their fate in their hands, reveling in their agency, taking advantage of opportunities seldom if ever previously seen in the course of history. They looked upon anyone presuming to rule them with deep skepticism: they had risen to the occasion together, proving to themselves, as much as to their British brethren, how well they could manage without direction from above, skeptical of all politicians but especially professional ones.

In that too they resembled the Jews, whose best leaders acquiesced to God's tasking them to guide the people only with great reluctance, afraid they had not been worthy. Though Moses is by far the best known, more than three millennia after the presumed date of the Exodus, the same humility would be championed by another guide to their ancestral home, Hungarian-born Theodore Herzl (1860-1904). After the antisemitic outpouring in the Dreyfus affair exposed the thinly hidden virulence of French antisemitism, Herzl saw that Europe was no longer safe for Jews. But it never crossed the mind of the secular Founder of modern Zionism to lead them himself.

For in Herzl's Jewish liberal imagination, writes Ruth Wisse, faithful to "the tradition of Moses and the Hebrew Prophets, only the reluctant leader wins the public trust. [Herzl had written:] 'Those who try to push themselves are gently ignored; while, on the other hand, we take great pains to discover real merit in the most obscure roots.'"[50] Only someone who does not crave power may be trusted to wield it; and even then, safeguards must be instituted against its possible abuse – even if well-intentioned, let alone by malign design.

In fact, Herzl's concern for Jews was inseparable from his commitment to liberalism more broadly, and thereby to everyone's well-being, Jew and gentile alike. As Wisse further explains, he "believed that in getting the Jews out of Europe, he would help to secure liberalism by removing one of its major irritants. The depth of Herzl's commitment to liberal ideas was touchingly on display in his utopian novel *Altneuland* (*Old-New Land*, 1902)."[51] In that fictional universe, there were no professional politicians; why should there be in this one?

It is not simply a question of personal character. Rather, someone who fails to appreciate that a ruler is no closer to God than any other man is conceptually and spiritually unequipped for the job. God's admonition in the book of *Samuel* against anointing a ruler represented a monumental advance in political theory. Explains Rabbi Joshua A. Berman: "Indeed, the king in many biblical passages—and especially in the Pentateuch [the first five books of the Bible]—was not deemed to be a necessary bond between God and the people. This dissociation of a people from its leader in relation to the divine is found nowhere else in the ancient Near East."[52]

Berman agrees with Jewish Theological Seminary Professor Yohanan Muffs that the new idea in the Torah is not monotheism, but "the idea of God as a personality who seeks a relationship of mutuality with human agents. In the neighboring cultures of the ancient Near East, man was merely a servant of kings. In the Bible, he is transformed into a servant king in relation to a beneficent sovereign…."[53] A political or military leader, therefore, has no spiritual guiding role. In books such as *Exodus*, *Deuteronomy*, and *Joshua*, argues Berman, "the covenant is clearly conceived to be between God as the sovereign and the people as the subordinate." No middleman is required, especially one overly authoritarian. These

> texts reflect a fear that a strong monarchy would result in the marginalizing of the common man. By articulating the metaphysical paradigms of the God-human encounter in terms of a suzerainty treaty or marriage, the biblical texts portray a relationship in which honor can be reciprocally bestowed between God and Israel; indeed, **between God and the common man of Israel.**[54]

Pastor Samuel Langdon, a former Harvard College president, commended the Old Testament to his New Hampshire congregation in 1788, not only for its spiritual but for its political guidance, providing "the basis of a law-based society with curbs on the corruptive influence of power as an integral part of its system." Writes Rabbi Berman: "Bringing the lessons of Deuteronomy to bear on the momentous decision facing the nation, [Langdon] remarked, 'If I am not mistaken, instead of the twelve tribes of Israel we may substitute the thirteen States of the American union.'"[55]

Unlike pre-Abrahamic conceptions of legitimate authority, the principle that most fundamentally

> animates the Israelite citizenry is that, like the Greek polis, it is law-based. The great twentieth-century political philosopher Friedrich Hayek saw Athenian political philosophy as the origin of the notion of equality before the law. But it is already present in *Deuteronomy*. All public institutions—the judiciary, the priesthood, the monarchy, the institution of prophecy—are subordinated to the law. No institution is self-legitimating. Moreover, the law is a public text, one read aloud before the entire nation (31:10–13). Its dictates are meant to be widely known, thus making abuse of power more obvious.[56]

The individual must be protected against the abuse of power. The covenant at Sinai had been made not so much between God and the nation of Israel in the collective sense as with each of its members. As noted above, the ultimate partner with whom God proclaims the sacred and binding political treaty is, in fact, ***the common man***. Stated more accurately, it was both at once. Specific details of governance would be worked out depending on circumstances, but the overarching guidance would transcend any one mortal human being and any one group at a particular time in history.

French political philosopher Pierre Manent best captured the centrality of the individual to the Western idea of liberty in his brilliant study *An Intellectual History of Liberalism* (1996):

> One of the principal "ideas" of liberalism, as we know, is that of the "individual." The individual is that being who, because he is human, is naturally entitled to "rights" that can be enumerated, rights that are attributed to him independently of his function or place in society and that make him the equal of any other man.... What are liberty and equality, after all, if not "biblical values" shaping civic life?[57]

It was but a short conceptual step, albeit travelled over the course of several millennia, from the Torah to the colonists' recognition that the locus of political sovereignty and thus the fountainhead of legitimacy could never rest in any single person. Kings and all other government officials were to have only as much legitimate power as they were allotted by those whose interests they served, by the people who endorsed the laws and chose their enforcers. The latter, in turn, were to confine their actions to what they were entitled and not exceed their mandate. God's acquiescence is implied in the observance of the community's covenant by all its members.

The Torah offers no guidance regarding specific electoral systems or constitutional structures. But what it does suggest is that ordinary people, regardless of pedigree and social standing, were perfectly eligible for any task, including that of king, if they must. But "[b]e sure to set a king over yourself from one of your own brethren" reads *Deuteronomy 17:15.* Family lineage is quite beside the point. What matters is that whoever is king must under no circumstances "stray from the commandments" (*Deuteronomy* 5:29; 17:11; 28:14). He must always bear in mind the good of all, or what today we might call the national interest, rather than his own aggrandizement and personal preferences. The exceptional rarity of such qualities explains why being weary of kings is wise.

To translate these principles into a pragmatic, workable system of interwoven authorities, balancing disparate groups and interests against each other to everyone's ultimate advantage, was the Founders' great task.

They lived up to the challenge, albeit imperfectly. Their collective genius, and that of their generation, eloquently captured by Temple University Professor Daniel Elazar, had been to begin "building institutions based upon neo-covenantal models a generation earlier and, by the time that the great seventeenth century political philosophers began their work, were already well along toward modifying those institutions in light of both New World and modern conditions." As a result, "[w]hat had been primarily an ideological expression of a grand theory became a fundament of culture, a shaper of institutions, and a major influence on political and other behavior."[58]

Chapter II:

New Eden across the Atlantic

Soul libertie

"*Enforced uniformity confounds civil and religious liberty and denies the principles of Christianity and civility. No man shall be required to worship or maintain a worship against his will.*"
– Roger Williams, *The Bloudy Tenet of Persecution* (1644)

"*Give me the liberty to know, to utter, and to argue freely according to conscience, above all liberties.*"
– John Milton, *Areopagitica* (1644)

Though John Locke is often credited with parenting liberalism, that honor might be more justly conferred upon his American predecessor Roger Williams (1603-1683). Through "carefully reasoned argument for the complete dissociation of church and State," argues historian W. K. Jordan, Williams indeed "surpassed John Locke." In fact, that argument "may be regarded as the most important contribution during the [seventeenth] century in this significant area of political thought."[1] Similarly, literary historian Vernon L. Parrington describes Williams as "one of the notable democratic thinkers that the English race has produced" – not only as "a forerunner of Locke and the natural rights school" but of Benjamin Franklin, Thomas Paine, and Thomas Jefferson, for his "theory of the commonwealth must be reckoned the richest contribution of Puritanism to American political thought."[2] *New York Times* bestselling author John M. Barry captures it succinctly: "Williams's ideas entered America's bloodstream."[3]

Additional historical research has further confirmed Williams's extraordinary contribution to liberalism, in both theory and practice. While his uncompromising Puritanism earned the ire of more pragmatic colonial leaders, including some influential co-religionists, his example fueled popular devotion to unqualified freedom of conscience. Even John Locke favored denying Catholics and atheists such a right, for fear it might endanger the state; Williams would have none of it.

To be sure, Williams differed in important ways from the Founders who were otherwise his conceptual heirs. Unlike Thomas Jefferson, for example, who advocated religious liberty based on political and social considerations, Williams's reasons were almost purely theological. Yet its applications were practical: his distaste for secularism notwithstanding, he argued that a church was fully a part of civil society, "like unto a Corporation, Society, or Company of East-Indie or Turkie-Merchants." To Williams, "Soul Libertie" was more than on a par with the more tangible sort, such as property; it was paramount.

Preaching about it, however, wasn't enough for Williams. He worked hard to obtain political support for what he considered the indispensable prerequisite to human flourishing: religious worship. His selfless, almost fanatical devotion was to cost him and his family dearly. But due to his exceptional persuasive skills and an almost providentially fortuitous set of circumstances, he eventually did succeed, almost miraculously. On March 14, 1644, he obtained for Rhode Island an official charter, signed by members of the body empowered to extend such a document at the time, the Committee on Foreign Plantations in London. Williams had made history.

The Charter gave Rhode Island (or rather, the awkwardly named colony of Providence Plantations in the Narragansett Bay, which included Providence, Portsmouth, and Newport) enormous latitude. Specifically, it had "full Powre & Authority to Governe & rule themselves, and such others as shall hereafter Inhabite within any part of the said Tract of land, by such a form of Civil Government, as by voluntary consent of all, or the greater Part of them shall find most suteable to their Estates & Conditions," provided only that the laws thereby passed "be conformable to the Laws of England, so far as the Nature and Constitution of the place will admit."[4] All decisions regarding freedom of religion were thereby within the purview of that "greater Part," which the committee knew well would remove the state from any interference with matters of worship.

Barry draws out the full import of this development:

> Williams had succeeded. **Providence Plantations thus exceeded any other known state in the world in its freedoms.** Holland tolerated different religions, but its toleration had limits and each province still had a state church; the Dutch government had even paid the salaries of some of the Puritan ministers who had fled to the Netherlands. The Committee on Foreign Plantations by not interfering, by leaving its status up to those living there, had now given official sanction to Williams's soul liberty. **Williams had created the only such society in the civilized world.**[5]

As if this had not sufficed to earn the Puritan zealot a place in the liberal pantheon, there was one more: Williams's passionate defense of the native Americans' equal rights to liberty on the basis of their common humanity. For example, he found that the natives' "desire of, and delight in news, is great, as [true of] the Athenians, and all men, more or lesse."[6] Adamantly opposed to slavery, Williams had anticipated the eventual implementation of the principles expressed in the Declaration, a full three centuries prior to the civil rights era.

But Williams did not speak for most, let alone all, Puritans. He was tried in Boston's General Court for "diverse dangerous opinions" on July 8, 1635, and eventually condemned by both magistrates and clergy. Worse yet, to his great astonishment as indeed that of his parishioners in Salem, Massachusetts, who were very fond of him, Williams was banished from the colony altogether. That he would eventually prevail he could not have known at the time. It was scant consolation to his wife and children.

For an idealistic religious community dedicated to free thought and individual rights to become a model for the European settlements in the New World seemed unlikely. In his aptly titled tome *The Barbarous Years*, Bernard Bailyn describes the motley crew as "a mixed multitude."

> They came from England, the Netherlands, the German and Italian states, France, Africa, Sweden, and Finland; and they moved out to the western hemisphere for different reasons, from different social backgrounds and cultures, and under different auspices and circumstances. Even those who came from England - the majority of the immigrant population of the founding years - fitted no distinct socioeconomic or cultural pattern. They came from all over the realm, bearing with them diverse lifestyles.[7]

Hardly all strict observers of the Ten Commandments, they showed no particular empathy for one another, and even less for the people they were surprised to find already inhabiting a land they had imagined bare of humans, albeit full of riches, ripe for the plucking. Though not all natives proved hostile to them, the often-fierce, internecine warfare that took place regularly even among rival tribes, let alone against strangers, exponentially exacerbated the settlers' perplexed attempts to co-habit.

The ensuing cruelty, which Bailyn illustrates in nauseating detail, refuted romantic illusions. The newly discovered lands were no Eden. Instead, the mix of disparate populations led to

> a brutal encounter - brutal not only between the Europeans and the native peoples, despite occasional efforts at accommodation, and between Europeans and Africans, but among the Europeans themselves, as they sought to control and prosper in the new configurations of life that were emerging around them. In the process, they created new vernacular cultures and social structures similar to, but confusingly different from, what had been known before, yet more effective in this outback of European civilization.[8]

That so inauspicious a beginning should have given rise to so singular, so intricate, and so successful an experiment, based not on the model of empire but of republican federalism, is all the more remarkable for having emerged after such a relatively short gestation.

Only later would it transpire that native Americans "contributed more to successful European settlement in North America than the Europeans perceived at the time," writes Daniel Elazar. And the main contribution was federalism itself, as "in many cases, [tribes]... were organized on a federal basis with tribal confederacies [sic] and leagues from coast to coast."[9] Albeit not strictly covenantal, these arrangements do "stand as testimony to the federal qualities of the country," a matter of considerable practical importance to the framers of the Constitution.

Unsurprisingly, Roger Williams's egalitarian religious idealism was not shared by all the settlers who landed in Virginia in 1607 and in Massachusetts thirteen years later. A large percentage had been driven mainly by economic necessity. Their sponsors were commercial enterprises, undertaken by private individuals for their and their partners' profit. But if enhancing English trade was presupposed, it was not required. And that made all the difference.

As the celebrated historian of colonial America Charles M. Andrews concedes, the Mother Country was fumbling and stumbling into becoming the world's greatest imperial power "without any fixed policy, in fact, without any clear idea of what she and her people were doing." The British Crown was actually "giving scarcely more than legal sanction to a migration for which it was in no way responsible."[10] It was default 209, , in its most salutary form.

So did the New World become an unwitting socio-political laboratory, no visible guide directing its growth. An accidental-experimental weed, the peculiar hybrid included several territories - Jamaica, New York, and Nova Scotia - that England had seized by force from Spain, the Netherlands, and the French, respectively. But most settlements had been privately funded by people whose motives were as motley as their lineages:

> Some of these people wanted religious and political independence; others aimed at commercial profit; many fleeing from the hard conditions of life in the old countries, sought land and a living for themselves and their families in the wide spaces of the New World; while a small number, in somewhat the spirit of the old Vikings, were stimulated to action by the salt of pure adventure and the glamour of the sea.[11]

In other words, these were ordinary folk, if singularly un-averse to risk, almost to the point of recklessness. Yet in that unprecedented crucible, within little more than a century, a strange alchemy would produce results worthy of a providential Invisible Hand. Bailyn marvels at how "commercial ambitions, the search for religious perfectionism, environmental circumstances, and the great flow of migrants, free and unfree, from Europe and Africa, had combined to produce variant ways of life, different from what had been known before."[12] Modern liberalism was about to sprout in a soil that few who landed on its hard, cold rocks had anticipated could yield such bountiful harvest.

No professional nation-builders, imperialists, let alone political theorists, the daring humans who poured out of the improbably rickety vessels that landed along the Atlantic coast had to fend for themselves. Coordination among them was practically nonexistent - the result of distance, religious and ethnic differences, and disparate economic conditions, climate and soil. Albeit spread out along the vast shore, necessity somehow forced them to meet their various challenges in roughly similar manner: "[A]lways, though more or less unconsciously," writes Andrews, "they tended toward uniformity of governmental procedure and used similar methods of increasing their self-governing powers."[13]

Simultaneously with the increase of those powers, exercised through popular assemblies, the largely separate colonies gained a taste for independence from both one another and their titular sovereign an ocean away. As time went on, the assemblies began to consider themselves akin to the British parliament - each, writes Andrews, a "miniature house of commons which was exercising full powers over legislation, membership, and finance, and claiming legislative equality with the highest body of the realm."[14]

It helped that the English government did not take serious notice of its overseas colonies till after 1660. By then, explains Bailyn, "the North American communities had existed for two or three generations, and distinctive, persistent patterns of life were beginning to emerge. The patterns were not entirely clear, the trajectories unpredictable, but certain fundamental lines could be perceived that framed the colonies' place in the world."[15]

The lack of British supervision had created a kind of pristine, if not exactly idyllic, state-of-nature. The king's indifference to their plight was a mixed blessing. On the one hand, writes Andrews, "during the colonial period, no one knew certainly what was law and what was not in the colonies."[16] On the other, "[n]o colonies hitherto established by any power in any part of the world had been permitted to govern themselves."[17] Yet, no chaos ensued; instead, the experiment in self-rule succeeded beyond expectation.

At last, the colonists articulated the justification they needed to declare independence from Britain: London had no right to tax them. Properly represented in their own local parliaments, they refused to be patronized from across the ocean, like so many savages. Surely not when they could manifestly govern themselves perfectly well, thank you.

But to what extent the Founders truly believed their own argument is an open question that will probably never be resolved. Andrews has his doubts, for "the right of parliament to legislate for the colonies was not expressly denied by the colonists themselves before 1765." He cites "former Massachusetts governor Thomas Pownall's observation in 1764 that the claim of freedom from the authority of parliament was of very recent growth," John Adams's 1775 assertion to the contrary notwithstanding. Rather, Andrews is convinced that "the colonists would have gone with their revolt, regardless of the conclusions of the intellectuals, for the impulses behind that movement did not originate in the question of parliamentary right."[18]

That ideas were crucial to garnering popular support for the revolt no one doubts. How else to explain the enormous success of Thomas Paine's pamphlet *Common Sense*, published anonymously in January 1776? To be sure, Paine's ideas consisted largely of emotion with a sprinkling of logic, all wrapped inside fetching biblical language. That said, the passion behind the rhetoric served to validate something far more important than rigorously argued philosophy: hard facts on the ground. Slowly but surely, a new social, political, and economic arrangement was manifestly emerging: *homo americanus*, albeit anything but homogenous, was turning into a people.

Consider the case of New York, as captured by Bailyn:

> There was no settled pattern of life in New York, only a slow and at times contentious process by which the mixed multitude of the Dutch years, soon to be supplemented by Huguenots and German Pietists, grew into a new community dominated by the English. Slowly and persistently English laws, language, and institutions were beginning to penetrate the lives of the minor ethnic groups and to press against the majority Dutch who clung to their inherited ways. The consolidation of economic interests and kinship among the major merchant families, Dutch and English, tended to weaken ethnic differences, as did the shared interest of the most successful merchants in establishing great estates on the Hudson, suitable properties for landed gentlemen of whatever ethnic origin and excellent soils for valuable grain production.[19]

Ethnic, class, and religious differences, however weakened, persisted within the colony. Eventually, however, changed circumstances would gradually recalibrate interests and identities. Soon trading networks would also link and realign intersecting Atlantic networks, such as New York, Boston, their satellite towns, and the Chesapeake ports, thereby strengthening inter-colonial ties. International ties increased as well - with western Europe, West Africa, the Azores, the West Indies, and ports on the Hispanic-American mainland. Although "[b]y the 1670s, the tangles of the overlapping trade routes were too intricate, too volatile, and too often extemporized to be described in clear, schematic form,"[20] they were nonetheless real. Globalization had reached a whole new level.

The colonists' unplanned experiment was unwittingly demonstrating the power of transnational trade, creating new connections and opportunities: "New York's great merchants, in all sorts of high-level transactions, roamed the distant ports of Europe, West Africa, and mainland Hispanic America, maintaining, despite political obstacles, their profitable contacts with the broad reaches of the Dutch-Atlantic trading network. They had grown rich in this Atlantic system." The same was true of "[a]ll the major merchants [, who] prospered by transnational ties, legal and illegal, maintaining affiliations not only with English creditors and suppliers but with the credit, supplies, and contacts of the Low Country's Atlantic trading patriciate."[21]

At the same time, the colonists were coming into contact with ideas, books, and events that broadened their perspective. For as Bailyn points out, the trans-Atlantic

> flow was not only material. The British Americans were informed, though often belatedly and in fragments, about events abroad, about the politics of the great states whose casual permutations could affect them directly, about the clangorous discourse of English political and religious thought in this fraught century, and about the long struggle for the grounds of legitimate authority.[22]

They would become increasingly cosmopolitan, gaining additional perspective on their own evolving philosophical framework. The more they saw and learned, the more certain they were that freedom was the right path for America.

Natural Liberty

"*[L]iberty is not a means to a higher political end. It is itself the highest political end.*"

- Lord Acton, "The History of Freedom in Antiquity" (1877)

"'*[T]is plain each one has a natural right to exert his powers, according to his own judgment and inclination, for purposes [of natural affections] in all such industry, labor, or amusements, as are not hurtful to others in their persons or goods, while no more public interest necessarily*

requires his labors, or requires that his actions should be under the direction of others. This right we call natural liberty."
- Francis Hutcheson, *A System Of Moral Philosophy* (1755)

The question of what differentiates legitimate authority from usurpation has preoccupied philosophers since time immemorial. It took on far greater urgency, however, as the bloody religious wars throughout Western Europe escalated the debate. Amidst all the ferment caused by political and scientific revolutions, it was the philosophers of the Scottish Enlightenment who contributed most to the development of American classical liberalism. Unlike most of their French and even some of their English counterparts, the Scottish thinkers acknowledged that reason alone did not suffice: the passions and the interests affect behavior at least as much, if not more. They saw, moreover, no conflict between individualism and empathy, prosperity and generosity.[23]

The most prominent among them was Francis Hutcheson (1694-1746), an immensely popular philosophy professor at the University of Glasgow. Possibly the first to teach in the vernacular rather than Latin, instead of straight lecturing he encouraged robust student discussions. A preacher of affable temperament, Hutcheson believed that religion should not inspire fear but rather should encourage a disinterested affection for others. His listeners, writes historian Arthur Herman, "would discover that the underlying principles of all human behavior were part of an 'immense and connected' moral system governed by the dictates of natural law. That included '*oeconomicks*, or the laws and rights of the several members of a family,' as well as 'private rights, or the laws obtaining in natural liberty.'"[24] Here, economics is used in its Aristotelian sense of household management. That term would be expanded by the man who inherited Hutchenson's chair, to launch a new science.

The seeds had already been planted in Hutcheson's *System of Moral Philosophy*, which declared: "'tis plain each one has a natural right to exert his powers, according to his own judgment and inclination, for purposes [of natural affections] in all such industry, labor, or amusements, as are not hurtful to others in their persons or goods, while no more public interest necessarily requires his labors, or requires that his actions should be under the direction of others. This right we call *natural liberty*."[25] 'Tis plain - which is to say, it is common sense.

Along with freedom of speech and religion, Hutchenson simultaneously condemned all forms of oppression against all human beings. His contribution cannot be overestimated, writes Herman: in effect, "Francis Hutcheson had created a new political and social vision...: the vision of a 'free society.' He is Europe's first liberal in the classic sense: a believer in maximizing personal liberty in the social, economic, and intellectual spheres, as well as the political."[26] Perhaps he could share the honor with Roger Williams, though others undoubtedly could claim it as well.

Thomas Jefferson fully agreed with Hutcheson that "man," as he wrote to his friend Peter Carr in 1787, "was destined for society... He was endowed with a sense of right and wrong merely relative to this. This sense is as much a part of his nature as the sense of hearing, seeing, feeling: it is the true foundation of morality."[27] Though also indebted to John Locke, Jefferson, like Hutchenson, had no trouble positing a "moral sense":

> The moral sense, or conscience, is as much a part of man as his leg or arm. It is given to all human beings in a stronger or weaker degree, as force of members is given them in a greater or less degree. It may be strengthened by exercise, as may any particular limb of the body. This sense is submitted indeed in some degree to the guidance of reason; but it is a small stock which is required for this: even a less one than what we call Common sense. State a moral case to a ploughman and a professor. The former will decide it as well, and often better than the latter, because he has not been led astray by artificial rules.[28]

It is on this basis that Jefferson and certain of the other Founders supported the principles of the Declaration,[29] summarized in the one phrase that has since galvanized the world: "We hold these truths to be self-evident, that all men are created equal, that they are endowed by their Creator with certain unalienable[30] Rights, that among these are Life, Liberty and the pursuit of Happiness. That to secure these rights, Governments are instituted among Men, deriving their just powers from the consent of the governed." He later explained in a letter that by "self-evident" he had meant merely "to place before mankind the common sense of the subject, in terms so plain and firm as to command their assent, and to justify ourselves in the independent stand we are compelled to take."[31] These truths were deemed self-evident because it was the common understanding of the subject, certainly in America. That made them also "sacred and undeniable," which incidentally had been the original wording.[32]

They had also been shared by one of Hutcheson's greatest disciples, Scottish philosopher Adam Smith (1723-1790), who opposed England's obsolete restrictions on inheritance and trade left over from feudalism. Smith defended the right to dispose of one's property without undue restrictions, to engage in trade freely without imposition of tariffs, as the best way to build the wealth of nations and individuals. That his great work *On the Wealth of Nations* was published the same year as the Declaration cannot go unmentioned.

Smith's theoretical defense of private property rights was evidently easier to apply in an environment that, unlike the United Kingdom, was unencumbered by trade and property customs going back centuries. Smith was also a celebrated moral philosopher, whose deep understanding of human action and ethical principles accounts for his well-deserved fame and influence. The best known of the Scottish Enlightenment theorists, writes Daniel Elazar, Smith became "part of the covenantal tradition one step removed, who sought a federal democratic republic in North America as the way to actualize civil society."[33] Among the Founders most influenced by his writings was the future U.S. president and principal framer of the U.S. Constitution, James Madison.

Whether an Invisible Hand was in any way behind Madison's decision to leave his native Virginia to attend Princeton University, then known as the College of New Jersey, is a matter of conjecture. But coming there under the powerful influence of Hutcheson's student, the Reverend John Witherspoon (1723-1794), proved a blessing to the future United States. Nor can it be entirely coincidental that the 1787 Constitutional Convention numbered no fewer than five Princeton alumni.

The only clergyman and only college president to sign the Declaration of Independence, Witherspoon had deliberately sought out students from throughout the colonies, and Madison was luckily among them. From Witherspoon, the brilliant young Virginian learned that a common, natural moral sense, alongside the ability to reason, rendered all human beings equal, meaning that none was entitled to decide for another without consent. His influence on Madison was at least equal to that of Adam Smith.

Like Smith, Madison agreed that competition operates through checks and balances. The result is hardly perfection, either in the market or the public square. But short of utopia, it may be superior to all other arrangements. In *An Inquiry into the Nature and Causes of the Wealth of Nations*, Smith had explained why allowing people to pursue their own goals as they see fit leads to the greatest prosperity of the whole. No crass materialist, Smith preferred such an arrangement less on utilitarian than on moral grounds, for it permits the greatest degree of individual freedom without prejudice as to social distinctions.

It follows that some form of democracy is the best system of government, for it is predicated on the preeminence of self-rule. Explains University of Chicago political theorist Joseph Cropsey, a noted Smith scholar (and my beloved professor): unlike those among "[t]he ancient moralists [who] coldly concentrated upon the distinction between the politically weighty people and the entire populace that dwelt within the frontiers… democracy [alone] has the merit of making possible the effacement of that distinction."[34]

A regime that minimizes the distinction between human beings was the ultimate aim of Smith's philosophy, often imprecisely referred to as capitalism, free enterprise, or laissez-faire. Smith of course never used those terms. What he proposed to defend was "the natural system of perfect liberty and justice," or more briefly, "the system of natural liberty."[35] But he didn't think himself an innovator: "[L]iberty," explains Cropsey, meant to Smith the same thing that "it had meant to Locke, to Aristotle, and to the long tradition of political philosophy: the condition of men under lawful governors who respect the persons and property of the governed, the latter having to consent to the arrangement in one way or another."[36]

Liberty also meant the same to the Founders as it did to Smith, which accounts for their creating a calibrated federal system based on the principle that all power rests with the people. Outlined in the elegantly concise federal Constitution, meant to be synchronized with state constitutions, the system was unprecedented in both scope and boldness.

It prompted Alexander de Tocqueville to declare, in a speech before the French Constituent Assembly on September 12th, 1848, that America was the one nation that both defined and implemented the idea of liberty as nowhere else on earth. It would become one of the most important speeches ever delivered on this topic, though why so few have ever heard of it remains a mystery.

The issue before the Assembly which Tocqueville was addressing on that day concerned the possibility of solving the unemployment problem plaguing the new – second – French republic following the overthrow of King Louis Philippe I, by setting up government work projects and guaranteeing employment at a fixed wage. In his extraordinary speech, Tocqueville confronted his fellow lawmakers bluntly: the real issue at hand was socialism. And he wouldn't stand for it.

Acknowledging that several different systems could qualify as socialist, he proposed examining only their common characteristics, which he proceeded to list: first, "an incessant, vigorous and extreme appeal to the material passions of man;" second, "an attack, either direct or indirect, on the principle of private property;" and third, "a profound opposition to personal liberty and scorn for individual reason, a complete contempt for the individual." In a word, socialism is quite "simply a new system of serfdom."

Tocqueville had understood better than most of his contemporaries the fundamental principle of liberalism that every person had a right to life, liberty, and property. He was thus also incensed by the racist theory of the infamous French ethnologist Count Arthur de Gobineau (1816-1882), with its implied historical determinism, predestination, and fatalism. One of the first European writers to interpret the historical development of mankind as being dependent on race, in his 1855 *Essay on the Inequality of the Human Races,* Gobineau denied that "the colored races" were part of the human species. Rejecting this view as preposterous, in a letter of January 24, 1857, Tocqueville asked scornfully: "[W]hat could be clearer than the unity of mankind in *Genesis* and that all men are descended from the same man?"

This led historian Joel Fishman, former editor of the *Jewish Political Studies Review*, to conclude that

> [t]aken in historical context, Tocqueville's letter to Gobineau of 24 January 1857 clearly recognizes the contribution of the distinctly Jewish

> idea of equality to the evolution of Western thought. This attribution is significant, because in *Democracy in America* he emphasizes its central importance to modern democracy, describing both its benefits and potential dangers… [For] when abused, equality in modern society could serve the ends of the totalitarian state.[37]

Fishman is encouraged as well by a renewed appreciation among historians for the influence of the Hebrew Bible on the American liberal tradition. But first, slavery had to go. A black blot on the nation's conscience, a dagger in the heart, its eradication was long overdue.

The Unoriginal Sin of Slavery

"*[T]hrough the Indulgence of GOD to our First Parents after the Fall, the outward Estate of all and every of the Children, remains the same, as to one another. So that Originally and Naturally, there is no such thing as Slavery.*"

– Samuel Sewell, *The Selling of Joseph* (1700)

"*Whenever [I] hear any one arguing for slavery I feel a strong impulse to see it tried on him personally.*"

- Abraham Lincoln, *Speech to the One Hundred Fortieth Indiana Regimen*, (March 17, 1865 – autograph draft)

The lofty ideals of the Declaration and the Constitution were lagging far behind their implementation. But the complexities of the debates surrounding slavery deserve more than the condescending scorn of hindsight. Which is what they mercifully receive from Princeton University historian Sean Wilentz in his impressively documented *No Property in Man: Slavery and Antislavery at the Nation's Founding*. By no means does Wilenz, a self-described liberal, minimize the ubiquity of slavery: "[B]etween 1660 and 1710, virtually every English colony in the New World enacted laws defining slaves as conveyable property," writes Wilenz. Yet he also reminds the reader that at the same time, "[o]rganized antislavery politics originated in America."[38]

In fact, the first written constitution in history to ban adult slavery by declaring that "all men are born equally free and independent" was approved in the state of Vermont in 1777. The 1770s were the great watershed moment after what John Jay, the first chief justice of the

Supreme Court, called "the great revolution." Previously, as Jay told his friends in the English Anti-Slavery Society in June 1788,

> the great majority or rather the great body of our people had been so long accustomed to the practice and convenience of having slaves, that very few among them even doubted the propriety and rectitude of it. Some liberal and conscientious men had, indeed, by their conduct and writings, drawn the lawfulness of slavery into question, and they made converts to that opinion; but the number of those converts compared with the people at large was then very inconsiderable.[39]

This Ciceronian use of "liberal" to mean "generous," implying surpassing what is strictly required, had long been common. For centuries, subjects had been accorded privileges by the powers that be. By contrast, equality before the law for everyone, not a matter of generosity but as a right mandated by nature and nature's God, was revolutionary. Even after becoming enshrined in the founding covenant of the republic, it took decades for states to include it in theirs, and longer still for the law to be applied and enforced.

That slavery contradicted this principle was appreciated by many, though abolishing it altogether at the end of the 18th century hardly anyone thought possible. And yet, notwithstanding the plethora of practical obstacles to outlawing it through the federal Constitution, some antislavery delegates to the constitutional convention opened the door to its future abolition by categorically refusing to acknowledge the legitimacy of owning property in another human being. Their tenacity and tactical savvy paid off, and their principled stand cannot be sufficiently applauded.

The argument for that important stance had been articulated with uncommon eloquence by the leading jurist of Massachusetts, Samuel Sewell, as early as 1700. It lay dormant in the colonists' collective unconscious until events ripened to permit its realization. Sewell's pamphlet was in fact the first anti-slavery tract in English North America. "The Selling of Joseph: A Memorial" invoked the Old Testament as movingly as a sermon:

> [T]hrough the Indulgence of GOD to our First Parents after the Fall, the outward Estate of all and every of the Children, remains the same, as to one another. So that Originally, and Naturally, there is no such thing as Slavery. Joseph was rightfully no more a Slave to his Brethren, than they

> were to him: and they had no more Authority to Sell him, than they had to Slay him. And if they had nothing to do to Sell him; the Ishmaelites bargaining with them, and paying down Twenty pieces of Silver, could not make a Title. Neither could Potiphar have any better Interest in him than the Ishmaelites had. *Gen. 37. 20, 27, 28*. For he that shall in this case plead Alteration of Property, seems to have forfeited a great part of his own claim to Humanity. There is no proportion between Twenty Pieces of Silver, and LIBERTY. The Commodity itself is the Claimer.[40]

But even biblical allusions did not suffice; anti-slavery sentiments, though nascent, were not solid enough. The Quakers, for example, in their Yearly Meeting held in Philadelphia in 1696, warned against encouraging anyone to import slaves, yet implied that slaveholders' claims to property rights in humans did not violate God's word. This remained basic policy among the Quakers for another half century.[41]

What about the Jews? American and Foreign Anti-Slavery Society's 1853 annual report assumes that they would stand categorically against it: "The objects of so much mean prejudice and unrighteous oppression as the Jews have been for ages, surely they, it would seem, more than any other denomination, ought to be the enemies of caste and the friends of universal freedom."[42] The report, however, notes that there was no organization representing the views of the community in an official manner.

There were many reasons, quite apart from the Jews' notorious propensity to disagree with one another, including themselves. (Whence the saying "two Jews, three opinions." It is a conservative estimate). Principal among them was the extraordinary increase in the numbers of immigrants to America. If in 1850, out of twenty-three million inhabitants, Jews numbered no more than fifty thousand, during the following decade their numbers tripled. And a motley crew they were.

By 1860, there were an estimated 150,000 living in the North and 25,000 in the South. Most so-called "greenhorns" (newcomers) settled in urban communities, primarily New York City. A large majority of new immigrants, mostly though not exclusively from Eastern Europe, were poor; others, mainly earlier arrivals, had been well-to-do, even wealthy. Considerable class differences, a multiplicity of languages and ethnicities, alongside various attitudes toward religion, all militated against a monolithic perspective and a univocal institution speaking in their name.

For if age-old prejudice enhanced Jews' tribal identity, it simultaneously reactivated their tried-and-true method of survival: laying low, out of the limelight, avoiding calling attention to themselves by contrarian attitudes and behavior. Writes the historian Rabbi Bertram W. Korn in his 1951 book *American Jewry and the Civil War*: "The insecurity which Jews brought from their European experience was an unconscious freight which they carried over the ocean. It is still among our possessions." Yet he also argues that despite the failure of all attempts to create a formal nation-wide Jewish organization, "there was already an American Jewish unity in an emotional sense."[43] And as could be expected, by far the greatest number of that community repudiated Black slavery.

Yet Rabbi Korn concedes that "Jews were as divided [on slavery] as the American population itself." Some – notably J. F. Moses of Lumpkin, Georgia - even traded slaves.[44] Unfortunately, it was none other than a rabbi, Morris J. Raphall, who told his congregation in New York on January 4, 1861, National Fast Day, that while he personally did not favor slavery, and even if southern slaveholders were wrong, he thought slave property had been "expressly placed under the protection of the Ten Commandments."[45] A consummate biblical scholar, Rabbi Raphall has been recognized, notably by Yale University Professor David Brion Davis, as offering "perhaps the most authoritative religious defense of black slavery ever written."[46]

The rabbi attempted to distinguish biblical slavery, which had been common practice throughout the ancient world, from the Southern variety. Yet he emphasized that despite recognizing its existence, the Bible unquestionably considered the slave as "a person in whom the dignity of human nature is to be respected." There is no doubt that Raphall personally opposed slavery; indeed, one of his sons would later serve as an officer in the Union. But the effect of his ill-timed words was hardly felicitous. Learned scholarly exegesis is not always good politics.

The general reaction among Jews was explosive. Rabbi David Einhorn of Baltimore, expressing his outrage, spoke for the majority:

> A Jew, the offspring of a race which daily praises God for deliverance from the bondage of Egypt ... undertakes to parade slavery as a perfectly sinless institution, sanctioned by God ... ! A more extraordinary

> phenomenon could hardly be imagined.... A religion which exhorts to spare the mother from the bird's nest, cannot consent to the heart-rending spectacle of robbing a human mother of her child ... Thus crumbles into a thousand fragments the rickety structure of Dr. Raphall ... To proclaim in the name of Judaism, that God has consecrated the institution of slavery! Such a shame and reproach the Jewish religious press is in duty bound to disown and to disavow, if both are not to be stigmatized forever. If a Christian clergyman in Europe had delivered a sermon like that of Dr. Raphall, all the Jewish orthodox and reform pens would have immediately been set to work ... to repel such a foul charge, and to inveigh against this desecration of God's holy name. Why should we, in America, keep silence when a Jewish preacher plays such pranks?[47]

Ultimately, defenders of the so-called "peculiar institution" set aside theological considerations as essentially irrelevant. Notes Lake Forest College Professor Arthur Zilversmit, an authority on African-American history, "all pro-slavery arguments turned on the question of property rights."[48] No southerner defended property rights by citing Scripture. In the Northern states with the largest percentage of slaves, New Jersey and New York, for example, the anti-emancipation stance all but "shed its coating of biblical justification and historical precedent and stood revealed as the armor of property, defending its interests."[49]

But could slaves, as human beings, ever be considered property? The colonists having adopted the classical liberal tri-pronged right to life, liberty, and property, articulated by John Locke in his *Second Theory of Government,* as self-evidently true, they could not avoid facing a crucial paradox. If slaves were property, their owners would have a right to hold on to them; but if they were not, that right evaporated. Any middle ground was logically impossible. The question remained whether logic would prevail over political expediency. Logic may have dictated against slavery, as did morality; political expediency, not so much. To be sure, in cases of war, victors had always considered it fully justifiable to do what they wished with enemies. It was quite different in peacetime.

The extent to which John Locke himself (as distinct from the citizens of the Carolinas, whose original constitutions Locke had drafted in 1669) had been tolerant of Black slavery is debatable, particularly given that he did invest in the slave trade. The same cannot be said of his later fellow-liberals in Britain and Scotland, who rejected it out of hand. Most famously, Adam Smith wrote that "[t]he property which every man has in his own labor, as it is the original foundation for all [i.e., everyone] over property [in general], so it is the most sacred and inviolable."[50]

It is precisely on such grounds that the abolitionists figured out a way to take advantage of the slaveholders' property claims. Two could play that game: as slaveowners hailed against violations of *their* property rights in their slaves, so too abolitionists argued that slaves were being robbed of *their* natural rights to property in their own persons.

The question was whether *any* person could legitimately become someone else's property. It led to a spirited debate among northern and southern delegates at the Federal Convention, whose secret minutes were mercifully recorded for all posterity by James Madison. Though at times it looked like a make-or-break proposition which would prevent agreement on a common text, the antislavery contingent did not budge on the question of slaves being referred to as "persons." They fully agreed with Madison, who had told his colleagues on August 25, 1787, that he had "thought it wrong to admit in the Constitution the idea that there could be property in men. … [S]laves are not like merchandize, consumed, &c."[51] In the final text of the founding document, no reference was ever made to slaves – only "persons." It would prove immensely helpful in the next century.

A year later, Madison's influence on the debates over Virginia's ratification of the federal Constitution was manifest in this provision: "By our present Government every man is secure in his person, and the enjoyment of his property."[52] By implication, a man of whatever hue should be "secure in his person," as would any woman in hers. The language was unmistakably laying the foundations for a future devoid of slavery. Wilentz concludes that Madison and his likeminded fellow "framers left room for political efforts aimed at slavery's restriction and, eventually, its destruction, even under a Constitution that safeguarded slavery. Those efforts, although sporadic through the early years of the nineteenth century, would eventually bring the advent of the Republican Party, the outbreak of the Civil War, and the completion of emancipation in 1865."[53]

The hapless Jews, meanwhile, were again assigned their time-tested role of everybody's favorite scapegoat. Validating popular English historian Paul Johnson's remark that "the language of anti-Semitism through the ages is a dictionary of non-sequiturs and antonyms, a thesaurus of illogic and inconsistency,"[54] Jews were attacked *en masse* by anti-Semites among both advocates and opponents of slavery. The assumption that no abolitionists could be antisemitic is simply wrong.

Leaving aside the many staunch abolitionist evangelicals who had sought assiduously to convert the Jews, a good number detested the whole lot. Their principal leader, William Lloyd Garrison, editor of *The Liberator*, once even called Mordecai Noah "that lineal descendant of the monsters who nailed Jesus to the cross between two thieves." The most influential Jew in early 19th century America, whose father had served in the Revolutionary War and contributed a great deal of money to the cause, Noah had been a respected editor, prolific writer, judge, a major in the New York military, and an ardent Zionist. True, the volatile Garrison had elsewhere expressed philosemitic sentiments. Highly intemperate and haughty, he was notoriously prone to lashing out uncontrollably, so the slur might have been untypical. But it cannot be dismissed as a mere fluke.

Historians disagree about the extent of abolitionist antipathy to Jews. Some portray the radical abolitionists as power-hungry politicians opposed to foreigners in general. Others, notably Louis Ruchames, emphasize their humanitarianism. Yet even he admits that "one sometimes finds, in their letters and other writings, expressions of racial stereotypes and prejudices, concerning both Negroes and Jews[. But] these are infrequent and atypical."[55] In the end, it was the abolitionists' antagonism to the Constitution that alienated not only Jews but also the principal leaders of the Black community, notably the iconic Frederick Douglass.

As proof of their acceptance by the larger community, Jews served in both Union and Confederate armies - many even became officers. Though most resided in the North, by far the most successful was a Southerner: Judah P. Benjamin, who in 1852 became the second United States Senator of Jewish origin. (The first, David Levy Yulee, was elected Senator in 1845.) In turn the Confederacy's attorney general, secretary of war, and secretary of state, Benjamin was a complex man, irreligious, though he never denied his Jewishness.

Despite his high positions in the Confederacy, he was no unequivocal proponent of slavery. In a court case that was later reprinted in the abolitionist press, he successfully argued in favor of slaves who revolted on the ship Creole in 1841, with words poignantly (and deliberately?) reminiscent of Shylock's:

> What is a slave? He is a human being. He has feelings and passion and intellect. His heart, like the heart of the white man, swells with love, burns with jealousy, aches with sorrow, pines under restraint and discomfort, boils with revenge, and ever cherishes the desire for liberty ... Considering the character of the slave, and the peculiar passions which, generated by nature, are strengthened and stimulated by his condition, he is prone to revolt in the near future of things, and ever ready to conquer [i.e. obtain] his liberty where a probable chance presents itself.[56]

Benjamin's legalistic position on slavery was at minimum paradoxical, arguably even cynical.[57] For while admitting that it was against the law of nature, he considered slavery as "the creature of the statute law of the several states where it was established,"[58] and was thus, implicitly, justified. A belief that Blacks were underprepared for liberty, however, was common indeed, shared by anti- and pro-slavery advocates alike. That prejudice transitioned seamlessly into the progressive eugenics movement championed at the turn of the century by the academic and political ideocracy.[59]

But if some Jews assisted the Southern cause, for whatever reason, the vast majority strongly supported the Union. True, many Jews in Charleston, South Carolina, like most whites there, owned slaves. But so too did a sizeable number of free blacks – for that, writes the foremost historian of American Judaism Jonathan Sarna, "was the southern way."[60] Tragically, the internal rupture affected not only the larger community; it would tear apart even otherwise close-knit families. Sometimes Jewish brothers literally fought one another, as happened with the family of Abraham Jonas, whom Lincoln had called one of his most valued friends. Yet only one of Jonas's five sons fought for the North; the rest joined the Confederate Army.

Lincoln and the Jews

"We are covenantally joined, thus collectively punished. The same covenantal bond means that, in our sinfulness and imperfection, we are obligated toward one another: 'with malice toward none, with charity

for all.' Lincoln's Second Inaugural remains the most biblical presidential address ever delivered; Frederick Douglass, who was there, reflected: 'There seemed at the time to be in the man's soul the united souls of all the Hebrew prophets.'"

- Meir Y. Soloveichik, "Lincoln's Almost Chosen People," Feb. 2021

Lincoln's affection for Jews whom he knew personally, like Jonas, and his trusted podiatrist Issachar Zacharie, was well-known. But so was his admiration for Jews generally. And it was fully reciprocated. Most, particularly Northern, Jews loved Lincoln from the outset and held out great hopes for him. The new president's conviction that Jews deserved equal rights with everyone else was tested as soon as he took office. Unbeknownst to him, an amendment to the 1861 military chaplaincy law had been passed stipulating that a regimental chaplain be a regularly ordained Christian minister - in effect rendering the Jewish faith illegitimate. The first Jewish chaplain, Michael Allen, promptly lost his job. When a second chaplain, Rabbi Arnold Fishel, applied, he was refused. Whereupon Fishel brought the matter to the president's attention, asking for remedy.

Unable to repeal the amendment by executive action, Lincoln got to work immediately, eventually succeeding in getting Congress to revoke it. When on July 17, 1862, the chaplaincy was opened to non-Christians, it constituted a great victory not only for Jews but for all minority religious sects, a triumph of liberalism as originally understood.

But a few months later, on December 17, 1862, the Jews faced an even more serious threat. An order issued by General Ulysses S. Grant expelled them from the entire territory under his control, alleging that "the Jews, as a class, violating every regulation of trade established by the Treasury Department, and also Department orders, are hereby expelled from the Department." Jews as a class? On what grounds were they all deemed guilty? Lincoln recoiled: "I do not like to hear a class or nationality condemned on account of a few sinners." He immediately had the order rescinded.[61] Fortunately, that was in his power.

But nothing captures the centrality of Lincoln's place in the sacred Jewish pantheon as poignantly as do the events of the fateful morning of April 15, 1865, when the nation learned of Lincoln's tragic death at the hands of an assassin. It was the beginning of Passover.

The country that had welcomed Jews more readily than any other in history had just lost its leader on the very day when they celebrated their great redeemer, Moses, who similarly would not live to see the promised land. At Temple Emanu-El in New York the congregation rose as one at the terrible news and recited in unison the *kaddish* memorial prayer for the dead. So too, in San Francisco's Temple Emanu-El, Rabbi Elkan Cohen, who had heard the news as he mounted the pulpit to deliver his sermon, "was so overcome that, bursting in tears, he sank almost senseless."[62]

It is impossible to overstate the sixteenth president's intellectual debt to the Hebraic tradition. As Rabbi Meir Soloveichik noted in his riveting 2020 Erasmus Lecture, Lincoln's legacy is "bound up with the children of Abraham. For the covenantal imagery of the Hebrew Bible, so essential to the birth of the American republic, found its fullest expression in Lincoln during the Civil War. He ultimately emerged as the theologian of the American idea."[63] That idea, of course, is the right of all human beings to natural liberty.

If only Lincoln could have carried it on to the next stage; but that was not to be. The president's message, observes Solveitchik, echoing Daniel Elazar's magisterial study, was to remind Americans of their covenantal legacy. The new birth of freedom that Lincoln proclaimed at Gettysburg, intimating the supremely elegant rhetorical cadence of the King James Bible, "fourscore and seven years ago" marked the signing of that Declaration, an act the president acknowledged as endowed "with covenantal significance." Unlike secular, temporary contracts which bind only the specific parties indicated in the parchment, a covenant spans across generations through the original sacred binding event. Evidently, continues the Rabbi, "in Lincoln's theology, Locke and the Bible, Enlightenment and covenantal language, are joined."[64]

Soloveichik joins the knighted Chief Rabbi of Great Britain, Sir Jonathan Sacks, in marveling at "how the joining of social contract theory *and* covenantal thought in America allows, at its best, for both freedom and collective purpose." What Sacks calls integration without assimilation thereby not merely permits but encourages religious pluralism. "In the double helix of the American idea," as Soloveichik eloquently describes it, "biblical covenant and American enlightenment,

Lockean liberty and scriptural symbolism, are always intertwined. At times they are in tension, and at times they sustain each other."[65]

But Lincoln goes one step beyond the Hebraic precedent, evincing deeply Christian humility in his reluctance to describe his countrymen as more than an "almost chosen people." There are no guarantees that God's promise will be fulfilled no matter what. God is no determinist. It is always possible for a people to lose their exceptional status if they transgress. The covenant needs to be repeatedly reaffirmed, rededicated, and defended. It serves as a consistent reminder of man's imperfection, both cognitive and moral, and a need to do better, respecting one other.

It also demands an appreciation of the biblical tradition, as explained by Rutgers University political scientist Wilson Carey McWilliams: "Our older biblical language—the first grammar of American life—speaks of virtues and righteousness, qualities beyond choosing, bound up with the fundamental order of things. From that teaching, we learned to regard our rights as unalienable, not made by us nor subject to our surrendering. But we also were taught that community is a fact of life."[66] He adds that restoring biblical language is the "first step toward rearticulating **the inner dialogue - the ambiguity and irony - that is the soul of the liberal republic**."[67]

But ambiguity and irony can only be restored if the American idea is understood to rest on a liberal vision that transcends both individualism *and* group identity, respecting the unique traditions of particular communities variously self-defined, while at the same time preserving the inalienable sanctity of each human being, created ineffably unlike every other. It was precisely this idea that had appealed to the former slave Frederick Douglass, who upon hearing Lincoln's Gettysburg Address, reflected: "There seemed at the time to be in the man's soul the united souls of all the Hebrew prophets."[68]

By then, Douglass had abandoned his earlier infatuation with Garrison's radical "no union with slaveholders" secessionist irredentism. The firebrand Garrison had denounced what he contemptuously regarded no more than "half-measures," as he called all moderate paths away from slavery, for in fact he opposed politics of all kinds. A pacifist and a teetotaler, he was haughty and dictatorial, repeatedly urging Douglass not to speak about anything more than his personal experiences as a Black man. Whether Garrison's condescending behavior reflected ideological rigidity or a tinge of racism, Douglass (who suspected the latter) grew increasingly bitter: "I could not always follow the injunction, for I was now reading and thinking."[69] Other Garrison followers felt the same way – notably, philanthropist Gerrit Smith of New York, who left the group and endorsed a pro-Constitution form of abolitionism that did not reject political, legal, or military action. Soon Douglass would join Smith.

Yet Douglass still hesitated to endorse the newly elected president, the lanky politician so little known beyond Illinois, with full enthusiasm. But so buoyed was Douglass by the Emancipation Proclamation that he immediately declared abolitionists were now "willing to allow the President all the latitude of time, phraseology, and every honorable device that statesmanship might require for the achievement of a great and beneficent measure of liberty and progress."[70] It would turn out that a great deal more patience was going to be required than anyone would have anticipated at the time.

Lincoln was reelected, and eventually the war would be won. A touching scene took place on the White House lawn, when Douglass attended his inauguration on March 4, 1865. Policemen first tried to throw out the dark-skinned activist, but Lincoln noticed and instantly stopped them, with these words: "Here comes my friend Douglass." Holding out his hand, he added warmly: "I saw you in the crowd today, listening to my inaugural address; how did you like it?" Deeply moved, Douglass responded: it had been "a sacred effort."[71] That was the last time the two titans of emancipation would ever meet. Lincoln's star eclipsed before it could light the way of millions just emerging from the darkness of bondage.

The torch of Lincoln's hope and faith was naturally taken up by Douglass, a worthy secular prophet. Of his countless stirring orations, none surpassed the stunning address delivered at the unveiling of the Freedmen's Monument in Lincoln's memory in 1876. His speech turned into a monument all its own, a paean to America's liberal idea, at once pragmatic and transcendent.

Douglass began by setting the scene in appropriately lofty terms: "We stand today at the national center to perform something like a national act

- an act which is to go into history; and we are here where every pulsation of the national heart can be heard, felt, and reciprocated."[72] Meant to honor a nation's martyr, the speech became a tribute to the nation itself, which had managed to mend after nearly hemorrhaging to death in an apocalyptic civil war. A paean for the eons.

He started by recognizing that two decades earlier such an assembly would have been unthinkable. Despite a lingering "spirit of slavery and barbarism" that might have prompted mayhem, there they were, together, acknowledging their common ground:

> [T]hat we are here in peace today is a compliment and a credit to American civilization, and a prophecy of still greater national enlightenment and progress in the future. I refer to the past not in malice, for this is no day for malice; but simply to place more distinctly in front the gratifying and glorious change which has come both to our white fellow-citizens and ourselves, and to congratulate all upon the contrast between now and then; the new dispensation of freedom with its thousand blessings to both races, and the old dispensation of slavery with its ten thousand evils to both races—white and black.[73]

His was no ordinary panegyric. Douglass readily conceded that Lincoln "was preeminently the white man's President, entirely devoted to the welfare of white men. He was ready and willing at any time during the first years of his administration to deny, postpone, and sacrifice the rights of humanity in the colored people to promote the welfare of the white people of this country. In all his education and feeling he was an American of the Americans." And sure, he "shared the prejudices common to his countrymen towards the colored race." That said, he continued:

> Looking back to his times and to the condition of his country, we are compelled to admit that this unfriendly feeling on his part may be safely set down as one element of his wonderful success in organizing the loyal American people for the tremendous conflict before them, and bringing them safely through that conflict. His great mission was to accomplish two things: first, to save his country from dismemberment and ruin; and, second, to free his country from the great crime of slavery.[74]

What comes next, however, is the crucial lesson of Lincoln for the Black community that no one but Douglass could have articulated with equal eloquence and poignancy, for it mirrored his own odyssey:

> Born and reared among the lowly, a stranger to wealth and luxury, compelled to grapple single-handed with the flintiest hardships of life, from tender youth to sturdy manhood, he grew strong in the manly and heroic qualities demanded by the great mission to which he was called by the votes of his countrymen. The hard condition of his early life, which would have depressed and broken down weaker men, only gave greater life, vigor, and buoyancy to the heroic spirit of Abraham Lincoln. He was ready for any kind and any quality of work. What other young men dreaded in the shape of toil, he took hold of with the utmost cheerfulness. … All day long he could split heavy rails in the woods, and half the night long he could study his English Grammar by the uncertain flare and glare of the light made by a pine-knot.[75]

It was precisely this spirit that Douglass considered necessary to be a good president but also to be a genuine human being. Douglass fervently believed that

> the tendency of the age is unification, not isolation; not to clans and classes, but to human brotherhood. It was once degradation intensified for a Norman to associate with a Saxon; but time and events have swept down the barriers between them, and Norman and Saxon have become Englishmen. The Jew was once despised and hated in Europe, and is so still in some parts of that continent; but he has risen, and is rising to higher consideration, and no man is now degraded by association with him anywhere. In like manner the Negro will rise in social scale.

He had no illusions: it was not going to happen without effort. "Manly self-assertion and eternal vigilance are essential to Negro liberty, not less than to that of the white man."[76]

The Jews rose by hard work and effort, just as he himself had done, as did the great president – proving to him beyond doubt that neither race nor poverty presented insuperable obstacle to personal success. The secret was education, respect for work, and self-confidence. The attitude, writes Virginia State University historian Oscar R. Williams, Jr., was not unusual among

> Blacks [who] have consciously and unconsciously held Jews as a success model in America.… Black religion has always been obsessed with Jews in Egyptland. Historian Miles Mark Fisher noted that Blacks were singing "'Let My People Go,' as early as the 1790s." Paradoxically, their admiration of Jews continued long after slavery ended. In the minds of Black slaves the Union victory was living proof that Blacks were the 'Modern Day Children of Israel.' 'The Promised Land' became the

> major theme of Black history in the Nineteenth Century. Likewise, slave narratives often compared the plight of Blacks with that of the children of Israel in Pharaoh's land.[77]

Like Douglass, so too Booker T. Washington intimated that to become influential like the Jews, Blacks should demonstrate both unity and pride, implying, writes Williams, "that Black failure to imitate Jews would insure failure in America." In brief, "Black leaders from Frederick Douglass to Martin Luther King have continued to use Jews as models for Black people."[78]

But the greater white community was hardly sanguine about accepting Blacks as equals, contrary to what Douglass and many others had hoped, if not necessarily expected. President Theodore Roosevelt learned his lesson the hard way. After his invitation to the great educator Booker T. Washington for a White House dinner in 1901 raised eyebrows, TR would never repeat the gesture. In 1906, when 167 members from a detachment of Black soldiers were falsely accused of involvement in a bar fight in Brownsville, Texas, the president felt he had no choice but to discharge them. But while Republicans, like TR, mostly wobbled on the issue, the Democratic party flaunted its bigotry. It was almost ostentatious. Southern leaders, still smarting from the Confederate defeat, were furious, unrepentant, and as the party's dominant wing, called the shots. Would they prevail and go so far as to eviscerate the war's gains?

The spin-masters went to work. What came to known as the "Lost Cause" theory of the war, developed by white Southerners, including former Confederate generals, represented a distortion of history. Legal scholar Timothy Sandefur, for example, describes it as "a reactionary doctrine, which came to dominate the political science and history departments of respectable universities throughout the country, [that] held that the war had not really been about slavery at all and that the enfranchisement of former slaves had been an immense mistake."[79] Though by no means restricted to the South, the theory would especially resonate with the son of a chaplain in the Confederate army and outspoken proponent of slavery.

The young man's name was Thomas Woodrow Wilson. An apple who didn't fall far from his slaveholding family's tree, Wilson embraced the outlook of his Southern kinfolk. He even argued that slavery was "not so dark a thing as it was painted," because slaves were generally "happy and well cared for."[80] Reflecting on the manifestly flawed Reconstruction, Wilson did not blame his fellow white supremacists. Instead, he accused those claiming to help the ill-used recently "liberated" freedmen who, truth to tell, were foolishly "excited by a freedom they did not understand."

Face it: those poor Black folk were "bewildered and without leaders, and yet insolent and aggressive; sick of work, covetous of pleasure, - a host of dusky children untimely put out to school."[81] Was it really humane to let them loose? Wilson thought it was high time for a whole new look at America's compact with its people by steering the ship of state along the trajectory of real progress toward the Common Good. Liberalism was about to mutate.

Chapter III:

Liberalism Gets Hijacked

Woodrow Wilson's Declaration of Interdependence

"The liberal party insists that the Government has the definite duty to use all its power and resources to meet new social problems with new social controls - to ensure to the average person the right to his own economic and political life, liberty, and the pursuit of happiness."

- Franklin D. Roosevelt (1941)

"Religious practice changed drastically during Wilson's lifetime as Protestant ministers began linking salvation to the doing of good works. They interpreted the Lord's Prayer, 'Thy kingdom come, Thy will be done on earth as it is in heaven,' as directing Christians to rid the world of evils including poverty, crime, racial tension, child labor, war and other concerns now typically associated with liberalism."

- Jeremy Menchik, "Woodrow Wilson and the Spirit of Liberal Internationalism" (2021)

Young Woodrow Wilson was duly groomed while sequestered at the University of Virginia, University of North Carolina, and Johns Hopkins. Under the tutelage of the disgruntled Confederate intellectual class, the future commander-in-chief had been ready for prime time long before he gained national stature. Princeton, by appointing him president, first provided the coveted title. The nation then offered him the big prize: a global platform. Its immense power and prestige thereby turned Wilson, observes Timothy Sandefur, into "a leading spokesman for the Progressive ideology that rejected the ideas of the Declaration of Independence and opted instead for the organic collectivism that was once the heart of the confederate cause."[1] Wilson openly rejected the Declaration's version of liberalism as "radically evil and corrupting." Nothing less.

Scholars have been struck by Wilson's admiration for Prussian chancellor Otto von Bismarck and the redoubtable Napoleon, whom he had praised for allegedly advancing their nation's General Will. By way of explanation, they point to his family circumstances, to bigoted Southern professors, his own narcissism, and especially Continental influences. At the same time, Wilson was just as solidly steeped as were his fellow American intellectuals in a British heritage they had never repudiated, having merely resented the Crown's prolonged parental supervision.

American nouveaux-liberals had remained attuned to the ideas that emerged from the Mother Country. In truth, it had been their British colleagues who first repudiated a strict form of Lockeian individualism, veering in a communitarian-collectivist direction far more popular on the Continent. Among them was John Stuart Mill (1806–1873), easily the most famous and influential British philosopher of the nineteenth century. That hardly any college student was until recently, as standards plummeted, exempt from reading Mill's "On Liberty" testifies to the precocious scholar's continuing relevance.

If only they had understood the real secret of its success. A typical bestseller, Mill's essay intoxicates with ambiguity. Writes the eminent scholar of the Enlightenment Alan Charles Kors:

> Perhaps Mill's *On Liberty* has had such a great influence not only because of the eloquence of his celebrations of individual liberty and autonomy, but also because *On Liberty* can be appropriated both by casual rights theorists - individual sovereignty over one's life, absent direct harm to others, has a ring to it - and by casual utilitarians - his stated goal is the long term well-being of mankind as a species. What surely appears as a weakness to more philosophically minded moral and political theorists - a possible conflation of utility and rights - probably functions as a great source of Mill's enduring appeal.[2]

Mill's disciples reflected that internal contradiction. Some opted for the strand that emphasized individual rights, which earned him the reputation as the Founder of classical liberalism, while others applauded his utilitarian collectivism, which promoted the greater good of the greatest number, which led to progressivism. But true to tradition, most agreed with John Morley who wrote, in 1873, that Mill's work deserves praise because it "reposes on no principle of abstract right, but like all the rest of its author's opinions, on principles of utility and experience."[3]

Except it was one thing for mere philosophers to argue about truths their predecessors thought self-evident. It was quite another for the leader of an increasingly powerful nation to forge policy while opposing the nation's basic principles enshrined in its founding document. Blithely redefining it, with a mere sweep of the semantic hand, amounted to nothing less than an intellectual *coup d'etat.* Although hardly alone, Wilson did more than anyone to propel into the mainstream of American public discourse the idea that some fuzzy notion of collective good collectively pursued, rather than individual freedom, was the paramount ideal of government action. He accomplished this sleight-of-hand by switching labels in mid-stream. From the highest bully pulpit in the nation, he was ideally positioned to affect both the legal and popular culture away from its roots.

Wilson's lexical *legerdemain* was arguably the most tectonic political act in American history to date. In plain daylight, within the space of a few months, the president switched from self-styled *progressive* in 1916 to new-style *liberal* in 1917. "I am a progressive," he said in one of his campaign speeches in 1916. "I do not spell it with a capital P, but I think my pace is just as fast as those who do."[4] A few months later, on January 22, 1917, he proceeded to ask, rhetorically of course, whether he might not "believe that I am in effect speaking for ***liberals*** and friends of humanity in every nation and of ***every program of liberty***," if not indeed "for the silent mass of mankind everywhere who have as yet had no place or opportunity to speak their real hearts out concerning the death and ruin they see to have come already upon the persons and the homes they hold most dear."[5]

What he proposed therefore was nothing less than total unity, "[w]hen all unite to act in the same sense and with the same purpose all act in the common interest and are free to live their own lives under a common protection." All must unite; with the same purpose; and act in the common interest. Not so much Exodus-on-the-(Plymouth)-Rock as pre-demolition Babel-on-the-Hudson, he proclaimed one mindset and one purpose *uber alles*.

Not that there was anything especially remarkable about refurbishing liberalism: such is politics. Humpty Dumpty had been correct when he reminded Alice that words mean "neither more nor less" than what their author can get away with. Her protest that "[t]he question is whether you *can* make words so many different things" is fair, but she had obviously missed his point. "The question is," retorted Humpty Dumpty abruptly, "which is to be master – that's all." The garrulous egg had admittedly overstepped the boundaries of good breeding, but the lesson is eminently worth heeding by creatures of all species, shapes, and sizes. Unconsciously channeling Machiavelli, Humpty was anticipating Saul Alinsky, to whom we will return shortly.

The odyssey of so-called liberalism parallels that of so-called conservatism in endlessly complex ways, which students of intellectual history underestimate at their peril. In his brilliant 1987 book *The Language of Politics in America: Shaping Political Consciousness from McKinley to Reagan,* political theorist David Green observes that hard as it may be to believe, "a hundred years ago Americans did not talk about 'liberals' versus 'conservatives.'" Words must change with the times. "Because politics is an ongoing struggle for power, the competition to define political terms is constantly being renewed."[6]

Like any tool, language may be repurposed – and it is, routinely. Since any politician knows that "the retention of an existing vocabulary need not mean fidelity to established policies," it follows that a label which "has been associated in the past with popular institutions, behavior, and values or appears to embody the dominant values of the moment"[7] is worth keeping, even if its application defies those values. If this sounds like subterfuge, welcome to democratic discourse.

Wilson's 1916 claim had seemed appropriate at the time, writes Green, since his "rhetoric candidly revealed his strategy." Namely, the absence of one. The quintessential politician, intent above all on winning, he had "neither a consistent policy framework nor a clearly articulated ideology." In 1912, his victory had come essentially by default, thanks to the Republicans' split following Theodore Roosevelt's defection. Once in office, however, Wilson gravitated increasingly toward his personal preference which had been, just like Roosevelt's, decidedly statist. Accordingly, "by early 1916 he was adopting more and more Progressive party planks from 1912, such as child labor legislation, workmen's compensation, and rural credits, all of which he had previously failed to support."[8]

It might not have come as much of a surprise to anyone really familiar with Wilson's thinking. For while Wilson had no consistent policy in 1912, and his ideology was not clearly articulated, he had actually revealed his underlying viewpoint decades earlier. In a paper entitled "Socialism and Democracy," admittedly never published in his lifetime, Wilson clarified what was really hidden behind the anodyne labels "progressivism" and "liberalism." Well versed in political theory, he knew its real name: state socialism.

> [S]ocialism is a proposition that every community, by means of whatever forms of organization may be most effective for the purpose, see to it for itself that each one of its members finds the employment for which he is best suited and is rewarded according to his diligence and merit, all proper surroundings of moral influence being secured to him by the public authority. "State socialism" is willing to act though state authority as it is at present organized. It proposes that all idea of a limitation of public authority by individual rights be put out of view, and that the State consider itself bound to stop only at what is unwise or futile in its universal superintendence alike of individual and of public interests.[9]

Believing that "all proper surroundings of moral influence" are and should be secured by public authority, any limitation on that authority by such gobbledygook as "individual rights [should] be put out of view." Given its "superintendence alike of individual and of public interests," therefore, the State might, if it so decides, stop only at "what is unwise or futile." Sounds good, but... what does it mean? Who decrees what is "unwise" and "futile?"

How does a community "see to it for itself" that each member finds the employment for which he is "best suited?" Will the community as a whole decide? Don't we each do that for ourselves, through trial and error, within myriad constraints? In sum, Wilson's proposal that "all idea of a limitation of public authority by individual rights" be "put out of view" is tantamount to rejecting the Bill of Rights and the basic purpose of the Constitution, namely, limited government. The General Will dressed as public authority is not supreme; the people are – each one of them.

Unfettered democracy is thus in principle limitless. If no one may curtail what "society," speaking through (or for) the majority, "wants," what's to stop it? However grandiose sounding, its "will" is ultimately tyrannical. If democracy/society speaks as one, the wills of particular individual considered contrary to it are deemed suspect. Thus the group is Leviathan. As Wilson puts it:

> The germinal conceptions of democracy are as free from all thought of a limitation of the public authority as are the corresponding conceptions of socialism; the individual rights which the democracy of our own century has actually observed, were suggested to it by a political philosophy radically individualistic, but not necessarily democratic. Democracy is bound by no principle of its own nature to say itself nay as to the exercise of any power.

The key is to use state power to combat social, economic, and other ills, of which there is never any shortage. His concluding question, therefore, cannot but be rhetorical: "[M]ust not government lay aside all timid scruple and boldly make itself an agency for social reform as well as for political control?" One wonders whether, had the paper been published during Wilson's lifetime, it would have changed the electoral outcome.

The philosophically trained will recognize traces here not only of British but also German idealism. This was to be expected; for as Clemson University historian C. Bradley Thompson documents in his brilliant study *America's Revolutionary Mind*, the first mention in America of Georg Wilhelm Friedrich Hegel, the enormously influential 19th century German philosopher, occurred as early as 1832. South Carolinian Rev. James Warley Miles (1818-1875) would adopt Hegel's view of a "determinate plan in history." which he saw as leading necessarily toward higher levels of freedom by a "progressive stream of civilization."[10] What Miles found most appealing was Hegel's view that man should be seen as "a member of the organic body of humanity." The enemy was individualism; like Hegel, Miles believed that "man can only develop all of his capacities in the organism of the state."[11] So too did Wilson.

Observes Thompson: "It is hard to imagine a philosophy or worldview more antithetical to the principles of the American Revolution." Miles's contemporary George Fitzhugh (1806-1881), a Virginian sociologist and lawyer, in his 1856 essay titled "Centralization and Socialism," had similarly railed against increasing aggregate wealth causing "continually its more unequal distribution."[12] For as long as capital is "in the hands of the rich and the skillful," wrote Fitzhugh, it cannot fail "to oppress the laboring class" - an argument eerily reminiscent of Karl Marx.

Thompson explains: "Many proslavery writers in the American South were, in effect, pre-Marxian socialists." Their break with the Declaration was presumably predicated on its most resonant passage, which so brazenly flouted the traditionally British antipathy to "abstract principles." It may seem ironic, at first glance, that pro-slavery intellectuals should make common cause with progressives allegedly dedicated to equity, democracy, and yes, socialism. But Jefferson fell into disrepute in many circles of the South.

Men like Wilson, whose understanding of political communication was highly sophisticated, were capable of providing the requisite rhetorical camouflage. To convince the audience, "socialism" would not do: it did not fly in the public square, and Wilson did not want to risk using it. Too many Americans were unable to shed that pernicious, radically individualistic political philosophy of the Declaration, so inconveniently entrenched in the pesky, senescent Constitution, which he believed prevented the nation from achieving the progress it deserved. If only the experts were allowed to take care of its march, all would be well.

Eager to wield power in the name of the people, and on their behalf pursue the greater good, however, Wilson needed democracy's moral imprimatur. And in order to win, he had to campaign. Which is where carefully honed rhetoric comes in. In 1912, Wilson knew that his vaguely collectivist views, at the time basically anti-war, were shared by the "great majority of [self-styled] progressives,"[13] according to historian Arthur Link. Wilson believed, as they did, that America's unique mission was to set an example of "social justice and peaceful behavior." So *progressive* it would be. And *democratic* too, sure. Wilson was comfortable with either term. Whatever works.

By 1917, however, circumstances had changed considerably. Given the way the war was unfolding, Wilson faced a new dilemma. The Allies were stalled, battles were inconclusive, and the president was itching to make a difference on the global scene. But how to explain the emerging geopolitical realities to his progressive constituents, stubbornly pacifist and still staunchly opposed to taking sides in a war that didn't seem to affect the United States? What occurred most readily to his academically trained mind was also the most obvious, if slightly cynical: find the most popular label, then redefine it, completely if need be, and then blithely appropriate it.

Green describes both Wilson's dilemma and the rationale behind his clever semantic solution:

> The rhetoric of liberalism gave him a maneuverability in the situation that progressive rhetoric could not. It would have been extremely dangerous to have argued foreign policy in the language of progressivism, especially as he moved closer to war. ... The liberal label was... relatively untainted at the time by domestic political controversy and could be used as a fresh means of refocusing public attention on international affairs.[14]

It was pure genius. The professor-president, preacher-*manqué,* applied his tradecraft with commendable skill. By casting the United States as the defender of freedom as against German imperialism, Wilson thereby "helped prepare Americans themselves for an unprecedented assertion of governmental authority in the name of liberty." Yet Green recognizes the irony in this extraordinary *legerdemain* of progressivism-cum-liberalism; for

> the substitution could not have worked unless the two labels could have been taken to have some common connotations, **however superficial**. Indeed that is what happened, for on a general level both appeared to connote sympathy for the underprivileged or oppressed. "Forward motion" could be interpreted as "liberation" from oppression.[15]

Note that it merely *appeared* to connote sympathy, little more. Increasingly, the new & improved American "liberalism" would become preoccupied with appearances. "Forward motion" was a synonym for "progress," with a nod to scientism and pragmatism. Most of all, there had to be compassion, which mandated *sounding* compassionate. Convinced of their own good intentions, the new autocrats thus felt morally empowered to decide what is best for the *demos*. Their trust in knowledge and technology was equaled, if not superseded, by trust in their own moral superiority. Hubris was thus camouflaged by self-validated altruism in the name of freedom.

It was not a new affliction. As Lord Acton warned, in an address before members of the Bridgnorth Institute on February 26, 1877: "If hostile interests have wrought much injury, false ideas [about liberty] have wrought still more." This passage applies equally today:

> The ancients understood the regulation of power better than the regulation of liberty. They concentrated so many prerogatives on the state as to leave no footing from which a man could deny its jurisdiction or assign bounds to its activity. What the slave was in the hands of his master the citizen was in the hands of the community. The most sacred obligations vanished before the public advantage. The passengers existed for the sake of the ship.[16]

Like the ancients millennia earlier, Wilson had chosen power in exchange for liberty, the community at the expense of its members, the ship over its passengers. What he sacrificed was not only his sacred obligation to his office and his nation but in effect, though he would never acknowledge it (except perhaps subliminally), to his God.

Scientism and Eugenics

"[W]e in America all know too well how often 'science' has been appealed to in the least calm of public assemblies to bear evidence in favor of one view or another of the way in which we ought to treat the inferior races that live with us."

– William James, *Essays in Religion and Morality* (1868)

"You respect the rights of man, I don't, except those things a given crowd will fight for – which vary from religion to the price of a glass of beer."

- Oliver Wendell Holmes, Jr., letter to Morris Cohen (1919)

The North-South peace had silenced the gunshots, but tranquility was still elusive, even if no one could yet foresee that another devastating conflagration was about to liquidate much of the European elite, inaugurating the bloodiest century in history. The Great War reflected tectonic shifts within the crust of Western civilization. Precipitated by the scientific and technological revolution, man's self-image and conception of liberty were about to change even more, almost beyond recognition.

Still the good news predominated after America's war with itself. Despite a near-brush with suicide, the nation had survived, emerging from its trauma even stronger in some respects. For ultimately, observes Harvard Professor Louis Menand in *The Metaphysical Club: A Story of Ideas in America*, "the outcome of the Civil War was a validation, as

Lincoln had hoped it would be, of the American experiment."[17] Once the Constitution was properly amended, all but the most intransigent of Garrisonians had to admit that it was no longer inconsistent with the Declaration.

But in other ways, continues Menand, the war seemed to many who lived through it "not just a failure of democracy but a failure of culture, a failure of ideas.... The Civil War discredited the beliefs and assumptions of the era that preceded it.... They seemed absurdly obsolete in the new, postwar era." Even the meaning of "meaning" was changing, alongside "truth" and "morality," as a utilitarian-pragmatist-instrumentalist model was emerging in the new, albeit not unequivocally improved, America.

The founder of American psychology, William James, shared with fellow philosophers Charles S. Peirce (1839-1914) and John Dewey (1859-1952) a newly acquired skepticism about ideas in general and truth in particular. Explains Menand:

> They believed that ideas are produced not by individuals, but by groups of individuals – that ideas are social. They believed that ideas do not develop according to some inner logic of their own, but are entirely dependent, like germs, on their human carriers and the environment. And they believed that since ideas are provisional responses to particular and unreproducible circumstances, their survival depends not on their immutability but on their adaptability.[18]

Ideas were thus considered equally subject to evolutionary selection: only the fittest survived, and therefore, only the fittest *should* survive. But if what *is* becomes synonymous with what *should be,* does history determine morality? For many ideocrats, the question became rhetorical, paving the way to a progressive version of liberalism that stood the Declaration on its head.

A century after America had declared independence from a decaying Old World, elites who floundered amidst upheavals, craving direction yet seeking a greater role in decision-making, returned to its shores for inspiration. Between 1865 and 1914, two generations of young Americans from the North caught up with their Southern brethren and went off to study in Europe, primarily to Germany. The result, writes J. Bradley Thompson, was that "[w]ithin a generation after the Civil War, American intellectuals, particularly in the North, came to reject not only the

Declaration's self-evident truths but the very idea of 'truth' itself – truth as absolute, certain, universal, and permanent. ... The moral and political principles of the old liberalism, or the Founders' liberalism, disappeared almost overnight from American universities."[19]

The newfound cavalier attitude toward truth, especially severe after the Great War, may also have reflected the kind of depression and anxiety that mass carnage is bound to elicit. No doubt it affected future Supreme Court Justice Oliver Wendell Holmes, Jr. (1841-1935), who had seen his closest friends slaughtered in that war and was himself seriously wounded. To be sure, his occasional callousness also reflected a character flaw. On one occasion, he declared casually to a friend: "All I mean by truth is the path I have to travel."[20] No sentimentalist, he saw the natural order of things as utterly amoral. Truth and goodness seemed equally relative to the cynical patrician. In the ruthless struggle of history, rights are just another social weapon.

Already in 1873, in one of his first law review articles, Holmes had stated that democratic means should be used in the evolution of society to allow every "social gene," as it were, to fight for survival. Everyone, of course, pursues his own (narrow) interest - "this is as true in legislation as in any other form of corporate action. All that can be expected from modern improvements is that legislation should easily and quickly, yet not too quickly, modify itself in accordance with the will of the *de facto* supreme power in the community…."[21]

De facto power comes first, becoming *de jure* when that power becomes officially enforceable. Its legitimacy, in sociological terms, is cemented by the "supreme power" of the majority. Holmes reiterated this idea in his magnum opus, *The Common Law,* published in 1881: "It seems to me clear that the *ultima ratio*, not only *regum,* but of private persons, is force."[22] Holmes was Dumpty with a sheepskin, chastening naïve Alice.

Ultimately, "the key to all his jurisprudence," argues Menand, "is that he thought only in terms of aggregate social forces; he had no concern for the individual."[23] Opposed to the concept of the individual on the level of theory, he also lacked faith in the notion of individual human agency. He accepted that some people must be sacrificed for the sake of group survival. Far too unfunny to count as a joke, the comment revealed

Holmes's concern-deficit - proof of a crippled soul. Undoubtedly affected by personal trauma during the Civil War, he had lamented that "every society rests on the death of men."[24] That said, he also seems to have clearly enjoyed upsetting his audience. As when he casually remarked in a lecture, that since successful people basically knew how to survive better than others, those who ended up drowning deserved to do so. It not only sounded heartless, most likely it was.

Thus on closer inspection, Holmes's reputation as a civil libertarian, argues Menand, must be placed in perspective. For when he ruled favorably in cases that involved civil liberties, his defense "had nothing to do… with the notion that such liberties were owed to people merely by the fact of their being human." Strikingly callous, Holmes "exhibited complete indifference to the suffering of, for example, Southern blacks victimized by de facto discrimination." True, "he disliked the self-righteous, but he had no sympathy for the weak. He reversed, in effect, the priorities of his youth: he took the Constitution for his text and rejected the Declaration of Independence."[25]

None of Holmes's rulings better illustrated his antipathy to the principles of the Declaration than his infamous decision to uphold a Virginia law, *Buck v. Bell* (1927), which promoted sterilization of the "feeble-minded,"[26] on the ground that such impaired human beings would "sap the strength of the State." Frankly speaking, wrote Holmes, sterilization is far and away the most humane course of action. For "[i]t is better for all the world, if instead of waiting to execute degenerate offspring for crime, or to let them starve for their imbecility, society can prevent those who are manifestly unfit from continuing their kind."[27]

The measure was all in the name of progress, shorthand for the good of the state. To justify his decision to permit and even encourage sterilization, he then proceeds to utter one of the most cold-hearted public statements in American history: "Three generations of imbeciles are enough." Never mind that the young woman whose case was before the high court for having been sterilized against her will, Carrie Buck, was neither feeble-minded nor handicapped! It had all been a travesty[28] - and its perpetrators, including Holmes, knew it. But eugenics had by then become widely accepted throughout the nation, specifically among the academic and professional elite. It was the most outrageous example of the new cult of science that captivated post-war culture.

"Eugenics," rooted in "well-born" (from the Greek, *eu,* "good" and *genos*, "birth"), refers to the (pseudo)science of improving a human population by controlled breeding, designed to increase the occurrence of desirable heritable characteristics. While originating in England, it really took off in the United States, starting with Indiana, which legalized the practice of forced sterilization in 1907. During the next six years, eleven additional states would adopt legislation authorizing sterilization of "undesirables," especially those of low intelligence. The glaringly un-technical word "feebleminded" was widely used despite having "no precise medical description. A catchall term that covered a wide range of purported deficiencies," writes bestselling author Adam Cohen in his carefully documented *Imbeciles: The Supreme Court, Eugenics, and the Sterilization of Carrie Buck,* it basically meant that "he or she behaved in ways that offended the middle-class sensibilities of judges and social workers."[29]

This proto-fascist practice would serve as a model for the Nazis, who were seeking to justify liquidating the mentally ill,[30] a dress rehearsal for the obscene "race-cleansing" Holocaust. It also served the purposes of Soviet political psychiatry.[31] Such practices, inconceivable in any society that dared to call itself liberal, reflect how science can degenerate into vulgar scientism. Defined as the cult of science, physicist Ian Hutchinson condemns this idolatry of "science, modeled on the natural sciences, [as]… the only source of real knowledge."[32] Sciences thus "modeled" soon included social science, sociology, psychology, and related fields such as physiology, neurobiology, and last but not least, statistics. Numbers trumped wisdom.

All these disciplines profited enormously from appeals to empirical data gathered by growing armies of graduate students and researchers. Increasingly sophisticated mathematical processing tools immeasurably (no pun intended) improved their potential predictive power. But scientism went one unconscionable step further: it denigrated non-quantitative, humanist insights as "not real science," contemptuously dismissing them as irrelevant, or worse. This attitude, that science alone held the key to all truth, did much more than impoverish analysis. It seriously damaged sober and effective policymaking.

Although the post-Civil War intellectual climate exacerbated its effects, scientism had emerged long before that conflict erupted. As science was fast gaining in prestige, American colleges were eager to catch up with the times. Hallowed Harvard, for example, had been seeking to establish a school of science since 1845. At the same time, the country's frontier was pushing westward, for the all-American exploring itch had to be scratched. And a nation on the move needed moving ideas, moving machines, not to mention moving rhetoric.

To the rescue came the charismatic Swiss-born naturalist Louis Agassiz, whose Boston lectures delivered in 1846, boldly titled "The Plan of Creation in the Animal Kingdom," mesmerized crowds numbering in the thousands. Having inherited an invaluable collection of fish fossils from the well-known French paleontologist Georges Cuvier, Agassiz had been keen to publicize his theories of science as based strictly on observation. So, when Harvard made him an offer, in 1847, to establish the first school of science in the United States, he accepted enthusiastically. It inaugurated the professionalization of American science.

Already a celebrity who could attract large audiences and money, Agassiz was perfect for the job. But his career really took off after meeting the most famous American anthropologist of his time, Samuel George Morton. A specialist in fossils, Morton had become fascinated by the bounty Lewis and Clark had retrieved from their Western expedition. His main passion was human skulls, which he measured and compared by "race." His methodology, unfortunately, relied on woefully incomplete, unverified, indeed unverifiable data, so risibly flawed that it is hard to understand how Agassiz could have been so readily enthralled by Morton's absurd conclusions. There could be but one reason: that however preposterous, they fit neatly with his own prejudices.

The shoddiness of Morton's research still astonishes. It involved correlating measurements of some six hundred crania with platitudes about "national traits" found in popular travel literature, on which he based his generalizations.[33] Yet Agassiz thought this was just what he needed to complement his own observations of fish fossils, which he believed threw light on human development. His own intriguing hypothesis that an embryo develops in ways that mimic the evolution of its species across time, later known as the "ontogeny recapitulates phylogeny" theory, was ingenious. But over-eager to venture into deeper speculative waters, Agassiz proved as casual about evidential scarcity - and as mesmerized by the illusion that mere numbers guarantee precision - as his newfound skull-obsessed, bigoted friend. Nor any less bigoted.

In 1847, for instance, Agassiz confidently declared to an awe-struck audience in Charleston, South Carolina: "[T]he brain of the Negro is that of the imperfect brain of a 7 months' infant in the womb of a White."[34] Evidence? None. Zero. Invited to return to that city three years later to address the newly founded American Association for the Advancement of Science, he had the chutzpa to tell the illustrious gathered scientists that "viewed zoologically, the several races of men were well marked and distinct."[35] No hint as to how those alleged markings could be discerned.

It was therefore not surprising that he would vigorously oppose social equality among the races. Yet he did not go so far as to support slavery. That emboldened Samuel Gridley Howe, head of the American Freedmen's Inquiry Commission (established in 1863 after Lincoln issued the Emancipation proclamation) to ask Agassiz's opinion on whether the Black population might become absorbed into the general population through interbreeding. Shocked by such an outlandish suggestion, Agassiz's response was unequivocal: the government ought "to put every possible obstacle to the crossing of the races, and the increase of half-breeds." He ranted on:

> It is immoral and destructive of social equality as it creates unnatural relations and multiplies the differences among members of the same community in the wrong directions. ... I am convinced also that no efforts should be spared to check that which is abhorrent to our better nature, and inconsistent with the progress of higher civilization and a purer morality.[36]

The logic seemed to him self-evident: progress meant higher civilization, which necessarily entailed a "purer" morality and thus purer genes. His conception of "social equality" was predicated on not multiplying differences "in the wrong direction." Progressivism could thus promote both eugenics and equity. To achieve maximum equity, i.e., social equality, the population should be as homogeneous as possible, thus legitimating eugenic measures. Agassiz thereby helped make racist eugenics respectable, notwithstanding the patently fraudulent "evidence" adduced in its defense.

Not everyone advanced the same arguments to defend the pseudo-science and its ghastly practices. For his part, Agassiz thought that each species had evolved separately. Others, by contrast, thought diverse species had derived from one common root that later branched out, which in the case of humans may or may not imply further racial divisions. In either case, however, the idea of evolution took hold long before Darwin published his ambitiously titled *On the Origin of Species, or the Preservation of Favoured Races in the Struggle for Life* in 1859. The beautifully written book, whose loving attention to detail has enthralled many a reader, argued that the world evolved throughout history toward a higher civilization and a purer morality.

Unlike any prior biological study, *The Origin of Species* offered a treasure-trove of archeological data documenting evolutionary development throughout the natural world. As a result, observes acclaimed Columbia University Professor Richard Hofstadter in his seminal *Social Darwinism in American Thought* (1945), the book rose to oracular status almost instantly, being "consulted with the reverence usually reserved for Scripture."[37] The temptation to draw normative conclusions from Darwin's data was irresistible.

Among the awe-struck was Charles Loring Brace, a leading social worker and reformer, who after reading it thirteen times concluded that "if the Darwinian theory be true, the law of natural selection applies to all the moral history of mankind, as well as the physical. Evil must die ultimately as the weaker element, in the struggle with good."[38] Progress is but another way of describing evolution: both aim upward, ineluctably, toward the Good. *Is* and *ought* coalesce.

Contrary to widespread popular opinion, however, the word itself, "evolution," its normative connotations manifest, hardly appears in Darwin. He certainly did not suggest that selection of favorable traits is either deliberately intended or progressive in the sense of morally superior.[39] Yet Darwin's protestations could not deny the political implications, to say nothing of the theological fallout, of intimating that humans were basically less-hirsute bipedal apes. Darwin did not need to spell it out; others would do it for him.

His most effective admirer was fellow-Englishman Herbert Spencer (1820-1903). Author of the infamous slogan "survival of the fittest," generally assumed to have been coined by Darwin, Spencer's own evolutionary theory of mind and behavior had already been developed by 1855. Like Darwin, Spencer's reputation was especially great in America.[40] Here, writes Hofstadter, Spencer was seen to have drawn out evolutionary theory's "ultimate purpose … of finding for the principles of right and wrong in conduct at large, a scientific basis,"[41] and it resonated with a public primed to believe.

What Spencer thought he had found, as he believed had Darwin, was a scientific proof for the morality of cutthroat competition: let the fittest competitor survive, come what may. It was caricature-capitalism, reified mockery. Yet many free-market proponents, who should have known better, found it irresistible. He even appealed to those who sought to justify certain kinds of coercion, even war. This outraged William James, believing it to be a misunderstanding of Darwin,[42] as it indeed was.

Misunderstanding Darwin seemed to have become a tempting, equal-opportunity pastime. As Hofstadter observes, "[i]f there were, in Darwin's writings, texts for rugged individualists and ruthless imperialists, those who stood for social solidarity and fraternity could [also]… match them text for text with some to spare."[43] Nor was the naïve solidarity/fraternity crowd the only cohort of the leftwing fan club that put Darwin to good use. Hofstadter observes that even "[o]rthodox Marxian socialists in the early years of the twentieth century felt quite at home in Darwinian surroundings."[44] Marx himself had reputedly told Friedrich Engels that *The Origin of Species* "contains the natural-historical basis of our outlook."[45]

Who had it right? Both political wings did so, each in their own way. Hofstadter, a self-described progressive critical of all opportunistic normative extrapolations by social Darwinists from both ideological camps, castigates all American "evolutionary" sociologists:

> Sound as the socialist criticisms may have been, they were nevertheless stereotypes, cast in the mold of the same nineteenth century monism that afflicted both Marx and Spencer. Only when biology seemed to agree with their social preconceptions were they ready to build a sociology upon it. They were willing to use the struggle for existence to validate the class struggle, but not individualistic competition.[46]

Whether from cynicism or self-deception, the result was the same: scientism superseded morality, and evolution led to progress, both descriptive and normative. Later is better. Native American optimism fused religiosity with secularism, the enforced altruism of "social justice" replacing irrevocably solipsistic egoism for a higher purpose. Marx in Spencer's garb thus inspired (besides, apparently, a popular British department store) an entire generation, forever changing the prevailing *weltanschauung*.

Not even William James, who rejected the overly simplistic sociology of eugenics, could fully escape its effects – particularly in its implications for racial hierarchies. While decrying demagogic ideological arguments for "one view or another of the way in which we ought to treat" anyone, he nonetheless referred to "the inferior races who live with us."[47] That James opposed using scientific reasoning to justify draconian genetic practices evidently did not imply that he rejected all racial assumptions, thereby providing a perfect illustration of their entrenched ubiquity. It is worth remembering, after all, that Jim Crow legislation was established in the antebellum North. Slavery may have been outlawed, and considered wrong, but "inferior races" were a given.

Racism was only the tip of the eugenicist fixation with genetic perfectibility, which had thoroughly permeated the academy by the 1920s. No fewer than 376 colleges and universities, including Harvard, Columbia, Cornell, and University of California-Berkeley, taught courses on the subject. Nor did they shun activism. The chairman of Harvard's anthropology department, temporarily dispensing with academic restraint, called for a "biological purge," lest Americans sold "their biological birthright for a mess of morons."[48]

It should therefore come as no surprise that segregation-sympathizer Woodrow Wilson, during his tenure as New Jersey governor, signed into law in 1911 the state's promoting sterilization of "certain categories of adult feeble minds." (Later struck down as unconstitutional, it was eventually upheld by Holmes in 1927.) Far from reluctant, Wilson's support for that law was reputed to have been "enthusiastic."[49] Small wonder that in 1915, he applauded the pro-Ku Klux Klan, scurrilously racist and xenophobic movie *The Birth of a Nation*,[50] which inspired a resurgence of that monstrous organization five years later. The reincarnated Medusa had merrily acquired a few additional heads: anti-Catholicism, nativism, and – of course – antisemitism.

But does eugenics square with the principle enshrined in the Declaration that all men are created equal? It doesn't, of course. A "survival of the fittest" policy assumes that undesirable "defectives" may be deemed unworthy of citizenship, and are even expendable altogether, since they allegedly harm society. The policy implies that these hapless humans should be removed by expulsion or extinction, voluntary or otherwise, lest they impede sacrosanct Progress.

Economists Art Carden and Steven Horwitz attribute this worldview to the influence of *The Origin of Species* on ideocrats who believed in government by science, or rather, by scientism:

> The advent and broad acceptance of Darwinism in the late nineteenth century, combined with a more general belief in the power of science and scientific management to solve social problems, led to a fascination with eugenics and the possibility of using public policy to ensure the "survival of the fittest" and the purity and strength of the human race. In the hands of many thinkers at the turn of the twentieth century, Darwinian theory became a rationale for using the power of government.[51]

Ultimately, according to this mindset, what matters is not the individual but the group. If it is in the best interest of the aggregate community to weed out undesirables, so be it. And who could be better qualified to decide which people fit that description than state bureaucrats, the selfless aristocracy of technocrats. A popular textbook from 1923 deplored that "[g]overnment and social control are in the hands of expert politicians who have power, instead of expert technologists who have wisdom. There should be technologists in control of every field of human need and desire."[52] The elected instrument of the people too should be just as scrupulously impartial, to properly and fairly represent, define, and enforce the "democratic" will of the majority.

Repurposing "Democracy"

"[T]he individual rights which the democracy of our own century has actually observed, were suggested to it by a political Philosophy radically individualistic, but not necessarily democratic. Democracy is bound by no principle of its own nature to say itself nay as to the exercise of any power."

- Woodrow Wilson, *Socialism and Democracy* (1887)

"To 'capture' a word such as democracy – that is, a word which has favorable emotive properties is per se to assure oneself of a formidable position of strength. And to 'surrender' to a word with negative associations - to accept for instance the term ideology as the proper label for all that we say in political matters – is in itself to start off with a handicap."

- Giovanni Sartori, *Democratic Theory* (1962)

The new ideology was bound to create confusion. Times were changing radically, prompting the enterprising wordsmith to try to influence their direction. While a stronger America was becoming increasingly integrated, through trade and travel, into the world community, its chattering class was busy distorting the nation's most fundamental liberal principles. On the eve of a world war, "liberalism" was being used to garner support for global action in a manner never envisaged over a century earlier. Though Wilson's original political focus had been domestic, the international dimension proved eminently suited to rationalizing the implementation of a collectivist vision.

The Mother Country had undergone a similar metamorphosis. "In nineteenth-century British thought," explains David Green, "the word 'liberal' was used primarily to refer to the individual's relationship to the sovereign state, and described a national rather than an international relationship."[53] Within a few decades, however, the concept extended to both. What they shared was a departure from the individual to the collective, stressing centralized power.

The globalized environment inevitably stretched the limits of the federal U.S. Constitution. Set up to provide an ingenious framework for protecting the rights of the American people and their states against encroachment by government overreach, its focus was originally primarily domestic. But by no means exclusively, as foreign affairs could never be ignored. They are assigned to an executive who is given considerable latitude of action. Though Congress maintains both the right to declare war and the power of fiscal appropriation, the commander-in-chief has the prerogative to make the momentous decisions whether to engage the nation in belligerent action to guard the nation's safety. His wide discretion recognizes that decisive action in time of peril is imperative.

For most of its short history, the United States was fortunate to focus mainly on affairs at home, and indeed lacked both the means and the desire to look far beyond. But with the advent of industrialization and increasing global interdependence, along with massive immigration resulting from assorted revolutions and massacres, the New World could no longer afford to mind only its own business. The world was encroaching on the lives of plain Americans, like it or not.

Business too was rapidly expanding in ways never anticipated. Railroads, oil, power companies, and banks were growing, adding jobs and boosting trade. But they simultaneously aroused populist fear of oligarchs who might be taking advantage of "the little guy." The rugged individual of lore felt increasingly subservient to faceless, not to mention heartless, corporations. Self-reliance was also losing its luster. New wording had to be found to conceptualize the unease and unrest, and then how to cope with them. Ironically, a communitarian message was being trumpeted just as the nation was becoming more divided, corporations larger, and immigrants distrusted. As Americans felt more unsettled in their private life, they sought relief from Big Brother, and a new language of altruism appealed to a people facing too many changes too fast.

At the turn of the new century, Teddy Roosevelt had sensed the opportunity to meet the demand. As he proclaimed, from his political pulpit, "that each must be his brother's keeper," he left it open whether he was referring only to American citizens or to the whole world. In effect, the aristocratic TR was engaged in delivering a missionary homily. Trumpeting the message that the ultimate purpose of all moral action lay in the greater good of the greater community, his aim and that of the Progressives whom he gathered into a political party meant to unite

Republicans and Democrats in the pursuit of the same National Interest. Anyone opposed to that Interest, whose lofty ring obscured the vacuity of its content, was obviously anti-American.

It was effective political rhetoric, tried and true. TR painted his political enemies with the broad brush of heartlessness. Denying being one's brother's keeper would become thereafter the essence of anti-Progressivism. Cain, Satan, anti-Christ, the label *du jour* changed but not the technique: the "reactionary" opposition was forthwith tarred with the indelible stigma of Egoism.

Individualism was rapidly losing ground. Though TR continued to invoke it, just to be safe, an onslaught of pejoratives was eroding the reputation of a concept once central to the nation's understanding of itself. Explains David Green:

> Since the emergence of the United States as an industrial power after the Civil War, five sets of labels have dominated political discourse. Roughly from the mid-1860s to the depression of the mid-1890s, the term "individualist" was the most popular self-designation, with the term "paternalist" as an accompanying pejorative to be hurled at opponents....With brief exceptions, the "progressive" versus "reactionary" polarity predominated from shortly after the turn of the century until the 1930s, when it was replaced by that of "liberals" versus "conservatives."[54]

TR had capitalized on the rising anxiety in turn-of-the-century America. He thundered "against the unfair profits of unscrupulous and conscienceless men, or against the greedy exploitation of the helpless by the beneficiaries of privilege."[55] Proclaiming "faith in the people," he held the moneyed elite responsible. "Our aim," spoke Roosevelt in the name of everyone, "is to secure the real and not the nominal rule of the people." Long live Democracy! It would become the new mantra for all progressives, whether or not they called themselves, as did Wilson, liberal.

In the great semantic reboot of liberalism, *democracy* was pitted against *individualism*. Progressives accused rapacious capitalism of undermining democratic governance through what they disparagingly dismissed as "radical individualism," which allegedly enabled the Few to look out for themselves at the expense of the Many. When Woodrow Wilson advanced the notion of democracy that "is bound by no principle of its own nature to say itself nay as to the exercise of any power,"[56] he implied that numerical majorities should decide who should rule them and how. Their leaders would then enforce the People's Will. Limited government was out the window.

He was thereby harnessing legitimacy from the people collectively and concentrating it into a technocratic elite under the guidance of a modern-day philosopher-king (e.g., himself). Thus defined, "democracy" refers to empowering the Many to delegate decision-making to the Best and Brightest, in effect using populist rhetoric to justify authoritarian practice. Plato's analogy between the human body and the body politic, outlined in *The Republic*, was being resurrected: an individual is like a human cell, whose existence is unthinkable apart from the whole living being.

That had been John Dewey's theory, as expressed in one of his earliest papers, "The Ethics of Democracy," published in 1888, a year after Wilson's essay, mentioned earlier, titled "Socialism and Democracy." "Society, as a real whole, is the normal order," declared Dewey, "and the mass as an aggregate of isolated units is a fiction."[57] Individuals must be seen to function as parts of a greater whole; democratic government applies to an intertwined, ever-changing and complex organism, which cannot be defined as merely the sum of its parts.

Neither is democracy a theoretical abstraction, but something that happens through the many working together, pursuing a common endeavor. Protection for minority rights concerning speech or property thus fell by the wayside: what mattered was society as "a real whole." The Bill of Rights was so eighteenth-century. According to newspeak-democracy, an elected representative who felt empowered to interpret the true interests of "the real whole" could even repudiate his own electoral promises.

Which is just what happened. Woodrow Wilson's decision to bring the United States into the Great War had reversed his solemn campaign promise. He had defied the very "democratic" sentiment that had delivered his electoral majority. Unsurprisingly, John Dewey came out in strong support of the president's decision, which he believed promoted the national interest. That *ipso facto* rendered it democratic in purpose, which is what ultimately mattered. Procedural or electoral democracy is only meant to select a leader; once he is in power, he embodies the General Will. It didn't bother Dewey that Wilson had flip-flopped. Politics is politics, after all.

But it bothered Dewey's devoted student at Columbia University, Randolph Bourne, who was frankly appalled. Where was the principle of fulfilling the nation's express will, he asked? Evidently, Bourne had not fully appreciated the real import of Dewey's redefinition of democracy. Principles aside, however, he was entitled to ask: how does a democratic leader who dispenses so cavalierly with campaign platforms intend to implement his vision? What's the plan?

In his 1917 essay "Twilight of the Idols," Bourne spells out his concerns:

> I search Professor Dewey's articles in vain for clues as to the specific working-out of our democratic desires, either nationally or internationally, either in the present or in the reconstruction after the war. No program is suggested, nor is there feeling for present vague popular movements and revolts. Rather are the latter chided, for their own vagueness and impracticalities. Similarly, with the other prophets of instrumentalism who accompany Dewey into the war, democracy remains an unanalyzed term, useful as a call to battle, but not an intellectual tool, turning up fresh sod for the changing future.[58]

Claiming distrust of theoretical constructs, progressives allegedly championed what they called pragmatism, which was supposed to be based on "democratic" decision-making. For it had been "one of the lessons the Civil War had taught them," writes Louis Menand. The Constitution was being sabotaged in the name of some vague collectivist notion: "The political system their philosophy was designed to support was democracy."[59] Bourne finally saw through this Hollywood-set charade of content-free democracy: mostly rhetoric, designed to arouse. It provided traditionally-populist cover, cleverly repurposed to fit new challenges, for behind-the-scenes executive overreach. Bourne would die in 1918, at age 32.

Wilson's entry in the Great War, though not unpopular, had been anything but universally endorsed.[60] If liberal republican democracy means anything at all, absent extraordinary circumstances, an electoral mandate surely cannot be treated as optional, lest the ballot becomes pure sham. By reneging on the pledge to keep the United States out of the European war, he was snubbing his supporters - and he knew it. But he had always intended to pursue what he believed was the best approach to governing, convinced that he was doing it in his nation's interest. His job was to try to convince them, as best he could, that they should trust him. If that required a bit of linguistic *legerdemain* – in plainer language, sleight-of-hand - so be it.

One way to finesse it was to switch "isms." By moving away from vague "progressivism" to an even more vague "liberalism," he was thereby shrewdly taking refuge in traditionally resonant lingo that he hoped would obscure a manifestly autocratic move. So does the linguistic tail wag the self-righteous dog.

Wilson's rhetorical acrobatics was of course pure politics, but it succeeded in effectively redrawing the entire ideological map of the United States at an opportune time of social and economic realignments. The political culture was in flux. A conceptual revolution was unfolding, seemingly without a shot being fired. Yet in fact, the shots had already been fired. In the aftermath of the Civil War, science had continued to gain in stature, as did the experts eager to become the new vanguard. Pursuing the common interest through politicians who placated the voters with slogans was becoming big business just when Big Business was losing popular ground.

Thus the Founders' democratic republic stealthily metamorphosed into its opposite: individual freedom was giving way to a vague notion of the General Will, with a subtle nod to the French revolutionaries of yore. Alan Charles Kors explains with singular clarity the radical "distinction between surrendering one's 'natural' rights to, in theory, an appropriately configured and an appropriately moral 'political' society, on the one hand, and surrendering the least possible individual liberty to secure the protections of society, on the other;" in fact, these represent "mutually exclusive uses and meanings of 'democracy.'"[61] And so they do, which Dewey knew as well as Wilson.

The idea-mongers managed this feat with exquisite skill. It was *chutzpa* at its most brazen, and it worked. The newfound audacity was based on a Promethean confidence, bolstered during the century after the fall of the Bastille, in man's ability to control his own destiny through scientific inquiry. Its proponents appear to have believed, with varying degrees of sincerity, that they were transcending their own individual, that is, selfish interests, and moving history "forward," toward the Good.

The stunning rapidity of scientific discoveries greatly increased the prestige of expertise, creating a new aristocracy of the intelligentsia. As the nation licked its near-terminal wounds in post-Civil War America, new elites were poised to assume a powerful political role. Government ideocrats wearing the toga of science shared not so much an ideology as a barely concealed egotism. Explains University of Michigan historian Arthur P. Mendel: "If there is one attribute that more than any other characterizes the modern radical intelligentsia, left and right, it is the conviction that the ideas and ideals they espouse are somehow irrefutably objective and necessary – in a word, scientific."[62]

The Ideocracy Takes Over the Administrative State

"'Totalitarian democracy' is not an oxymoron."

- Alan Charles Kors, "The Ethics of Democracy" (2020)

The post-Civil War climate of opinion had evolved in paradoxical ways. The Thirteenth and Fourteenth Amendment - the former having abolished state-sanctioned slavery, while the latter recalibrated the relationship between Washington and the states - disrupted the delicate balance both positively and negatively. On the plus side, the Union's victory ensured that "the United States" would be used henceforth as a singular noun. One of the war's principal "effects on American culture," observes Menand, "was to replace the sentiment of section with the sentiment of nation."[63] A horrible wrong had been outlawed, which could only be done through amendment. On the other hand, as the national interest and national survival became wedded to the evolutionary-progressive mindset, the measure turned out to precipitate the centralization of power in the federal and away from local government.

An administrative state would thereby be set in motion. Its much-taunted, superficially seductive theoretical advantages proved illusory. For unfortunately, given the propensity of human nature for wishful thinking that defies reality, allegedly apolitical servants who claimed devotion to nothing but advancing the Common Good, obeying only the objective dictates of the latest data, was more fiction than reality.

The innocuous sounding "administration" joined other progressive words that would later be called Orwellian, meaning euphemisms designed to conceal unsavory denotation. Like "liberalism," the term had first been used in this modern context by Woodrow Wilson. In 1886, in an essay with the deceptively pedestrian title "The Study of Administration," he proposed separating a seemingly anodyne, innocuous synonym for management, connoting mere number-crunching and filling in the dots, from rough-and-tumble pyrotechnical politics.

Why argue about policies when it could be scientifically demonstrated whether one or another is superior to alternatives in achieving the greatest good? The deficient options, by implication, would only benefit private, selfish ends – and that had to stop. Thus Wilson proposed that political candidates should enact measures designed to curb the power of the "unscrupulous" and the "greedy," all those heartless beneficiaries of "unjust profits," by empowering impartial, selfless paper-pushers to work out the messy details using the latest and best technology and accurate data.

With administration thus liberated from partisan politics, civil servants were to be anointed as the new secular priests, worshipers at the altar of Science. It was but a step away from a system whereby the people's elected representatives would be similarly apolitical technocrats. After all, science speaks with one voice. All one needs is to listen and follow its guidance.

Wilson conceded that a strict "distinction between constitutional and administrative questions" is difficult. Nor is it always obvious which branch of government and which agency should exercise authority over one or another issue; "one cannot easily make clear to every one [sic] just where administration resides in the various departments of any practicable government."[64] Yet he dismisses the problem as a mere technicality. Administration is a scientific enterprise that cuts across all branches of government: Congress needs staffers; the judiciary uses clerks; and the executive agencies writes all the statutes. So then, let them all work out the specifics among themselves. They know best what is needed. Blindfolded, as it were.

An eerily similar idea had been revealed in an essay published that same year across the ocean, in Leipzig, Germany. It predicted a future time when "state interference in social relations becomes, in one domain after another, superfluous, and then dies out of itself; the government of persons is replaced by the administration of things, and by the conduct of processes of production." Bearing the cumbersome title "Anti-Dühring: Herr Eugen Dühring's Revolution in Science," the essay's author was Frederick Engels.[65] Whether either had ever heard of the other, Engels and Wilson both seemed to agree about where History was headed. Inefficiency would be reduced to a minimum, and as politics became obsolete, individual interests would gradually fall by the wayside, eventually absorbed in the whole.

Soon V. I. Lenin would adopt the same approach in the essay *State and Revolution*, which he wrote after the February coup of 1917 that effectively put an end to the tsarist regime. The Communist plan, wrote Lenin, was simply "to organize the whole national economy on the lines of the postal service."[66] The idea was elementary: once egoism was abolished and everyone pursued the good of all, the business of running a state was mere logistics - like sorting out mail. One wonders whether Lenin had read Wilson's essay. (And whether Lenin would have reconsidered if he had known about FedEx; not likely.)

By Wilson's time, the old-fashioned New World of decades past was New no more. Ironically, as it aged, America was finding ideas from an Old Europe more tempting. Intellectuals especially were becoming increasingly receptive to jumping on the bandwagon of Progress. Wilson, for one, expressed great admiration for the Continent's patently pioneering "governments [that] are now in the lead in administrative practice which [admittedly] had rulers still absolute but also enlightened." Enlightenment was in – but not unambiguously. Flipping Lord Acton's dictum of "absolute power corrupts absolutely," Wilson suggested that absolute power might actually be *required* in order to *un-corrupt* absolutely. He praised the strong leaders of Prussia who, like Napoleon, should rather be commended for having bestowed upon future generations an "administration [that] has organized the general weal with the simplicity and effectiveness vouchsafed only to the undertakings of a single will."[67] How else can "the general weal" be expressed if not by "a single will?"

James Madison would have been appalled. Slowing down government action, he fervently believed, far from being bad is actually a very good thing. The time that it takes to sort out differences is spent on compromise, process, and deliberation – a price very much worth paying for the advantage of greater opportunity to accommodate additional perspectives. The diminutive Founder would never have imagined that a fellow Princeton alumnus and U.S. president, precisely a century later, would so categorically disagree.

Wilson and the progressives flatly rejected the Founders' approach to the problem of special interests not only on the basis of inefficiency but, more importantly, on moral grounds: a new, enlightened communitarian spirit had to replace the cacophony of selfish individuals. A single, lovely plainsong, the Voice of the People, its liturgy composed by the noblest souls whose sole mission was the People's Good, would be sung in unison using one sublime score. Society must be guided by objective facts instead of subjective passion, because if anything can lead us to a safe and happy future, science can. Certainly not subjective, egoistic impulse.

Checks-and-balances pluralism had been getting a bad reputation for a few decades, as checks were not balancing very well, and lax governance led to corruption. In creating the Progressive Party, TR hoped to supplant both the Democratic and Republican establishments, thinking them equally mired in graft and favoritism. In Hegelian-speak, the new party would constitute a "synthesis" transcending the nefarious, antagonistic, politics of his era. Virtue would triumph over special-interest politics in dialectical harmony. This seemed to fit the prevalent mood of the time.

Parties deserve their label, being partial in both senses: incomplete as well as biased. A multiparty system cannot but deflect citizens' zeal away from the national interest, argued the journalist Herbert Croly (1869-1930) in 1914. The obsolete political arrangement that "demands and obtains for a party an amount of loyal service and personal sacrifice which a public-spirited democrat should lavish only on the state," must be abandoned. Croly advocated its immediate abolition, the Constitution be damned.[68]

Though less extreme than Croly, Wilson tacitly agreed. By way of compromise, as second best, he praised the parliamentary electoral model whereby the prime minister is selected by the majority party, thus effectively uniting the legislative and the executive. Though not explicitly an advocate of total electoral revamping, TR similarly attacked "both of the old parties" for having turned away from their true purpose as "instruments to promote the general welfare," becoming little more than "tools of corrupt interests."[69]

While the two progressive presidents diverged on many issues, both targeted Big Business. Roosevelt's trust-busting campaign that broke up major railroad, oil, and steel conglomerates was followed by other business restrictions under Wilson's presidency. So too, both men ardently believed in using public education to mold young minds. And yes, they both loved wielding power. On balance, they had more in common than not.

On November 4, 1916, *The New Republic* ventured to guess that future historians "will interpret the work of President Wilson as a continuation of the work begun by ex-President Roosevelt."[70] This continuity was especially true in domestic policy, opined the editors, who went on to praise TR for "his exceptional gifts as an agitator [which] were devoted to concentrating public opinion on the all-important task of democratizing the political system of the country and socializing its economic system." ("Socializing" was definitely the right word.) They concluded that the Wilson administration "is clearly a continuation, if not a consummation, of that begun by Mr. Roosevelt. By a skillful use of Presidential initiative and sustained by an aroused public opinion, Mr. Wilson wrote into law the connection between a progressive economic policy and national unity."

But if the Progressive Era was so diametrically opposed to the Founders' view of individual liberty as enshrined in the Constitution and the Bill of Rights, could the same political label apply to both? In fact, the original idea of natural liberty, liberalism *avant la lettre*, was slowly being replaced altogether, deliberately and strategically. As John Dewey revealed in his book *Liberalism and Social Action,* published in 1935, activist government and social reconstruction had "virtually come to define the meaning of liberal faith."[71] They had come to define it because ideocrats like Dewey saw to it that they would.

It had been long in coming. On August 9, 1900, *The Nation* published an article by its Founder Edwin L. Godkin (1831-1902) deploring that

> [a]s the nineteenth century draws to its close it is impossible not to contrast the political ideals now dominant with those of the preceding era... [when] doctrine of natural rights was set up. Humanity was exalted above human institutions, man was held superior to the State, and universal brotherhood supplanted the ideals of national power and glory. These eighteenth-century ideas were the soil in which modern Liberalism flourished. Under their influence the demand for Constitutional Government arose. Rulers were to be the servants of the people, and were to be restrained and held in check by bills of rights and fundamental laws which defined the liberties proved by experience to be most important and vulnerable. ... [Alas,] recent events show how much ground has been lost. The Declaration of Independence no longer arouses enthusiasm; it is an embarrassing instrument which requires to be explained away. The Constitution is said to be outgrown.[72]

Embarrassing; to be explained away: such words would have pierced the Founders' hearts like daggers. Once instrumentalism, or pragmatism, progressivism, socialism, and other similar isms did away with covenantally proclaimed and constitutionally enshrined respect for the natural rights of mankind who are all created equal in God's Image, the floodgates were open.

Again, Randolph Bourne explained it well:

> To those of us who have taken Dewey's philosophy almost as our American religion, it never occurred that values could be subordinated to technique. We were instrumentalists, but we had our private utopias so clearly before our minds that the means fell always into its place as contributory. And Dewey, of course, always meant his philosophy, when taken as a philosophy of life, to start with values. But there was always that unhappy ambiguity in his doctrine as to just how values were created, and it became easier and easier to assume that just any growth was justified and almost any activity valuable so long as it achieved ends.[73]

The ambiguity was unhappy, but hardly accidental. Thereafter, the classical liberalism of the Scottish philosophers would be replaced by a new pseudo-liberal faith clad in scientism, turning to government solutions for social problems, to be implemented by ostensibly selfless public servants. The new political class consisted of entrenched defenders of the established status quo, as hostile to rapacious capitalists as to the IQ-challenged lower rung of society.

But the bureaucrats were supposed to be merely doing the bidding of a politically motivated elite. The new ideocracy, salivating at the aroma of a utopian omelet, believed to be facilitating the march of Progress no matter how many proverbial eggs it took. That same elite, though focused primarily on the United States, would export its ideas and rhetoric beyond the nation's shores even without a clear strategy, solid intelligence, or appreciation for all the instruments of power. Convinced of its own virtue and unimpeachable intentions, this humility-challenged crew often paid less attention to reality than would have been expected from self-declared devotees of empirical evidence. The results were often disturbingly, even lethally, anti-liberal.

Chapter IV:

National Socialism

Common Good Nationalism

"The president's [Wilson] proposals were not a program but a creed. He had not given, and for a long time was not to give, any thought to their concrete implementation. ... He was unaware of the revolutionary implications of this principle if applied to the Austrian or the Russian and Ottoman Empires."
- Victor S. Mamatey, *The United States and East-Central Europe 1914-1918* (1957)

"When I gave utterance to those words [that all nations had a right to self-determination], I said them without a knowledge that nationalities existed, which are coming to us day after day."
– Woodrow Wilson to Robert Lansing (1918)

For more than a century since its birth, America had given ample proof that it wasn't at all interested in venturing abroad in search of monsters to destroy, thereby confirming John Quincy Adams's prediction to that effect in a speech celebrating the fourth of July in 1821. The future president, then-Secretary of State, had captured the rationale for what seemed like an isolationist stance. Once having enlisted itself under any banners other than its own, he warned, "were they even the banners of foreign independence," the United States would risk becoming involved in "wars of interest and intrigue… which assume the colors and usurp the standard of freedom. The fundamental maxims of her policy would insensibly change from liberty to force."[1]

Read by Woodrow Wilson, however, these words took on a very different resonance. By the time he assumed the lofty office of commander-in-chief, liberty had taken second place to democracy, which he along with his progressive colleagues understood no longer as an electoral system but shorthand for the putative Common Good. At the turn of the twentieth century, exercising force in order to promote social welfare for the greatest number was seen as a net positive, even necessary. If the purpose was worthy, the means were an afterthought. The cause of democracy abroad, and thus the pursuit of "foreign independence," was worth the risk of using force to achieve it.

Although Americans remained focused on their own affairs, a century had done much to reduce the nation's traditionally more insular state of mind. The inevitable monsters lurked closer, and even if America was not looking for them, they were eyeing America. As the nation's wealth and power increased, so did its worries. Industrialization affected many social groups in nineteenth century America, as did a massive influx of refugees from Asia and Europe, especially after the failed revolutions of 1848. The simultaneous emergence of social Darwinism and the huge popularity of eugenics, promoted in the academy and enforced by the courts, bolstered prejudices and eroded the sanctity of individual rights, further undermining the principles of the Declaration.

Aggrieved constituencies who sought government assistance to weather economic hardships were bound to obscure the liberal vision that had inspired the nation's founding. Over the course of several decades, radical self-styled reformers would refurbish traditional language for political purposes. But semantic overhaul was risky: whenever possible, politicians opted for preserving the linguistic outer shell while stealthily changing meanings. A subtle *trompe d'oeil* that preserved the façade as it completely rebuilt the intellectual architecture underneath, it worked wonders.

It was a triumph of marketing. Indiana University Professor Michael McGerr credits the ubiquity and effectiveness of the movement's success to its method of dissemination: "[B]ecause the progressive agenda was so often carried out in settlement houses, churches, and schoolrooms, in rather unassuming day-to-day activities, the essential audacity of the enterprise can be missed. Progressivism demanded a social transformation that remains at once profoundly impressive and profoundly disturbing a century later."[2]

Woodrow Wilson was ideally suited for the conceptual transition. Steeped as he was in German philosophy alongside the Anglo-Saxon idealist tradition, John Stuart Mill's utilitarianism appealed to him, particularly in its American incarnation as pragmatism. It fit the times: while predicated on a quintessentially idealist staple - the Common Good and its synonyms - pragmatism sounded suitably hard-nosed. William James thus dedicated his 1907 book *Pragmatism* to Mill as "our leader were he alive today."

James was speaking for most of his fellow progressives who, notwithstanding disparate individual preferences, applauded Mill's rejection of abstractions and absolutes, which endowed the method with an empirical aura. If one didn't look too closely, the vacuous idea of "the greatest good for the greatest number" sounded vaguely objective, perhaps even measurable. American intellectuals, eager to get away from liberalism's Scottish origins, had been in search of a secular religion.

Not that the general population, in England or America, paid much heed to philosophy in their daily life. More and more people were hurting as the century progressed. Unemployment was rising. The economic malaise, culminating in a depression through most of the 1880s, had shaken people's confidence in the promise of the much-vaunted American Dream. Between 1870 and 1900 alone, nearly 12 million immigrants had arrived mainly from Germany, Ireland, and England, far more than prior to the Civil War. Among the first contingents was a relatively large group of Chinese, following the California gold rush in 1849, and then again in 1882. At that point, the Chinese Exclusion Act stopped their immigration for nearly a century. It was a watershed decision, about which more later.

And then there were the Jews - always the Jews.

Antisemitism as Litmus Test

"*The most certain test by which we judge whether a country is really free is the amount of security enjoyed by minorities.*"

- Lord Action, "History of Freedom in Antiquity," Feb. 26, 1977

"*[As in the book of Daniel,]in the broader historical context, an augury of civilizational doom has indeed repeatedly correlated with damage of danger to the Jews.*"

- Ruth R. Wisse, "Is the Writing on the Wall for America's Jews?" Aug. 8, 2022

If successful, which most of them were, but especially if they were not, Jews were increasingly being shunned even in America, the nation that had welcomed them most warmly. As usual throughout the centuries, they were damned if they did and damned if they didn't. Their relative homogeneity too, resulting from intra-faith marriage in restricted communities, could and often did count against them, especially since many tended to "look Jewish" and were easier to single out as "different." Growing European obsessions with race had managed to cross the ocean, fertilizing antisemitic and anti-Black bias, which could be conveniently merged as needed. Though many Jews were blond and blue-eyed (like my mother's mother), others had darker complexions (like my handsome olive-skinned father and very brunette mother, once a stunning-looking fashion model). Pseudo-scientific rationalizations for discrimination naturally followed.

Writes Leonard Rogoff of the Jewish Heritage Foundation: "Ideologies born in the salons of European intellectuals and the academies of New England professors found their way into the sermons of backwoods Southern preachers."[3] Among them was Arthur T. Abernethy, who used pseudo-ethnology and biblical "proofs" to argue in *The Jew a Negro* (1910) that "the Jew of to-day, as well as his ancestors in other times, is the kinsman and descendant of the Negro."[4]

This was still largely a minority view, but antisemitism had been growing for about half a century. Already in 1850, the same august audience in Charleston, South Carolina, that had been awed by the racial speculations of Agassiz in 1846 and of Morton in 1847 gave the latter's disciple, Josiah Nott, a platform for expounding on "scientific" racism. Determined to "cut loose the natural history of mankind from the Bible,"[5] Nott was deeply versed in continental "racial demography." The term had been coined by Count Arthur de Gobineau, one of the first European writers to interpret the historical development of mankind as being dependent on race. He declared that whites, especially aristocrats, were superior because they possessed more of the coveted Aryan genetic traits. In 1856, Nott eagerly edited and published selections from Gobineau's infamous, widely read *Essay on the Inequality of Races* (1853-55).

Such ideas were bound to affect attitudes toward the Jews; at minimum, they provided a patina of legitimacy, a fig leaf for deeper resentments. Truth be told, Southern whites were bothered far less by the amount of melanin present in the skin of their Hebrew step-brethren than by the latter's irritatingly successful economic habits. In 1846, for example, then-U.S. Senator John C. Calhoun declared that Jews were "notoriously a race of brokers, bankers, and merchants." (Tell that to the shtetl rag-peddler, but why quibble?) By 1862, a public meeting in Thomasville, Georgia, called for the "banishing of the town's Jews."[6] Religion wasn't the problem; their money was.

America was by no means alone. Social Darwinism metastasized rapidly, exacerbating racial hysteria and antisemitism throughout the world. Francis Galton, who had coined "eugenics" in 1883, was becoming increasingly popular in Europe. Though not openly antisemitic, he had confided to his friend Alphonse de Candolle on October 17, 1884: "It strikes me that the Jews are specialized for a parasitical existence upon other nations, and that there is need of evidence that they are capable of fulfilling the varied duties of a civilized nation by themselves"[7] – unavailable prior to 1948. (Though not entirely. Lord Acton, for example, praised the Jewish proficiency in self-government predating that of all other peoples.[8])

"Parasitical existence." That is how German anti-Semites liked to describe the Jews in their midst. (Some parasites! Legally restricted to a few professions, they were disproportionately represented in journalism, law, medicine, and retailing.) Officially, anthropology was being invoked to provide "scientific" justification for removing Jews from the body politic, especially from positions of authority. It didn't help that many assimilated Jews, in both Austria and Germany, at least tacitly, seemed to agree with their detractors. Most did so only from expediency, but many had internalized the accusation, to the point of self-hatred.[9] The converted Karl Marx, for example, called fellow-Jew Ferdinand Lassalle "the Jewish nigger," questioning his head shape and genealogy. Sigmund Freud studied Jewish obsession with their identity, which he took as evidence that they (and therefore he) constituted an "impure" race, mere half breeds with "Jewish-Negroid features."[10] Though few rivaled their influence, Marx and Freud were hardly atypical. We will return to this disturbing pathology.

In America, as elsewhere at the time, race provided a far better excuse for discrimination than did unfounded accusations of greed. Writes

Rogoff: "Certainly the social discrimination that American Jews began experiencing in the late nineteenth century owed to class resentments against Jews as parvenus, but the distaste was expressed as racial. Hoteliers Henry Hilton and Austin Corbin set off a national storm when they excluded Jews beginning in 1877 with the celebrated rebuff of Joseph Seligman in Saratoga."[11] The arrival of two million Jews from Eastern and Central Europe between 1880 and 1924 only made internecine hostility worse, as native-born Southern Jews of German origin found themselves categorized with their newly arrived co-religionists.

The eugenics movement played into native xenophobia by fueling fears of race "pollution." Anti-Black Southerners made common cause with anti-Catholics, labor unionists, upper-class New Englanders, anti-Mexicans, anti-Asians, and a motley assortment of equal-opportunity bigots. Pseudo-scientists gladly supplied the jargon. "Eugenics and race science provided a vocabulary that reinforced Southern antiimmigrant prejudices," notes Rogoff. "Particularly Southern was the sexual obsession with racial intermingling."[12] Northern antisemites preferred the German narrative which blamed Jews for rapacious capitalism. The ideology seemed more highbrow.

But wasn't the Constitution designed to protect against government encroachments on the rights of all, however intellectually challenged? Apparently not. Eugenics provided the perfect rhetorical camouflage to members of both major parties in the United States, as the mantle of science could be tailored to fit all manner of policies that transcended partisanship. The ideocracy had manufactured the perfect conceptual virus, capable of rapid and ubiquitous transmission. It soon infected the global political culture, not only throughout Europe where it had actually originated, but also Latin America, Japan, China, and Russia.

Among its immediate effects in America was to bolster support for immigration restriction, as a preventative measure against harmful human specimens. Another tool of so-called "negative eugenics" was prohibiting marriage and breeding among "defective stock." A prominent supporter of all forms of eugenics, positive as well as negative, was Theodore Roosevelt, whose zeal for biological purification extended beyond sterilization… to justify armed conflict itself. "[A] great war," wrote Roosevelt in 1914, "may do for the whole nation a service that incalculably outweighs all possible evil effects," by purifying it of inferior specimens.

TR's prime example was none other than the American Civil War. His regret at the magnitude of the carnage seemed secondary to its composition: what he most deplored was… that the *wrong* people had died. Explains Roosevelt:

> That war cost half a million lives. It is certainly a sad and evil thing that timid and weak people, the peace-at-any-price and anti-militarist people who stayed at home, should have left descendants to admire well-meaning, feeble articles against militarism, while their valiant comrades went to the front and perished…. Worthy writers on eugenics must not forget that heroes serve as examples."[13]

To deplore the death of some over others on the basis of the victims' relative enthusiasm for armed combat sounds like something Friedrich Nietzsche might have endorsed, and even he only half-facetiously. But TR was serious, a chilling exemplar of a new mindset. It is one thing to memorialize the best and most valiant soldiers who now lay dead, declaring them heroes; quite another to bemoan that "antimilitarist" and hence implicitly timid, weak people would go on living, spawning spineless, and thus socially undesirable, progeny. Nor is it helpful to suggest that the two sides are morally equivalent. Whatever any individual soldier may have felt about slavery, dying to defend it was not unequivocally heroic. For TR to gloss over that fact was deplorable.

But it was no oversight. For TR supported eugenics without any reservation. Unabashedly in favor of sterilizing criminals, he regretted that "as yet there is no way possible to devise [a way] which could prevent all undesirable people from breeding" in the first place. This was a profoundly ominous prospect, given his prejudices and that of others in position of authority. Should politicians be trusted to decide who is too "undesirable" to procreate? TR went one logical step further, suggesting a few effective ways of "getting desirable people to breed."[14]

Encouraging breeding among superior human specimens and discouraging the riffraff, though cringeworthy, may have sounded sensible to some people. But war?! Roosevelt's penchant for combat, even for eugenic purposes, remained generally unpopular among progressives, whose main focus was domestic. Most were still pacifists at century's turn. TR was ahead of his time: his arguments for ousting Spain from Cuba, in late 1897, seemed perfectly consistent with what progressivism would become a few years later, under Woodrow Wilson.

Wrote Roosevelt:

> I would regard war with Spain from two viewpoints: first, the advisability on the grounds both of humanity and self-interest of interfering on behalf of the Cubans, and of taking one more step toward the complete freeing of America from European dominion; second, the benefit done our people by giving them something to think of which is not material gain, and especially the benefit done our military forces by trying both the Navy and Army in actual practice.[15]

TR's macho-liberalism was expansive, self-confident, and aggressive; it was also eminently idealistic. He believed that America should be a force for progress, that it must stand for righteousness and justice, and stop obsessing about material gain. In his eyes, the Cuban cause was surely just, the perfect opportunity for the United States to fight against enemies abroad whom he suspected to be aligned with enemies within, some of whom were notoriously focused mainly on profits. Could he have meant the Jews?

He could, and he did. On November 4, 1897, TR told Capt. French E. Chadwick of his conviction

> that the Jew money lenders in Paris, plus one or two big commercial companies in Spain are trying to keep up the war [Cuban insurrection]. I more than agree with you as to the iniquity of our country allowing these people a hold on Cuban finances, but I don't believe that my words will be listened to. We ought to go to war with Spain unless she were to get out peaceably within the next month.[16]

Whether or not he really embraced this conspiracy theory, he was evidently not above alluding to it. Eric Alterman of the Center for American Progress observes that TR had a penchant for "channeling Populist rhetoric to mobilize the American people, [by] deriding the 'malefactors of great wealth' in ways that foreshadowed FDR's chiding 'economic royalists.'"[17] National pride, humanitarianism, idealist trust in progress, and xenophobia, with a sprinkling of antisemitism and anticapitalism, were a mighty mixture which the exuberant blue-blood applied with alacrity as soon as he became president in 1901.

TR's expansive interpretation of the Monroe Doctrine meant declaring U.S. primacy in Latin America. This included exercising police power over its southern neighbors to insure sound fiscal policies. By implication, the United States could even act preventively, explains British historian Adam Quinn, "to avert the occurrence of any legitimate justification for European creditor-states' intervention, potentially a pretext for land-grabbing."[18] Henry Kissinger's admiration for TR as an American Otto Bismarck, a practitioner of *realpolitik* in search of maximum leverage in a world of balanced powers,[19] is nonetheless misplaced: TR was no less idealistic than Wilson.

Their pragmatic rhetoric notwithstanding, the two progressive presidents shared a universalist, messianic vision. Writes Quinn:

> [I]t was [TR's] explicit assertion that the moral standards incumbent upon the good nation and the good man were one and the same. He was also emphatic that he believed himself to be chiefly a moralist in his political thought, not a cold calculator of interest. His most prominent views, concerning the importance of military strength and a struggle for national greatness, were based on an ideology which emphasized forgoing material self-indulgence in favor of a striving ethic of martial values and self-improvement, aimed ultimately at a place in history.

TR advocated a putatively "liberal" version of imperialism predicated on a benevolent democratic paternalism that involved, "in its intentions at least, a program of imposed reform, societal uplift, and liberation." The liberation that both he and Wilson had in mind, along with their fellow progressives, entailed certain specific goals to forge a particular sort of society. Liberty was no longer seen, as had been the case with the Founders, as a means to secure the life, liberty, and property of citizens to pursue happiness as they saw fit. "Rather," explains Quinn, "liberty was taken to contain within itself a fixed outcome, or at least narrow parameters limiting acceptable outcomes within which free nations would develop. To put it more pithily, it was assumed by American thinkers that liberty for a state must produce a utopian vision within that state, for such was 'progress.'"

The ideal ends of this new progressive liberalism were to be based on the common national interest, which involved at once the greatest possible material equality and a repudiation of selfishness. TR, moreover, believed his nation, or at least his nation's (progressive) vanguard, to have superior insight as well as virtue – the two had to be inseparable. The U.S. deserved to be the world's leader, and had a responsibility to act accordingly. It was foremost a matter of morality.

Though TR was both less naïve and more knowledgeable than Wilson, especially about international affairs, the two agreed that the best means of settling disputes among antagonist states were transnational. Writes Quinn: "in his discussion of the subject during the final years of his life, it is striking that the international structures he advocated were not at all dissimilar to those Wilson in fact sought to negotiate."[20] However much the two presidents disliked one another, near polar opposites in temperament and heritage, they essentially shared a worldview.

Alongside the much-vaunted Common Good, the other critical concept used to fashion the face of *nouveau* liberalism was equality, increasingly used interchangeably with equity. University of Nevada sociologist Dmitry N. Shalin explains the rationale by citing its principal apostle, John Dewey, who

> saw Progressive reformers as working for "a more balanced, a more equal, even, and equitable system of human liberties"[21] and determined "to limit and control private economic power as the Founders had limited political power."[22] ... In their fight against *laissez faire* capitalism, progressives borrowed many insights from Socialism; some claimed that "we are in for some kind of Socialism, call it by whatever name we please."[23]

John Dewey's description of the new "system of human liberties" touched all the right buttons. First, it was pronounced "more balanced;" because who, pray tell, prefers an "unbalanced" one? Then, it had to be "equal," because that's what we all believe in: equality. And of course, a system should be "more even." Seldom, if ever, is anything "uneven" much good, to say nothing of "odd"! The synonymy with "equitable" closes the virtuous synonym circle, whose ultimate goal is "to limit and control private economic power." The implicitly ideal new alternative is public economic power. Public equals good. End of story.

Social Reconstruction

"The next advance in the art of human association demands the introduction into capitalist industry of the same government by the consent of the governed as that which the Founders of the American republic intended to introduce into the state. If liberalism implies an interest in human liberation, the wage-earners who are fighting the battle for this advance deserve the sympathy and support of liberals."
- Herbert Croly, "The Eclipse of Progressivism," (1920)

What John Dewey and his fellow progressives sought was nothing less than social reconstruction, a reconfiguration of American life and political system. This "meant bringing government into the marketplace, broadening the scope of economic activity, democratizing education, and transforming the public into an agent of social control," explains Dmitry Shalin. They imagined being able, somehow, to "secur[e] these goals without breaking the constitutional framework of democracy…[That is] the most enduring legacy of the Progressive movement. It is also a source of perennial tension and contradiction in Progressivism as well as in the kindred pragmatist and interactionist movements."[24] Contradiction indeed, a paradox with no solution.

Albeit highly susceptible to populist demagoguery, progressivism was nonetheless embraced by many genuinely admirable, generous and earnest people. At times their ideology and rhetoric sounded (and was) confused - that often happens when a big heart silences a head of even average size. They included social workers, teachers, and philanthropists, whose assistance ranged from useful to miraculous. These exceptional individuals were often idolized by the grateful recipients of their kindness and abnegation, earning them a worthy place in history.

Unsurprisingly, many became politically involved. Unusually committed "men and women longing to socialize their democracy," as the much-admired Jane Addams lovingly described her fellow social workers and activists, these were disciples in search of a church. When joined by American writers, journalists, and wealthy, philanthropically-minded reformers, who made common cause with similarly motivated Europeans, the synergy proved highly effective in advancing the new agenda and changing the culture. The Old World gladly stepped up to its traditional role as incubator of radicalism. French social theorist Charles Fourier (1772-

1837) and the philosopher Etienne Cabet (1788-1856), alongside the Welshman Robert Owen (1771-1858), a cotton mill owner and social crusader, three valiant musketeers from across the Channel, were in the frontlines.

But ominously enough, the name that Fourier chose for the communal associations that he saw as key to the reconstruction of society was "phalanges." A term from anatomy referring to the whole row of finger joints which fit together like a phalanx - in ancient Greece, a body of heavily armed infantry formed in close order – it was innocuous enough at first glance. Around 1600, the word began to be used more broadly, figuratively, to mean "number of persons banded together in a common cause" - like a bundle of sticks. In 1933, however, it was also appropriated by the Spanish fascist party, whose members became known as Falangists.

In fact, "fascist" itself comes from a very similar root: the word is Latin for "a bundle of sticks." An ancient Roman symbol of authority, it became *fascismo* in Italian. It was first used in 1921 by Benito Mussolini (1883-1945), for the splinter socialist party which he called National Fascist, in an effort to distinguish it from the pro-Bolshevik Italian Socialist Party (ISP) founded in 1892, which he had headed from 1912 to 1914. Both parties purported to pursue the common interests of workers, but unlike the ISP that targeted the entire capitalist world and was therefore internationalist, Mussolini's socialists were Italian patriots who prioritized the national interest.

A few differences notwithstanding, the "economic program of Italian Fascism," according to the eminent Austrian economist Ludwig von Misses, "did not differ from the program of British Guild Socialism as propagated by the most eminent British and European socialists."[25] Mussolini's was merely one variety of the same brand. The ambitious *El Duce* (a title he assumed in 1925 when proclaiming himself the people's leader) saw early on that nationalism, not internationalism, was on "the right side of history." And coincidentally, it would also appeal to a large popular constituency that would catapult him to power, as well as attract the most ruthless war ally of all. It was a mistake of millenarian proportions.

Unlike the Falangists and other fascists, the European progressive idealists had been focused mainly on promoting an egalitarian lifestyle rather than war. Unsuccessful in England, the Fourierists decided to try their luck in America. Here they hit the jackpot. The communitarian message greatly appealed to the utopian writer and social reformer Albert Brisbane (1809-1890), who agreed to become a co-editor of the Fourierist magazine *The Phalanx*, based in New York City, in 1843.

Especially helpful in that effort was Horace Greeley (1811-1872), the highly regarded editor and publisher of *The New York Tribune*, who in 1872 ran for president on the short-lived Liberal Republican Party ticket. (The LRP vanished immediately after the election). Albeit not a self-described socialist, Greeley was highly sympathetic to the ideology. Indeed, in 1851, the *Tribune* hired Karl Marx as London correspondent. The decision was more significant than Greeley could have anticipated.

During the following decade, Marx's writings in the *Tribune* inaugurated a new style of journalism, ably described by the writer James Ledbetter in an interview for *Jacobin* magazine (which advertises itself as "a leading voice of the American left, offering Socialist perspectives on politics, economics, and culture"):

> [T]he basic Marx approach to his *New York Tribune* column was to take an event that was in the news - an election, an uprising, the second Opium War, the outbreak of the American Civil War - and sift through it until he could boil it down to some fundamental questions of politics or economics. And then on those questions he would make his judgment. In this sense, Marx's journalism does resemble some of the writing that is published today in journals of opinion, and it's not hard to see a direct line between Marx's journalistic writing and the kind of tendentious writing on public affairs that characterized much political journalism (especially in Europe) in the twentieth century.[26]

As too would the twenty-first, testimony to the stunning resilience of the dialectician's masterful rhetoric. It was politically malleable to fit any "us vs. them" scenario as circumstances dictated, demonizing the latest satanic scapegoat targeted for expulsion from the human species – all in the name of either equality or racial purity, take your pick.

Throughout his career, Greeley promoted Progress. In the words of Washington University of St. Louis Professor Iver Bernstein, "Greeley was an eclectic and unsystematic thinker, a one-man switchboard for the international cause of 'Reform.' He committed himself, all at once, to utopian and artisan Socialism, to land, sexual, and dietary reform, and, of course, to anti-slavery."[27] Through what he called "Association," a European-inspired "far-reaching program of social reorganization," continues Bernstein, "Greeley hoped to do away with the wages system and the accompanying evils of 'unjust division of toils, unequal distribution of profits, isolation, and opposition of interests.'"[28]

The socialist experiment had started out on a purely voluntary basis. A large number of communal colonies sprang up during the 1840s to implement these idealistic reformers' egalitarian ideas, of which the Brook Farm Experiment, home to the Transcendentalists, became the most famous. In Red Bank, New Jersey, the Phalanx commune was established in 1843. Most did not last long, but the yearning for cooperative living and egalitarian distribution of resources remained. Among the new German immigrants who arrived in the United States after the failed European uprisings of 1830 and 1848, there were many socialists who would eventually help organize working men's unions with socialist objectives in cities of the East and the Midwest. The progressive wave was inching its way across America, its tide increasingly higher, but would not reach political peak until after the Civil War.

It could not have happened without the intelligentsia. Buoyed by Eugene V. Debs's nomination as presidential candidate of the Socialist Party of America[29] in 1904, the movement gained increased momentum in the early twentieth century. A year later, several writers established the Intercollegiate Socialist Society (ISS), whose first president was the world-renowned novelist Jack London and its first vice president the bestselling writer Upton Sinclair. Endorsed by such major figures as the celebrated critic Walter Lippmann, Clarence Darrow of Scopes "monkey" trial fame, writer Charlottle Perkins Gilman, along with millionaire financier James Graham Phelps Stokes, who later replaced Sinclair as ISS's second VP, and the Socialist republican William English Walling, the ISS was symptomatic of a pervasive progressive reorientation on the part of the American intellectual elite.[30]

According to ISS's organizing secretary, Harry W. Laidler, its members viewed Socialism's "aims and fundamental principles with sympathy, and believe[ed] that in them will ultimately be found the remedy for many far-reaching economic evils." It had been established "for the purpose of promoting an intelligent interest in Socialism among college men, graduate and undergraduate … [a]nd the encouraging of all legitimate endeavors to awaken an interest in Socialism among the educated men and women of the country"[31] more generally. In short, it sought to create a new left-oriented ideocracy.

In 1921, Laidler, now Executive Director, renamed ISS, to be known thenceforth as the League for Industrial Democracy (LID). Its main mission also changed to promoting "Education for a New Social Order Based on Production for Public Use and Not for Private Profit."[32] While less radical sounding, the LID became the base for the highly influential, no-holds-barred Muckrakers, journalists who aggressively uncovered economic, political, and every other kind of corruption.

After morphing once again in 1933 into the Student League for Industrial Democracy (SLID), the organization focused primarily on students, and in 1935 merged with the Communist National Student League (CNSL) to form the American Student Union. Reverting to SLID after World War II in 1946, its 1960 reincarnation was the infamous Students for a Democratic Society (SDS), many of whose members were my U of C colleagues. (Full disclosure: I even found stashed away among some old files an SDS membership card inscribed… with my own name! How that ever happened, I cannot for the life of me recall. My friends now cannot believe it, and I can't blame them.)

The ISS-SLID thus became, in effect, the cultural arm of the Socialist Party's less radical wing. As Laidler explains, they were

> moderates [who] believed that progress toward Socialism would come primarily through political action, the election of Socialists to public office, and the gradual peaceful and democratic transfer of industry from private to public ownership. The extremists, like William D. Haywood, the leader of the IWW [International Workers of the World] … laid more emphasis on economic action than… on parliamentary activity. He believed with syndicalists that strikes, leading to a general strike, and such tactics as sabotage, would be more effective in bringing about fundamental change.[33]

In 1912, some left-leaning Republicans joined TR's Progressive Party, while other socialists cast their votes for Woodrow Wilson. But this new political faction was only one facet of a far more momentous ideological reconfiguration that inaugurated what Richard Hofstadter called "the Age of Reform." If we adopt Hofstadter's expanded definition of progressivism to encompass "that broader impulse toward criticism and change that was everywhere so conspicuous after 1900, … [the movement] affected in a striking way all the major and minor parties and the whole tone of American political life."[34] The change within America's political culture was tectonic.

In the former Confederate states, after the Civil War, middle class and agrarian resentment of the moneyed northern elite merged with the gentle communitarianism of Southern literati into a nativist nationalism tinged with anti-business animus. Northerners holding a variety of grudges, legitimate or otherwise, joined soon thereafter. During the 1890s, fifteen states instituted taxes on large inheritances. By the 1910s, more than forty states had inheritance taxes in place.

Gaining momentum at the state level, national redistributionist legislation was only a matter of time. In 1894, Congress included a 2 percent tax on annual incomes over $4,000 as part of a new tariff bill. On December 3, 1906, TR took to the bully pulpit provided by the traditional presidential annual address to Congress, and called for graduated taxes on incomes and inheritances. "The man of great wealth owes a peculiar obligation to the State, because he derives special advantages from the mere existence of government," declared the President. "Not only should he recognize this obligation in the way he leads his daily life and in the way he earns and spends his money, but it should also be recognized by the way in which he pays for the protection the State gives him."[35] Placing a disproportionate reliance "on the inheritance of those swollen fortunes which it is certainly of no benefit to this country to perpetuate," he proposed an income tax amendment in 1909. The "certainly" was designed to dispense with empirical backing for the argument.

A precedent had actually been set earlier that year, on June 17, when Nebraska Senator Norris Brown introduced a resolution giving Congress a new power, to enact taxes on income without apportionment. Snubbing the Tenth Amendment, the resolution passed. Four years later, in 1913, the Sixteenth Amendment was ratified with almost equal ease. It read: *The Congress shall have power to lay and collect taxes on incomes, from whatever source derived, without apportionment among the several States, and without regard to any census or enumeration.* The brevity belied its revolutionary import. The following year, 1914, the nominally small but conceptually monumental 1 percent tax was to be levied on annual incomes from $4,000 to $20,000, incrementally larger up to a maximum 10 percent on estates over $5 million. The issue was not whether or not to levy taxes; that running a state takes money is a given. Rather, the question was how and to what ends.

Before long, Woodrow Wilson expanded the reach of federal legislation, mostly by using the pretext of wartime expenditures. But the wealthy were not alone in resenting the income tax; so too did many ordinary consumers. After 1914, the cost of living rose by 102 percent, largely due to inflation; it was "unquestionably the middle class that were the chief victims of the war-time high cost of living," wrote sociologist Ross Finney in 1922. "Ministers perhaps suffered as badly as anybody. Thousands of capable middle-aged men left the teaching profession, discouraged and in many cases embittered.... Civil service employees had cause to worry, too; in fact, all salaried employees."[36] Funny how taxes end up hurting everyone, but especially those who imagine they will reap the benefits, yet never do. The *demos,* it seems, never learns until it is too late.

After it became clearer that monetary conditions, rather than an increase in domestic spending, contributed most to ending the economic depression of 1880s,[37] *laissez faire* capitalism returned briefly. But the momentum of government expansion could not be reversed. The income tax would never go away. The issue at hand was not so much whether or how to help the needy, but the moral opprobrium attached to wealth. The assumption that disinterested bureaucrats would redistribute it to advance the common good, unlike private individuals whose very affluence defined them as incorrigibly selfish and thus untrustworthy, left the door wide open to crony (pseudo)capitalism.

Soon populist egalitarianism would become entrenched. Men like George Creel (1876-1953), born into a poverty-stricken midwestern family from Missouri, inevitably became attracted to progressivism, which claimed to care about the underprivileged. Favoring "the highest degree of socialization,"[38] he was on his way to join the virtuous elite.

Despite receiving only a primary school education, Creel rose quickly to become a successful journalist. In 1916, he joined the Democratic National Committee as a writer, and the following year was appointed chairman of the Committee on Public Information (CPI). By then, he had already gained a reputation, according to Princeton historian Arthur S. Link, as a leading figure "of the advanced wing of the progressive movement in the United States."[39] In fact, so "advanced" a progressive was Creel that even *The New York Times* protested, in an editorial on April 16, 1917, his appointment by Wilson's appointment to the CPI, objecting to the young man's "radicalism."

The Times turned out to have been right. CPI would end up engaging in such crass propaganda that it came close to paralyzing future efforts at public diplomacy through the United States Information Agency.[40] George Creel's anti-German harangues were notorious, whipping up hatred against the "Huns." Under his leadership, writes Columbia University historian Leo Ribuffo, the Committee on Public Information encouraged Americans to believe that "Kaiser Wilhelm's domestic allies undermined national security."

From Germanophobia it was but a short step for the nation to slide into the Red Scare, notes Ribuffo. Justifying mass arrests and deportations, Attorney General A. Mitchell Palmer warned in 1919 that the "'sharp tongue of revolutionary heat' licked church altars, played in school belfries, and crawled 'into the sacred corners of the home.' The campaigns against Huns and Bolsheviks obviously encouraged the suspicious dispositions of '100% Americans'"[41]

Though not personally bigoted, Creel's hysterical jingoism ended up fueling nativist ire and extremism which included antisemitism. For if "Huns" was shorthand for Germans, "Bolsheviks" typically stood for Jews. Once again, as usual, Jews got it from both sides. Seen as mere hyphenated Americans, the enterprising rich Jews, invariably portrayed as rapacious, were as resented as the poor new immigrants. Sometimes the reason was just that they were all considered interlopers. Once again, Jews were the Jolly Jokers of scapegoating, all-purpose objects of resentment.

First to be shunned by the old, largely WASP, superrich Northern upper class were the successful and most assimilated Jews. From the other side of the divide, Southern populist agrarians and the urban poor both worried about the negative influence of newly arrived city-dwellers on the nation's moral health. Many simply distrusted anyone whose lifestyle was not in accord with strict Christian values, and who thus seemed to endanger the nation's integrity, if not its very survival.

Neither TR nor Wilson was particularly sympathetic to immigrants as such. The deeply religious Wilson, steeped in southern agrarian white-supremacist culture, just like the Knickerbocker-aristocrat TR,[42] detested the nouveau-riche capitalists with their presumed egoism and vulgar money-grubbing, albeit for somewhat different reasons. Antisemitism proved a bipartisan aberration.

The newly arrived Jewish immigrants from Eastern Europe and Russia, with their peculiar customs, large families, and apparent lack of marketable skills, sadly inspired little sympathy. Huddled inside overcrowded city neighborhoods that drove even their wealthy co-religionists into distant exclusive residences, the already-radicalized pogrom survivors often spoke up against their exploiters. But neither were the wealthy Jews spared. The Boston brahmins and JP Morgans made common cause with the blue-collar beer-lover who was competing against the skinny new kid on the block with the funny Yiddish accent. Attacks were thus once again channeled by the tried-and-true lightning rod of antisemitism, from all quarters, above and below.

But progressive ideology did not require philo-semitism. TR's distaste for Jews may have differed from Wilson's in both intensity and motivation, but they shared the widely prevailing view that races should not be mixed. Even proximity should be limited, let alone matrimony. The majority of their native constituents were worried that ever-increasing number of refugees were threatening to take away scarce jobs and would overcrowd cities already bursting at the seams.[43] The progressives' much-vaunted empathy was not quite as universal and equitable as they claimed.

Though surely concerned that poor immigrants with limited linguistic and professional skills would interfere with his plans to expand welfare benefits to existing voters, TR was also bigoted. Dutch historian Hans Krabbendam finds evidence in TR's public statements, including his autobiography, that his "support for [immigration] restriction was based on his conviction that people in substantially different stages of civilization should not be mixed, especially when immigrants were bound to come in great numbers and their economic position was weak."[44]

TR's reputation as a friend of immigrants is thus unwarranted. For while true that he generally refrained from blatantly racist arguments (except for strongly defending Chinese exclusion, which had preceded his tenure), Krabbendam blames him for having "paved the way for the end of free emigration."[45] TR's foreign and domestic policies were intertwined. "Throughout his career he used civic reform to build a strong nation. Immigration regulations also served this end. As it was difficult to curb democratic voting rights for legal white, male citizens, TR's solution was to select them at the gate, allowing racial stereotypes of fitness to guide the selection process." He thus "balanced immigration policy with foreign policy and skillfully used public opinion to advance harmony."[46] Never mind melting the pot; better stick with plain gruel, cleansed for purity.

Most Jews saw through it, but over the course of a couple of millennia one gets used to discrimination. They had, after all, witnessed far worse. So, the immigrants kept coming, joining family members who had helped those unable to save enough by paying for their boat tickets in advance. The deracinated took their chances once again, trusting in their own wits, the kindness of strangers, and an uncanny ingenuity honed by hardship. Though many failed, most survived, and many even thrived, taking full advantage of the country's economic opportunities.

My own grandfather had left a wife and five children behind, hoping to bring them along later when he could afford to do so. Three followed soon. Then the Second World War trapped my mother, her sick brother, and my grandmother. "It was so strange," my mother told me. "Watching American bombs fall on the hill across the valley from our shelter, we were terrified that we would be killed. Still, we rooted for their victory. They would bring our liberation – provided we survived."

With bags packed, ready, should they be "relocated" (to Auschwitz) with no prior notice, my parents had no inkling of their eventual fate. They prayed and hoped. My father's family home had already been expropriated. But they had survived, at least so far. A miracle might happen yet, and there would be peace again.

Chapter V:

Internationalized "Liberalism"

Exporting National Democracy

"This is the time of all others when democracy should prove its purity and its spiritual power to prevail. It is surely the manifest destiny of the United States to lead in the attempt to make this spirit prevail."

- Woodrow Wilson, "State of the Union Address" (1920)

Their manifest appetite for power aside, both TR and Wilson genuinely believed in America's leading global mission as a force for good, singularly consecrated to enlighten the less fortunate everywhere. Democrat Woodrow Wilson, who continued his progressive predecessor's domestic policies after defeating him in 1912, eventually also emulated his foreign policy. Though Wilson's appointment of the pacifist William Jennings Bryan as secretary of state at the start of his first term appeared to ensure against unwise meddling in other nations' affairs, it didn't last long. Bryan soon had to go, as Wilson began flexing his executive muscles abroad.

Little did his voters know that their new president's crusading spirit had not been entirely dormant. Though Wilson's campaign for a second term, in 1916, advanced the popular platform "He kept us out of war!," he had been itching to play a major role on the global stage. Listing several unsuccessful international activities, Cato Institute Fellow Jim Powell notes that even before the breakout of the Great War, "Wilson couldn't resist interfering in the affairs of other nations."[1] His appalling ignorance of the facts and lack of military experience led to a number of disastrous initiatives in the southern hemisphere - Nicaragua, Haiti, Mexico ("somewhere along the way, Wilson realized he had approved of an act of war against Mexico"[2]). Undaunted, the ambitious Wilson was convinced that he could act as righteous peacemaker. He boldly proposed that

America join the Allies against the Axis powers. The weakness of his arguments notwithstanding, on April 8, 1917, events precipitated to the point that Congress had little choice but to declare war.

Yet Powell's accusation that "consumed by ambition to be a world statesman, Wilson was simply pursuing his self-interest as a politician,"[3] fails to acknowledge that the president's idealism was rooted in both religion and scientistic secularism. One of Wilson's advisors, Congregationalist minister George D. Herron, believed that Wilson's support for democracy was at bottom a reflection of his faith. "The uttermost democracy, the democracy that scales the whole human octave, is to him the certain issue of the idea for which Jesus lived and died," wrote Herron. The Great War, therefore, "will become a crusade for a democracy whose application shall at last comprehend all the facts and forces of life—all moral and social and economic relations; a democracy, in fine, which shall be an approach to the early Christian idea of the kingdom of heaven. It is precisely this idea which President Wilson has brought into the sphere of practical politics."[4]

For him, socialism and Christianity went hand-in-hand. In 1912, Wilson proclaimed that "if you do socialism justice, it is hardly different from the heart of Christianity itself."[5] In his second term, "the courtship between Wilson and the leftists," argues Columbia University Professor Fred Siegel, was further intensified: "The very speech in which he asked for a congressional declaration of war also welcomed the Russian revolution that had overthrown the czar and put the socialist Alexander Kerensky (temporarily) in power." Wilson effusively, if inaccurately, described the revolution as the fulfillment of the Russian people's long struggle for democracy. It was for this reason, writes Siegel, that when "then-Russian War Commissar Leon Trotsky coined the now famous concept of the "fellow traveler," he was referring to Wilson." Later, the term would apply primarily to Western Soviet sympathizers who carried the regime's waters, mostly wittingly.

Eventually, Wilson soured on Bolshevism. But he remained a crusader. For he fervently believed in "the Christian provenance of democracy, human progress, and international cooperation," explains Boston University Professor Jeremy Menchik. Just as he promoted eugenics in the name of genetic progress, Wilson "supported the development of democracy abroad in populations with homogeneity of race and community of thought. He believed that democracy was made possible by an organic connection between society and the state, not republican institutions. He supported the annexation of foreign territories in order to civilize heathen populations and to tutor the lesser races and religions." And just as he deplored the two-party system in the United States, he sought international cooperation through dialogue facilitated by a League of Nations.

Ultimately, Wilson was convinced that "Christianity was the source of justice and liberty in the world, missionaries the mechanism for its expansion, and progress achieved through Christianization."[6] But democratic liberty cannot be attained until a society reaches a high enough stage of development, which allows it to achieve "national organic oneness." As Wilson describes it in "The Modern Democratic State,"[7] true democracy is based not so much on the Constitution as on values:

> Justly revered as our great Constitution is, it could be stripped off and thrown aside like a garment, and the nation would still stand forth clothed in the living vestment of flesh and sinew, warm with the heartblood of one people, ready to recreate constitutions and laws.[8]

Why wear an old rag instead of a gorgeous new outfit? Dump the *shmata,* put on the finery.

As he expanded his executive reach, Wilson increasingly unleashed his inner preacher to create an aura of supranatural legitimacy, inspiring the electorate to solidarity. In his 1920 Annual State of the Union address, Wilson described what he declared to be the nation's faith that world peace was attainable:

> By this faith, and by this faith alone, can the world be lifted out of its present confusion and despair. ... This is the time of all others when democracy should prove its purity and its spiritual power to prevail. It is surely the manifest destiny of the United States to lead in the attempt to make this spirit prevail.[9]

The lofty rhetoric, however, could ill conceal his own lack of foreign policy experience, on full display in Versailles, which had contributed significantly to the "confusion and despair" he was now proposing to alleviate. Wilson's insistence on the preeminent role of empiricism and science belied his appalling ignorance of world history, geography, and much else. The one key principle for which he is best remembered, national self-determination, was mainly an ideological extension of his deeply felt conviction that America had a moral responsibility to liberate the world.

Albeit some version of this sentiment had long been a staple of the national self-image, it referred mainly to providing an example to others and offering moral support – what Harvard Professor Joseph Nye would later call "soft power."[10] When Wilson seized the opportunity to move beyond serving as an example of good governance, however, and sought to spread democracy using interventionist methods, to the point of embroiling the country in a world war, he was changing the course of American foreign policy in ways even he could not have fathomed.[11]

If Wilson's rhetoric was damaging, so too were his actions. Grandly proclaiming a new universal "right" of so-called "self-determination of peoples," he hadn't any idea what he was talking about. Though immediately evident to anyone with a shred of knowledge about Europe in general and Eastern Europe in particular - never mind the Orient, Africa, and "the rest" - the fractious ethnic compositions of most states insured that extracting "peoples" for purposes of "self-determination" (whatever that meant) would lead to continued insecurity and strife. Alas, Wilson was clueless.

Laments University of Virginia Professor Allen Lynch: "sheer ignorance as well as conceptual ambiguities informed Wilson's course"[12] – or, rather, uninformed it. To his credit (or was it shame?) Wilson admitted as much in a letter written to Secretary of State Robert Lansing in 1918:

> When I gave utterance to those words [that all nations had a right to self-determination], I said them without a knowledge that nationalities existed, which are coming to us day after day ... You do not know and cannot appreciate the anxieties that I have experienced as the result of many millions of people having their hopes raised by what I have said.[13]

No knowledge that nationalities ***existed*?** How could Wilson have failed to appreciate the role nationalism had already played in starting the very war he was now trying to quell? Though Wilson could not be blamed for the disastrous Versailles treaty whose short-sighted European drafters mainly ignored him, he was certainly responsible for lighting the conceptual match of national so-called self-determination in such a flammable global atmosphere. It was a mistake of monumental proportions. The USSR would take full advantage of it during the 1960s to legitimize "liberating" former colonies into its orbit, to the benefit of kleptocrats spouting communist slogans.

But Wilson's crusade and its rhetorical justification did serve a crucial domestic function, which may have been his main goal anyway. Far from repudiating progressivism – on the contrary, implementing its policies with greater vigor than ever – his semantic switch to liberalism allowed him to continue enacting the already entrenched statist agenda, while simultaneously bolstering the sense of national unity that was its core. Ultimately, nothing unifies a constituency quite as effectively as does military mobilization. As an added bonus, the rapid need for massive new revenue presented a ready rationale for government spending on a grand scale.

The Great War thereby gave a serendipitous boost to the new Promethean ideology, offering an unexpectedly effective opportunity for systemic rehaul at home. Writes Indiana University Professor Michael McGerr:

> From the 1890s to the 1910s, the progressives managed to accomplish much of their ambitious agenda. World War I marked the high point of the progressive movement. As American soldiers fought overseas to make the world safe for democracy, the administration of Woodrow Wilson worked feverishly to create a wartime model for a peacetime progressive utopia. Against the backdrop of wartime struggle and sacrifice, reformers managed to outlaw alcohol, close down vice districts, win suffrage for women, expand the income tax, and take over the railroads.[14]

Thus when Wilson justified the use of force to advance democracy and national self-determination, notwithstanding the absence of clear and present danger to the United States, he was inaugurating a doctrine sometimes known as *liberal internationalism* – also, internationalism *tout court*, democratic internationalism, or globalism, all of them ambiguous. At bottom, however, he was enacting a personal vision. Appealing at once to the universalist humanism of the Founders and the Christian evangelism of his father, Wilson reveled in the opportunity to evangelize from the great pulpit of Versailles.

Declaring that America's purpose in entering the war was "to make the world safe for democracy," he had revealed the utopian core of progressivism. The president's expansionist policy also precipitated, even if it did not inaugurate, the use of double standards - a trend that would eventually deal a potentially fatal blow to the prestige of liberalism in an international context. Writes Lynch: "the fact remains that 'national self-determination' was applied only to the defeated powers, the victors being free to practice self-determination as they saw fit."[15]

Their short-sighted tactic was soon to boomerang against the interests of Western democracies. The arrogant great powers, basking in their victory, had long regarded their Central and Eastern neighbors with indifference, if not contempt. Dire consequences would follow much earlier than anyone could have imagined. Their source was Russia.

The vast empire had been sorely neglected, all but unknown in America. Wilson failed to see it as anything but a backward lump, a unitary mammoth. When Lenin signed the 1918 Treaty of Brest-Litovsk in 1918, which offered Russian withdrawal from the war in exchange for German restoration of independence to the Baltic States that it had occupied since 1915, Wilson at first refused to recognize their sovereignty. According to official documents, the United States even questioned whether the Baltic states were "morally justified" in proclaiming their independence during what Wilson considered to be the hour of Russia's weakness! Why, didn't they owe allegiance to Moscow? How were Estonia, Lithuania, and Latvia any different from the American states? Wasn't this Russia's equivalent of the Southern secession?

If Wilson had no conception of Baltic nationalities, he knew less than nothing about other ethnic, religious, and linguistic groups. The only thing that seems to have mattered to him was "the territorial integrity" of Russia – this even after becoming the Union of Soviet Socialist Republics, which he never understood (though, to be fair, neither did almost anyone else at the time).

To most Americans, the USSR was just a name-update, which they continued to use interchangeably with the old. Referring to all its citizens as Russians, they unwittingly advanced the Politburo's russification policy. When the United States finally, and reluctantly, did recognize Baltic independence in 1922, the State Department released the following statement:

> The United States has consistently maintained that the disturbed conditions of Russian affairs may not be made the occasion for the alienation of Russian territory, and this principle is not deemed to be infringed by the recognition at this time of the Governments of Esthonia, [sic] Latvia, and Lithuania, which have been set up and maintained by an indigenous population.[16]

The implications of this blind spot and profound misunderstanding of Soviet reality for American foreign policy must be understood in its ideological context. The meaning of democracy would evolve once more, reflecting Communist Russia's deft manipulation of language. Psychological warfare known technically as "active measures," (Russian: активные мероприятия - Romanized: *aktivnye meropriyatiya*), which included but was not limited to disinformation (*dezinformatsia*),[17] became the KGB's most valuable weapon in a war whose apparent coldness belied a radicalism that turned liberalism itself into a dagger pointed to America's own heart.

But even before the USSR had a chance to further manipulate our political discourse, the Depression would provide countless new opportunities for semantic warfare. The immediacy and enormity of the shock that followed the unexpected collapse of Wall Street electrocuted the country into conceptual paralysis, rendering it highly vulnerable to ideological subterfuge. Not even the widely admired Herbert Hoover knew how to deal with such a devastating economic disaster.

He had originally seemed the perfect choice for president. Appointed head of the Commission for Relief in Belgium by Wilson during the Great War, Hoover excelled in saving the population of that occupied country from starvation. After the war, as head of the American Relief Administration, he provided food to the inhabitants of Eastern and Central Europe. A reputation for managerial talent earned him the confidence of Republican president Warren Harding, who appointed him Secretary of Commerce in 1920. Eight years later, Hoover easily won the party's nomination for president, defeating Democrat Al Smith in the general election by a comfortable margin.

Hoover's timing could not have been worse. The impending apocalypse would forever seal his fate. Irredeemably linked to the Great Depression, his reputation would never recover. Before long, his earlier self-descriptions as progressive and liberal were dismissed. Ignoring his protestations, he was consistently being labeled conservative and even reactionary, if not pro-fascist. The fact was, he didn't know how to get the country back on track economically. And people craved presidential leadership. Progressives took full advantage of the situation. Labels be damned – and labels damned him.

The Depression seemed to have jolted the population into a mindset of dependence. The Founders' proud self-reliance was far in the past, a relic of a bygone era. David Green reflects on the semantic realignment that emerged amidst the unprecedented national trauma:

> Panic is seldom conducive to serious reflection; it more frequently propels people down the path of least resistance. All one had to do was correlate the persistence of the depression with Hoover's insistence on individual responsibility and on the individual as the natural political unit; once this was done, it became all too easy to believe in the nation as the natural unit and the federal government as the focus of all responsibility.[18]

The country had been utterly unprepared for the collapse. Observes Green: "the panic was as much intellectual as financial." When FDR was elected in 1932, he inherited the progressive and liberal label, taking his success as an overwhelming mandate to appropriate the labels for the Democrats. Republican Senator George Norris of Nebraska, conceding defeat, spoke for a great majority of his ideological brethren when he said: "We of the progressive faith have to look to the Democratic Party."[19]

The door was thus open to the grand synthesis for which few were as ideally qualified as FDR. Endowed with an uncanny ability to galvanize the country, exuding optimism and sheer willpower, FDR used the new medium of radio to project his soothing, mesmerizing voice inside each family's living room to stunning effect. If only he had not been duped by his own instincts, advisors, and ideology to commit some spectacular mistakes.

If only. To cite one of my father's favorite jokes: if my grandmother had wheels, it would be a bicycle. FDR's mistakes were, as Communist Party members liked to say, "no coincidence, comrade."

Old Liberalism's Raw New Deal

"Generally speaking, in a representative form of government there are usually two general schools of political belief – liberal and conservative.... The liberal party is a party which believes that, as new conditions and problems arise beyond the power of men and women to meet as individuals, it becomes the duty of the Government itself to find new remedies with which to meet them."
– Franklin Delano Roosevelt (1941)

After Hoover, FDR revived progressivism with help from several members of Wilson's administration, notably George Creel. The chief propagandist during the Great War, Creel had campaigned enthusiastically for FDR in 1932. It earned him the directorship of the West Coast Administration under the National Industrial Recovery Act, which he applauded as

> a gigantic effort to reorganize the whole industrial structure of the United States on higher, finer lines, substituting a cooperative order for an unlimited competitive order, a determined drive for the adoption of a planned, well-balanced, national economy as opposed to pep talks, high pressure salesmanship and other phases of the hit or miss, devil take the hindmost, dog eat dog plan under which America has been operating.[20]

Six months later, Creel left the administration, apparently miffed by FDR's insufficient appreciation for his hard work, though he remained loyal to the president and his ideals. After joining *Collier's* magazine, he became one of FDR's favorite reporters. But Creel credited Wilson, not FDR, with inaugurating the new liberalism: "What we call the New Deal," wrote Creel, "as well as all other progressive thought, derives from Woodrow Wilson's vision of a fairer, finer world."[21] He was right.

Creel's progressivism, however, was not especially egalitarian. Indeed, what eventually alienated Creel from FDR was Roosevelt's indulging "the desires of blacks and organized labor," writes Rochester Institute of Technology Professor Frank Annunziata. "Creel applauded Donald Richberg's insight - the President sought 'superior rights for inferiors,'"[22] which Creel found appalling and rather unexpected from someone with such an elite pedigree.

The final straw was Creel's alarm at the encroachment of pro-Soviet agents and fellow travelers in the government, securing many, sometimes highly sensitive positions. That turned the old progressive into a committed supporter of Senator Joseph McCarthy. Creel felt betrayed by FDR's inability to appreciate the danger from home-grown enemies. The histrionic propagandist's adulation for the no-less-unhinged senator was unbounded: "I may sound the call for a Society for the Protection and Preservation of McCarthyism, for pointing out that it stems from the same sturdy Americanism that led plain men to risk all at Lexington and Concord while 'loyalists' raced for the Canadian border."[23]

Just as Creel's name would thenceforth be associated with jingoist propaganda, and Hoover's with banks defaulting, FDR became America's savior. It became "a cliché that 'twentieth-century liberalism' began with Roosevelt," observes David Green. And specifically, this reflected the president's success in having "transformed people's expectations of government." A stunning feat of polemical engineering, it was not the Founders' liberal idea, nor even the refurbished version of his immediate predecessors. For while "Wilson and Hoover were both defining 'liberal' in terms of voluntary action," continues Green, everything changed after the Great Depression managed to sap trust in the very system of free enterprise and personal philanthropy. Taking advantage of the shock, Roosevelt saw to it that "**liberalism [would] emerge redefined as the politics of governmental generosity**. This is what the public works programs, the job creation programs, social security, and the various other efforts at redistribution of wealth were all about."[24] This was Wilson's liberalism on steroids.

In a brilliant case study that focuses on FDR, Chapman University Law Professor Ronald Rotunda explains the calculus behind the crafty president's semantic reboot. Above all, "Roosevelt needed to introduce a political label that would allow voters to think in terms other than Republican or Democrat. By associating his policies with a word such as 'liberal,' instead of 'Democratic,' a sympathetic Republican could more easily justify his vote for FDR"[25] It had been, for FDR as before for Wilson, a semantic adjustment based on political expediency.

It worked miracles, testimony to FDR's uncanny marketing talent. His economic advisor Rexford Tugwell, who had actually advised the president against using that label, much preferring "progressive," writes

Rotunda, "recalled once talking to Roosevelt about the origin of his use of 'liberal,' but Roosevelt did not answer him, though 'he laughed and asked if it mattered.' Roosevelt probably did not answer because he had not consciously chosen the liberal symbol."[26] His political genius was instinctive.

But a word whose value lay in ambiguity needed careful recalibration before it could gradually become associated with one party over the other. First it had to be appropriated from Hoover and the Republicans, who were not giving up easily. They stubbornly resisted having "conservative"– to say nothing of "reactionary"[27] – vengefully thrust upon them by their opponents. Roosevelt deftly finessed the challenge. With characteristically exquisite sense of timing, FDR chose the perfect moment to announce and establish the creedal makeover: his acceptance of the Democratic Party's nomination as presidential candidate. He nonchalantly proceeded to christen the party "the bearer of liberalism and progress."

Though he implemented the transition deftly, it would take a while for the concept to be properly fleshed out, endowed with new meaning, and longer still for its titular owners to react. Writes Rotunda:

> Willard Kiplinger, who wrote an influential business newsletter, argued that it was not until March 1, 1934, that business reaction against Roosevelt became significant. That this thunder on the right did not appear until 1934 was of great advantage to the New Deal, for it furnished a period of grace in which Roosevelt's programs could be identified with liberalism unhampered by any serious challenge to the New Deal's power to define this term.[28]

Ever the politician, FDR consistently refused to define his words, taking the high road and declaring that he was simply doing what was best for the country. But since his policies increasingly looked, walked and quacked like a socialist duck (the unpopular S-word), it was left to Roosevelt's academic supporters to step in and explain how his New Deal was nonetheless liberal in a true, traditional American sense – appearances to the contrary notwithstanding. The master wordsmith John Dewey gladly obliged.

After identifying the two strands of liberalism, humanitarianism and *laissez faire*, he declared that the United States had always been humanitarian, but not the latter – certainly not anymore. Everyone knows, wrote Dewey in the *New York Times Magazine* on February 3, 1936, that "liberalism has been identified largely with the ideal of the use of governmental agencies to remedy evils from which the less-fortunate classes suffer." As for that other strand, added Dewey, sure it was tried for a while, but as FDR has recognized, it's over: "laissez-faire liberalism is played out."[29] That brand was passé. So yesterday. Uncool. Can't even remember if it ever caught on.

No mention was made of the inherently coercive nature of government action – whether for the sake of "remedying evils" or any other motive. Besides, in true progressive fashion, FDR saw nothing sinister in coercion. Writing in June 1941, Roosevelt explained that a liberal party by any name believes "in the wisdom and efficacy of the will of the great majority of people." As opposed to those (and you know who **they** are) who "believe that control by a few," who trust "in the judgment of a small minority," in a word, "stand in the way of all social progress."[30] Liberalism is not centrally orchestrated redistributionism but democratically ordained generosity. Just don't call it "coercion," that sounds so heartless. (Orwell, stop rolling your eyes.)

FDR knew his audience. Far from refuting his detractors who accused him of taking from the rich to give to the poor, he relished the Robinhood analogy. It suited him. Borrowing language from the preamble of the Constitution, he proudly admitted that he sought to promote "welfare" as mandated by the founding document. In contrast, members of the opposite party, more principled than astute, opted to dig in their heels, heedless of the quicksand. Their reputation for tradition and constitutional order mocked, non-progressives found themselves despised as rapacious, heartless, retrograde, in short, **conservative.**

The result was pure political gold. Explains Green:

> This vocabulary not only reinforced the idea of inevitable corporate combination under minimal government but established Roosevelt as the champion of countervailing power. Even more important, the vocabulary made the New Deal itself synonymous with a more effective and equitable distribution of wealth. … [As a result,] to the extent that the economic situation improved, the New Deal got the credit; to the extent that the depression continued, Roosevelt's use of labels ascribed responsibility to corporate greed and shortsightedness as well as to the intransigence of procorporate [sic] politicians (the Republican party).[31]

Eventually, FDR overplayed his hand. Frustrated by court decisions that struck down proposed New Deal legislations that strained the Constitution's language to the breaking point, FDR turned up the heat. Increasingly, he took to calling conservatives not only reactionary but full-fledged fascists. He portrayed himself and his fellow Democrats as opposed to "old-line Republicans and Communists alike – for they are people whose only purpose is to survive against any other Fascist threat than their own."[32] By 1941, he was using Nazi terminology to discredit opponents of his proposal to increase the size of the Supreme Court to 16 by accusing them of engaging in a propaganda "putsch." He might have been applying the tactic preferred by both Goebbels and Stalin colloquially known as the Big Lie. If so, he proved a quick learner.

But smearing opponents and finger-pointing could go only so far. As the war progressed, and the failure of New Deal social programs could no longer be denied, [33] FDR had to temper his ideology with capitalistic realism. He had to navigate carefully. Moving the camera away from domestic woes to international threats, he followed in Wilson's footsteps, making increased use of war rhetoric. The public's anti-war sentiments were palpably weakening, as the growing Nazi threat could no longer be concealed even by State Department, which minimized it as long as it could.[34] It was a good time to channel the national malaise by preparing for military action – and gather the requisite, much-needed expenditures. Opting for the progressive politician's last and most effective resort to economic disaster, he set the stage for war. It had obviously been a good decision, but it came with an ideological catch or two.

FDR had just the words for his new focus: antifascism. "As rearmament replaced the New Deal," notes Green, 'antifascism' began to emerge as both the new freedom and the new generosity." At the same time, however, "the antifascist rhetoric also camouflaged Roosevelt's surrender to large corporations." With a faint yet unmistakable touch of sophistry, FDR had managed to deftly obscure the fact that not only Herbert Hoover but the vast majority of Republicans were antifascist as well. Far from wanting to allow Nazis free reign in Europe, a preposterous notion, they feared America's becoming itself a national socialist state.

And there was one more issue at stake. The pro-Bolshevik left had been hedging their bets in a complex strategic dance since 1935. On August 2 of that year, a report released by the Seventh World Congress of the Communist International (CCI), which followed a secret Franco-Soviet pact signed exactly three months earlier, signaled new tactics to its members. The Communist parties saw the anti-Hitler front becoming the center of the battle. This meant "provisionally collaborating with their own bourgeoisies,"[35] explains French historian and University of Chicago Professor Francois Furet in his incomparable *The Passing of an Illusion: The Idea of Communism in the Twentieth Century* (1997).

The CCI report defined fascism as no longer a mere political tendency in all capitalist countries, but rather as it played out in the specific regimes of Mussolini's Italy, Nazi Germany, and even Poland. In effect, explains Furet,

> through anti-Fascism, the Communists had recovered the trophy of democracy without renouncing any of their basic convictions. During the Great Terror [of the 1930s], Bolshevism reinvented itself as a freedom by default. Even while drawing strength from what it despised [i.e., freedom] – the homage of vice to virtue – it was intimidating its adversaries by spreading the rumor that anti-Sovietism was the prelude to Fascism. Not only was Hitler useful in reviving the idea of democratic Communism, but he also provided a pretext to incriminate democratic anti-Communism.[36]

In other words, Moscow sought an alliance against the fascists to hedge its bets against German attack. Stupid Stalin was not.

And then the wily Georgian did an about-face, stunning the world by forging an agreement with Hitler! The Molotov-Ribbentrop Pact, signed on August 23, 1939, was supposed to prevent a German invasion, simultaneously weakening the Allies. And through a Secret Protocol, whose existence the Soviets denied until the imminent demise of their empire in 1989,[37] the two totalitarian governments agreed to carve up Eastern Europe. It thus precipitated Poland's invasion by both sides, Hitler and Stalin annexing different slices of the oft-divided country at the heart of Europe.

Once again, the means justified by whatever ends Stalin was pursuing, and anti-fascism was put on hold. It was ideological whiplash for the

Communist Party USA, which now had to adopt Moscow's line to keep the U.S. out of the war. At the same time, it proved a boon to progressives who placed themselves against isolationists on both right and left. In truth, prior to Hitler's unsurprising (except to Stalin) invasion of the USSR in June of 1941, America had already cast its lot with the Allies, yet still awaited a provocation to go all-in.

Although the number of Nazi sympathizers throughout America was astonishingly high - including not only writers, politicians, and businessmen, but a huge proportion of the diplomatic corps and the foreign service – by no means were all who cautioned against precipitous military engagement outright Nazi sympathizers. Even the celebrated human rights defender Ambassador Max Kampelman (1920-2013) had been a pacifist throughout World War II.

His was a fascinating story. I remember meeting the Ambassador in the early 1980s, when I had the opportunity to interview him for a study I was writing for the Heritage Foundation about the United Nations' Human Rights Council's double standard. A man of considerable warmth and evident commitment, he was utterly without airs. I didn't know then that we both hailed from Romania, and that he had attended yeshiva as a boy. I was also unaware of his sympathy for what he called "the Quaker approach." Only later would I learn that when young, his "total instinct was against dictatorship and against the communists. I found myself," wrote Kampelman,

> actively engaged in an anti-communist clique on campus.... I also had a professor who taught social legislation and remained my friend until he died.... He recommended that I spend a month during my last summer in college with a Quaker work camp.... We were fixing up slum buildings.... [The Quaker approach] influenced me. ... I became an anti-communist conscientious objector [CO].... [W]hat persuaded me to be a CO at the time was that wars and violence don't solve the problem. The elimination of evil requires something different from killing people.[38]

But few saw it this way. The progressive *New Republic* chose to throw the whole lot of what it called "appeasers" into one satanic pile, charging in a February 3, 1941, editorial that "whatever their other differences, it is the absolutist philosophies of our time that are united for isolation and appeasement. These included Communists and the dogmatic socialists of the Norman Thomas stripe; the pacifists; the Nazis," to mention but a few. The editorial contrasts this nefarious motley crew with the good guys who chose to label themselves "instrumentalists," meaning those "who know we can use only the instruments at our command, and who are determined to use them in the unending struggle to come closer to a decent world."[39] During the rest of 1941, these instrumentalist-pragmatists, eager to appropriate the mantle of liberalism, focused on disrobing the Republicans, who stubbornly insisted on keeping that label for themselves.

Eventually Republicans rose to the bait and (neither for the first nor last time) provided their adversaries the rope. When Arthur Schlesinger, Jr., writing in the *Nation* on December 6, 1941, linked "non-interventionism" with "conservatism" hurling both at the Republican Party wholesale, Senator Robert A. Taft bristled. On December 13, a week after Pearl Harbor, the *Nation* happily published his passionate rebuttal. Taft was denying that he was "correct in attributing the position of the majority of Republicans to their conservatism." Far from it, he protested. Only "[t]he most conservative members of the party – the Wall Street bankers, the society group, nine-tenths of the plutocratic newspapers, and most of the party's financial contributors – are the ones who favor intervention in Europe."

He had stepped into it. With typically dubious tactical acumen, Taft was more eager to castigate pro-war sentiment than to save "conservatism" from pejorative connotations. Go ahead, blame the fat-cat conservatives who favored war, he thundered, not "the average man and woman – the farmer, the workman, except for a few pro-British labor leaders, and the small business man – who are opposed to the war." He denounced "the war party" as "the business community of the cities, the newspaper and magazine writers, the radio and movie commentators, the Communists, and the university intelligentsia." Like Hoover, Taft fought tooth and tail not to surrender the word "liberal" to the opposition. But by lumping fat-cat conservatism together with Red communism, he was unwittingly playing into the opposition's narrative that big money was evil.

The Jewish community, worried sick over Nazism, became even more alienated from Republicans. They knew that "fat cats" included financiers, code-word for their co-religionists. Taft had been easy prey. Hoover, however, was a much bigger fish, deserving the use of far more powerful instruments of political warfare. The *Nation* shrewdly resorted to deploying journalist Herbert Agar. Once the victim of baiting for allegedly "Fascist" views[40] himself, Agar was eager to subject others to similar tactics. Justifiably reserving a special circle in ideological hell to Henry Ford, whose rabid antisemitism was no secret, Agar turned on Hoover, of whom he declared: "Hitler has no more stubborn helper in all the world."[41] Calling this accusation preposterous is a gross understatement: it was obscene. But politics is a contact sport, and the rules are up for grabs.

The old Republican liberals held out a little longer. By 1945, it seemed futile to continue thrusting themselves against the progressive windmills. Hoover threw in the towel, albeit reluctantly. Furious that the New Dealers had stolen his preferred designation, he nonetheless capitulated. The postscript to an editorial Hoover sent to Norman Chandler for the *Los Angeles Times* of October 14, 1945, deserves a special place in the annals of liberalism:

> We do not use the word "liberal." That word has been polluted and raped of all its meaning… Liberalism was founded to further more liberty for men, not less freedom. Therefore, it was militant against the expansion of bureaucracy, against socialism and all of its ilk. … Lenin's instructions on propaganda included the deliberate distortion of accepted words and terms and Lenin has surely had his way with the word "liberalism." The Socialists and Communists daily announce that they are "liberals." They have nested in this word until it stinks. Let them have the word. It no longer makes sense.

In this, Hoover was wrong: it still "made sense" in the most important respect, which is to say, emotionally. Lenin and his Western fellow-travelers were better psychologists, and decidedly more astute politicians. Green's assessment of Hoover's failure is unassailable: "To concede the liberal label to Roosevelt and his supporters was not only to aid them in justifying all sorts of government action in the name of liberalism, but to validate their long-standing claim that opponents of their policies were, after all, self-confessed opponents of liberalism."[42]

Green is on shakier ground when he charges that "Hoover's insistence on linking New Dealers with 'socialists and communists' was to be equally self-defeating." It was one thing to make the best of "conservative," given its respectable historical pedigree in an America: being respectful of tradition, preserving the classics, encouraging biblical learning, and being realistic rather than utopian. It was quite another to surrender and abstain from exposing one's enemies candidly, with solid arguments, allowing them to turn the word into a smear. Here, Hoover was on solid ground.

Hoover had understandably resisted adopting "conservatism" for so long because he fully appreciated the danger of so volatile, open-ended, and relative a label. Its savvy hijackers divined its intrinsically chameleonic ability to accommodates diametrically opposed ideological stands. Unsurprisingly, it has since allowed its enemies in the academy and the media to stigmatize the foundational American liberal traditionalism enshrined in the Declaration and the Constitution, based on scrupulous regard for individual freedom, by painting it with the same brush as Politburo Stalinism, Islamist totalitarianism, and the increasingly ubiquitous stalworth, Fascism.

It didn't help that Hoover was hardly the prototype of classical liberalism. As prize-winning economist Amity Shlaes explains in her superb 2009 bestseller *The Forgotten Man: A New History of the Great Depression*, Hoover proved incapable of either understanding or countering the market collapse which his own monetary policies had exacerbated. In fact, charges Shlaes, "the New Deal [was merely] a more intense, less constitutional version of Hoover policy, [which] also failed to yield recovery - for seven more years." Tragically, "[t]here is plenty of evidence that neither in the 1920s nor the 1930s did the U.S. economy require an octopus expert or even a Great Engineer. Yet Hoover's urgent need to show off his knowledge by mounting rescue operations - whether of the food-aid or stock-market variety - overwhelmed his common sense."[43] That in Hoover's case the fault was less ideological than personal is largely irrelevant.

But his utter lack of political acumen bordered on the ludicrous, as demonstrated by his meeting in Berlin with Adolph Hitler at the Reich Chancellery in March 1938, topped off by dinner with Hermann Göring at the Nazi minister's hunting lodge, in Carinhall. In an astonishing display of stupidity, in his chat with Hitler, Hoover reportedly spoke up for... personal liberty! His cluelessness before the Nazi menace tainted not only his own reputation but that of his ideological label, smearing his party.

Senator Robert A. Taft held out longer, hanging on to liberalism as late as 1948. But he was fighting a losing battle. Even though Republicans sought solace in Hoover's attempt to rescue as positive a connotation as possible for conservatism, it was far too late. "[T]he Rooseveltian definitions had already triumphed," notes Green. "For most Americans, the conservative label was no longer a positive self-designation at all because it connoted no more than opposition to the New Deal," which had long ago lost most of its stigma as the economy revived. Few had either the ability or inclination to understand the economics. Besides, politically it was far more useful to embrace it rather than keep opposing it in vain.

The New Conservativism, same as the Old Liberalism?

"[The New Conservative consensus] posits ... that the freedom of the person, not the asserted authority of 'society,' of some 'mysterious incorporation of the human race,' is primary in political thought and action. ... At the source to which American conservatism inevitably returns - The Declaration of Independence, the Constitution and the debates at the time of its adoption – this simultaneous belief in objectively existing moral value and the individual person was promulgated in uncompromising terms. From that source it irradiates the active present scene of American conservatism."

– Frank S. Meyer, *In Defense of Freedom: A Conservative Credo* (1962)

To the rescue came William F. Buckley, Jr., the witty, erudite, urbane founder of *National Review,* who intuitively grasped the essence of the challenge: "Conservatives in this country – at least those who have not made their peace with the New Deal, and there is serious question whether there are others – are nonlicensed nonconformists; and this is dangerous business in a Liberal world." The year was 1955. General Dwight Eisenhower had ably united a country relieved to return to the business of business, which seemed to augur well for a revival of normality. But much had changed. Observing that the new "Liberal world" did not look kindly on anyone practicing nonconformism without a license, Buckley decided to take on the challenge. Almost single-handedly, he succeeded in resuscitating a moribund classical liberal mindset with renewed intellectual respectability.

But only almost. Another, less visible hand behind the maverick new magazine belonged to an Austrian Jewish émigré journalist named

William S. Schlamm (1904-1978). According to the celebrated historian of American conservatism George H. Nash, it was Schlamm who "conceived the idea" of *National Review*, persuaded Buckley to become its editor-in-chief, then "worked assiduously with him to launch the enterprise."[44] Invaluable help soon arrived from another, most unlikely source: the prize-winning screenwriter of such Marx Brothers masterpieces as "Night at the Opera," and "Cocoanuts," Morrie Ryskind (1895-1985). Famous for his hilarious one-liners, a welcome contrast to the turgid prose of the other, sinister Marx, Ryskind organized fund-raisers at his home in Beverly Hills for wealthy Hollywood friends. It turned the magazine into a financial success.

Though Buckley never doubted the appeal of classical liberal ideas to ordinary people (he once famously quipped that he would rather be governed by the first one hundred names in the Boston telephone book than by the Harvard faculty), he rejected what he called "the popular and cliché-ridden appeal to the 'grass roots.'" He sought rather to target intellectuals. For it was they "who have midwived and implemented the revolution. We have got to have allies among the intellectuals," he confided to a friend on December 1, 1955.

Among those allies were former Communists, ex-Trotskyists, and other anti-statists. In addition to Schlamm and Ryskind,[45] other remarkable Jews who joined the ranks of the *National Review* included Eugene Lyons, a senior editor at the *Reader's Digest*; political theorist Frank S. Meyer, whose books sought to reinvigorate classical liberalism for a post-liberal era; and Frank Chodorov, founder of the Intercollegiate Society of Individualists (ISI), which later became the Intercollegiate Studies Institute.

Eugene Lyons (1898-1985), who emigrated with his parents from Belarus, had been one of a significant number of former radicals whose illusions about communism were shattered in the most incontrovertible way: direct experience. He was appalled by the famine, show trials, and mendacity that characterized Soviet totalitarianism. At the same time, he valiantly confronted the vulgar "hobgoblin of red-baiting" that had given fighting against that very real danger a bad name. He reserved his greatest contempt, however, for the new liberals who ignored or even apologized for the enormities perpetrated by that tyrannical regime.

Frank S. Meyer (1909-1972), born to a well-to-do German Jewish family, had attended Princeton, then Oxford, where he turned to communism, and eventually joined the Communist Party USA (CPUSA). But during World War II, while serving in the U.S. Army, he encountered F. A. Hayek's monumental *A Road to Serfdom* (written between 1940 and 1943). By 1945, he was cured. Meyer joined the original staff of *National Review* a decade later, to help Buckley redefine conservatism in a manner that sought to preserve the liberal idea of the Founders, which they both felt had been thoroughly betrayed. It is no exaggeration to claim, as does the Acton Institute leadership, that "Frank S. Meyer defined the goal of postwar conservatism: to create a society in which men are free to pursue virtue but not enforce virtue at the point of a gun."[46]

His intention in writing his seminal book, *In Defense of Freedom: A Conservative Credo* (1962), explained Meyer, was "to vindicate the freedom of the person as the central and primary end of political society," fully appreciating that the ideal name for such a creed was of course liberalism.

> Liberalism was indeed once, in the last century, the proponent and defender of freedom. But **that which is called liberalism today has deserted its heritage in defense of freedom of the person, to become the peculiarly American form of what in Europe is called democratic socialism**. This transformation was the result of a fatal flaw in the philosophical underpinnings of 19th century liberalism. It stood for individual freedom, but its utilitarian philosophical attitude denied the validity of moral ends firmly based on the constitution of being. Thereby, with this denial of an ultimate sanction for the inviolability of the person, liberalism destroyed the very foundations of its defense of the person as primary in political and social matters.[47]

He preferred to call the bastardized, hijacked form of liberalism as "collectivist," and often used scare quotes around "liberal" to distinguish it from its original version, which Meyer sought to rekindle.

So too did Frank Chodorov (1887-1966), the son of poor Russian-Jewish immigrants. Like Morrie Ryskind, he had also attended Columbia. The two shared a passion for free speech and individual liberty. In 1953, Chodorov founded the Intercollegiate Society of Individuals (ISI) with William F. Buckley as president. This is how Chodorov diagnosed the illness of the age:

> At the beginning of the last century, when liberalism was emerging from adolescence, its only tenet was that political intervention in the affairs of men is bad. It traced all the disabilities that men suffered from to the power of the State. Hence, it advocated the whittling away of that power, without reserve, and proposed to abolish laws, without replacement. This negativeness was all right until the liberals got into places of power, and then it occurred to them that a little positive action might be good; they discovered that only the laws enacted by non-liberals were bad. The fact is—and this is something the State worshippers are prone to overlook—that the comforts, emoluments and adulation that go with political office have great influence on political policy; for the State consists of men, and men are, unfortunately, always human. And so, liberalism mutated into its exact opposite by the end of the nineteenth century. Today it is the synonym of Statism.[48]

Like Meyer, Chodorov never abandoned true liberalism. It had been liberalism that had "mutated into its exact opposite." What united all these Jews, once leftists, was a staunch opposition to communism, whose Soviet incarnation horrified them. All were willing to suffer the consequences of the hostility they would necessarily face from their fellow ideocrats.

Morrie Ryskind, for example, would be confronted by Hollywood and duly punished. His still strong socialist leanings notwithstanding, he had come to thoroughly distrust the Communists. Reading Eugene Lyons's revelations in *Assignment in Utopia,* describing his experiences during six years spent inside Stalin's Russia, further enflamed Ryskind's animosity. In 1947, he decided to testify before the House Un-American Activities Committee's hearings on Communist infiltration in the motion picture industry. Having categorically refused to heed suggestions by motion-picture industry representatives to "soft-pedal" his testimony, he was promptly blacklisted.

Up to then, as one of the ten highest paid writers in Hollywood, Ryskind had been earning as much as $75,000 per script – a fortune in those days. After he testified, he never received another cent. It was McCarthyism in reverse, with one notable exception: he was not making baseless accusations. He simply told what he knew.

McCarthyism Muddies the Ideological Waters

"The so-called McCarthy Era [narrative implied] that the Red-hunting Republican senator from Wisconsin was himself singlehandedly

responsible for the evisceration of ideological opposition to Communism – anti-Communism – rendering said anti-Communism into a kind of disease. The remedy was said to be a steady dose of anti-anti-Communism."

- Diana West, *American Betrayal: The Secret Assault on Our Nation's Character* (2013)

"[A]nti-communism is an essentially conservative stance, which uses the experience of Soviet-type regimes as a further means - there are many others - of combating as utopian, absurd, dangerous, and sinister any transformative project which goes beyond the most modest attempts at 'piecemeal social engineering.'"

- Marcel Liebman and Ralph Miliband, "Reflections on Anti-Communism," *Jacobin* (2017)

A very different type of nonconformism to that of Buckley and his colleagues was being practiced with a sort of license so appallingly audacious that it almost looks like a KGB operation. Only demagoguery of the sort practiced by a drunken, if shrewd, politician the likes of Joseph McCarthy, a Republican senator from Wisconsin, could manage to distort the sinister effects of KGB meddling in the United States with such spectacular success. Lacking in adequate evidence to validate his over-inflated claims, rude and histrionic, he was easily ridiculed.

Scholars of American communism Harvey Klehr of Emory University and Library of Congress expert John Earl Haynes painstakingly document in their 2003 book *In Denial: Historians, Communism, and Espionage*, [49] how McCarthyism became a "useful" epithet against all manner of anti-communist views and actions. It was wielded as a weapon "to discredit or ignore the new information" revealed after the collapse of the Soviet regime opened sensitive Soviet archives. He was heaven-sent to his enemies, and a boon to naïve *nouveaux* liberals.

Yeshiva University Professor Ellen Schreckner, for example "called on [her fellow revisionist] historians to use 'McCarthyism' as the term of choice for 'the movement to eliminate communism from American life during the late 1940s and 1950s,' thereby taking all varieties of opposition to communism with this one 'pejorative' label."[50] Klehr and Haynes conclude that "the charge of McCarthyism is a diversion from the broader issue of anticommunism," which has infected modern liberalism. "Operating as they do in an overwhelmingly liberal and leftist academy," these historians have appropriated "the myth that politically conscious persons could not have known ... the totalitarian character of Soviet communism" during the Cold War. Yet "in fact," write the authors, "in the 1930s and 1940s a great deal was known"[51] by many people indeed.

Among them was the iconic, brilliant, if far too little known, Herb Romerstein, my former colleague at the Institute of World Politics, who during 1983 to 1989 headed the Office to Counter Soviet Disinformation at the U.S. Information Agency. Like so many of the Brooklyn Jews growing up in the 1940s, he joined the CPUSA only to leave it after 1949, disgusted by its tactics and mendacity.[52] Shortly thereafter, he was hired by the House Intelligence Committee to investigate Soviet activities in the U.S. In 1963, he prepared a seminal study for congressional hearings on the "Communist International Youth and Student Apparatus," among many others.[53] He became a veritable living encyclopedia of American communism. Humble to a fault, the only thing surpassing his copious knowledge was his personal warmth and inimitable sense of humor.

Romerstein's invaluable experience served him well in the 1990s, after President Boris Yeltsin in 1992 and 1993 opened some of the secret Soviet archives to American experts. The National Security Agency similarly released its own documents, doubling the treasure-trove. The NSA documents were explosive, revealing that the intelligence services had engaged in a secret counterintelligence operation, code-named *Venona,* starting in February 1943, and not ended until 1980.[54] Venona shed light on communist infiltration inside the American elite. Among other things, the documents linked American agents' real and cover names.

Notable among them was Harry Hopkins, FDR's close friend and advisor, who provided secret government information to a Soviet handler. As Romerstein notes in *Stalin's Secret Agents* (2012), co-authored with historian M. Stanton Evans (whose jokes rivaled Herb's) the Soviet penetration of America's bureaucracy was astonishingly successful. "The now available documentation to this effect is massive. ... A striking pattern in the record is the extent to which Soviet agents attached themselves to naïve U.S. officials who were highly susceptible to disinformation."[55]

Indeed, what emerges most acutely is not only the activity of agents and so-called fellow-travelers inside the bureaucracy, but, equally important, their cultural impact, especially through the media. Among the most important was *New York Times* correspondent I. F. Stone (1907-1989), whose code-name, according to *Venona,* was "Blin" (Russian for "blintz"). The son of Russian Jewish immigrants, born Isidor Feinstein, Stone's value to the USSR was mainly to promote Soviet disinformation themes, specifically in relation to the Korean War.

As Herb Romerstein notes in another remarkable book, *The Venona Secrets*: *The Definitive Exposé of Soviet Espionage in America* (2000), "perhaps the most outrageous was [Stone's] book *The Hidden History of the Korean War.*" Co-authored with his congressional colleague (and also my friend, before his tragic untimely death from cancer) Eric Breindel, a son of Holocaust survivors, *The History* included taking a statement by John Foster Dulles completely out of context to imply that the South Koreans attacked North Korea at America's bidding. "Some of the false statements supporting the Soviet line were traceable to Soviet disinformation," write Romerstein and Breindel, "but others appeared to be Stone's own inventions."[56]

In 1992, retired KGB general Oleg Kalugin revealed that Stone did not really sever his ties with the USSR until 1956. Temporarily anyway. Kalugin reports that in his capacity as official press attaché at the Soviet embassy during the 1960s, he succeeded in persuading Stone to renew those ties, at least, until the invasion of Czechoslovakia in 1968. Not that Stone stopped cooperating; he merely "said he would never again take any money from us."[57] He would start donating his services.

Soviet sympathies aside, Stone never abandoned his anti-Americanism. Even in 1968, his principal concern was that "the strengthening of the hard-liners in Moscow will strengthen the hard-liners in Washington."[58] In their book on Venona, also published in 2000, Haynes and Klehr similarly confirm that Stone had been fully aware that his Russian contact during the war years, Sergey Pravdin, was no journalist. "No left-wing or even mainstream journalist in America would have been afraid to meet a TASS correspondent [journalist] or think that meeting with one in 1944 would incur the wrath of the FBI. Stone was perfectly willing to meet with Kalugin during the 1960s, when the climate for Soviet government officials was far less hospitable."[59]

Haynes and Klehr further note that "because the deciphered Venona messages were classified and unknown to the public, demagogues such as [Joseph] McCarthy had the opportunity to mix together accurate information about betrayal by men such as Harry [Dexter] White and Alger Hiss with falsehoods" about many others. As a result, "[a] number of liberal and radicals pointed to the excesses of McCarthy's charges as justification for rejecting the allegations altogether."[60]

The term "McCarthyism" was first popularized by a cartoon in the *Washington Post* by the talented Herbert Lawrence Block, best known as Herblock, becoming synonymous with illiberalism as demonstrated by reckless and unsubstantiated accusations of anti-Americanism and even treason. Anyone who questioned the new progressive-liberal consensus was thereby suspected of illiberalism, and easily labeled McCarthyite.

Herblock's influence on the popular conception of liberalism was extraordinary by any measure. "Block may have insisted that his work was unbiased," notes Creighton University historian Simon Appleford, "but his contemporaries—as evidenced by both the praise of such luminaries as [Arthur M.] Schlesinger [Jr.] and [Connecticut Governor Chester] Bowles and the reactions of his readers—and later commentators have been almost unanimous in their assessment that his cartoons reflected a strong liberal ideology." Bowles, for example, had written on March 6, 1951: "I honestly do not know anyone in the publication field or radio field who is presenting a liberal viewpoint more effectively and consistently than you."[61]

Herblock protested that he was entirely evenhanded. But Appleford's analysis demonstrates that his "cartoons produced during the presidencies of Democrats were more varied in their focus and commented upon a broader range of topics and issues, indicating a reluctance on Block's part to criticize the actions of these administrations and negating his claims of 'independence.'" By using images, a mindset was created far more effectively than words ever could.[62] In becoming politicized through one of the two major parties, however, the original progressive vision of unity was being undermined. The new ideology, which had first been deemed liberal by a Democratic president, was now openly partisan.

This is how it worked, explains media expert Chris Lamb: "By reducing the vast right-wing conspiracy to a single word, Herblock turned McCarthy into a metaphor for the abuses of the Red Scare. One of McCarthy's confederates was Richard Nixon, who came to Washington from California as a Communist-hunting congressman. Nixon smeared opponents with gutter politics. In a 1954 cartoon, Herblock sketched a stubbly-faced Nixon climbing out of a sewer."[63] The pencil was surely mightier than the sword in the political war of impressions. Herblock took full advantage of demagogic exaggerations, resulting in the most egregious paradox: *les extremes se touchent (*extremes meet). Show trials were being likened to Congressional histrionics.

At first, both right and left profited from the caricaturized oversimplification. On one hand, the extent of infiltration by communists and their sympathizers inside the government was exaggerated, while on the flip side the intellectuals succeeded in ridiculing overreaction as stupid and baseless. Write Romerstein and Breindel: "The political Left spawned the term 'McCarthyism' and infused it with dire and even evil connotations and then used it effectively to define an entire period."[64] And, more to the point, a political party: the Republican.

As the celebrated journalist Norman Podhoretz points out in *Why Are Jews Liberals?* (2009), President Harry Truman had won Jewish support because of his strong stand against McCarthyism. This had been an excellent move, since "all the surveys showed that the Jews were far more hostile than any other segment of the population to McCarthyism."[65] This despite the fact that, as Romerstein and Breindel point out, "Truman was ironically, in the long run, a more effective foe of Soviet subversion than McCarthy…. [But McCarthyism] was too useful a weapon to waste by substituting 'Trumanism.'"[66]

Similarly with Nixon, writes Podhoretz: "[I]n retrospect we can see that Nixon was closer to the Center-Right than to the Far Right, but that was not how he looked at the time to Jewish eyes. To them he was a McCarthyite *avant la lettre*, having earned that reputation even before Senator Joseph McCarthy himself had appeared on the scene."[67] The Jews were driven to vote for John F. Kennedy in droves in 1960, despite the fact that "Kennedy showed no sign of being a liberal cut from the Rooseveltian cloth or – apart from the usual campaign pandering – of being a great friend of the Jews."[68] The new liberalism was becoming curiouser and curiouser, as image-crafting increasingly replaced reasoned argument and facts. The Jews were voting Democratic as if by default.

But to return to the war era, the nagging question remains: why were American intellectuals in general and Jews in particular so seemingly prone to sympathize with Russian communism for so long? Not even the consummate student of Western leftism Francois Furet fully understands why "the United States presented what was perhaps the most paradoxical form of the Communist illusion." Perhaps the American ideocracy had "placed their hopes in the USSR when it came to defending liberty against Fascism," he speculates, "as though anti-Fascism were inseparable from an inevitable tendency toward Communism." But rather than reflecting geopolitical considerations, it was merely vaguely Marxist. Their pro-Sovietism was ultimately "based on two elements external to the USSR – hostility to Fascism and the critique of capitalism."[69]

The fly in the proverbial ointment was the Stalin-Hitler pact, which opened many a fellow-traveler's eye. By the time Hitler violated the infamous agreement by invading the USSR, which obliged the communist dictator to join the Allies, some Western sympathizers refused to swallow the propaganda machine's shameless about-face. Stalin's master disinformation professionals went to work. Without blinking, the KGB recycled the old meme of fascism/racism vs. progress/equality. Partly to attract Western support, Stalin "adopted the language of his new allies – the language of liberty. He had no intention of applying its principles, however," writes Furet. Ever the shrewd operator, "[h]e had altered his tactics and language but not his methods or ambitions."

Clad once again in the mantle of anti-Fascism, Stalin's victorious totalitarianism benefited enormously from the support of Western democracies in legitimizing his propaganda, for "the military victory allowed the USSR to turn to its own advantage the idea of nationalism, an idea shunted around by the Nazi occupation even among the nations once allied with Germany."[70] The USSR would thereafter engage in what philosophers call systematic ambiguity (in the vernacular, double standard): supporting it for de-colonization purposes to create new satellite regimes in Africa and elsewhere, excoriating it when invoked by Westerners. Hailing it for "Palestine," denouncing it for Israel.

After the end of World War II, as Western empires were disintegrating, Stalin emerged as the war's biggest victor by enlarging his own. He lost no time colonizing the nations of East-Central Europe, including my native Romania, ignoring the Yalta Agreement that promised multiparty regimes in the countries "liberated" by Soviet soldiers. Far more rapidly than anyone had anticipated, the Soviet occupation proved as brutal as its new captives had feared, leaving many people nostalgic for the resurrection of the Austro-Hungarian Empire. The Jews who had a chance to get away did so as soon as they could.

One Jewish Soviet soldier who marched into Romania, speaking to my grandmother in Yiddish, counseled her, at the risk of his life: "Run while you can." He had seen the Future and it was, if you pardon the expression, *genem* (hell). My parents started proceedings to emigrate the moment they were able to do so, once they received official documents, and tried to ask for a visa to go to Israel. That request being stalled for over a decade and a half, they finally mustered the courage to apply for permission to leave for the United States, where my mother's father and three siblings had been living since the mid-1920s. My grandmother had never stopped praying, each Sabbath, that she might one day see her long-gone children again.

The magnitude and bestiality of the massacre of Jews in World War II had yet to be grasped, their tragedy not yet been even given a name. But the nagging question could not be avoided: what had taken so long? What about Roosevelt, "who since 1943 had had some idea of the extent of the tragedy, said and did nothing about it?"[71] Furet denounces the affable progressive: "The American president was both ignorant and naïve about the Soviet Union and its leader."[72] Furet is being far too kind: naïve and ignorant, surely, but also morally challenged to an extent that would not become clear until many years later.

Not that American Jews themselves were exactly blameless.

Chapter VI:

America's Jewish Problem

Post-Marxist Antisemitism

"For us the Jewish Problem means this: How can we secure for Jews, wherever they may live, the same rights and opportunities enjoyed by non-Jews?"

- Louis D. Brandeis, "*The Jewish Problem: How to Solve it*" (1915)

"... in the [Germany of the] 1890s, 'philosemitism' became identical with the apologetic defense of rich Jews and the dishonest whitewashing of capitalistic injustices. ...[I]n 1894 [Eduard] Bernstein pointed out that it had become difficult to differentiate between the use of the term 'philosemitism' by socialists or by [rightist] antisemites... From the young Marx to [Franz] Mehring (and beyond) this anti-Jewish stereotype [as the embodiment of the worst features of capitalist behavior] had continued to haunt the socialist movement like a ghostly specter."

- Robert S. Wistrich, *From Ambivalence to Betrayal: The Left, the Jews, and Israel* (2012)

The same year, 1955, that William F. Buckley deplored the use of "conservative" as a slur against all non-licensed non-conformists, the well-known sociologist Seymour Martin Lipset noted the simultaneous conflation of that political label with antisemitism. The progressive ideocracy having thus managed to add one more accusation to the rapidly proliferating pejorative connotations, the C-word would become tantamount to a mark of Cain, the ideological equivalent of the Nazi yellow star worn by Jews during the German occupation. To this day, conservatives are castigated as *ipso facto* bigots, extreme (a.k.a., radical, bomb-throwing) rightists, alt-rightists, fascists, and of course, racists. (All are vernacular for human vermin.)

American ideocrats emulated their much-admired European mentors. Explains Lipset:

> As a number of European political commentators have suggested, anti-Semitism has often been the extreme rightist functional equivalent for the socialist attack on capitalism. The Jewish banker replaces the exploiting capitalist as the scapegoat. In the United States, the radical right had to find some equivalent method of appealing to the groups which have a sense of being under-privileged, and McCarthy's principal contribution to the crystallization of the radical right in the 1950's has been to hit on the key symbols with which to unite all its potential supporters. McCarthy's crusade is not just against the liberal elements of the country, cast in the guise of "creeping socialists;" he is also campaigning against the same groups mid-west Populism always opposed, the eastern conservative financial aristocracy.[1]

Little wonder that a vast majority of Jews, alongside most of the academic and media elite to which many belong and many more aspire, still cannot bear being labeled right-wing.

Especially once President Harry S. Truman decided to cast a vote supporting Israel in the United Nations, ensuring its membership and thus international recognition for the newly established state, the Jews' love affair with the Democratic Party was all but sealed. In reality, the State Department under the direction of its Secretary, George Marshall, had opposed Israel's admission. It was Truman's fellow soldier and trusted old friend Edward Jacobson, the only Jew who was always welcome into the White House, who convinced the president to meet with Chaim Weizmann, the leading international figure championing Jewish statehood. It was reminiscent of Abraham Lincoln being strongly affected by individual Jews he had come to respect and cherish.

This is how the celebrated historian David McCullough, in his bestselling biography of Truman, describes the scene:

> "Harry, all your life you have had a hero…I too have a hero, a man I never met, but who is, I think, the greatest Jew who ever lived….I am talking about Chaim Weizmann….He traveled thousands of miles just to see you and plead the cause of my people. Now you refuse to see him just because you are insulted by some of our American Jewish leaders, even though you know that Weizmann had absolutely nothing to do with these insults and would be the last man to be party to them. It doesn't sound like you, Harry, because I thought you could take this stuff they

> have been handing out." As Abba Eban later wrote, the comparison between Weizmann and Andrew Jackson was unimaginably far-fetched. And it worked. Truman began drumming his fingers on the desk. He wheeled around in his chair and with his back to Jacobson sat looking out the window into the garden. For what to Jacobson seemed "like centuries," neither of them said anything. Then, swinging about and looking Jacobson in the eye, Truman said what Jacobson later described as the most endearing words he had ever heard: "You win, you baldheaded son-of-a-bitch. I will see him."[2]

Weizmann was then secretly ushered into the White House. On May 14, Truman overruled Secretary Marshall, whom he otherwise revered, and voted in favor of recognizing the Jewish state.

The deck was thus stacked against Republican President Dwight D. Eisenhower – albeit unfairly. For as Australian historian Ian J. Bickerton demonstrates, the traditional view that the president "showed least inclination to befriend the Jewish community," expressed by American University Professor Melvin Urofsky, was simply wrong. So too was the anti-Zionist Jewish activist Alfred Lilienthal's claim that Eisenhower "strove to steer the country on a neutral course in the Middle East away from the Truman blatant bias toward Israel."[3]

"Far from being indifferent to the Jewish community," argues Bickerton, "President Eisenhower maintained contacts and held meetings with American Jewish leaders if anything on a more frequent basis than had been the case during the final years of the Democrats under Truman. There were changes, of course, but they were more in style than substance." Still, once again, impressions (and spin) matter; "it was indicative of the persuasiveness of American Zionists that so many Americans believed that a 'special relationship' had been created between the U.S. and Israel during the Truman administration."

The GOP had become all but *treif* (Yiddish for unkosher, "anathema") after the war. *Thou shalt not be a conservative (Republican)* became an unwritten commandment - and not only for secular Jews, but for those who considered themselves conservative and traditionalist. Binyamin Rose, editor of the Orthodox magazine *Mishpacha*, for example, remembers growing up in a very pro-Democrat atmosphere during the Sixties: "If an Orthodox Jew were to vote Republican in those days, they would have been considered on par with having converted to Christianity."[4]

Things are slowly beginning to change, albeit mainly among the most religiously devout. At the end of 2019, a survey of more than 700 Orthodox Jews across 15 states conducted by *Ami Magazine* found overwhelming support for Republicans not only when asked which president has "accomplished the most for the security of Israel" – to which over 80 percent responded it was President Donald Trump, followed by former presidents Ronald Reagan and George W. Bush. Even on the all-important question of fighting antisemitism, over 92 percent said Orthodox Jews trust Republicans over Democrats.[5]

While similar to anti-Judaism and Jew-hatred, which some fine scholars have carefully defined,[6] antisemitism tends to obscure the inconvenient fact that Semitism as an ism doesn't actually exist. What does is semitic *languages*, notably Hebrew and Arabic, so people who speak them may be called semites.[7] But while Arabs and Jews share many things, such as the lovely greeting "peace be upon you" (*Salaam alaikum* and *shalom aleichem*, respectively), not to mention foods like hummus, falafel, and tabouleh, their differences are too many to mention. The defect, however, is far from accidental. By omitting specific reference to Jews, who are the obvious target, leaving it merely implicit, the neologism seeks to deemphasize the personal content of the attack. It isn't Jews as such but their mindset, or ideology if you will, the ism, which is being rejected: a monolithic, racial-ethnic-(im)moral, dangerous and inescapable stigma.

Though routinely assumed to be the province of rightwing bigots, the term *Antisemitismus* according to the premier scholar of antisemitism, Robert S. Wistrich,[8] "had its origins on the German Left."[9] The atheist journalist William Marr (1819-1904) is often credited with coining it, but he mainly popularized the term,[10] by giving the name "The Antisemites League" to a group proudly dedicated to that purpose. His aim was to differentiate Jew-hatred based on racist political ideology from the ordinary kind.

Basically, Marr was a lunatic. In his 1879 rant *Victory of Jewry over Germandom*, for example, he denounced the Jews' "eighteen-hundred-year war" as a racial conspiracy. The myth that he perpetrated by insisting that it was the Jews, not their enemies, who had been the real racists, would be neither the last nor the most preposterous of its kind.

Marr's later notoriety notwithstanding, he was only one of many leftists who embraced the word with alacrity. In 1874, the German publicist Otto Glagau, among the most prominent and effective according to Wistrich, "specifically identified the 'Jewish Question' with the 'social question.'" The Jews had the money, which they used to exploit the have-nots. Q.E.D. In Glagau's "pamphleteering works about the stock-exchange swindles of the era… the identification of Jewish merchants and bankers with *Homo capitalistus* is palpable."[11]

But no one succeeded like Karl Marx in linking Jews and Judaism to bourgeois capitalism as all but synonymous, a demonstrable redundancy. In his essay "On the Jewish Question," Marx blamed the Jews' supposed "cult of money" as the principal obstacle to achieving the collective redemption promised by communism. The abolition of capitalism amounted to the elimination of Judaism, if not Jews themselves. The two are intimately interrelated, argues Catholic University Professor Jerry Z. Muller: "On the Jewish Question" is at the root of Marx's entire philosophy, for it "contains, in embryo, most of the subsequent themes of Marx's critique of capitalism… If Marx had one big idea, it was that capitalism was the rule of money – itself the expression of greed."[12] And greed was the essence of Judaism: it was the ideology of the Jews. But since greed had to disappear, to be eliminated, draw your own conclusions.

Chaos is bound to accompany the last stages of capitalism, as "disasters occurring regularly will be repeated on a vaster scale, eventually lead[ing] to the violent fall of capital." Having declared contemptuously that "the bill of exchange is the real god of the Jew," Marx concludes that "as soon as society succeeds in abolishing the empirical essence of Judaism—huckstering and its conditions—the Jew becomes impossible." Observes Muller: "That would be the theme, with variations, of subsequent anti-Jewish authors from Richard Wagner down to the Nazi ideologist Gottfried Feder."[13]

How someone can "become impossible" is left unexplained, though abolishing an "empirical" essence is only marginally more comforting than "liquidating." It may offer a clue as to why Hitler, in *Mein Kampf*, credited Marx with revealing to him the solution to the world's ills.[14] Abolishing the "empirical essence" of six million Jews could be a good start.

To be sure, the conflation of Judaism with usury had long preceded Marx. Martin Luther (1483-1546) retreaded ancient Jew-hatred with peculiar venom. Two centuries later, the poison infected the otherwise enlightened Voltaire. The witty Anglophile *philosophe* had contemptuously accused the Hebrews, that "ignorant and barbarous people," of having "long united the most sordid avarice with the most detestable superstition." The accusation was especially ironic given his notorious stinginess.

But he could not hold a candle to his German contemporary philosopher of sometime Jacobin persuasion, Johann Gottlieb Fichte. In 1793, Fichte picked up the conspiratorial torch from Wilhelm Marr and then upped the ante. He accused the Jews of constituting "a powerful state . . . continually at war with all the others, and that in certain places terribly oppresses the citizens."[15] If the Big Lie had yet to become a tool of statecraft for the Politburo, few claims can rival this one for sheer absurdity.

By the 19th century, the image of Jews as a *Volk* (nation) afflicted with terminal egoism and obsessed with commerce and business had become commonplace. The radical journalist Ludwig Börne's assault on the semitic "money-devil" had fed the rising tide of "progressive" Jew-hatred in Germany as early as 1808. It became increasingly prominent in Socialist writings after 1840 linking Jews "with the all-devouring Moloch of Mammon," according to Wistrich. The first German socialist, Moses Hess, writing in 1843, went so far as to identify "the Jewish Jehovah-Moloch" and the Christian God with human sacrifice, capitalistic cannibalism, and social parasitism.[16] Sadly, inexplicably, Börne and Hess were both Jewish.

But Karl Marx surpassed them all, building his whole ideology on antisemitism. "Marx's form of antisemitism," wrote British historian Paul Johnson, "was a dress rehearsal for Marxism itself."[17] The virulence of Marx's ire is astonishing. How anyone as familiar with Judaism as Marx, whose grandfathers had both been rabbis,[18] could write these words, he needs to explain to them:

> What, in itself, was the basis of the Jewish religion? Practical need, egoism. Money is the jealous god of Israel, in face of which no other god may exist. Money degrades all the gods of man – and turns them into commodities. Money is the universal self-established value of all things. It has, therefore, robbed the whole world – both the world of men and

> nature – of its specific value. Money is the estranged essence of man's work and man's existence, and this alien essence dominates him, and he worships it. The god of the Jews has become secularized and has become the god of the world. The bill of exchange is the real god of the Jew. His god is only an illusory bill of exchange.

Marx then delivers the final coup:

> Once society has succeeded in abolishing the empirical essence of Judaism – huckstering and its preconditions – the Jew will have become impossible, because his consciousness no longer has an object, because the subjective basis of Judaism, practical need, has been humanized, and because the conflict between man's individual-sensuous existence and his species-existence has been abolished. The social emancipation of the Jew is the emancipation of society from Judaism.[19]

Johnson, who refers to this as "almost a classic anti-Semitic tract," argues that it "contains, in embryonic form, the essence of his theory of human regeneration: by abolishing private property society would transform human relationships and thus the human personality." In his later writings, Marx "retained the fundamental fallacy that the making of money through trade and finance is essentially a parasitical activity, but he now placed it, not on a basis of race or religion, but of class." The distinction seems to be one without a difference. He set out to change human nature, which meant abolishing egoism and spirituality. His was a crusade to create *homo post-religiosus*, at once selfless and soulless.

Wistrich similarly denounces Marx's notion that the God of the Jew is money as an "ugly and baseless libel," a severe case of Jewish self-loathing. Not even the anti-Semitic sociologist Werner Sombart, who a century later sought to hold Jews responsible "for the entire development of modern financial capitalism—especially its less appealing features,"[20] went as far as to demonize an entire people. He recognized the admirable tradition of learning, discipline, sobriety, and varied talents of the Jews. Marx never did; his apocalyptic vision amounted to intellectual murder-suicide.

The poison spread fast. By the 1880s, even the more moderate German Social Democratic Party (SPD) had become thoroughly imbued with antisemitism. Most SPD members of all faiths believed that the Jews deserved the contempt of the German masses as payback for the "murderous role" their usury had played under feudalism, when they allegedly mercilessly abused the peasants. Ironically, the SPD were more worried about philosemites, whose sympathy for Jews protected the ruling class and hence undermined the ideology of anticapitalism, than about antisemites.

They argued that philosemitism was the last ideological disguise of exploiting capitalism. So long as antisemitism could serve a politically unifying role to precipitate an anti-bourgeois uprising, so went the reasoning, the ugly prejudice could serve as a welcome catalyst to the great Marxist upheaval. In the long run, therefore, being despised could actually be beneficial to Jews who were eager to be liberated alongside all humanity. As if swallowing poison would heal – assuming it doesn't kill. It appears these patients were prepared for the mad gamble. The upshot was that many socialist Jews abstained from criticizing antisemites and attacked their own friends instead. It was hard to tell where wishful thinking ended, and masochism began.

Not to be outdone, France had its own, anticapitalist antisemites, their zealotry rivaling that of their German counterparts. The same Charles Fourier who had inspired the New England Transcendentalists similarly identified capitalism with the new Jewish elite. So too did his follower Alphonse Toussenel (1803-1885), who penned what "can be considered the first proposal of a socialized economy based on the expropriation of wealth and the redistribution of the capital of Jewish families."[21]

This led the infamous journalist Edouard Drumont (1844-1917), Founder of the Antisemitic League of France in 1889, to consider Toussenel his "inspired precursor." Drumond was joined by the socialist writer Auguste Chirac (1838-1910), who argued that all capitalists can be considered Jews *without actually being Jewish,* because usury, thievery, social parasitism, and capitalist exploitation are all Jewish practices. Explains University of Pisa Professor Michele Battini in *The Socialism of Fools*:

> All capitalists can therefore be legitimately defined as "*juifs*" [Jews] and treated accordingly: discriminated against, persecuted. The process of generalization and abstraction transforms the *juifs*, as real men, into a symbol of exploitation: *le juif*, and usury at the same time, becomes the figure of speech of all the types of exploitation.[22]

As for the next step? If America, having achieved the highest stage of capitalism, embodied it at its purest, didn't it follow that communists had to be anti-American? Yet this went counter to everything that Jewish Americans had believed since the nation's founding. America had been good to them; should they return the favor by being ungrateful?

The Jews' Assimilation Dilemma

"Freedom, the same quality that made America so alluring for persecuted faiths, also brought with it the freedom to make religious choices... American Jews, as a result, have never been able to assume that their future as Jews is guaranteed."

- Jonathan D. Sarna, *American Judaism* (2004)

"We consider ourselves no longer a nation, but a religious community.... We recognize in Judaism a progressive religion, ever striving to be in accord with the postulates of reason."

- "The Pittsburgh Platform" (1885)

My family and I had been immediately embraced by our new countrymen upon arrival, oblivious to our nonexistent English (except for my polyglot father, who managed to speak English fluently despite having learned it merely on his own). They looked past our awkwardness, happy to help. No one quite knew where Romania was, or why we had emigrated, but they weren't especially interested. I wasn't sure whether to find that comforting or alarming, but it was decidedly an improvement over the hostility of Parisians who treated immigrants like us, even temporarily sojourning in their precious city, like intruders.

In America therefore we became instant patriots. It took a while to realize that the sentiment was not as common among our compatriots as we had imagined - not even among our co-religionists, who could always find a reason to complain.

Jews have traditionally felt quite safe in their new country, their political affiliations not markedly different from those of their gentile neighbors, no more monolithic than other groups or "nationalities." Probably less so, given the occasionally exasperating, if often endearing, peculiarity of our notoriously argumentative lot. Jews have tended to divide along religious and ethnic lines: Sephardim felt superior to German Jews, who in turn looked down on Ashkenazim from Eastern Europe and

Russia, who naturally subdivided in myriad additional ways, all but inscrutable to the uninitiated. Yet a penchant for internal squabbles did not substantially weaken the ancient tribal bond, especially since external enemies could easily take advantage of such divisions. This encouraged washing our *mishpocha* (family) laundry behind closed doors.

Their members' individual petulance checked by prudence, the American Jewish community as a group have traditionally, wisely, sidestepped unwelcome attention, largely avoiding divisive politics. While respecting private beliefs, their leaders stayed away from taking public stances on contentious matters. Even the Pittsburgh Platform of 1885, which outlined the major principles of Reform – the largest and most secular of the three Judaic sects that also included Conservative and Orthodox - basically ignored political and social issues except in rather general terms.

During most of that time, Jews spanned the political spectrum, though ideologically the majority could have been described as more or less classically liberal. The prominent political analyst Michael Barone (a friend and fellow Detroiter) found that some Jews had become Republicans "out of support for the Union cause and its opposition to slavery," while others preferred the Democratic Party, which "in the nineteenth century was a laissez faire party, for free trade and free markets, for tolerating local policies."[23] This included saloons in the North, although in the South, it meant segregation. Ultimately, most Jews were keen not to become "a Jewish voting bloc" in either party, not to attract undue attention, and accommodate to their surroundings. Changing one's name, as much to enhance ease of spelling and pronunciation as to blend in, was not uncommon.

Most of the Russian, Romanian, and other Eastern European immigrants who descended in droves upon the New World at the turn of the century proved decidedly less chameleonic. Their ideology was as forthright as their personal style, their sheer numbers further emboldening the most recalcitrant among them to abandon appeasement when faced with severe economic struggles. To these hardened survivors of poverty and persecution, trade union activism and socialism had already become second nature.

In any event, it was no longer possible for these Jews to keep a low profile even if they tried, which most did not. Having grown up in Orthodox households, many of the largely Yiddish-speaking, feisty newcomers, especially the young, had become disillusioned with what they took as the self-defeating meekness of their parents and grandparents in the Old Country. Old-fashioned piety and strict observance of Jewish law seemed to them exactly the wrong way to defeat the contempt and violence to which the Jews had been subjected for centuries. Many turned to social action as a substitute for religion.

A similar process was simultaneously taking place in Western and Central Europe, albeit for somewhat different reasons. There, what prompted Jews to appropriate more of what they believed was the superior culture of their gentile host nations was the Enlightenment's glorification of reason, science, and progress. Embracing what they took to be socialism, many who had already chosen cultural assimilation – known among German-speaking Jews as *Bildung* – looked askance at orthodox Judaism as mostly an anachronistic superstition. Hebrew University Professor Steven E. Aschheim, in his erudite book *At the Edges of Liberalism,* explains that *Bildung* was

> the Jewish internalization of middle-class respectability and morals.... Jewish reformers stressed manners, politeness, decorum, refinement, self-control, and low decibel levels – and contrasted these modes of civility with the purported crudity, boorishness, loudness, and unrestrained nature of traditional communal Jewish life.[24]

Their differences notwithstanding, both Eastern and Western Jews saw in America a new dawn of equality that could finally, they hoped, elevate them to the same level as everyone else. Their sympathy for the downtrodden, the have-nots, call it the proletariat, was understandable. Hence the Marxist arguments against selfish "capitalist" individualism could resonate equally with the tortured souls of Russia and the assimilated Jews of Vienna, Berlin, London, or New York's Lower East Side.

European patriotic universalism, Aschheim believed, enabled "vulnerable minorities in a post-emancipation world" to conceptualize challenges. For this reason, Jewish leaders like France's three-time prime minister Leon Blum (1872-1950) declared in 1899 that Judaism above all was focused in "this world... which must one day be ordered in accordance with Reason, and make one rule prevail over all men and give to each his due. Is this not just the spirit of Socialism?"[25] Paradoxically, the rosy prospect promised by that slippery, treacherous ism was bound to sabotage the very classical liberalism that was actually, not just nominally, predicated on that spirit.

It took a few more decades before Western and Central European Jews would finally concede that socialism would place them literally in its crosshairs. Not all were able to escape in time to the United States - nor, of those who did, were all uniformly appreciative. Nonetheless, most thrived and contributed immensely to their new host country and to the world at large. In America, Jews could expect not to be ill-treated, despite occasional outbursts of antisemitism. Even so, Jews had experienced too many reversals during their centuries-old exile ever to rest easy. Would the gentile majority in the New World continue to welcome them, even into the unforeseeable future?

A rift predictably began to take place after the mid-1800s between Jews who had arrived earlier, most of German descent, and Eastern European Jews, primarily from Russia and Poland, who were nearly all Yiddish speakers. The former, more secular than religious, were eager to assimilate, while the latter generally came from an Orthodox cultural tradition. The youngest among them tended toward a radical form of socialism, even advocating what some – alarmingly - called a "revolution." The finely-honed policies of the predominantly Reform "liberal" American Jews were being threatened by rabble-rousers in unprecedented ways, requiring adjustment.

The newcomers gradually prevailed, less because of their superior numbers than by pushing along the leftward conflagration sweeping the country, stoked by the ideocracy. By the late 1800s, even the Reform Jews had already been "influenced by social progressivism," observes Brandeis University Professor Jonathan D. Sarna. Rabbis were increasingly railing against child labor and supported striking workers, who were in turn organized by Socialist Jews. And "[c]alls to apply modern standards of 'justice, equality, and fraternity' also rang out internally within Reform temples."[26] Equality became a rallying cry for Jews in the Diaspora who sought to be considered bona fide citizens despite their minority status. Equity was but a short conceptual step away.

Having started as a pious evolutionary egalitarianism of a Protestant variety, the commingling of justice and economic equality was also appropriated by many Catholics and others willing to worship at the altars of the new secular political religion, socialism. Lasting through the Great War, the hybrid concept at last congealed in what would become formally known as the Social Gospel movement, providing a spiritual foundation to progressivist liberalism. It turned Dewey's philosophical underpinnings to the rhetoric of Wilson and FDR into electoral dynamite.

The major spokesman for that movement was theologian Walter Rauschenbusch (1861-1918), who advocated "socializing property" to advance social goals. Convinced that true Christianity eschewed attachment to property, he explained why social action was not only a political but a religious imperative:

> By "socializing property," we mean, then, that it is made to serve the public good, either by the service its uses render to the public welfare or by the income it brings to the public treasury. … [As a result,] instead of serving the welfare of a small group directly, and the public welfare only indirectly, it will be made more directly available for the service of all.[27]

To carry out this task, far from opposing government action, he applauded it. After all, "[t]he whole institution of private property exists because it is for the public good that it shall exist."[28] He called for the public ownership of essential industries, and the "cooperative ownership of other businesses." Explains Hillsdale College Professor Ronald J. Pestritto in *America Transformed: The Rise and Legacy of American Progressivism*: "For these revolutionary economic policies, Rauschenbusch laid the foundation in a social Christianity which necessitated throwing off traditional theology and concentrating on the achievement of God's kingdom here on earth."[29]

Economist Richard T. Ely (1854-1954), another major figure of the Social Gospel movement, meanwhile, urged the church to exceed its spiritual function and take up the abolition of poverty as a central element of its earthly mission to establish a general system of social welfare. In blending religion and sociology, piety and activism, Ely sought to create an effective instrument for political change. The new movement "at its core was quite radical," writes Pestritto, for "it crossed the line into matters of economic justice." It "turned part of the Protestant church against capitalism"[30] no less deliberately and effectively than its secular counterparts, if not more.

Pestritto notes that the movement was at bottom utopian-millenarian: "Social Gospel posited evolution as a divine plan for rational social advancement and suggested that it had become possible, through an empowered central state, to realize the Christian hope that 'thy will be done on earth as it is in heaven.'"[31] While repudiating Spencerian "survival of the fittest" determinism, it opposed the "religious individualism" of mainstream Christianity, thus echoing progressive criticism of the Constitution. A new collectivism had apparently replaced classical liberalism.

And where were the Jews on all of this? In brief, mostly sympathetic. Romanian-born Rabbi Solomon Schechter (1847-1915), president of the Jewish Theological Seminary, for example, reflected the views of most of his Reform colleagues when he expressly professed agreement with the aspirations of the Social Gospel movement. For "man to work towards establishing the visible Kingdom of God in the present world," argued Schechter, was "the highest goal religion can strive to reach." Castigating "bad government" as vehemently as did his Christian brethren, equally concerned by a "state of social misery engendered through poverty and want," he offered similarly political solutions: "All-wise legislation in this respect must help towards its speedy advent."[32]

And yet, could a movement so deeply rooted in Christianity be good for the Jews? Did it not portend ill? In the early twentieth century, the jury was still out. On the one hand, "[l]iberal American Jews, it would appear at first glance, could hardly have felt themselves estranged during the era of social gospel,"[33] observes University of Wisconsin Professor Egal Feldman. They were certainly encouraged by the attendant revival of interest in Judaism that accompanied the new religiosity. The most enthusiastic Judeophile among the Social Gospel leaders was the influential editor of a popular magazine, Lyman Abbott, who offered this assessment of America's debt to the Hebrew tradition: "Every legislative hall, every courthouse… to say nothing of less visible and tangible manifestations of our national life and temper are monuments of our indebtedness to this ancient people,"[34] he wrote in 1905.

Yet even Abbott expressed serious reservations about the actual Jews of his own time, whom he considered overly absorbed in commerce, oblivious to the teachings of the prophets.[35] Similarly, Rauschenbush, describing Judaism as "fixed, monotonous, shut off from the spontaneity and naturalness of the general life," attributed lingering anti-social elements in Christianity to Jewish influence. Concludes Feldman:

> If social reform and human betterment were earnest objectives of the social gospel, there is little evidence that the elimination of bigotry and prejudice against the Jew was a significant part of their goal. … In examining the pious utterances of that age, one might even conclude that they succeeded in rekindling ancient animosities and supplied a new rationale for an old aberration – anti-Semitism.

It was still the greatest country. Ultimately, most Jews thought of America as home, their personal ideological views aside. "All major movements and ideologies within American Judaism," wrote Sarna, "insisted that Americanism and Judaism reinforced each other, and annually, on days like Thanksgiving, this message was reinforced."[36] On the centennial of George Washington's inauguration, in 1889, Chief Rabbi Jacob Joseph gratefully acknowledged the first president's respect for "our holy Torah." Declaring all Jews to be eager "to become like other citizens of the country," the Rabbi spoke for the entire community. Adds Sarna: "[T]hey could be both American and Jewish, their dual identities complementing and mutually enhancing each other."[37]

The newly arrived Jews had responded to the challenges they encountered in their new Golden Land (*goldene medina*) with the political and religious language they knew, and the tenacity that had traditionally insured the tribe's survival. But even the hardcore leftists among them meant no harm. No loudmouthed radicals had come to overthrow anything, only to build a new life. Marxism-shmarxism, they all wanted to thrive. Though a large portion did describe themselves as socialists, Jews disagreed among themselves as did everyone else about the meaning of this notoriously slippery concept.

In truth, it was the sorry plight of the newcomers, far more than their shtetl-leftist arguments, that eventually led the remaining Jewish community to opt in favor of government relief for struggling immigrants. This had deep roots in the age-old biblical tradition of compassion for one's fellow human being. Addressing the Conference of Eastern Council of Reform rabbis on April 25, 1915, Louis D. Brandeis (1856-1941) recognized as much, noting that the Jewish "teaching of brotherhood and righteousness has, under the name of democracy and social justice, become the twentieth century striving of America and of western Europe."[38]

He was echoing the 1885 Pittsburgh Protocol, which had declared "Judaism a progressive religion, ever striving to be in accord with the postulates of reason." The same Protocol had stated that the Jewish community saw its "duty to participate in the great task of modern times, to solve, on the basis of justice and righteousness, the problems presented by the contrasts and evils of the present organization of society."[39] But overconfidence had been premature. Antisemitism had crossed the Atlantic after all.

The Jewish Problem would not spare even America, the original-but-no-longer-classically-liberal and no-longer-quite-so-New World. Though Brandeis conceded that "manifestations of the Jewish Problem vary in the different countries, and at different periods in the same country," he worried that "the differences, however wide, are merely in degree and not in kind. The Jewish Problem is single and universal."[40] In the United States, even the occasional exceptions seemed to be on the wane. As recently as "half a century ago the belief was still general that Jewish disabilities would disappear before growing liberalism," reflected Brandeis. Equality before the law seemed sufficient to guarantee it. But the hope had proved unwarranted.

Why? asks Brandeis. "[B]ecause the liberal movement has not yet brought full liberty." The solution, he argued, was not to abandon liberalism but to change it. Individualism no longer seemed sufficient, he reasoned. Instead, Brandeis advocated securing group rights: "Jews collectively should likewise enjoy the same right and opportunity to live and develop as do other groups of people." There was but a minor obstacle: deciding what makes someone a Jew.

During the heyday of eugenics, which celebrated hematic purity, Brandeis opted for showcasing the obvious purity of "Jewish blood." While "Jews are not an absolutely pure race," he conceded, "the percentage of foreign blood in the Jews of today is very low. Probably no important European race is as pure," he somewhat sheepishly reminded his fellow non-black Americans. But Jews were pretty close, and that, he figured, had to count for a great deal.

He wasn't just wrong, but dead wrong. The future Justice had failed to realize that race "purity" was nothing to brag about. In fact, it would soon boomerang against the Jews with a vengeance. Of course, there was nothing racist in his own argument, for he went on to underscore the cultural tradition of the community. He defended the common core of Jewish identity in terms of nationality: "Can it be doubted that we Jews... are 'conscious of a community of sentiments, experiences and qualities which make us feel ourselves a distinct people,' whether we admit it or not?" Every cultural tradition deserved to be respected, argued Brandeis, sure to be met with uniform approval. That was not what purity meant to the bigots.

But by 1915, he had already thrown in his lot with the progressives. A firm believer in regulating large corporations, in the 1912 presidential race he switched his support from Teddy Roosevelt, who considered trusts inevitable, to Woodrow Wilson - on the strength of the latter's vow to "destroy the trusts." During Wilson's first year as president, Brandeis was instrumental in shaping the new Federal Reserve Act. He also served as Wilson's chief economic advisor until 1916, when the president nominated him to the U.S. Supreme Court.

But Brandeis's progressive inclinations had already become so controversial that upon his nomination to the Court, the Senate Judiciary Committee, for the first time in its history, held a public hearing prior to his confirmation. Previously, a president's nominees had been accepted outright. Brandeis's opponents had objected to what they saw as his radicalism. Justice William O. Douglas, for example, explained that he "frightened the Establishment" because he was "a militant crusader for social justice."[41] The objections, however, were purely philosophical rather than racial or antisemitic, and no one resorted to *ad hominems*.

Anti-immigrant storm clouds, however, were gathering fast, to the point that even some Jews supported more selective criteria for admittance into the U.S. - not fully realizing, one must assume, the tragic implications for their own co-religionists. For as early as 1917, when Congress mandated a literacy test for new immigrants, Eastern European Jews were, inevitably, severely affected. Soon entrance quotas reduced Jewish immigration to the U.S. by as much as eighty percent. A new ideological wave, moreover, would sweep over the leftward-oriented American Jewish community, as the Russian Revolution gave new hope to socialist Jews for whom the Soviet experiment seemed to fulfill a promise for the equality and justice they had long dreamed about.

It was a time of enormous upheaval. Political allegiances were shifting, along with party labels and affiliations. Though socialism appealed to a large portion of the newly arrived Jewish immigrants, those already here leaned Republican. This led both main political parties, whose membership was yet uncertain, to court this tiny yet vocal minority of Hebrews more vigorously. Michael Barone estimates that "the tipping point, when Jews moved away from the Socialists and Republicans and toward the Democrats, probably came in 1922."[42]

The pivotal moment was marked by the election of the Democrat Al Smith as governor of New York, who advocated factory and welfare legislation. After losing in 1920, he was reelected three more times with a sizeable number of Jewish votes. It was the same percentage of Jewish Democrats who contributed to Franklin Roosevelt's narrow win in 1928. But ironically, FDR's Republican opponent this time happened to be Jewish. The victory of a Democratic WASP - whose Judeophilia had been more illusory than real - over a Republican Jew was not a little portentous.

The Jewish vote continued to waver between the two major parties that were themselves ideologically elastic, but the general direction was unmistakable. Writes Barone: "Jews in overwhelming numbers embraced a common view on issues that can be summed up in the word liberal – for civil liberties and civil rights, against immigration restriction and for protection of the Jewish people abroad, for labor unions and government efforts to protect workers, for public housing and public works projects."[43]

Eventually, the last would overwhelm all the rest, government emerging as the panacea of first resort. "Liberal" had been decidedly redefined.

Yet ideology was merely a reflection of the continuing allure of the American Dream, which every immigrant sought for his family and himself or herself.[44] The economic disaster that was the Great Depression prompted many who had been apolitical to question the viability of capitalism. Perhaps the Invisible Hand needed some guidance from a vanguard whose much-vaunted pure motives could be trusted to pursue the interests of the little guy. Confidence in America's promise and founding principles had been seriously undermined, leading previously pro-American Jews to become more skeptical of those principles.

This is especially true of the Jewish intelligentsia who joined their gentile colleagues in embracing nouveau-liberalism. True, some changed their minds once they realized that progressive policies were unwittingly contributing to the demise of what they had set out to solve in the first place - namely inequality. Unfortunately, many others did not.

Socialists, Progressives, Liberals?

"*[T]he traditional content of [Judaism] has been quite reduced. It has been replaced, on the one hand, by the common content of a universal ethics, which has nothing distinctively Jewish about it, and, on the other, by survival – remember the Holocaust and save Israel.*"
- Nathan Glazer, *American Judaism* (1989)

In his penetrating analysis of American Judaism, Nathan Glazer focuses on the influence of its mainstream denomination, Reform, which he describes as "the religion of the economically comfortable Jews who wanted to be accepted by the non-Jewish world."[45] The increasing social exclusion of Jews after the 1880s had come as a complete surprise to many. Had they not tried hard enough to fit in? Something had to be done. Major revisions in the ritual had already been made, pre-emptively, even though "no one in America would have charged the Jews with being a nation apart," writes Glazer. The changes in the Union Prayer Book had been prompted by rabbinical ideology. "One cannot underestimate the sheer force of the rationalist and progressive position adopted by the rabbis, a position all of whose implications they worked out and tried to realize."[46] Eventually, however, some of those implications, as "it turned out, contradicted the original intention of Reform, that is, to make Judaism a dignified middle-class religion."[47]

Among them was the demand that the Jews, who in in America were primarily well-to-do middle-class merchants, should be in the forefront of the fight for social justice. Small wonder that by the turn of the century, when Reform rabbis attending annual meetings of a Liberal Congress of Religion would meet with Unitarian and Congregational ministers as well as liberal laymen, they found they "had far more in common with their liberal Protestant colleagues than they had with traditional Judaism." Some were forced by the logic of the Reform position to abandon it altogether, "and become apostles of a religion of progress."[48]

They included major figures like the German-born Rabbi Charles Fleisher, who in 1911 left his congregation of Temple Israel to found a community church. He was following in the footsteps of his predecessor, Rabbi Solomon Schindler. Also German-born, having similarly "become a leader among Boston's non-Jewish, reformers, [he then] left the pulpit to become a propagandist for the national socialism of Edward Bellamy."[49] Schindler agreed, notes Glazer, that Americans needed to be educated before they would be ready for radical change: "A great many things will have to be unlearned, and a great many lessons will have to be patiently drilled into the minds of the people before they will be ripe to take matters into their own hands and go even to the extent of nationalizing railroads, telegraph, etc." He advocated education, organization, and agitation, methods of the British Fabians, rather than political action.

That German Jews were flabbergasted by the ideological fervor of their Eastern co-religionists is no surprise. Their words, like their breath, smelled of garlic and the shtetl. Clearly, chutzpa radicalism needed a serious makeover. But their sheer number and energy were powerful. They could not fail to move the already largely progressive community further leftward still. As Glazer points out, "socialism, anarchism, Zionism, and other radical secular political movements flourished among East European Jews, particularly among those who moved to the cities from the small towns."[50] Yiddish-speaking Jews were hard-core. They had survived against terrible odds and had no time for hair-splitting. They weren't going to be pushovers to some timid German Jews, who were in any event already leaning their way. It was not so hard to nudge them a little further.

When the tsarist regime fell in 1917, Jews who populated New York's Lower East Side had cheered. A sizeable portion of Eastern European Jews (*Ostjuden*) had been Soviet-sympathizing fellow travelers, certainly prior to Stalin's notorious purges of his personal enemies in the late 1930s. Many had believed that Soviet communism was on the right side of history, which meant that its path should be followed by everyone, all humanity. They did not feel themselves to be traitors to the United States by supporting communism or socialism (not everyone made fine distinctions).

Nor did debating among themselves imply tribal disloyalty. The factionalism that inevitably accompanies the passion for debate and disagreement had earned their people alternately praise and opprobrium over millennia and could be safely practiced inside the "family." As economic hardship magnified the need of the (relatively) like-minded to stick together, Jews became increasingly leftwing. After all, advocating for free enterprise and self-reliance could be seen as heartless. How would they survive without compassion in a world where God seemed to be MIA?

Thus was socialism gaining ground, under the fig leaf of liberalism. Not that Jews repudiated their identity - they simply reimagined it. In his historic memoir, *Radical Son: A Generational Odyssey* (1997), for example, David Horowitz describes the atmosphere in New York's borough of Queens where he grew up, during the 1950s. His radical parents, who were atheists, finally joined a newly established *shul* (synagogue), like many of their neighbors not so much for religious as for political and social reasons. Their *shul,* recalls Horowitz, "was designed to teach us our Jewish heritage from a radical perspective, without religion. Even the Yiddish we were taught at *shul* was a way of dividing our tribe of radicals from nonprogressive Jews" – which was everyone to their right. Did it make sense? To them, apparently, it did.

While they never really discussed their decision to become Communists, or the factors that motivated them, he speculates:

> What my parents had done in joining the CPUSA and moving to Sunnyside [another part of Queens] was to return to the ghetto. … [T]here was the same conviction of being marked for persecution and

> specially ordained… the same fear of expulsion for heretical thoughts, which was the fear that riveted the chosen to the faith. … [For d]espite our disdain for religious belief, the creed we lived by was not dissimilar from that of our ancestors, the "People of the Book" who were forever analyzing the meanings hidden behind the text of life. We had our own guide to these meanings which was not the Torah and the Talmud, but Lenin and Marx.[51]

When asked why she had joined the party, his mother "confined herself to generalities like 'injustice,' and 'the Depression,' as though anyone who was concerned about either would naturally have joined." Neither she nor his father, nor any of his parents' other friends who were all Party members, ever used the word "communist" to describe themselves or their political agenda. Rather, "in identifying themselves to the political *goyim* [gentiles] they used the term 'progressive.'"[52] They justified it by citing fear of punishment for holding such beliefs, especially after the establishment of the ominously named the House Un-American Activities Committee in 1938, ominously reminiscent of the dreaded Inquisition.

"And yet, what else could they have expected? Even before they had really sunk roots in American soil, they had rejected its fruits. If the faith they had embraced was not 'un-American,' as the committee claimed, it was certainly alien to most Americans." Could they have entertained the possibility that they might have lived less ideologically-driven lives, accepting their good fortune to have landed in the freest country on the planet? The simple answer is, no. "[T]o the end of their days, they remained incapable of real self-reflection about the radical commitments that had defined their lives. In this they were typical among the inhabitants of the progressive ghetto, who believed in their truth with a ferociousness that left no room for dissent."[53]

The vast majority of Jews did not wish this country ill. The few who did in fact spy for the USSR, such as Julius and Ethel Rosenberg, were unrepresentative. Although American Jews had played an important role in the CPUSA, constituting as many as half of its members and a quarter of its leadership, they were still a minuscule percentage of all the Jews in America. Moreover, many of them had joined in the mistaken impression that the CPUSA was anti-Nazi.

A much greater danger came from the naïve among them who believed the liberal-sounding Soviet propaganda. According to Romerstein and Breindel, even Albert Einstein "was a frequent victim of Communist manipulation."[54] (Thereby proving that my father was right, as always: brains don't guarantee wisdom.) Ultimately, the Soviets' suspicion that American Jews were not reliable partners proved correct: "among the many Americans who were arrested or identified as mercenary agents of the KGB during the 1980s and early 1990s, virtually none were Jews."[55]

This is unsurprising. No one who knew anything about those immigrants would believe for a moment that they actually sought a revolution in the New World. They had basically become tired of being confined to their overcrowded, unsanitary, stultifying shtetls alongside other miserable fellow Jews squeezed in together as if they were cattle. They wanted to be able to support their families, to no longer have their teenaged sons conscripted to die in the tsar's army - in a word, to be treated as human beings. So, whoever could leave that wretched life, did. They wanted normalcy, not utopia.

The *Ostjuden* had arrived here with enthusiasm and hope. A verse popular in the *shtetls* after the 1871 pogrom went as follows: "As the Russians, mercilessly/ Took revenge on us/There is a land, America/ Where everyone lives free."[56] The Jews had made huge sacrifices to leave family and friends behind, sell everything they could and save every penny to pay the expensive fares, eager to try their luck in the New World, and as soon as they could afford it, bring their relatives along.

There was nothing especially radical about these aspirations. True, the former ghetto inhabitants, having despaired that no change would arrive in the tsar's feudal realm without drastic overhaul, had no place to turn but to socialism and Marxism. Once they reached America, however, the newly arrived greenhorns, expecting no handouts, set out to support themselves. They worked inhuman hours, attended night school to learn English, sacrificed.[57] Singularly uninterested in philosophical discourse, they mostly tried to adapt to their new surroundings, overwhelmed by the challenges but used to hard work and unafraid of pain. American novelists Anzia Yezierska's *Bread Givers* (1925) and Henry Roth's heart-wrenching *Call It Sleep* (1934), both literary masterpieces, offered heart-wrenching testimony of tenacity and courage despite horrific odds.

Life trumped talk. Their heated Talmudic arguments notwithstanding, most Jewish workers "cared less, if at all, about ideology than about improving their lot," writes Norman Podhoretz. Admittedly, "[t]hey might nod piously at the Socialist rhetoric that the leadership kept spouting, and they might even vote for a Socialist candidate in a local election, but it was higher wages, shorter hours, and better working conditions they were after, not the overthrow of capitalism."[58]

It was not easy to adapt, even in the crowded Lower East Side of New York where most of the former *shtetl* Jews arrived and stayed. Near relatives and townspeople, fortunately, gave one another a feeling of security. Many found work as cutters and pressers in the "needle trades" of ready-made clothes, for low pay and as many as seventy hours a week, in terrible conditions, but at least they could hope for a better future. And while this was indeed hard sweated labor, writes Paul Johnson in his splendid book *A History of the Jews*, "[i]t was also the great engine of upward mobility." Johnson credits Emma Lazarus with prophesying "a revival of Jewish civilization through mutual action from America and the Holy Land. In the wretched refuse of Ashkenazi Jewry accumulating in New York slums she saw not only life but hope."[59]

So did most Jews by far. By the turn of the new century, Jewish immigrants were gradually moving out of the crammed settlements.

> [T]he submissive spirit had gone. An entire Jewish-led labour movement had been created and established its power through four dramatic strikes. By their needles, too, the eastern Jews pushed their way into independence and respect. ... Their children went to colleges and universities; vast numbers became doctors and lawyers. Others became small businessmen; then big businessmen.[60]

Yet with greater visibility came heightened danger. As Americans recoiled from the immigration explosion, stunned by the Great War and what they saw as the imminent dangers of Bolshevism, Black unrest, and the uncertainties of modernity generally, xenophobia blighted the culture. First founded in 1865, after a decline of several decades, the Ku Klux Klan was revived once again in 1915, fiercely opposed to minority groups, including Jews, Catholics, foreigners in general, members of organized labor, and above all, Blacks. KKK membership crossed class and regional lines, from small farmers and laborers to planters, lawyers, merchants, physicians, and ministers from the Deep South to the Midwest.

Most painful, particularly for Jews who had gained both financial and political success, such as the brilliant financier Bernard Baruch, who advised successive presidents, was the refusal of patrician clubs, Ivy League colleges, and other exclusive establishments to accept them on an equal footing. While discrimination brought the community closer together, Jews were mortified by the depth of hostility they had never expected to encounter in America. It led to insecurity and diminished self-esteem. Even as eminent a writer as Walter Lippmann admitted that "I do not regard the Jews as innocent victims," for they had "many distressing personal and social habits." In a private letter, he painfully confessed that he found the manners and habits of gentiles "distinctly superior to the prevailing manners and habits of the Jews."[61]

Accordingly, Lippmann, like Baruch and many others, tried to obliterate their Jewish identity, or at best deflected it, as did Lillian Hellman. Her notorious plays written in the 1930s, for example, "tortured her Jewish humanitarianism to fit the prevailing Stalinist mode," writes Johnson, adding: "as did many thousands of Jewish intellectuals." He continues:

> She would not allow her love of justice to find its natural expression in outraged protest at the fate of her race. So it was perverted into a hard-faced ideological orthodoxy defended with rabbinical tenacity. The need to avert the face from the Jewish facts led her to doctor truth with fiction. These confusions, divisions and opacities in the American Jewish community, not least among its intellectuals, help to explain why American Jews, despite the enormous positions of power they were beginning to acquire for themselves, were so curiously incapable of affecting events in inter-war Europe, or even of steering opinion in America itself.[62]

Hellman herself joined the Communist Party in 1938 until 1940.[63] But even Jews who did not go to such extremes reacted with outrage against bigots whose vicious rhetoric was indistinguishable from European fascist slogans. When the likes of William Dudley Pelley, leader of the American

Christian Defenders and the Silver Shirts, for example, described himself as the American Hitler, and ran for president on the Christian Party ticket, Jews concluded that the enemy was on the "right," whatever that meant.

Not even putatively shared progressive values mattered to the demagogic Father Charles E. Coughlin: the Jews were evil no matter how liberal, charitable, or whatever. The charismatic reverend spewed his venom on the pages of a weekly newspaper titled *Social Justice*, which he founded in 1936. With Coughlin, the Social Gospel movement bared its antisemitic teeth with a viciousness that shocked even its most faithful followers. And Father Coughlin claimed to be a progressive Democrat.

In one of his many radio broadcasts, on November 11, 1934, for example, he rejoiced over the death of the Republican party "with its rugged individualism," and declared that "the Democratic party, now composed of progressive men and women of all political affiliations, is merely on trial." Summoning everyone "to organize for social united action which will be founded on God-given social truths" into a National Union for Social Justice, he includes among its principles "preferring the sanctity of human rights to the sanctity of property rights; for the chief concern of government shall be for the poor because, as it is witnessed, the rich have ample means of their own to care for themselves."[64]

He believed in "upholding the right to private property but in controlling it for the public good." A hardcore progressive, Father Coughlin supported a guaranteed income for every able-bodied American. He also advocated "an annual wage system that is just and equitable and thus permit American workmen to preserve the American standard of living. The annual wage shall not be one that will permit us merely to subsist. It must be one that will keep us on the level of the American standard of living." *Just and equitable* was the new mantra, but he defined it in a racist context.

The Catholic radio-evangelist shared the Social Gospel Protestants' aversion to the moneyed Jews, whom they blamed uniquely, if not exclusively then certainly primarily, for the various ills afflicting the nation. Coughlin, however, went much further. By 1938, he was openly peddling scurrilous lies. His magazine, *Social Justice*, began serializing a Tsarist-era forgery known as *The Protocols of the Elders of Zion,* first published in 1903. It would become by far the most powerful and influential weapon against the Jews ever created. Its lethality persists to this day.

Purportedly the "minutes" of a secret speech (in some versions, preposterously attributed to Theodore Herzl, the father of Zionism!) before the Elders, or Sages, of Zion, the document purportedly reveals a two-millennia-old conspiracy. A cabal of (anonymous, but surely no one could possibly doubt their authenticity, could one?) bloodthirsty and money-crazed Jews, who by the way already run the world, were allegedly planning the last steps before achieving total global victory. It was appalling that, despite having been discredited in 1921, such preposterous claptrap was still in circulation more than a decade later - let alone a century.

It was testimony to the incalculable harm done by industrialist Henry Ford's decision to publish it and disseminate it on a staggering scale. Starting in 1920, Ford had financed an enormous international campaign to publicize the obscenely absurd rag, along with sympathetic commentaries, in a compilation called *International Jew*, which he had arranged to be translated into sixteen languages. Ford eventually recanted his views, but not until 1927. Or so he said. For even then, he acknowledged the *Protocols*' fraudulent origin only grudgingly. It evidently failed to make an impression on Father Coughlin, who continued to refer to the lie as fact.[65] Pastor Louis Farrakhan still does - about which more later.

By the 1930s, writes Norman Podhoretz, it was becoming increasingly clear that among the Protestant establishment, "no trace remained of the philo-Semitic attitude of their Puritan forebears."[66] When accused by their worst enemies of manipulating FDR, Jews could not avoid supporting the WASP president. After all, if those wretched people thought he was their best friend, surely he must be! So, when Father Charles E Coughlin accused the Democratic Party candidate FDR of being "a tool of the Jews ('the Kuhn-Loebs, the Rothschilds…the scribes and Pharisees, the Baruchs')," going so far as to express support for Hitler's war against "world Jewish domination," the choice was clear. "[H]ow could Jews fail to conclude that casting their lot with Roosevelt was in their best interests, when the 'Jew Deal' had become the prime target of anti-Semitic agitation?"[67]

Some deal. The full truth would emerge later, but by then it was too late; the narrative had been set.

FDR, Good for the Jews? Not Exactly

Roosevelt's unflattering statements about Jews consistently reflected one of several interrelated notions: that it was undesirable to have too many Jews in any single profession, institution, or geographic locale; that America was by nature, and should remain, an overwhelmingly white, Protestant country; and that Jews on the whole possessed certain innate and distasteful characteristics.

- Raphael Medoff, *The Jews Should Keep Quiet: Franklin D. Roosevelt, Rabbi Stephen S. Wise, and the Holocaust* (2019)

It helped that FDR's own progressivism conformed to most Jews' liberal-socialist leanings. When Jewish labor leaders decided to support him "not out of any specifically Jewish concern but rather because Roosevelt's program included legislation that would – and did – strengthen the hand of the unions," it had been an ideological matter. For the New Deal, writes Podhoretz had "included a number of welfare measures that they, as Socialists, had long been advocating."[68] The member of a Knickerbocker family supporting unions and even socialism seemed too good to be true.

A new breed of progressive patrician, Roosevelt's long-standing affinity with the radical Social Gospel movement was well known. In a 1912 article that appeared in Lyman Abbott's *Outlook*, for example, Roosevelt had railed against property rights as the last defense of the "special interests" who put their own personal advantage ahead of the Common Good. He placed the blame squarely on the system itself, the constitutional framework of protecting private property. For any meaningful reform to take place, he argued, the only solution was "changing the rules of the game" so as to bring about "a more substantial equality of opportunity and reward."[69]

Not that Roosevelt objected to hierarchy and caste. He considered the best, brightest and whitest to be naturally superior. Famously proud of his lineage, which the family traced to the days of William the Conqueror in the eleventh century, he disapproved of "the mingling of white with oriental blood." His socialist brand of *noblesse oblige,* packaged for populist, electoral consumption, amounted to advocating elite control of government policies to advance the Common Good. That some of the most powerful Jews in the United States, including intellectuals, shared this mindset blinded them to the profound differences lurking just underneath the surface.

Foremost among them was the president of the American Jewish Congress Rabbi Stephen Wise (1874-1949), who in 1936 wrote a colleague that Roosevelt's election "is not only essential to the well-being of America, but to the highest interests of the human race."[70] It was a dangerous infatuation indeed. As Rafael Medoff demonstrates in his meticulously documented new book *The Jews Should Keep Quiet: Franklin D. Roosevelt, Rabbi Stephen S. Wise, and the Holocaust,* Roosevelt "took advantage of Wise's adoration of his policies and leadership to manipulate Wise through flattery and intermittent access to the White House," all of which made the rabbi "especially susceptible when the president implored him to help silence those in the Jewish community who challenged his administration's policies."[71]

In an astonishing display of pusillanimity, Wise complied, despite the president's breaking every promise he made to him and other Jewish leaders, completely disregarding the plight of their brethren being slaughtered by the millions. Medoff does not disguise his contempt:

> By taking upon himself the task of making excuses for Roosevelt and shielding him from Jewish criticism, Wise was in effect implementing what FDR said to him in 1936 about "the necessity of Jews lying low." He was also helping to facilitate policies that neither he himself nor most American Jews, supported, from Roosevelt's pursuit of cordial – sometimes even friendly – diplomatic and economic relations with Nazi Germany in the 1930s, to his closing of America's doors to refugees despite unfilled quotas, to his refusal to take even minimal steps to interrupt the mass murder process.[72]

Roosevelt's appalling record cannot be excused on the basis of expediency: "He would not have had to incur substantial political risks had he permitted immigration up to the limits set by U.S. law, admitted refugees temporarily to a U.S. territory, utilized empty Liberty ships to carry refugees, or authorized dropping bombs on Auschwitz or the railways from planes that were already flying over the camps and its environs."

The evidence suggests that the president, who had admitted pride in having "no Jewish blood," feared the presence of too many Jews (along with too many Japanese (?)) in any one university or profession. He preferred that such people be "spread thin" around the United States lest they dilute the native race. FDR obviously didn't like minorities very much, observes Medoff.[73] Nor was it an issue of genetics alone, but also of culture and religion. Roosevelt saw America as "a Protestant country," with "the Jews" and people of other backgrounds and religions (notably Catholics) present only "on sufferance." The record indicates that saving Jews was no more a priority for him than for the Ivy League-groomed foreign service crew ensconced inside the State Department.

Wise had not been alone in placing excessive trust in Roosevelt. So did practically all other Jewish leaders. Wise was evidently not responsible for the decision by *The New York Times* and other major Jewish-owned newspapers, for example, to under-report news of Jewish persecution and annihilation before and during the Holocaust.[74] Was it insecurity about their status in American society, an empathy deficit, or both? None could possibly count as an excuse.

Exhaustive research by eminent Holocaust historians, notably Haskel Lowenstein, provides ample evidence of culpability:

> In the America of the 1930s Jews put their skullcaps in their pocket upon leaving home, synagogue, or school.... For most Jews the desire was to blend in with the majority, to be assimilated into the larger culture, to be as American as possible and to conceal or obliterate the obviously Jewish characteristics of language, accent, clothing, behavior, and sometimes even group loyalties.[75]

But even conceding that no one could have even imagined the impending horror about to engulf civilization, the muted reaction to early signs of Nazi antisemitism such as Kristallnacht was shocking. Unwilling to extend benefit of doubt, Lowenstein believes it to be "more the result of fear than of incomplete knowledge. The American Jew of 1938-1939 was a cowed figure, who was destined to remain in that state for most of the war years." Did that anxiety ever disappear completely?

If anything, it worsened. The sense that America was no longer welcoming to Jews could not fail to dampen their commitment to their adoptive nation. They saw that America's celebrated religious pluralism notwithstanding, Christianity could easily be invoked by antisemitic demagogues. Medoff thus notes that "Rabbi Wise was profoundly uncomfortable at the thought of developing relationships with Republicans and conservative Christians."[76] That discomfort persists to this day. Jews continue feeling far closer to self-described social justice advocates than to religious Christians. Though many eventually came to realize that FDR had mesmerized them with lofty rhetoric and promises he never kept, it came too late to affect their political outlook or behavior.

The Jews were struggling to cope in a perilous environment, which fostered greater internal solidarity against threats to their survival, while at the same time having to avoid alarming their hosts by appearing unduly recalcitrant. It was a delicate balance. In 1934, in an effort to articulate a common ideological framework, Rabbi Mordecai Kaplan, a European-born professor educated at the City University of New York, published *Judaism as a Civilization: Toward a Reconstruction of American-Jewish Life.* In that seminal work, Kaplan argued that being accepted in America did not require abandoning either piety, Zionism, or any other Jewish concern. For ultimately, as Nathan Glazer sees it, "it was essentially Kaplan's liberalism, both in politics and in religion, that led him to feel that Jewish separatism would not create a serious problem."[77] Kaplan believed that progressive liberal ideas would guarantee that Jews would be seen by the ideocracy as its allies.

And then, he added: "It is the feature of interest, rather than that of the supernatural origin of rationality, which is – and must be – the essential factor in the approach to Judaism." This was no trivial afterthought. Once *interest* becomes a substitute for the transcendent, politics steps in to fill the spiritual vacuum. Glazer reflects that secularism, alongside socialism by whatever name, had thus triumphed. When the leftwing Yiddish newspaper *Forward* endorsed FDR in 1936, Glazer observes, "it symbolized the fact that socialism had become simple liberalism."[78] Jews, imagining they were being good liberals, were stuck genuflecting before the Golden Calf of government.

Choosing between the Scylla of progressivism and the Charybdis of religious bigotry was no easy task. The linguistic legerdemain of Wilson and FDR would ensnare idealistic Jews seeking emancipation from an Establishment conservatism that seemed, and often was, contemptuous of them as but another "inferior" race. Unfortunately, the promise of a rationally organized, socialist system based on secular egalitarian principles was seductive to the point that many were attracted not only to the ideology but to the one country that purported to have adopted it: the USSR.

What most Western Soviet sympathizers, among them American Jews, did not know then was that within days of the Bolshevik coup of October 1917, "a far more pervasive and virulent form of the Okhrana was reinstituted as the Cheka,"[79] led by the brilliant F. E. Dzerzhinsky, with full support from Red Army Commissar Leon Trotsky (1879-1940). They should have realized that it was only a matter of time before they too became its targets – would, in fact, be among the first in line.

That included Trotsky (Leon Bronstein's *nom de guerre*) himself. Though he appealed to gentiles, Christian and atheist Socialists alike, and widely influential among Western intellectuals, he especially inspired his ideologically kindred co-religionists who either repudiated their Judaism or subsumed it into a sort of mishmash Marxism. (It persists to this day; Trotskyites continue operating as members of the International Marxist Tendency.[80]) Accordingly, during the Soviet years, when someone was accused of being a Trotskyite, it often meant simply that he was a Jew.

The successor of the much-hated Okhrana, the tsar's ruthless secret police, the Cheka was an entirely novel system of espionage and political warfare that targeted enemies both within and without the borders of the state. On its first anniversary in December 1920, Dzerzhinsky ordered the creation of a Foreign Department specifically designed to conduct foreign intelligence and counterintelligence operations. A core objective was cultivating Communist Parties and their sympathizers throughout the world. "In a very profound sense," explains the brilliant counterintelligence expert John J. Dziak (my admired colleague and also close friend of Herb Romerstein) "foreign intelligence, from the earliest years, was more of an external projection of state security." Unlike anything known before anywhere in the world, these activities were "so qualitatively different from its Western counterparts… that they tend to be unintelligible when approached on the basis of Western bureaucratic or interest group models."[81]

In 1935, Stalin escalated his outreach to sympathizers inside what he called "bourgeois democracies" through a new strategy called Popular Front. "Communists everywhere were to stop acting and talking like revolutionaries," explains Podhoretz. "Instead they were to portray themselves as no different from the formerly despised liberals except in their impatience to bring about the same reforms: they were 'liberals in a hurry.'"[82] The Jewish leader of CPUSA, Earl Browder, would proclaim communism itself as "twentieth-century Americanism," the phrase becoming a slogan of the party's membership and their fellow travelers.

In 1938, Browder offered an eye-opening explanation of its meaning: "We Communists, taking our place as an integral sector of the progressive and democratic camp, claim the common title of 'Good Americans,' and further add to it the claim that our particular principles and program embody the future development of our country. Thus our claim is, first, one of unity with the masses of the people, and with their historical development, and, secondly, the claim to be in the vanguard - a claim which we must continuously prove by our work."[83]

It wasn't merely his idea, but that of the Soviet Union's sainted leader: "In his famous Letter to American Workers," writes Browder, "Lenin reminded us of the rich revolutionary traditions of our country, and advised us to claim the heritage of 1776 and 1861." It was left to his successor to carry out the details: "Stalin's history-making works on the national question furnished us with the modern instruments of thought, hammered out in the course of actually changing world history, which armed us for the task."[84] Weaponized history, weaponized language, for progressive ends: sound familiar?

Sheep-like, Browder's minions went out their way to look as American as possible. The Young Communist League was renamed American Youth for Democracy, and its local chapters took on the names of American heroes like Paul Revere. The Party's "educational" institution set up in New York bore the name of… Thomas Jefferson. The men recruited to fight in the Spanish Civil War on the side of the Soviets against Caudillo Francisco Franco innocently joined the Lincoln Brigade. Podhoretz explains what this meant for American liberalism, and specifically for Jews:

> [T]he most important consequence of the Popular Front was its creation of an ecumenical Left in which the old distinctions and conflicts among the various factions of the Socialist movement, and between them and "bourgeois liberalism," were set aside so that they could all be comfortable subsumed *under the newly honorific rubric of liberalism (minus any qualifier).* Thus the Jews, for the majority of which Socialism had been the default political positions, were now almost compelled to regard themselves as liberals.[85]

Before long, the centrality of liberalism in the self-image and self-definition of American Jews would become entrenched to the point of all but replacing Jewish practice itself. Writing in 1997, Elliott Abrams, a senior official in several Republican administrations, now Chairman of Tikvah, described this secular turn as a "flight from Judaism." He cited a 1989 American Jewish Committee survey which found that nearly two thirds of respondents said that what they considered most important to their Jewish identity was "social justice;" a mere 17 percent cited "religious observance."[86]

The result, writes Abrams, is that Jews have come to politicize their tradition, "virtually identifying it with the program of American liberalism and with support for the democratic Party. In congressional elections since 1980, Jews have cast 74 percent of their votes for Democratic candidates."[87] Hebrew Union College sociologist Steven M. Cohen had written in 1983: "[P]olitics – in particular pro-Israel and liberal activity – have come to constitute their principal working definition of Jewishness. In this sense modern Jewish political movements have served as functional alternatives to conventional religion."[88]

Frank Chodorov though them short-sighted. For he firmly believed that

> Jewish culture is definitely not socialistic, even though tribal adherence has always been emphasized as a matter of self-preservation. That many Jews have advanced socialistic ideas is true, but I believe this can be explained as an inclination to protect against injustices, which is

> characteristic of the individualist.... Among the Old Bolsheviks were a number of Jews, more than their proportionate population would entitle them to; but it is significant that very few of them escaped the Stalinist purges; the Jew is too individualistic to be tolerated by the collectivism he sometimes urges.[89]

In America, even a Jew could flirt with socialism without fear. But Chodorov saw what too few of his fellow Jews either could not or would not admit: that they were merely succumbing to the age-old human temptation of idolatry. "We have it on the authority of the Lord, as recorded in Genesis, that idolatry is a corruption far more reprehensible than even the sins of the flesh," he wrote in his 1952 autobiography *One is a Crowd.* A splendid title, it captures the infinite complexity of each individual, but also his own sense of alienation from his own community.

He describes that lethal temptation by appealing to the Torah:

> Man has done a lot in accumulating a knowledge of things in general, but he seems incapable of ridding himself of the need of a golden calf. He still yearns for "gods which will go before us," gods that are uninhibited by the laws of nature, gods that are accountable only to our appetites, gods that speak not of consequences or the long run. In that respect we are like the Jews in the wilderness. Witness the pervasive religion of our times, the worship of the State. Is not the State an idol? Is it not like any graven image into which men have read supernatural powers and superhuman capacities?[90]

Too many Jews had succumbed to the temptation, seemingly convinced that equality of possessions and government hand-outs constitute fair substitutes for spiritual equality. To that end, they were willing to all but deify the State, which possesses the power to mold society in the image of some self-appointed vanguard with democratic pretensions. In the name of progress, they seemed not to notice that they were repudiating the key value of Western civilization: freedom. Chodorov saw what so many of them did not, that "liberalism mutated into its exact opposite by the end of the nineteenth century. Today," he wrote in 1952, "it is a synonym of Statism."[91] It still is.

The eleventh child of a Russian Jewish immigrant peddler in New York, Chodorov had started a new magazine in 1944, *Analysis,* which he described as "an individualistic publication," declaring it, dispensing with false modesty, "the only one of its kind in America." The mission was indeed unique. It "looks at the current scene through the eyes of historic liberalism, unashamedly accepting the doctrine of natural rights, proclaims the dignity of the individual and denounces all forms of Statism as human slavery."[92]

Throughout his quixotic career, Chodorov never abandoned that stance. And he could not help wondering

> what will happen to the Judeo-Cristian tenet of the primacy of the person?... In the darkness and the stillness of universal Statism, will it be whispered that once there was a world built on the faith of the human being in himself and his God?[93]

Many of his fellow Jews, even those who originally opposed him, would later share his dismay, eventually recognizing that they had indeed been worshipping a calf whose golden veneer was oxidating before their very eyes.

Chapter VII:

Revolutionary "Liberalism" and the Jews

The Kountercultural Reboot

"In 1965 two new political movements, the anti-war movement and black power began to gain great backing among culturati in New York."
- Tom Wolfe, "*Radical Chic: That Party at Lenny's*" (1970)

Though Woodrow Wilson first sought to replace progressivism with liberalism in 1917, its official entry in the academy took another two decades. Ironically, the first major text to use the term, George Sabine's *A History of Political Theory* (1937), amounted to a combined birth announcement-obituary, for it merely described a relic of 19th century Britain. Apparently oblivious to its American reincarnation (didn't he get the memo?), Sabine thought it already *passé.* Not so the general public, according to City University of New York Professor Helena Rosenblatt. She writes that the newly refurbished ideology was about to assume center state - and not only at home, but abroad: "The Second World War only fortified and spread the view of America as the prime representative and defender of liberalism, democracy, and Western civilization."[1]

Rosenblatt is careful to warn, however, that "it would be wrong to conclude from the growing association of liberalism with America that there was a consensus over what the word actually meant." (Semantic hijacking 101: Appropriate a word with positive connotations; start the obfuscations; steer stealthily, full speed ahead, forget about definitions.) It was unclear, she continues, "how, for example, liberalism differed from democracy, or what it meant in terms of a government's role in the economy." In brief, there was near-total confusion about the difference between the traditional, so-called classical, liberalism of the Founders and the progressives' disingenuous substitute. In Europe, by contrast, "powerful voices continued to spread the idea that liberalism meant laissez-faire," writes Rosenblatt. "Those who meant something else had to add a qualifier such as 'progressive' or 'constructive' or speak of 'liberal socialism.'"[2]

This country, however, had John Dewey. To legitimize the new statism using the most sacred concept at the heart of America, which was freedom from government intrusion on individual liberty, and standing that concept on its head, took nothing less than rhetorical genius. Dewey rose to the occasion. His 1940 essay on "The Meaning of Liberalism" begins: "The meaning of liberalism then consists in quiet and patient pursuit of truth."[3] Note: pursuit of **truth** vs. what, "pursuit of falsehood?" Argue with that if you dare. And needless to say, truth must be pursued with decorum: **quiet**, not loudmouthed, not tentative but confident; **patient**, not rushing headlong into revolution, unlike those dangerous self-described socialists. And the wise **pursuit** of truth is hardly precipitate. Why, it's almost conservative, if you pardon the word. Only those too (thank the Lord for those fine antonyms) impatient, hotheaded, stupid, venal, or complacent to care for truth could oppose so tautologically perfect an ism: Liberalism as Truth, Goodness, and Beauty. Protagoras the quintessential sophist, Socrates's nemesis, would have winked approvingly.

As to what exactly is actually being pursued by liberalists under the mantle of truth, Dewey carefully advances a normative argument by invoking the progressive's moral guidepost: History. Not left on its own, helter-skelter History at the mercy of some imaginary "invisible hand," but History whose true path is only revealed to its patient pursuers, those virtuous, altruistic philosopher-experts republican--kings. Surely the Founders had the same idea, didn't they? "The word [laissez-faire] has never been associated in this country with laissez-faire economics and hands-off governmental action, as it has been in England and especially on the continent of Europe. It [liberalism] has been used in connection with what is vaguely called a forward-looking and progressive attitude, and in opposition to the kind of conservatism that looks back in time to the extent of being reactionary."[4]

In a sleight-of-hand worthy of a Houdini, Dewey accurately though disingenuously states that the word itself, "liberalism," had not been associated "in this country" with laissez-faire. Of course not. It had been Dewey, aided by Wilson, who together launched that nefarious ism as a decoy. He makes no mention of the Founders' commitment to free trade and the popularity Adam Smith's "system of natural liberty" throughout the colonies.[5] What was that if not liberalism properly understood?

Dewey's liberalism was designed to connote the opposite of conservatism, whose very etymology reeks of "looking back in time," if not "reactionary." The unspoken message: since the Declaration and the Constitution themselves "go back in time," they must be obsolete. End of discussion.

Proving that displaying chutzpa doesn't require being Jewish, Dewey declares the author of the Declaration himself a proto-progressive. Wouldn't you know it, Thomas Jefferson was "not an 'individualist' in the sense of the British ***laissez-faire liberal*** school"[6] at all. Dewey proceeds to deconstruct the Virginian's "democratic faith" with seemingly innocuous paraphrases: "[T]he connection of justice – or equity – with equality of rights and duties was a commonplace of the moral tradition of Christendom. Jefferson took the tradition seriously."

But obviously, for every right there must be a correlative obligation – duty, if you prefer – to respect it, lest the claimed right is no better than a blank check drawn from a non-bank. And Jefferson was no exception - after all, this is merely a definition of the concept. What does that prove? Certainly not that Jefferson repudiated the system of natural liberty. Yet, condescendingly commending the former President for taking tradition "seriously," Dewey breezily enlists Jefferson in the progressive camp.[7] There was still one small problem. Not only did Jefferson never refer to himself as a "liberal," he abhorred centralized power - of which he accused his rivals John Adams and Alexander Hamilton. (Yet his own mixed record as president all but obliterated whatever theoretical differences there might have existed between them.)

Moreover, John Dewey's casual synonymy between "justice – or equity" being connected with "equality of rights and duties" similarly ignores the fact that Jefferson never used the word "equity" either – *any more than did anyone else at the time*. But Dewey nonchalantly seeks to disarm the objection. Why sure, "*the terms* in which Jefferson expressed his belief in the moral criterion for judging all political arrangements... are not now current." All the more reason, he argues, to translate it all into modernese. If a little distortion happens along the way, that's just the price we have to pay for – what else? – progress.

To keep up with the times, suggests Dewey, "we have to find *another set of words* in which to formulate the moral ideal served by democracy."[8] Better yet, keep the old words and change their meanings; ensuing ambiguities could then serve new goals. Liberalism, democracy, and progress had been repurposed with the exquisite subtlety to be expected from so masterful a pragmatic ideocrat.

Repudiating the Ideology of Tolerance

"*Part of [the struggle for a real democracy] is the fight against an ideology of tolerance which, in reality, favors and fortifies the conservation of the status quo of inequality and discrimination.*"
- Herbert Marcuse, "An Essay on Liberation" (1965)

"*[R]eligion can and should disappear from earth... only by the collective effort to establish justice, equality, and happiness here on earth.*"
- Herbert Marcuse, "Repressive Tolerance" (1969)

A decade later, to the chagrin of the great Austrian economist Ludwig von Mises (1881-1973), it was already too late to turn the clock back. In his 1951 book *Socialism*, Mises balked at the brazen, disingenuous expropriation of liberalism and democracy by its foes. Only the original, classical meanings, bemoaned Mises, permit the true expression of individual choice which in turn is the real essence of democracy. For "the power to dispose of the means of production, which belongs to the entrepreneurs and capitalists, can only be acquired by means of the consumers' ballot, held daily in the market-place."[9] Each of us votes daily, with our pocketbooks. That too is democracy.

The game of labels had been played and won by the champion obfuscators. Liberalism would thenceforth have to wear the ill-fitting cloak of "capitalism," however thoroughly infused with venom by its coiner, the author of *Das Kapital*. This makes advocating the system of natural liberty nowadays doubly difficult. Defending the freedom to fail while others succeed, and championing personal choice when most people prefer to be spared the bother, are hard enough without having to redefine words that hamper conversation from the outset.

Without doubt the most accurate synonym for the system of natural liberty is classical liberalism, which best describes the U.S. Constitution. The definitive explanation may be found in University of Chicago law professor Richard A. Epstein's magisterial and seminal tome *The Classical Liberal Constitution: The Uncertain Quest for Limited Government* (2014), "which defends with a passionate intensity the classical liberal vision of the Constitution against its rival, and ascendant, progressive alternative."[10] But the term, alas, intimates anachronism and obsolescence – and who wants to be passé? By contrast, its antonym connotes "modern, new, cool."

Of course, "classical" is also implicitly elitist – who, after all, reads the "classics" except nerdy eggheads? Scholarly disputations regarding who counts as a classical liberal compound the problem. Do utilitarians qualify? The not-always-consistent J.S. Mill aside, what about his teacher, the curmudgeonly Jeremy Bentham? Surely the author of "[n]atural rights is simple nonsense: natural and imprescriptible rights, rhetorical nonsense, nonsense upon stilts"[11] would seem a strange candidate for inclusion. Liberty without rights sounds like a bicycle without wheels.

The ostentatiously foreign expression *laissez-faire,* famously scoffed at by Dewey, is also flawed fare. Launched sometime in the 1690s and popularized in the 1700s by Jean-Claude-Marie Vincent de Gournay, when used in the place of the British-pedigreed "free market system," the French adoptee seemed designed to deliberately mock the Anglo-Saxon mutt. Unsurprisingly (certainly to a Francophobe) it was all-too easily distorted as the "anything goes," no-holds-barred, crude anarchism rejected even by most libertarians. Whiggism, briefly adopted by free-market proponents in England, flourished from the 1680s to the 1850s, but once they were absorbed into the Liberal Party in 1859, it mostly disappeared, victim to its eccentric and arcane etymology.

Nor is "neo-liberal" much help, for reasons both logical (being parasitic on defining "liberal") and political: the term is understandably rejected by its presumed denotees who tend to detect the not-so-subtle antagonism of its coiners. Most, though by no means all, opponents of socialist-style, progressive, government-centric economic models thus fall back on "capitalism," resigned to being misrepresented, misunderstood, and worse. Having been coined as a synonym for the secular equivalent of the Antichrist, it isn't doing its stubborn advocates many favors. But what then?

In a language game that pits greed against compassion, pessimism about human rapacity against optimism regarding government-sponsored altruism, and siding with progress rather than against it, the decks are manifestly stacked. No wonder, writes George Washington University Professor Samuel Goldman, the new "theories of progress associated with optimistic liberals such as the philosophers John Stuart Mill and John Dewey"[12] appealed more broadly than did a more traditionalist defense of natural rights. Once the latter, centered as it was on limited government, were declared pessimistic and even reactionary, it didn't have much chance. The vision thus mutilated didn't go over well in modern America; optimism has by far the better batting average.

And Jews like Ira Glasser fell for it. As president of the American Civil Liberties Union from 1978 till 2001, Glasser was both a worthy successor to Dewey and a symbol of Jewish progressivism. He "served as the public face of liberal tolerance, in the process giving civil libertarians a distinctively Jewish appearance," writes Goldman. Glasser was emblematic of an entire generation, at least for a while:

> An idealistic product of booming mid-century America, his liberalism was essentially confident of future success, and his secular, Jewish, lower-middle-class background was more important to that optimism than any formal philosophy of history. Even when they flirted with Marxism, his generation and class of American Jews displayed intense cultural patriotism. The task of the left, as they saw it, was not to replace America. It was to help America become more fully itself by exposing and combating religious bigotry, racism, and economic exploitation.[13]

That upbeat, patriotic brand of socialist liberalism, an oxymoron that still affords countless hours of overheated, high-decibel arguments that often end in family excommunications, would be replaced within a few decades by what came to be known as the New Left, whose hot-headed proponents turned heretical. Heroes of the counterculture, they scoffed at their unforgivably compliant parents and held America's traditional liberal values in contempt. "Though they joined together in the campus Free Speech movement [of the 1960s] and later opposition to the Vietnam War, liberals of Glasser's type and the avatars of the various 'liberation' movements held fundamentally different views of the American promise," writes Goldman. "For the radicals, it meant transforming a form of life that they saw as not just contingently but essentially implicated in oppression."

The deeper reality, however, was revealed by the celebrated art critic Hilton Kramer of *The Nation* magazine, reflecting on the reaction of Columbia University Professor Lionel Trilling's brainy colleagues to his seminal book *The Liberal Imagination*, which appeared in 1950. There, Trilling had dared suggest that intellectuals might profit from being exposed to other perspectives as well. "In the United States at this time liberalism is not only the dominant but even the sole intellectual tradition. For it is the plain fact that nowadays there are no conservative or reactionary ideas in general circulation," wrote Trilling. This, reports Kramer, "instantly earned its author the enduring enmity of the intellectual Left."[14] Another point of view? What heresy!

Kramer and Trilling had both belonged to the distinguished and highly influential set of Jewish contributors to the now defunct magazine *Partisan Review* (born communist in 1937), nearly all New Yorkers. In Ruth Wisse's assessment, they soon "became perhaps the largest community of intellectuals in modern times," comparable to Britain's Bloomsbury social set and Jean-Paul Sartre's Parisian coterie. [15] None had rejected Judaism outright, yet they believed that true art could never be "parochial," which inclined them toward Trotskyite socialism of the Marxist internationalist variety. After all, writes Kramer, "socialism was the ideal toward which all liberal sentiment was inevitably inclined."

Ironically, however, this was ultimately a form of "cosmopolitan parochialism," Wisse's apt *bon mot*. In truth, it detracted both from their art and their ethics. For surely "no one can be trusted to benefit mankind who is not prepared to protect his small part of it," observes Wisse. Consider their reaction to the Holocaust: "So great was the distance these Jews felt between themselves and their community that they voiced no sense of special responsibility toward the fate of their fellow Jews in Hitler's Europe," incredible as that may seem.

As for their art, she offers her good friend Saul Bellow (once my teacher), as prime counterexample. Bellow's later novels about Jewish life were his greatest, earning him the Nobel Prize in 1976. That same year saw the publication of his riveting *In Jerusalem and Back,* which Wisse describes as "an intellectual's attempt to destroy the ideas that seek to destroy the Jewish state."[16] Those ideas, he knew, were ultimately seeking to destroy the American liberal idea itself.

He and most of his fellow intellectuals around the *Partisan Review* understood the attraction of socialism better for having flirted with it. They had come to appreciate Kramer's insight that "the Stalinism of the 1930s and the New Left radicalism of the 1960s, …[despite] differences in style and tactics, … were alike in one essential respect: in their power to persuade liberals to betray their professed ideals of liberty, democracy, and the rule of law by worshipping at the altars of illiberal gods." They had seen the betrayal. The next generation would not be as wise.

The Sixties radicals, not intellectuals so much as narcissists, rebelled against all constraints: discipline, inequality, materialism, and sexual repression (above all). Members of this restless generation recognized their own self-described "alienation" in the writings of Existentialist philosophers then *en vogue*, from Nietzsche and Kierkegaard to Sartre, Camus, and the tantalizingly inscrutable Heidegger. I recall reading them in high school along with my equally befuddled colleagues. Though intrigued, I found these books depressing, nihilistic. Forget it.

But most impressionable college students, eager to be mesmerized, were easy prey for the charmingly oleaginous Herbert Marcuse, whose 1965 essay "Repressive Tolerance" had catapulted him to unprecedented fame. His German-accented, jargon-filled lectures around the country were invariably packed. But behind the self-canceling title of his essay lurked Marcuse's thinly veiled darker side. Sure, he advocated equal freedom for all members of society. But: only after the demise of capitalism. Meanwhile, tolerance had to be "repressive" of all that stood in the way. The radicals, he believed, needed to start by suppressing "authoritarian" speech (anything that went counter to radical ideology) – presciently anticipating the ever-more draconian thought-crushing political correctness of America's campuses a full half-century later. Contradiction would usher in utopia by canceling dialogue altogether.

The wily, urbane professor supported his argument by citing from J. S. Mill's "On Liberty," the very gospel of free speech. "Liberty, as a principle," wrote the venerable British utilitarian liberal, "has no application to any state of things anterior to the time when mankind have become capable of being improved by free and equal discussion."[17] The sentence preceding it was particularly revealing: "Despotism is a legitimate mode of government in dealing with barbarians provided the end be their improvement, and the means justified by actually effecting that end." Total repression, then, is no sin if the end is the "improvement" of the masses as defined by Marcuse & co.

Marcuse's subsequent attack on toleration is bone-chilling. His rant against America's culture reeks of contempt especially unbecoming in a German-Jewish émigré who had been warmly welcomed in this country:

> The toleration of the systematic moronization of children and adults alike by publicity and propaganda, the release of destructiveness in aggressive driving, the recruitment for and training of special forces, the impotent and benevolent tolerance toward outright deception in merchandizing, waste, and planned obsolescence are not distortions and aberrations, they are the essence of a system which fosters tolerance as a means for perpetuating the struggle for existence and suppressing the alternatives.[18]

It takes chutzpah for a master propagandist to condemn "publicity and propaganda." His alternative to toleration he attacks as merely hypocritical was its sheer obliteration. For the revolution, everything; against the revolution, silence. Unanimous applause hailing "liberation."

Yet Marcuse was hardly unique, as University of Massachusetts Professor Paul Hollander, a Hungarian-born Holocaust survivor (who became a good friend shortly before his death), demonstrates in his important 1981 book *Political Pilgrims: Travels of Western Intellectuals to the Soviet Union, China and Cuba*. Instantly acclaimed, it was one of the first studies of Western leftist intellectuals who became mesmerized by communist/socialist regimes. Hollander describes Marcuse as "the main spokesman and theorist of the spiritual horrors of the West." Noting that his "critique of capitalism, often merges into a more general critique of modern industrial society," i.e., bourgeois liberalism, when Marcuse wanted to illustrate capitalism's "most evil and stultifying incarnation, his model was the United States."[19]

Marcuse had been a prominent figure in the Institute for Social Research, later known as the Frankfurt School of Critical Studies. Founded in 1923 with funds from Jewish leftist philanthropist Felix Weil, scholars in order to develop Marxist studies in Germany. After Hitler forced its closure in 1933, the Institute was welcomed at Columbia University. Before long, however, the Institute was cozying up to the USSR. One of its principal researchers, Franz L. Neumann, was recruited by the KGB in 1943.[20] By 1944, he would also be employed by the American Office of Security Services (OSS), for which he produced shrewdly misleading analyses of German political culture to Moscow's benefit.

Marcuse also joined the OSS as an analyst. Though he too had been a "Target of recruitment" by the KGB, according to entries in the notebooks of Alexander Vassiliev,[21] no evidence suggests that he ever became an actual spy. He didn't have to be. Actually, it was better that he be seen as nothing more than an academic. Marcuse did an excellent job in advancing an outlook deeply hostile to capitalism, which the young hip radicals relished. He and his colleagues from the Frankfurt School advocated precisely the kind of subversion the baby boomers were waiting for. The KGB could be proud of them, and probably was.[22]

Taking up the torch of the vanguard, Marcuse knew his audience, providing their raging hormones a ready outlet. They loved him for it, as I saw up close when witnessing one of his performances at the University of Chicago. To me, he sounded like some of my parents' old friends from Transylvania who used to kibitz over a game of rummy. I was disappointed that my otherwise smart undergraduate colleagues found him messianic. He seemed more like a shoe store salesman.

Marcuse advised promoting "a future better society" by using America's form of democracy to undermine it. If that "may require apparently undemocratic means," so be it. Sure, these

> would include the withdrawal of toleration of speech and assembly from groups and movements which promote aggressive policies, armament, chauvinism, discrimination on the grounds of race and religion, or which oppose the extension of public services, social security, medical care, etc. Moreover, the restoration of freedom of thought may necessitate new

> and rigid restrictions on teachings and practices in the educational institutions which, by their very methods and concepts, serve to enclose the mind within the established universe of discourse and behavior--thereby precluding a priori a rational evaluation of the alternatives.[23]

In 1965, such language was novel; it would take a few more decades before cancel culture became the norm. Unlike his post-modernist followers, whose gobbledygook (British philosopher Roger Scruton's perfect phrasing) served to camouflage their sinister anti-liberal intentions, Marcuse fully admitted justifying "cancellation of the liberal creed of free and equal discussion," which meant "intolerance against movements from the Right and toleration of movements from the Left." "Right" being defined, presumably, as "the liberal creed of free and equal discussion" which deserves "cancellation."

He warned his elite audience to resist having their minds "clouded by ideologies which serve the perpetuation of violence." But violence cannot be avoided when "[e]ven in the advanced centers of civilization violence actually prevails: it is practiced by the police, in the prisons and mental institutions, in the fight against racial minorities; it is carried, by the defenders of metropolitan freedom, into the backward countries. This violence indeed breeds violence." In plainer language: the system is rotten; it deserves to die. No one can oppose ending violence. But… completely?

He is careful to distinguish between two kinds of violence - progressive and regressive, good and bad, respectively. "There is a difference between revolutionary and reactionary violence, between violence practiced by the oppressed and by the oppressors. In terms of ethics, both forms of violence are inhuman and evil - but since when is history made in accordance with ethical standards?" History necessarily marches in the right direction: forward!

As always with progressivism, History thus comes to the normative rescue. When progress is at stake, ethical standards are redefined. "To start applying them at the point where the oppressed rebel against the oppressors, the have-nots against the haves[,] is serving the cause of actual violence by weakening the protest against it." If scruples against using violence stand in the way of History's march, so much the worse for scruples. To the barricades, comrades!

Undaunted by objections that radicals are elitists who offer "a dictatorship of intellectuals as an alternative" to the prevailing ethos, Marcuse is proud to plead guilty as charged. Here he appeals once again to the conflicted liberal J. S. Mill, who believed that "individual mental superiority" justifies "reckoning one person's opinion as equivalent to more than one" – meaning nothing less than "some mode of plural voting which may assign to education as such the degree of superior influence due to it, and sufficient as a counterpoise to the numerical weight of the least educated class."[24] So starkly undemocratic a suggestion, however, was not likely to appeal far beyond the campus.

Chances are that Marcuse might not have attracted quite so large a following, even among students, had it not been for his 1955 book *Eros and Civilization: A Philosophical Inquiry into Freud*, which argued that sexual drives cannot be satisfied within the psychological confines imposed by capitalist forms of social organization. Though it arrived at a time of post-war economic growth, anti-communism, and general middle-class contentment, the book became an instant bestseller.

Comfort tends to fade as restlessness sets in – and Americans are notoriously impatient. It didn't take long for the culture to veer left, in a heedlessly hedonistic direction. While still barely in middle school, baby boomers had already watched their older siblings swooning to Elvis, and Annette Funicello growing out of the Mickey Mouse Club into a well-fitting bathing suit. By the time their parents drove them to college, the kids were plenty ripe for Marcuse's "non-repressive mode of existence," which included a lot more than staying out beyond the girls' dorm's far-too-early curfew time. I recall watching their sensuous gyrations on "American Bandstand," and remembered how in communist Romania, when parties were organized in school on Christmas Eve - to insure no one attended church which was anyhow illegal - boys and girls were separated if they approached closer than two inches. (The gyrations won my vote, hands down.)

Eros had taken over from stern Apollo. Applying psychology to political theory, Marcuse repurposed Sigmund Freud's identification of civilization with repression, intent on radicalizing the young. Offering them "the vision of a non-repressive culture…[amounting] to a "civilized morality,"[25] he believed that America is the ideal flagship, though not until "a subversion of culture..., *after* culture [that is, counterculture] had done its work and created the mankind and the world that could be free." Most Americans having achieved a high level of prosperity, it was time to follow History on its preordained march. That doesn't mean stopping it in its tracks. On the contrary, it meant abandoning the rat race that enslaves corporate culture, wrest free and fly. History's onward course is naturally "predicated not upon the arrest, but upon the liberation, of progress." We are already rich enough; it is time to be truly "free." Morality itself has to be reexamined, redefined, reconsidered – indeed, if need be, abandoned for something still "higher."

Marcuse wrote that mankind should and "would ask again what is good and what is evil." Deftly turning *Genesis* on its head, he had still another proposition up his learned sleeve. That it bordered on the preposterous only increased its shock-value. "If the guilt accumulated in the civilized domination of man by man can ever be redeemed by freedom, then the "original sin" must be committed again." Actually, the idea was not new; in fact, it belonged to Henrich von Kleist, whom he duly quotes: "We must again eat from the tree of knowledge in order to fall back into the state of innocence."[26] Did that mean knocking at Eden's door to ask for a second helping? If that was a joke, it wasn't very good.

It wasn't, exactly – or at least, not entirely. Kleist's *Ueber das Marionettentheater* had been published in 1810 as a whimsical exploration of personal liberation. He had thought it reasonable to wonder whether one might attain the infinite self-consciousness of the divinity, in effect becoming godlike, by means of metaphorically tasting the fruit of the Tree of Knowledge all over again. That would mean first returning the human self to its paradisal innocence – essentially, attaining either a pre-moral or an amoral consciousness.[27] Coming three decades before Karl Marx's materialist abandonment of traditional morality in favor of progress and history, Kleist's bizarre fantasy was later echoed by Friedrich Nietzsche, who in 1886 called for transcending "beyond good and evil." Marcuse was next in line, perhaps sensing a headline-grabber.

In advocating abandoning the moral hang-ups that were now hampering progress and preventing the emergence of "a new stage of civilization," Marcuse proscribed the same kind of humanist utopia imagined by Kleist and then Marx, whose youthful musings were captured in his early manuscripts. True, that "might mean the subversion of the traditional culture, intellectual as well as material, including the liberation of instinctual needs and satisfactions which have hitherto remained tabooed or repressed,"[28] argued Marcuse.

No wonder students found the old but hip professor so irresistible. The critic Paul Berman explains:

> Marcuse, when he considered the depths of capitalist alienation, could only imagine one possibility [for redemption], which was for privileged young people to follow their own deep Freudian instincts instead of the social conventions – and in that way create zones free of psychological repression. A few zones like that might stimulate the larger population to rebel against the general repression. That was Marcuse's hope. It was a theory of countercultural revolution.[29]

It worked: a sort of revolution did happen. But was it liberal in any way? Obviously not in the classical sense. Appropriately forward-looking, its perpetrators called themselves "the New Left." Marcuse himself had described them mostly in negative terms as "not orthodox Marxist or socialist," and not "defined by class at all." Membership consisted "of intellectuals, of groups of the civil-rights movement and of the youth, especially the radical elements of the youth, which at first glance do not appear political at all, namely the hippies."[30] But only at first glance. Marcuse considered them all very political indeed. In fact, he declared the New Left to be "the only hope we have" for reaching the next historical stage.

The New Left

> *"The Red Terror is the terror that 'idealistic Communists' (like our parents) and 'anti-Stalinist Leftists' (like ourselves) have helped to spread around the world. You and I and our parents were totalitarians in democratic America. The democratic fact of America prevented us from committing the atrocities willed by our faith."*
>
> **- David Horowitz and Peter Collier, *Destructive Generation* (1989)**

The task of the New Left, wrote Marcuse, was "to prepare itself and the others… for the time when the aggravating conflicts of corporate capitalism dissolve its repressive cohesion and open the space where the real work for libertarian socialism can begin." He then declared that "libertarian socialism has always been the integral concept of socialism, but only too easily repressed and suppressed."[31] While confusion is unavoidable when resorting to oxymorons, words are essential weapons for change. "The Left must find the adequate means of breaking the conformist and corrupted universe of political language and political behavior."[32] Redefine away, comrades.

The paradox-obsessed Marcuse specialized in blending opposites, juxtaposing thesis and antithesis and dispensing with synthesis in a dialectic whose shock value was worth the price of incoherence. Wasn't the very success of capitalism an obvious proof of its failure? In an interview published by *The New Left Review* in 1967, on "The Question of Revolution," Marcuse declared that "[n]either the ideological veil of pluralist democracy nor the material veil of extravagant productivity alters the fact that in the realm of advanced capitalism the fate of man is determined by the aggressive and expansive apparatus of exploitation and the policies interwoven with it."[33]

A year later, in 1968, perhaps emboldened by the success of his devotees, Marcuse spelled out his political philosophy with even greater candor in a Postscript to the book *A Critique of Pure Tolerance* that had included his essay on "Repressive Tolerance." Marcuse answered critics who had objected to his advocacy of "restraining the liberty of the Right" by clarifying that no, he did not favor

> discrimination that would also be applied to movements opposing the extension of social legislation to the poor, weak, disabled. As that such a policy would do away with the sacred liberalistic principle of equality for "the other side," I maintain that there are issues where either there is no "other side" in any more than a formalistic sense, or where "the other side" is demonstrably "regressive" and impedes possible improvement of the human condition. To tolerate propaganda for inhumanity vitiates the goals not only of liberalism but of every progressive political philosophy.[34]

That's all rhetorical because of course lines have only one side. Thus the only question is whether to go forward or backward. Good or bad, progressive or reactionary.

If liberalism means pluralist democracy, marked by "extravagant productivity," it amounts to little more than the stealthy veil of "advanced capitalism," which is necessarily exploitative. Marcuse's was not your parents' - let alone your grandparents' – soft leftism of raising workers' wages and providing social services to the poor. Addressing the World Jewish Congress in Geneva in 1968, Avraham Schanker, a leader of Americans for Progressive Israel,[35] reflected: "By its very name, the New Left differentiates and separates itself from the 'Old' Left. The New Left stated quite bluntly that the 'Old' Left had failed. The ideological parties were not providing the answers."

Hopes that the young and hip President John F. Kennedy might have inaugurated a new, more radical ethos were dashed early on by his bungled attempt to topple Cuban dictator Fidel Castro. What upset the radicals was not the bungling per se but the operation itself, which they "considered an attempted repression of the Cuban revolution ... [and thus] another example of the failure of liberalism." So arose "the phenomenon we call the New Left – an amalgam of ideas, opinions and cultural style which reflected the failure of liberalism as well as the failure of the traditional ideological Left to provide answers to the great problems of the day."[36]

What Marcuse offered this hard-core super-ideological New Left, however, was not so much new ideals as new justifications for rejecting the old ones, repudiating even the older new liberalism of the progressives, many of whom had joined FDR, then JFK, and now President Lyndon Johnson. Marcuse warned the youngsters to use language strategically. Today we might consider it cynical, but at the time, many young utopianists genuinely harbored illusions of global peace-and-love.

They loved Marcuse's vision of an alternative world where "men who could speak a different language, have different gestures, follow different impulses; men and women who have developed an instinctual barrier against cruelty, brutality, and ugliness."[37] During the Sixties, recalls the German Lutheran theologian Oswald Bayer, Marcuse

> was on everyone's lips; in fact, he was not only a popular leader but almost a cult figure, because he was virtually without peer in the way in which he was able to orient and represent, conceptually as well as rhetorically, the general emancipation of society, which was the object of people's hopes and strivings. He did this by somehow combining the

> two main streams of influence, Marxism and psycho analysis, into a single package, which was expected to be nothing less than the solution of the world's problems.[38]

Marcuse knew his audience and provided what it wanted. Who knows what he genuinely felt. Was Belfast University professor Vincent Gheogegan right to believe that reading Marx's early manuscripts, previously unpublished, immediately after they appeared nearly a century later, in 1932, "was a pivotal moment for [Marcuse's] theoretical development"[39]? Among those manuscripts was "On the Jewish Question." What did Marcuse really think of it? Though he had celebrated his bar mitzvah, Marcuse's family was assimilated. Moreover, he had been a student of the Nazi-sympathizer Martin Heidegger. Gheogegan notes that Marcuse admired Marx's analysis of the complex dialectic of freedom and unfreedom in liberal capitalism described in the essay, and specifically commended the infamous work's "religious dimension." But what aspect of that dimension? Its boundless hatred of all religion, Judaism above all?

Perhaps Marcuse shared Marx's vision of a new human being, of a new morality without any categorical constraints, those "don'ts" of the biblical commandments. In a speech delivered at a forum called "Radical Perspectives: 1969" held in New York on December 5, 1968, Marcuse told an audience that included the top leadership of the New Left: "[O]ur goals, our values, our own and new morality, our own morality, must be visible already in our actions. The new human beings who we want to help to create—we must already strive to be these human beings right here and now."[40] The human beings Marcuse was addressing, however, were mostly interested in rejecting morality altogether. They loved being New and Left. So was a label born, and a movement.

Middle- and upper-class college students, eager to act out their fantasies, inebriated with self-importance, were easily seduced by Marxists like Herbert Marcuse – European-born, sophisticated prophets of liberation. A master of academic language, who sounded profound through paradox and contradiction, the affable old philosopher validated the youngsters' primeval urge to not conform, to break rules, and start something completely different. The kids were hell bent on being radical. Liberalism was for suckers.

In *Why are Jews Liberal?* Norman Podhoretz recalls how

> in those days a distinction was still being drawn between liberalism and radicalism. Unlike the Communists in their popular-front phase of the '30s, the radicals of the '60s (myself included to a large extent) did not present themselves as "liberals in a hurry." On the contrary: they identified liberalism with the "establishment" they were trying to topple and which they blamed for everything they believed had gone wrong with America.[41]

The radicals' mantra in the '60s, the trifecta of "war, racism, and poverty," blamed it all on the establishment. As the Sixties wore on, however, their violent hatred of America (spelled "Amerika" to reflect their belief in its affinity with Nazi Germany) led to an increasingly dangerous "conviction that nothing short of a revolution could eradicate the evils that were now seen not as deviations from the country's ideals but as manifestations of its very essence." Within a few years, recalls Podhoretz, "I and a number of other intellectuals on the Left were finding ourselves increasingly repelled by this development."[42]

But they represented only a small minority. The community was diverging. While "establishment liberals like those in the AJC [American Jewish Committee] were breaking ranks with the Left on the nature and quality of American society, establishment liberals were moving in the opposite direction – toward the formation of what was in effect a new and updated Popular Front. …[T]he liberal label was being applied to and accepted by radicals who … had previously scorned it."[43] So would radicalism become camouflaged, through linguistic sleight-of-hand, under the resilient, yet increasingly vague, label of liberalism. Though Marcuse had condemned it as thinly veiled capitalism, the New Left took a page from the Progressive playbook to use it for subterfuge.

At the time, Podhoretz was still a self-described intellectual of the left. But the distance he had to travel after abandoning Marxism was not quite as long as that of Peter Collier and David Horowitz. The two leading radicals had been close to the Black Panther Party when it was hailed by New Left leaders as "the vanguard of the revolution." Having founded and edited the movement's magazine *Ramparts,* Collier and Horowitz were radical royalty. As insiders, intimates of Bill Ayers, Bernardine (née Ohrnstein) and other leaders of the Weather Underground (Weathermen), a violent offshoot of Students for a Democratic Society (SDS), the two became privy to what really happened out of the limelight. And it wasn't pretty: drugs, cruelty, even murder. It was harder and harder to ignore; their eyes gradually opened. Once admirers of counterculture heroes Huey Newton and Eldridge Cleaver, the pair became increasingly disenchanted and finally, horrified. By the early to mid-1980s, they became, as Horowitz put it, freed "from the chains of an Idea."

It had been extremely difficult to abandon: "Life without the Idea of the socialist future felt to me like life without meaning," writes Horowitz. He understood then in what sense the antisemitic "Marx was a rabbi after all. The revolutionary Idea is a religious consolation for earthly defeat. … A passage home."[44] He recalls how his own father had travelled along a strangely similar path. As the only male child of poor immigrants who fled Russia in 1905 during the pogroms, speaking no English, he had been nearly as fearful of the strange new world as of the old one he had left behind. For years he was still adrift. And then, as he turned thirty, he suddenly decided to join the Communist Party (CPUSA). Only then, writes David Horowitz, did he feel he had at last "achieved what his own father had not, his self-esteem as a man." One cannot live without a higher aim.

But how could a Russian-Jewish immigrant gain self-esteem by adopting an ideology that identified his religion with money-worship and "capitalism" - the very system that provided a haven for the persecuted, particularly Jews, in America? If he felt the inconsistency, he didn't let on. He wouldn't tell his own son about the CPUSA membership for three decades. Nor did any of his friends breathe a word of it even at his funeral: "It was like a secret they all were keeping from themselves."[45] The mystery died with him. Perhaps there was no solving it.

Similarly mysterious was the story of another descendant of Russian (actually, Ukrainian) Jews, whose father had owned a hair salon: Leonard Bernstein. The world-renowned genius, whose magnificent operetta *West Side Story* would forever change modern music and catapult American entertainment to stratospheric heights, Bernstein was also a strong supporter of anti-American radicalism. After the great conductor-composer's death in 2008 at age 72, the *Social Activist* traced Bernstein's lifelong commitment to radicalism "as early as 1939, his last year at Harvard when he organized a defiant production of Marc Blitzstein's radical and recently banned opera *The Cradle Will Rock*, which dramatized the struggle of workers to resist corruption and corporate greed."[46]

As his fame grew, so did his ability to influence the intelligentsia and the fashion-conscious super-rich, whose money and power could and did shift the ideological winds. He would reach the top of the social and cultural pyramid. Before long, Bernstein became part of a growing circle of celebrities, sharing their complex mix of insecurity, intellectual myopia, and post-traumatic-disordered groupthink. But they were in for a surprise when, on June 8, 1970, *New York Magazine* published an article titled "Radical Chic: That Party at Lenny's," which revealed goings-on at one of those plush fundraisers, becoming an instant sensation. The super-rich West Enders' fatuous admiration for the haughty "revolutionaries" was undiminished by the latter's nonchalantly open contempt for greedy capitalists like them. Brazenly asking for money, they seemed to be doing the groveling fat-cats a favor. The spectacle was captured with razor-sharp irony by a literary genius of humble background: Thomas Wolfe. He unveiled and dissected the clash of these two decadent cultures - one post- and the other under-civilized - using unadorned, stark, steely prose. His exposés were funny – or rather would have been, had the reality not been quite so pathetic.

Wolfe begins the article by setting it in context, noting first the powerful effect of the new industry which, by the late Sixties, had taken over New York. That industry was communications. The rapid proliferation of television channels and radio, alongside newspapers and magazines, allowed many upstarts to gain eminence in the media. These were mostly Jews, but also Catholics like himself. Simultaneously changing was how the elite was being spotlighted. No longer mere venues of free publicity for *noblesse oblige* philanthropic gestures by condescending plutocrats, syndicated columns in newspapers across the country alongside magazines like *New York Magazine* could provide the occasional iconoclastic master of the writer's scalpel a chance to dissect some hard truths in witty prose.

It was perfect for Tom Wolfe, who took the opportunity and ran with it. This, for example, is how he describes the liberalism of his time as it evolved with the changing social landscape:

> Among the new socialites of the 1960s, especially those from the one-time "minorities," this old social urge to do well by doing good, as it says in the song, has taken on a more specific political direction. This has often been true of Jewish socialites and culturati, although it has by no means been confined to them. Politically, Jews had been unique among the groups that came to New York in great migrations of the late nineteenth and early twentieth centuries. Many such groups, of course, were left or liberal during the first generation, but as families began to achieve wealth, success, or simply, security, they tended to grow more and more conservative in philosophy.[47]

Jews, as usual defying expectations, "have tended to remain faithful to their original liberal-left world-view." For it had become, as Tevye sang in the made-for-Broadway take on Shalom Aleichem's bitter-sweet masterpiece, nothing less than their post-shtetl *Traditioooon.*

Three decades after graduating from Harvard in 1939, Leonard Bernstein was still a radical. Eager to emulate his posh friends among the culturati - notably John Simon of Random House, Richard Baron the publisher, Sidney Lumet the director and his writer-wife Gail, among others – Bernstein and his wife decided to virtue-signal by hosting a fundraiser for the gang of lives in their plush East Side home. It was this event that "Radical Chic" described in all its decadent absurdity.

The occasion was prompted by the Panthers' need for money, especially after their recent crime spree. Twenty-one of them had been arrested and charged with conspiracy to kill several police officers and destroy a number of buildings - including four police stations, five department stores, and the Bronx Botanical Gardens. Though the judge had released eight of the hooligans, he set bail for the remaining thirteen at $100,000 each. This was the hefty sum that Lenny (Bernstein) and his well-heeled friends were seeking to raise at their elegant soirees.

Wolfe's description of the motley crew surrounding the expensive *hors d'oevres* at the Bernsteins provides a deliciously incongruous background to the radically chic denunciations of liberal-capitalist-racist-evil Amerika by Don Cox, the Black Panthers' Field Marshal. "We think that this country is going more and more toward fascism to oppress those people who have the will to fight back," pronounces Cox. To which Lenny obligingly responds: "I agree with you one hundred percent!" (Fascism? Seriously?)

The Panthers' chief counsel, Gerald Lefcourt, then explains that his clients "are firmly convinced that there can be no change unless the system is changed. Less than five percent of the people of this country have ninety percent of the wealth, and ten percent of them have most of the ninety percent. The mass of the people by following the system can never make changes, and there is no use continuing to tell people about constitutional guarantees, either."[48] Ergo, they have to resort to violence - or, as they prefer to call it (and mean it), Revolution. No pushback from the embarrassed members of the .0001 percent shifting uncomfortably in their super-expensive chairs.

The New York Times's reporter in their midst duly covered the party, having been invited for that purpose. But what the hosts had not counted on was that news could now reach far beyond the culture capital thanks to a new practice: sending out articles through newswire across the country. Widespread negative reaction from places far removed from the Big Apple prompted the *Times* to issue an editorial on the following day. Seeking to distance itself from the fiasco, the "newspaper of record" blasted the party as "a sort of elegant slumming," which "might be dismissed as guilt-relieving fun spiked with social consciousness, except for its impact on those blacks and whites seriously working for complete equality and social justice." The coup de grace fell next: "It mocked the memory of Martin Luther King Jr., whose birthday was solemnly observed throughout the nation yesterday."[49] That really hurt.

But the *Times* had it exactly right: Reverend MLK had firmly opposed the Black Power approach to civil rights injustice. His liberalism was egalitarian in the traditional sense, as was the case with a majority of Jews. When Black Power proved incorrigibly antisemitic, supporters of MLK - notably ordinary Jews (outside the very wealthy and an assortment of supercilious intellectuals) - were incredulous. Yet that was only one symptom of a deeper malaise. The putatively upgraded liberalism was taking on a new, dangerous path all around the world. In retrospect, writes

Paul Berman, the signs were clear: "Almost everywhere the movements began by promising to construct a new kind of democratic or libertarian socialism." (That oxymoron again.) "And almost everywhere (except in the Communist world, where the student movements followed a path all their own), the democratic and libertarian aspects dropped away."[50] The United States, as usual, was in the forefront, endowed with a disproportionate number of fellow travelers.

Throughout the Sixties, students had been rejecting not only the so-called right-wing but even the social-democratic new (meaning, progressive) liberals. In 1961, for example, in a "Letter to the New (Young) Left," student activist Tom Hayden wrote approvingly of Marx's early writings - which included, of course, "On the Jewish Question." The future SDS leader (later elected to the California General Assembly and the Senate, also known as Mr. Jane Fonda) scorned the "inhibiting, dangerous conservative temperament behind the façade of liberal realism which is so current."[51] He accused "false liberals" of abandoning "the great optimistic tradition of liberalism."

No establishment liberals (meaning social-democratic progressives), the radicals blamed JFK's brain trust for the Vietnam War, which fellow-Democrat Lyndon Johnson had by then disastrously escalated. Unbeknownst to them, they had indeed been correct, but for the wrong reasons.[52] To them, the war was pure evil, Amerikan colonialism, fueled by greed, murderous, imperialist. The radicals' hatred of their own government was unprecedented in the nation's history. The war provided a convenient catalyst for a long-simmering visceral disenchantment with the very project of Constitutional liberalism, which had begun half a century earlier. But that was little more than a pretext. As the brilliant cultural critic Roger Kimball, currently editor of *Encounter Books*, observes: "More than any other event, it legitimated anti-Americanism and helped insinuate radical feeling into the mainstream of cultural life.... [In sum,] the war helped to 'normalize' a spectrum of radical sentiments."[53]

Even at that time, novelist Susan Sontag had candidly admitted that "Vietnam offered the key to a systematic criticism of America."[54] Yippie[55] leader Jerry Rubin concurred: "If there had been no Vietnam, we would have invented one. If the Vietnam war ends, we will find another war."[56]

So did Richard Barnet and Marcus Raskin, Founders of the radical Institute for Policy Studies: "The Indochina War is not the chief cause of the American crisis but a symptom of that crisis… a visible manifestation of a systemic disorder."[57] (Marcus's son Jamie Raskin is now my congressman from Montgomery County, Maryland. And no, I didn't vote for him.)

Sontag and her fellow leftists were not talking about any old form of criticism, which every human enterprise not only should but must permit to function optimally. It wasn't premised on America's guiding principle that we are all created equal, or more precisely, equally unequal, certainly equal before the law – an ideal that most Framers embraced even if they knew it couldn't be fully implemented at the outset. Though still far from being reached today, it served as a lodestar then and now. Meanwhile, the web of checks and balances constructed by the Constitution is proof that the nation's lofty ideal is firmly rooted in the hard reality of flawed human nature, which in turn is capable of both great evil and great good, in roughly equal measure.

Instead, the radicals proposed to embark on a wholesale criticism, if not a revamping, of America's system of government. Far from merely opposing the current leadership, or some particular segment of American society, they rejected *Amerika* itself.

The Even Newer Left

"*The moral revolution consists in a demand for a total transformation – a transformation from a totality of undifferentiated evil to a totality of undifferentiated perfection.*"

– Edward Shils (1969)

"*One has to belong to the intelligentsia to believe things like that: no ordinary man could be such a fool.*"

– George Orwell, "*Notes on Nationalism*" (1945)

Novelist, filmmaker, teacher, political activist, essayist Susan Sontag and her husband, University of Chicago Professor David Rieff, were the quintessential power couple. In 1955, they hosted Herbert Marcuse in their home while Marcuse worked on his *Eros and Civilization.* She later conducted research for Rieff's book *Freud: The Mind of the Moralist,* published in 1959. All of which likely contributed to her lifelong interest in pornography and distaste for capitalism. Sontag's writing amounted to a kind of manifesto for the post-liberal anti-liberalism and anti-bourgeois hedonism typical of the love-and-peace crowd.

In her aptly titled essay, "The Pornographic Imagination," published in 1967, Sontag denounces

> the traumatic failure of capitalist society to provide authentic outlets for the perennial human flair for high-temperature visionary obsession [read: pornography], to satisfy the appetite for exalted self-transcending modes of concentration and seriousness.[58]

Whereupon she swoons over pornography's "peculiar access to some truth," leading Roger Kimball to declare the entire essay quite simply "the perfect camp gesture: for if camp aims to dethrone the serious" it is also, by her own admission, 'deadly serious' about the demotic and the trivial."[59] Kimball's devastating opinion of Sontag extends to the decadent new ideology of the *avant garde* as a whole: "Sontag has been an emissary of trivialization, deploying the tools of humanism to sabotage the humanistic enterprise" and with it, liberalism itself.

If only she had stuck to vapid, low-content quasi-cultural commentary; instead, she dabbled in politics, visiting Cuba and North Vietnam in 1968, China in 1973, and other oases of nonfreedom, predictably displaying the same embarrassing moral vacuity. It was an accomplishment of sorts, observes Kimball: "Few people have managed to combine naïve idealization of foreign tyranny with violent hatred of their own country to such deplorable effect."[60] Thereafter, the New Left and its Newer Leftist successors would be on the side of whoever opposed the United States. Unfortunately, however, what started in the academy did not stay in the academy.

Did Susan Sontag ever have second thoughts as did fellow-radicals Collier and Horowitz? Not unless she had any that were strong enough to change. Her "deadly seriousness" (when not about pornography) was utterly unserious, even if she did confess a decade later to having long sensed the fundamentally "fascist cultural impulse" at the core of the protest movement. "Some of the activities of the New Left," she told a *Rolling Stone* interviewer in 1979, "were very far from democratic socialism [sic] and were deeply anti-intellectual, which I think of as part of the fascist impulse. They were also anticultural and full of resentment and brutality, reflecting a kind of nihilism." But she hastened to add: "Of course, our society is based on nihilism: television is nihilism."[61] She could never quite stoop to praising the United States; it would cramp her style.

Subsequent events have since shown that all that marching and support for communism led to the slaughter of millions, the dreams of those pampered, stoned, and aimless flower children thus proving hallucinatory. Sontag concedes "that everything that was hoped for and attempted in the Sixties basically hasn't worked and couldn't work out." This was, however, little more than half an admission. For next she adds: at least, it couldn't *at the time*. "But who says it won't work?" Perhaps it will, sometime in that ever-elusive future, pushed further and further up the infinite ladder by millenarian utopianists. Having once embraced an ideology, it's hard to let go.

As to radicals who mainly wanted to do "their thing" (read: bumming), she is nonjudgmental. "Who says there's something wrong with people dropping out?" In the end, she is magnanimously tolerant of deviant behavior. As the saying goes, she believed in letting it all hang out.

> We have to allow not only for marginal people and states of consciousness, but also for the unusual or the deviant. I'm all for deviants. There's no reason for people on this planet to live at a subsistence level. Instead of becoming more and more bureaucratic, standardized, oppressive and authoritarian, why don't we allow more and more people to be free?

"No reason for people on this planet to live at a subsistence level" seems to confirm her next generalization, that "Americans tend to think that everything is possible, and that's something I like a lot about them [*laughing*]. I know I'm very American, in that respect, because I like to think I have as many options as possible." She may well like to think that - don't we all. But claiming that "no reason" exists for people living "at a subsistence level" **anywhere** is embarrassingly silly even for an ostentatiously naïve American writer.

Rather more realistically idealist was my fellow-University-of-Chicago-alumnus Saul Alinsky. His extensive work with community organizers throughout the Sixties on behalf of Blacks, seeking to end poverty and political disempowerment, earned him the respect of many Democrats. A shrewd activist who taught revolutionary leftists how to win, he was a complex figure. His reasons for not joining the Communist Party are tinged with healthy skepticism:

> I've never been sure I'm right but also I'm also [sic] sure nobody else has this thing called truth. I hate dogma. People who believed they owned the truth have been responsible for the most terrible things that have happened in our world, whether they were Communist purges or the Spanish Inquisition or the Salem witch hunts.[62]

Basically, he didn't like communists because he found them "doctrinaire" and "rigid." Alinsky "knew that in this kooked-up [sic] irrational world, you really have to have a sense of humor to survive. And doctrinaire people have no humor."[63] They might win, but not persuade. It is unlikely that the new generation, self-righteous and immature, understood him. He may have sensed that.

By the time his how-to manual Revolution-for-Dummies, *Rules for Radicals*, appeared in 1971, the disconnect between the old and the young had become entrenched. "To the young the world seems insane and falling apart,"[64] wrote Alinsky, but don't forget that the older generation, "whose members are no less confused," also ask legitimate questions:

> "What do you want? What do you mean when you say 'I want to do my thing.' What the hell is your thing? You say you want a better world. Like what? And don't tell me a world of peace and love and all the rest of that stuff because people are people, as you will find out when you get older – I'm sorry, I didn't mean to say anything about 'when you get older.'"

Doing one's thing, as Sontag observed, is for the marginalized. It sparks neither change, reform, nor anything else. The clueless narcissist can at best disrupt, at worst destroy, but never improve.

To his credit, Alinsky does not demonize. He does not blame parents for wanting answers from their kids, nor the young for not knowing even what the questions are. But if any among them be truly "committed to the fight, committed to life," they must "remember we are talking about revolution, not revelation."[65] And that means starting where the world is, as it is. Only then can it be changed "to what we think it should be." To bring on a cultural change, the committed radical must "agitate, create disenchantment and discontent with the current values, to produce, if not a passion for change, at least a passive, affirmative, non-challenging climate."[66]

Alinsky cites President John Adams's observation in a letter penned late in life, in 1818, that the American "Revolution was effected before the war commenced." For it was "in the hearts and minds of the people," through painstaking, relentless, sophisticated efforts expended by countless of his fellow Founders, notably his irascible but brilliant second cousin, Samuel Adams.[67] Ultimately, wrote Adams, "the radical change in the principles, opinions, sentiments and affections of the people was the real American Revolution."[68] It was the spirit, not merely the letter, that mattered. Revising both Lenin and Hitler, Alinsky declares: "A revolution without a prior reformation would collapse or become a totalitarian tyranny." He saw his task as reformatory. Assuming, of course, that his apprentices were actually reformable.

Painting him as a duplicitous radical has become *de rigeur* among conservatives understandably miffed at his easily, commonly, and consistently misunderstood – to say nothing of nefariously applied – handbook for conducting effective political warfare. Smacking of Machiavellian politics, it is admittedly difficult to resist reading *Rules for Radicals* in any way other than cynically. But this is not entirely fair to Alinsky, whose own work on behalf of disadvantaged Blacks living in the heart of Chicago's South Side (whose terrible squalor I have glimpsed, when living in close proximity), stands testimony to his sincere desire to help them change their own lives.

He also recognized the tendency of community leaders to become coopted by the Establishment, too eager to get "their piece of the economic pie." Not all shared his idealism. He also disapproved of the myopia displayed by impatient young radicals rioting in Chicago during the 1968 Democratic Party convention. Met with police brutality and tear gas, they had been ready to blow things up, and played up to the cameras. But what did that accomplish? His advice: "Go home, organize, build power, and at the next convention, *you be the delegates.*"[69]

Though most radicals had no use for such advice, one did – and she would make history. In 1969, Alinsky's keen eye for talent spotted a bright Wellesley College senior who was looking for a thesis topic, a job, and a career path. Her name was Hillary D. Rodham. Alinsky had hit the jackpot – and so had Hillary.

She started her honors thesis analyzing his ideas by highlighting the surprising simplicity and familiarity of their message, its extremism deftly camouflaged:

> [M]uch of what Alinsky professes does not sound "radical." His are the words used in your schools and churches, by our parents and their friends, by our peers. The difference is that Alinsky really believes in them and recognizes the necessity of changing the present structures of our lives in order to realize them.[70]

"Changing the present structure" - read: revolution. Not immediately, and not violently – at least not at first. Accordingly, Hillary's definition of a radical as someone "not interested in ameliorating the symptoms of decay but in drastically altering the causes of societal conditions," might not seem to apply to Alinsky. The operative word here is "drastically altering," as opposed to "ameliorating" – corresponding to the divergent wings of progressive, modern liberalism. For Alinksy, she explains, "the non-radical means [i.e., tactics] involve the traditional quest for power to change existing situations. ... The question is how one acquires power, and Alinsky's answer is through organization." But eventually, the change *must* be drastic. It must lead to something new and fresh, healthy and good, rather than merely ameliorating what is intrinsically flawed. The ultimate goal is eradication.

At bottom, the real conundrum regarding power is not *whether* to be or not to be acquired, but *how*. Everyone wants it, needs it, craves it, but like sex, power must be sought with subtlety, and often stealth. (My analogy, not hers.) Especially mindful of "the popular distrust of amassing power" in this self-righteous New World settled by insufferable Puritans with their insufferable covenants, Alinsky, writes Hillary, "cautions against allowing our tongues to trap our minds." She cites from his *Rules*:

"We have become involved in bypaths of confusion or semantics.... The word 'power' has through time acquired overtones of sinister corrupt evil, unhealthy immoral Machiavellianism, and a general phantasmagoria of the nether regions."[71] That's a shame.

Semantics may be inescapable, but tongues should not "trap our minds," as she puts it, and – to change metaphors - tie our thoughts in knots. To avoid confusion, of others as much as of ourselves, what we say and what we think should be carefully calibrated. Once a particular target is selected for maximum effectiveness, words must be chosen with caution, for they will have disparate impact depending on the experiences and make-up of the particular target audience. Some people are ready to accept that fighting for power by any means, including open conflict, is inescapable and legitimate, while others need to be coaxed more gingerly. The eventual goal, empowerment of the "have-nots," serves to justify whatever means prove necessary to achieve it.

Reflecting on Alinsky's relationship to progressive liberalism as applied in the War on Poverty, she concludes: "That he greatly influenced the legislation seems evident. That he despises the effects of that legislation is undeniable." She concedes that he left little room for equivocation when he labelled the entire effort a "prize piece of political pornography… a huge political pork barrel, and a feeding trough for the welfare industry, surrounded by sanctimonious, hypocritical, phony, moralistic."

Nor did he stop at expletives, citing specifics. In his 1965 speech,[72] he observed that most city halls, acting through committees composed of the party faithful, controlled the local antipoverty funds which were frequently used to stifle independent action in the name of "community consensus." If programs did bypass city hall, the officials would disown them in order to "take themselves off the hook." He balked at the Poverty War's "vast network of sergeants drawing general's pay," contemptuous of those who didn't have the stuff for true leadership. But was his approach ultimately any better?

Many of those he criticized fought back, deprecating Alinsky's own organizing efforts, particularly The Woodlawn Organization (TWO). Philip M. Hauser, chairman of the University of Chicago's Sociology

Department, for example, objected to "[t]he methods by which Alinsky organized TWO," believing that they may actually have "delayed the attaining of Woodlawn's true objectives." So too did the activist social psychologist Frank Reissman, who speculated, notes Hillary, that "the Alinsky model's emphasis on local issues and goals determined locally diverts energies from wider or coalition organizing," deploring the negligible rise in local community participation.

Both critics considered Alinsky's methods, however well-intentioned, insufficiently effective in practice. Reissman in particular rejected his "opposition to large programs, broad goals, and ideology [which] confuses even those who participate in the local organizations, because they find no context for their actions." Reissman's solution: the "organizer-strategist-intellectual" who is able to "provide the connections, the larger view that will lead to the development of a movement." Translation: the vanguard must take a far more pro-active role, and not hesitate to use all available means to achieve the "true objectives" that elude the less enlightened.

Hillary came to the same conclusion, and it appears that so too, eventually, did Alinsky. For she mentions that his original belief, that the poor can translate apathy into power and then use it responsibly, has only "in some cases, proven true. In others, the transition has been dysfunctional either for the community or for the cause of radical change." Especially in lower-class areas, he admitted that his model often became "an almost bootstrap formula which is too conservative for our present situation." Too conservative? She clarifies: "[L]ocal organizations can at best create new levels of harmony among its members and secure a few material gains. It is not oriented toward harmonizing competing metropolitan interests in a concert of governmental restructuring."

But poverty is only one – albeit the most basic – problem. There is no shortage of grievances, reflects Hillary. "[T]here is no lack of issues[. W]hat is missing are politically sophisticated organizers." To fill that gap, Alinsky founded a school, which he called the Industrial Areas Foundation Training Institute. Based in Chicago, it garnered support from the Midas Corporation. Three years before his death, Alinsky described IAF's vision in his private conversation with Hillary: "[H]is trainees might be 'transmitters' digesting, communicating, and acting on information they receive. Logistically, there might be a cadre of organizers in a given area working on a cluster of issues maintaining close touch with another cadre whose cluster need not be similar. What is similar throughout the network is the goal of radicalization."

What she took away from him, however, was not so much the goal as the means: a trained transmitter, she would digest, communicate, and act on information she at first received then later initiated. She would become a highly sophisticated political organizer.

Though ostentatiously manipulative, Alinsky was not wholly cynical. At least he had not been so initially. Increasingly disillusioned as he aged, it may well be that he never completely abandoned the idealistic radicalism of his youth. Postponing the Revolution, working "within the system," was for him a necessary, and hopefully temporary, evil. Not so for his most successful pupil Hillary Rodham, who showed little sign of having thought it temporary, let alone evil.

As she notes in her 1969 dissertation, "[t]he Depression demonstrated the feasibility of federally controlled planning, and a massive war effort convinced us of its necessity." What she regrets is that "[n]ow we are no longer so convinced." Given that federal control worked, what's all this rush back to local control? It should be obvious: "Decentralization and democracy are not synonymous as those who use the words interchangeably would have us believe."[73] Centralization, of course, means power on a large scale. It means control.

Incidentally, it can also prove lucrative.

Chapter VIII:

Statist "Liberalism"

Equality as Equity

"'Equality,' 'liberty,' - what precisely do these words from the Declaration of Independence mean?... Are equality and liberty consistent with one another, or are they in conflict?"

- Milton and Rose Friedman, *Free to Choose* (1980)

"[I]t is necessary to begin where the world is if we are going to change it into what we believe it should be. That means working within the system."

- Saul Alinsky, *Rules for Radicals* (1971)

Hilary understood that short of revolution, redistribution was the only practical means to pursue inequality. For it to work on a national scale, that meant central government intervention. Those who preferred allowing individuals discretion to influence their local communities directly, rather than let Washington decide, would "have us believe" that federally controlled planning isn't working, dismissing even such overwhelming evidence as "a massive war effort [which] convinced us of its necessity." This is like saying that since central control over the economy works in wartime, it must be best in peacetime as well. Then should a doctor prescribe the same regimen during the course of an illness as in a state of health?

Besides, what happened to democracy from below? It seems to have fallen by the wayside. Even Saul, the consummate grassroots organizer, reports Hillary, eventually

> expanded his radical commitment to the eradication of powerless poverty and the injection of meaning into affluence. His new aspect, national planning, derives from the necessity of entrusting social change to institutions, specifically the United States Government. Alinsky's trust

> in the "people" must be distinguished from his distrust of the status quo and the people who make up that mysterious condition.

"Necessity" indeed. Distrust of that status quo is why those "people" whom Alinsky presumably could trust had yet to be born. Centralized "democracy" was the best default solution.

As for those who "make up that mysterious condition" known as the status quo, it seemed obvious to the hard-headed Hillary that too many, especially the most naively idealistic, were insufficiently pragmatic. The overly doctrinaire forget at their peril that voters must be won over. Some of Senator Eugene McCarthy's proposals during his 1968 presidential campaign, notes Hillary, were overly "'radical' within the [then-]current American political system. Societal comparisons raise again questions about the meaning of 'radical' and even 'revolutionary' within a mass production/consumption state, particularly the United States." Alinsky had replied: "Must definitions perhaps be as fluid as the actions they purport to describe?" Was that a question or, more likely, an answer?

Hillary's own answer would soon become evident. Radical chic went retail: Leviathan turned out to be as lucrative as those who sought its overthrow a decade or two earlier had said it was. Genuflecting to the icon of Equity also helped their bank accounts, whose size was significantly boosted by proceeds from the ostensibly charitable Clinton Foundation, its "nonprofit" status deliciously ironic.[1]

To be fair, it was not quite what Alinsky had thought radicals should be accomplishing. As recently as 1967, he had told his audience that in his view, the freest man was "one who would break loose from the terrestrial, chronological existence of security and status."[2] Whether he still thought that when he died suddenly, five years later, at age 63, no one knows. Hillary certainly did not share this kind of otherworldly liberalism. It might work for poets and idealists, but not for her. Nor for most of the aging baby boomers who retained the New Left's New-Ageist rhetoric minus the adolescent utopianism. The Establishment soon caught up with them as they married, had children, and wizened up. They are back, more respectable than ever. Mainstream. But liberal?

That's hard to say for Sixties poster-children Bill Ayers and his wife Bernadine Dohrn, famous founders of the militant Weather Underground.

Telegenic and charismatic, the two had planned and participated in numerous acts of domestic violence that left people dead and public buildings badly damaged during the hellish "days of rage" of Hate America First.[3] To evade the FBI, they fled underground, waiting for the cultural weather to change. It did, rather rapidly in fact. Bill is now a professor of education, Bernardine a retired law professor, both celebrities again – or rather, still.

Though known less for philosophizing than for hell raising, Ayers was asked by an interviewer from University of Chicago-spawned magazine *The Point* in 2012: "You keep mentioning that you are not a liberal. What is it about liberalism that you – well, what is liberalism according to you?" Comes the response:

> I'm not sure I can define it better than you guys can. There are things about classic liberalism that obviously I'm drawn to and I bet all of you are as well. Those are things like liberty, freedom, the Bill of Rights. But the reason that I reject the label is that I grew up cutting my teeth against the liberals. I wasn't part of John Kennedy's vision of the world, or Lyndon Johnson's. I thought of them as anti-Communist imperial monsters.[4]

That Bill Ayers is not now, nor has he ever been, an anti-Communist is no more surprising that is his view that Kennedy and Johnson had been "anti-Communist imperial monsters," in his lexicon an obvious redundancy. Though claiming that he doesn't much care for labels, he makes a point of explicitly rejecting liberalism. "[T]he reason that I keep joking and rejecting this idea that I'm liberal," explains Ayers, "well partly that's because I think of myself as a radical, and by that I mean, not even in the terms of Left-Right that you might imagine - but someone who wants to go to the root of problems." So then, "radical" is a label he can accept, consistent with his view of himself as "anti-establishment," not bothering to add that radicals like himself "go to the roots" not for edification, as does the etymologist or botanist, but to perform deracination.

When asked specifically what he thought about Barack Obama, who was president at the time, he told the interviewer: "After I had known him for a while, I remember saying to my partner, 'You know, this guy is really ambitious, I think he wants to be mayor of Chicago.'" Does he consider Obama a radical, or even a liberal? These labels don't fit, argues Ayers, because Obama is a politician – and "[e]very politician - FDR, Lyndon Johnson, Abraham Lincoln, Barack Obama - they're all conservative by nature. They are part of the big thing and they're moving in a very constrained world." If so, given Obama's leftist rhetoric, professional history, and policies, is Ayers suggesting that his "conservatism" is opportunistic, even cynical? Given Ayers' own closeness to him, both before and after his two terms in the White House, the answer seems to suggest itself.

The Sixties generation was principally motivated by negation: they knew, or thought they knew, what they did not want to be, where they did not want to live, and whom they despised. They considered themselves the antithesis to the thesis of the status quo, with synthesis comfortably out of range. Their agenda rose from particular to general, from tantrum to revolution. Down with oppression, up with anything else. Whatever. Liberation for all, shackles for none, peace and love.

"The ostensible political issues" at the time, including Vietnam, minority housing, and other signature liberal causes, writes Roger Kimball in *The Long March*, "were quickly assimilated to a much broader emancipationist program" amounting to "a generalized antibourgeois animus, and an attack on the intellectual and moral foundations of the entire humanistic exercise."[5] If it walked, talked, and quacked like the Chinese Cultural Revolution that had been unleashed simultaneously on the other side of the globe, that's because they were in many ways ducks of a feather.

What especially astonishes Kimball is how quickly the new academic ethos crumbled before the narcissistic, hirsute, raving radical hordes: "What had been a society defined and guided by allegiance to classic liberal ideals – the ideal, for example, that distinguished sharply between disinterested academic inquiry and political activism – suddenly found itself at the mercy of a distinctly illiberal activism." At its core, this drama "concerns the fate of liberalism itself."[6] Where would this all lead? Whether the capitulation of the education establishment, starting with the university, "bespoke an essential weakness in liberal ideology or only a failure of particular men faced with difficult decisions is perhaps an open question."[7] So it seemed at the time, though in retrospect both contributed in roughly equal measure.

The radicals moved the goalpost: no longer interested merely in improving the lot of the underprivileged, they sought to end inequality altogether. The ideal of social justice was thus upgraded to what the distinguished Stanford University economist Thomas Sowell called "cosmic justice" - the kind that went far beyond social inequities to include economic, political, and every other calamity. The goal was to do everything possible to place "particular segments of society in the position that they would have been in but for some undeserved misfortune."[8] Only such all-encompassing, galactic justice deserved being deemed "fair." And it can be attained only when everyone is as fortunate as everyone else: the good of all must also be the good of each.

Unfortunately, such a scenario is inconceivable in a society that still permits at least a modicum of freedom. For "[t]his conception of fairness requires that third parties must wield the power to control outcomes, overriding rules, standards, or the preferences of other people."[9] And while constituents may agree democratically, even by consensus, to provide judiciously calibrated safety nets for its most unfortunate citizens in small communities, on a larger scale the spectrum of coercive interventions can range from the minor to the draconian. A body politic can stand a little bloodletting with few or no serious repercussions, but there are limits to the hemorrhage.

That wealth disparities, let alone other kind of inequalities, abound in every society, including the most prosperous, is too obvious to mention. The question before a policymaker is not "the abstract desirability of equality" which, writes Sowell, "like the abstract desirability of immortality, is beside the point when choosing what practical course of action to follow. What matters is what we are prepared to do, to risk, or to sacrifice, in pursuit of what can turn out to be a mirage. Processes designed to create greater equality cannot be judged by that goal but must be examined in terms of the processes created in pursuit of that goal."[10] If those processes, no matter how well-intentioned, end up causing more harm than good, they must be abandoned. But this presupposes respect for empirical evidence, not wishful thinking, let alone hypocrisy. Some means are demonstrably more effective than others in producing a desired goal. Assuming it is the real goal.

Socialism Becomes Entrenched

"Wherever the free market has been permitted to operate, wherever anything approaching equality of opportunity has existed, the ordinary man has been able to attain levels of living never dreamed of before."
- Milton and Rose Friedman, *Free to Choose* (1980)

In a truly liberal society, the preference of the citizens themselves is paramount. Suggesting that "a more equal society is a better society even if its citizens prefer inequality," as does New York University Professor Ronald Dworkin,[11] exudes contempt for the very constituency he purports to protect. We don't all have to have the same amount of everything. So long as the standard of living increases over time, most people are satisfied. For example, I'll take the spiffy Jeep over the old jalopy any day (I did, for some two decades). You want a road-hugging, roaring two-door Lamborghini with just enough trunk space for a purse? Mazel tov, enjoy. It seems altogether reasonable to prefer wealth inequality, provided aggregate national well-being also rises.

Which just happens to be what the data indicate. Cato Institute scholars Chris Edwards and Ryan Bourne explain the statistical methodology in a 2019 study: "Poverty and inequality are different things, but they are often conflated in political discussions. High poverty levels, which are clearly undesirable, are often caused by bad policies, such as a lack of open markets and equal treatment. Wealth inequality is different - it cannot be judged good or bad by itself because it may reflect either a growing economy that is lifting all boats or a shrinking economy caused by corruption."[12]

But just how did equity become so central to the American vision in the first place? And how could it have so thoroughly replaced the original notion of freedom as the right to pursue one's own goals unfettered? It took nearly two centuries for 1787 to be turned upside down. By invoking progress, America regressed. The new Jacobins became the old reactionaries. How could it be?

Perhaps it takes a Frenchman to understand. In 1995, Francois Furet observed that "the French revolutionaries' obsession with equality seems to have taken over American society."[13] The problem is that some self-proclaimed liberals claim to want civil and political but not economic freedom. In truth, liberty is all-encompassing. Clearly, "liberals and democrats share the same philosophical world; the socialist critique knows it and so takes aim at both of them." What these socialists opposed then, and still do was

> the very idea of the rights of man as a subjective foundation of society; they regarded it as a mere cover for the individualism governing capitalist economy. The problem was that capitalism and modern liberty were both subject to the same rule, that of the freedom – or plurality – of ideas, opinions, pleasures, and interests.[14]

Socialist critics of classical liberalism may describe themselves variously as socialists, democrats, or both, while others downplay labels – sometimes "Independent" is deemed politically optimal. A refurbished "liberal" preferred by others is losing steam. Increasingly popular is the ideology of the mediagenic Alexandra Ocasio-Cortez's party, Democratic Socialists of America. DSA's website predictably advertises "a profound commitment to democracy, as means and end. As we are unlikely to see an immediate end to capitalism tomorrow, DSA fights for reforms today that will weaken the power of corporations and increase the power of working people." Adding that democracy is "our means of restructuring society," the DSA defines "a humane international social order" as achieving first and foremost an "equitable distribution of resources."[15] If property cannot be abolished, cosmic justice is the next best thing, a close facsimile.

Rejecting revolutionary means, DSA members have adopted liberal tactics, but kept the utopian ends. Both "are punting the elimination of capitalism – supposedly the goal of the 'party of opposition,' to capitalism – to an ill-defined future," observes Zephyr Institute historian Nathan Pinkoski. "Certainly the anticapitalist rhetoric persists, but the emphasis on an open-ended equality, rather than a strategy for eliminating capitalism, has changed socialism's characteristics and aims."[16] No longer doctrinaire Marxists, American leftists dissatisfied with the status quo do not seek to abolish property so much as redistribute it. The New World's "Bourgeois Bolsheviks," as Pinkoski calls them, have repurposed

> the political theology of the 1960s into the potent categories of contemporary identity politics. The irony, however, is that in pursuing its political and cultural revolution for individual self-creation, Bourgeois Bolshevism fuses its goals to the goals of American liberalism. American socialism is parasitical on American liberalism.[17]

That theology, argues Pinkoski, became "increasingly abstract. The generations that missed the Sixties turned the civil rights era into a readily applicable analogy to all other fights against inequality." The old neo-Marxist messianism for the working class and Black Americans became generalized. Thus "displaced from the Black experience and coupled with an open-ended, abstract passion, applications of the concept [of victimhood] multiplied," explains Pinkoski, and "the old moral authority of some minorities passes on to new minorities (in [Francois] Furet's example, from Jews to Muslims)."[18]

It was only a matter of time before Jews, once deemed equal to everyone else, lost their status as minority-victims, which had stigmatized them for millennia, then (very) briefly protected them. The miraculous emergence of Israel as a tiny oasis of democracy in the Middle East, "the Zionist entity" built largely by Holocaust survivors and their descendants, became too successful too rapidly to continue being perceived as victim. After a few years of socialist experimentation, it became much too capitalist, too close to the United States, and too effective militarily, economically, and every other way not to risk being demonized. It could not avoid being recast as the Satanic oppressor of hapless Palestinians who joined the privileged constituency of victims that provide ersatz-moral sustenance to the post-liberal left.

With Moscow's help, anti-Zionism became the new euphemism for Jew-hatred. That Israel would also be labeled "Nazi" was no mere insult: it was obscene.

Threat Code: Red (and Green)

"*American socialism transforms the anti-bourgeois passion... [T]he American left wishes to extend, not condemn bourgeois life. ... [T]he major transformation of the American left came from its desire to imitate the civil rights era....[by condemning] the systems of minority oppression that characterize American life.... [T]he new socialism's confidence in statism departs from the skepticism of the old.*"

- Nathan Pinkoski, *The Strange Rise of Bourgeois Bolshevism* (2020)

"*It is no mystery: the American left not only supports the grievance of those others – blacks, women, gays, etc. – but also unites them in a movement against the Jews, using the identification of Zionism with racism as its lever.... In its current bid for power, the progressive*

American left follows the Soviet example of embracing the Islamist-Arab war against the Jews in Israel as part of the fight against Western imperialism and capitalism – now repackaged to focus on an America that is "systemically racist." And just as in the 1930s, these Jews fall in with their assailants."

- Ruth R. Wisse, *A Threat Assessment for American Jewry* (2021)

It defies logic. Why, asks professor Wisse, is the behavior of Jews "unlike that of other Americans"[19]? African Americans stand up for their own, as do Asians, and other groups – but not the Jews. What gives? For David Horowitz's parents, Marxism as a "political religion was really the center of their moral life." Wresting free of it was not an option. Nor could Horowitz fail to adopt it. For when even the most mundane topics were infused with ideological significance, it would be hard for any child to avoid concluding that "this meant – without their necessarily intending it – that the condition of their parental love was that I embrace their political faith."[20]

Harder to explain is what he would later call his own "self-aggrandizing romance with corrupt Third-Worldism, … the casual indulgence of Soviet totalitarianism, [and…] the hypocritical and self-dramatizing anti-Americanism which is the New Left's bequest to mainstream politics."[21] Self-dramatizing, patently. But was it always hypocritical? Not necessarily, though perhaps misguided. For Horowitz, Peter Collier, and many others, the Vietnam war became "a universal solvent – the explanation for every evil we saw." Vietnam was the symbol of "the system," of capitalist exploitation, which the New Left invoked "to support the domestic extortionism and violence of groups like the Black Panthers, and to dismiss derisively Martin Luther King, Jr., as an 'Uncle Tom.'"[22]

Was it naivete? That "can be debated," concedes Horowitz, "but by the end of the 1960s we were not political novices." Radicals caught on to the political utility of supporting the Communists of Southeast Asia and started doing it more loudly and outrageously, in order to provoke the maximum mayhem and provide footage for the nightly news. Chaos was part of the plan, good for the business. For "the more repressive our government in dealing with dissent at home, the more recruits for our cause and the sooner the appearance of the revolutionary Armageddon."

And then the unexpected happened. The United States pulled out of Vietnam. Losing no time, the wolf shed the wool and bared its teeth. Stunned, Horowitz and Collier could no longer ignore what truly motivated radicals. "[L]eftists seemed so addicted to finding an American cause at the root of every problem that they couldn't recognize indigenous evils. As the Khmer Rouge were about to take over, Noam Chomsky wrote that their advent heralded a Cambodian liberation, 'a new era of economic development and social justice.' The new era turned out to be the killing-fields that took the lives of two million Cambodians."[23] Fellow-radicals blithely turned their backs on a region they never particularly cared about, the ensuing carnage not their problem. Idealism indeed.

The clear-eyed *Ramparts* editors had learned two invaluable lessons about their nation. First, that "basically, the country tolerated us. And listened to us." And second, "far from increasing the freedom and wellbeing of Third World nations, as we on the left had predicted, America's withdrawal resulted in an international power-vacuum that was quickly filled by the armies of Russia, Cuba, and the mass-murderers of the Khmer Rouge, not to mention the non-Communist but no less bloodthirsty fanatics of revolutionary Islam."[24]

They saw how American liberal institutions thrived amidst an open-minded and generous political culture that responded to, in fact encouraged, dissenting voices. These had been exponentially magnified through a free press, even to the point of permitting, thanks to legal loopholes, the publication of highly classified military information seriously damaging to American interests. Most important, however, they saw the global importance of American liberal leadership. Nowhere was it as clear to the naked eye as in Cuba which, along with other Central American countries, was thoroughly beholden to Moscow. Yet leftists idolized Castro. Why? Giving free reign to a despotism that, under the banner of liberation, had already murdered millions of its own people, to say nothing of others? Where was the logic?

If only David's parents could have understood. "My parents and their comrades believed that mankind's conflicts would be resolved by a universal class whose revolution would abolish all nations and unite all peoples and thus remove the distinctions that made them Jews."[25]

Horowitz credits the Polish communist Isaac Deutscher (1907-1967) with helping him see that this was not going to happen. He identified with Deutscher, who called himself "a non-Jewish Jew" in the tradition of the philosopher Baruch Spinoza and the poet Heinrich Heine. But as Horowitz saw it, "he meant Marxists like us – Jews who were of Judaism but not in it."

Deutscher had revealed what being Jewish meant to him. "Religion? I am an atheist. Jewish nationalism? I am an internationalist. In neither sense am I therefore a Jew. I am, however, a Jew by force of my unconditional solidarity with the persecuted and exterminated. I am a Jew because I feel the pulse of Jewish history; because I should like to do all I can to assure the real, not spurious, security and self-respect of the Jews."[26] Horowitz felt very much the same at the time.

During the interwar years, when the European left was divided among those urging emigration to Israel and others advising staying behind and fight for the socialist revolution, Deutscher had an advantage. He had seen Stalinism up close, having survived the raving dictator's purges and the death camps. He became a Zionist, albeit a thoroughly confused one, because he couldn't quite come to terms with nationalism. One thing was crystal clear to him. Jews could no more be freed from distinctiveness than any other potential scapegoat. And that was a problem. The only solution was a universalist perspective with no national or ethnic distinctions, where everyone was equal.

Horowitz understood, yet asked: why should Jews – indeed anyone - wish *not* to be distinctive? Isn't freedom all about being yourself, hence different from everyone else? That could never happen in a monolithic, totalitarian society that forbids dissent, where distinctiveness of any kind is verboten. Gradually at first, both he and Deutch would soon come to recognize that so-called universalism led ineluctably to the abolition of pluralism and individuality, enforced by terror.

By the end of the 1980s, the colonies of the Soviet empire were having enough of the charade. They were fed up with shortages and manifest bankruptcy of the system propped up by lies. Horowitz and Collier were having second thoughts, as were Ronald Radosh, the art critic Michael Medved, and a few others. I had met them in 1988 when I joined the National Forum Foundation as executive director; their attention was already focused on the place where real dissidents yearned for freedom: Eastern Europe.[27] We all traveled to Krakow, where these former leftists expressed their solidarity with people who wanted self-determination, personal and national. Without a national home, how could they exercise democracy? National self-rule is by no means sufficient, but it is a necessary condition for liberalism. Post-communism would obviously be nationalist.[28]

Ruth Wisse also argued that a healthy nationalism provides the best path to freedom. For example, "[i]t was Jewish nationalism rather than Jewish socialism that proved the more powerful force of liberation in this century….Whereas ideological internationalism, which sought the dissolution of Jews as the first step toward an undifferentiated humanity, invested its good intentions in projects that were at best quixotic, at worst murderous, the defense of the Jews remained the surest test of liberal values."[29] And those values could not be pursued on a global level and still be democratic in the traditional sense of covenantal community self-rule. Her book, *If I Am Not For Myself,* is aptly subtitled *The Liberal Betrayal of the Jews.*

Except that the liberal betrayal in America today is also perpetrated *by* Jews themselves. Many seem still enamored of a utopian kind of universalism they imagine will finally liberate them from the dreaded stereotype of the greedy *yid*, from the stigma of success, and exempt them from what is nonchalantly called cancelation. Perhaps one reason for this pathology is a result of having left untreated the enormous wounds inflicted upon the entire community during the Second World War. Children and now grandchildren of the Holocaust generation, in various ways survivors all, could not be expected to have emerged from the most devastating trauma in human history unscathed.[30] Instinctively short-circuited by anything that even hinted at rightwingism, liberalism defined as anti-conservatism and anti-fascism became like chicken soup, imagined to promote the equality that Jews had always craved. But unlike chicken soup, this illusion doesn't cure anything.

Writing in 2009, Norman Podhoretz reflected that if at one point "all socialists had despised liberalism as the ideology of the bourgeoisie and as a cover for capitalist rapacity," they no longer need to shun the term.

Liberalism has undergone a slow but unrelenting metamorphosis for decades. Increasingly, "liberalism in America had steadily been moving to the Left and was looking more and more like European socialism and less and less like the American liberalism of an earlier day."[31] No longer soothing, it has become toxic.

Podhoretz is here referring to a progressivism that turned to amending and reinterpreting the U.S. Constitution as a means of changing the system through increasing encroachments on individual freedom. Like the proverbial frog inside the boiling pot, gradually abandoning their tradition in exchange for a dangerously antithetical political religion, the Jews seemed not to notice how they were being cooked themselves. Describing liberalism as their "natural home," the founding editor of *Dissent*, the eminent literary critic and historian Irving Howe observes that it had become in effect the '"secular religion' of many American Jews."[32] So too does Podhoretz:

> Indeed it was; and the Jews of America were holding on to it for dear life because beyond the liberal faith there was nowhere to go but into the outright apostasy of conservatism. To them this was as deeply repugnant, and even horrifying, as conversion to Christianity had been to their grandparents in the shtetls of Eastern Europe. ... To most American Jews, then liberalism is not, as has often been said, merely a necessary component of Jewishness: it is the very essence of being a Jew.[33]

Liberalism having been properly identified as a religion, it still needed one more thing for the claim to pass muster: textual validation, couched in appropriately rhetorical garb, obviously in Hebrew. Enter *tikkun olam,* roughly translated as "repair of (or to heal) the world." It was an inspired choice.

Tikkun Olam

> "*Tikkun olam represents the bastardization of an ancient civilization and, for all the talk of liberation, the enslavement of Judaism to liberal politics.*"
>
> **- Jonathan Newman, *To Heal the World? How the Jewish Left Corrupts Judaism and Endangers Israel* (2018)**

The unanointed king of the movement generally associated with this concept is Rabbi David Saperstein, once described by the *Washington Post* as the "quintessential religious lobbyist on Capitol Hill" and by *Newsweek*

Magazine as America's most influential rabbi.[34] The savvy networker nurtured the nonprofit Religious Action Center (RAC) of Reform Judaism, which he directed for over four decades, to become "one of the most powerful Jewish bodies in Washington," whose influence soon extended far beyond the nation's capital. Its website states: "For more than six decades, the Religious Action Center of Reform Judaism (the RAC) has worked to educate, inspire, and mobilize the Reform Jewish community to advocate for social justice."

Known also as *tikkun olam*. Rabbi Saperstein tugs at the heart's strings: "I continue to believe what I learned from my mother: that our traditional commitment to social action is a key asset in the work of Jewish continuity. So many of my generation were taught by their families, as I by mine, that the 'doing of Torah' was the doing of *tikkun olam.* Polls have repeatedly found social justice activity to be by a large margin the most common expression of Jewish identity in America. The power of social justice as a means of strengthening Jewish identity is affirmed to us at the Center in the experience of the thousands of youth leaders who annually come through our programs."[35]

Chances are that it would not have crossed Rabbi Saperstein's mother's mind to translate the "doing of Torah" into *tikkun olam*, any more than would those of most Jews throughout the centuries. Rabbi Jonathan Neumann explains why: "[U]ltimately social justice and its Jewish variant *tikkun olam* are about designing an economic and political system that guarantees certain economic and social outcomes."[36] He can barely contain his outrage at the use of a beautiful expression derived from the traditional prayer *Aleynu,* a lovely liturgy that calls for perfecting the world under God's Kingdom, for unabashedly progressive purposes. His book's title - *To Heal the World?* – takes the form of a question to convey not marvel but barely veiled scorn.

Why would Reform Jews would turn to a sacred Hebrew prayer for so politically controversial a concept? Perhaps to adorn the project with a semblance of authenticity to satisfy Jews who don't know much about Judaism, and even less about its language. Hence the joke about the Reform Jew who goes to Israel and asks how to say *tikkun olam*... in Hebrew. If so, it seems to have worked. The political scope of this pseudo-religious concept is indeed as vast as it is one-sided: "The agenda of Jewish social justice is all-encompassing, and naturally the approach is uniformly leftist," writes Rabbi Neumann. He doesn't mince words: "We're talking higher taxes, increased regulation of business, big labor… [etc.] The tools needed to repair the world are all liberal ones. This isn't charity – it's leftist politics. And it's all in the name of Judaism."[37]

But it is invoked in vain. The subtitle of Rabbi Neumann's book promises to demonstrate *How the Jewish Left Corrupts Judaism and Endangers Israel*: by misappropriating scripture to defend "stridently universalistic aspirations [that] undermine Jewish Peoplehood." He accomplishes this with impressive erudition and clarity, tracing the original idea to the influential Rabbi Mordecai Kaplan (1881-1983), the Founder of Reconstructionist Judaism. Kaplan had felt a need to reorient Judaism "from an other-worldly religion, offering to conduct the individual to life eternal" through observing the commandments "into a religion which can help Jews attain this-worldly salvation" by perfecting this world.[38] This worthwhile endeavor, however, has so degenerated that its latest reiteration amounts to practically turning Reform Judaism into a sect of the Democratic Party.

The steepest decline in religious observance and turn to social activism occurred in the 1950s, when Shlomo Bardin (1898-1976), a Jewish educator and Founder of the Brandeis Camp Institute in Simi Valley, California, turned *tikkun olam* into the go-to ersatz religion of socially active Jews. Within little over a decade, it infiltrated the more traditional Conservative movement as well. By the 1960s, radicalism had gone mainstream, reminiscent of its early days when socialism and communism had sought to satisfy the spiritual yearnings of non-Jewish Jews.

Prominent among them was Michael Lerner, Herbert Marcuse's teaching assistant at the University of California, Berkeley. As philosophy professor at the University of Washington in 1969, Lerner founded the Seattle Liberation Front and was soon joined by the radical professor of religion Rabbi Arthur Waskow, a contributing editor to Horowitz and Collier's then-newly launched *Ramparts* magazine, and an early member of the Institute for Policy Studies founded in 1963. At IPS, he joined other radicals whose aim was described by IPS Founder Richard Barnet in his book *Intervention and Revolution* (1968): "[T]he first imperative is that the world must be made safe for revolution."[39] Observes the prolific writer Joshua Muravchik, my former colleague at the Institute of World Politics: "The 'revolutions' that IPS admires are all virulently anti-American and the revolutionaries virtually all ally themselves with America's most deadly enemy."[40]

Though Lerner and Waskow, both supporters of Communism in Southeast Asia, shared a similar worldview and both engaged in politicizing Jewish holidays, it was Lerner who contributed most to popularizing the name *tikkun olam* as a synonym for American Jewish social justice. By 1980, its meaning was spelled out explicitly in the *Third Jewish Catalogue*:

> The Jewish ideal is in some senses a political one: not the perfection of individual souls, but *tikkun olam*… [for] Jewish teachings have always been concerned with personal morality, social responsibility, and "political" questions of leadership, power, and control of property.[41]

Not the perfection of individual souls? Yet the very next sentence concedes that Judaism has always been concerned with *personal* morality. The thinly veiled political radicalism of *tikkun olam* was designed for leftist groups like the New Jewish Agenda. Founded that same year, 1980, NJA "took a liberal – and usually politically extreme – approach by claiming "many of us base our convictions on the Jewish religious concept of *tikkun olam* (the just ordering of human society and the world) and the prophetic traditions of social justice."[42]

In 1986, Lerner established *Tikkun* magazine. Still published today, it continues to serve as a venue for a variety of "social justice" causes, including, most tragically, antisemitism in anti-Zionist garb. In 2010, for example, Harvard law professor Alan Dershowitz, a longtime proponent of liberal causes, charged that the magazine, which he readily admits having "long criticized for spewing hatred against Israel," had falsely accused him of effectively wanting to kill Lerner, when in fact the opposite is true. It has been "*Tikkun Magazine* [that] has incited hatred against me and others who support Israel," threatening him with "real violence," necessitating "armed bodyguards, policemen with bulletproof vests and other forms of protection from those incited by Lerner and his crew."[43]

How to explain the paradox of this pseudo-religious, toxic, self-destructive word-game, which in the name of preserving Jews destroys Judaism itself and attacks Jews who refuse to play along, including some of the most famous defenders of civil liberties in America and staunch defenders of Israel and the Jews? Concludes Rabbi Joshua Berman: "*Tikkun olam* represents the bastardization of an ancient civilization and, for all the talk of liberation, the enslavement of Judaism to liberal politics."[44] Can there be an explanation outside psychopathology?

A self-described "red-diaper baby," the Anti-Defamation League's new Jewish outreach director, Tema Smith, for example, has defended claims that "Jews uphold white supremacy" in Israel. She has also defended the Muslim murderer who had shouted "Allahu Akbar" after violently beating the retired kindergarten teacher Sarah Halimi and then throwing her out of the window. Smith argued that he, not Halimi, was the real victim.[45] Concludes journalist Daniel Greenfield: "Smith's leftist politics and her identification as a black woman matter far more to the ADL than her position on any Jewish issues."[46] Not that the two diverge. Charges Greenfield: "Instead of opposing leftist antisemitism, the ADL would like leftists to moderate it, to draw lines between appropriate and inappropriate hate, but as the history of its own collaborators in leftist antisemitism show, that line is as imaginary as the ADL's Jewish commitments."[47]

He cites as a prime example the conference organized in November 2021, which he suggests should have been entitled not *Never is Now* but *Now Again.* For "[t]he ADL's decision to not only stock its virtual conference with radical leftists who wage a disinformation war against Jews, but to invite high school students to attend shows just how destructive to Jewish life the organization's wokeness under [its new director Jonathan] Greenblatt has become." The conference invited not a single pro-Israel group.

Not even the ADL, however, comes close to Jewish Voice for Peace (JVP), whose antisemitism is beyond the pale. Founded in 1996 in Berkeley, California, the birthplace of Sixties radicalism, JVP is described by Neumann as "among the most virulent of all Jewish social justice groups focusing on Israel."[48] "It views the founding of the Jewish State, he continues, "as an event of comparable iniquity to the Holocaust, maintains that is Israel is guilty of genocide, … and refuses to describe [Hamas, a] genocidal militia[,] as a terrorist group (preferring to apply that label to the U.S. government instead)."[49]

The self-described liberal Jewish political commentator Peter Beinart clarifies what this has to do with liberalism. He blames Israel's hawkish policies for alienating American Jews, particularly the young: "For several decades, the Jewish establishment has asked American Jews to check their liberalism at Zionism's door, and now, to their horror, they are finding that many young Jews have checked their Zionism instead."[50]

Jewish groups who define their social justice ideology as *tikkun olam* do indeed consider themselves liberal. Most, however, are anti-Zionist and not especially concerned with Judaism as traditionally understood. Instead, they substitute a secular form of compassion for religious observance. Rabbi Neumann cites "two important studies - one in 2001 and the other in 2011 – [which] found that most liberal Jews involved in general social justice activism are either indifferent to pursuing their agenda within a Jewish context or positively opposed to doing so."[51] There is indeed an irreconcilable difference between social justice and traditional Judaism: "the very existence of Jews as a distinct people ultimately conflicts with Jewish social justice's universalist aspirations," writes Rabbi Neumann. Yet paradoxically – or rather, contradictorily – "[w]hereas the Jews are subject to extreme universalism, the particularism of other communities is, apparently, to be protected at all cost."[52]

The expectation that pursuing social justice will render Jews immune to expressions of antisemitism is wishful thinking. "Whereas the Jews may once have benefitted from liberalism," argues Rabbi Neumann, "the growing illiberalism of the American Left and its hostility toward the Jews" render modern-day leftist-liberalism truly dangerous – even more dangerous than neo-Nazi and white supremacist animosity because far more powerful and pervasive.

It is hard to avoid agreeing with Ruth Wisse that American Jews are behaving irrationally. Too often they seem incapable of facing their own contribution to what is increasingly proving to hurt them as well as the country that has given them shelter, embraced them, and helped them more than did any other in history. When during the Cold War, charges Wisse, "Jewish leftists protested American injustice, they incidentally were deflecting attention from the Soviet persecution and murder of its Jewish intelligentsia" and other dissidents in that totalitarian state. Jewish leftists in America as elsewhere also watched silently while the USSR "incited Arab aggression against Israel in 1967 and 1973. Without the Soviet bloc, the Arabs could not have passed the 1975 United Nations resolution charging that Zionism was racism. A Jewish Communists Anonymous could have aired the truth about all this mendacity, freed mind and conscience, and helped to 'repair the world'"[53] in the authentic, real sense of that concept. But they didn't.

As for the histrionic anti-racism, pro-BLM, and other woke causes, Wisse accuses all those

> individual Jews [who] were best positioned to expose the Soviet role in fomenting the racism it professed to oppose. The Soviets saw in Jews and African-Americans the two American minorities that could best pit Communism against capitalist America, the former because of their alleged influence, the latter because they were the most genuinely aggrieved. Soviet agents cultivated the two groups separately and encouraged their cooperation—including their intermarriage as the highest enactment of the interracial ideal.
>
> Jews fell for it and did everything to support Black Americans who were invited to treat Jews as the class enemy. The same was true of Jewish Communists in Israel who promoted Arab-Jewish friendship in the face of escalating Arab violence. Jews were the willing scapegoats of Communism, singing kumbaya as they joined their attackers, inventing the slogans to demonize their own people—all in the name of ideals that had calcified into totalitarian policing. Blame America, shame America, condemn America—the more miserably the Soviets failed in governing their regime, the more ingeniously their American cadres were required to pump up the ideological war against the land of the free.

How could the Jews be so gullible? Wisse is worried, because

> [i]t is by now too late to undo all the rot that the Soviet-controlled Communists and their biological and ideological progeny pumped into American and Jewish culture and politics, traces of which have by now filtered into large swaths of the ideological left, and even into the Democratic party. Totalitarian intolerance of competing ideas; vicious anti-Zionism; politicized racism; bureaucratic halts to initiative; hatred

of freedom - what the Bolsheviks imposed by force, their American handlers brought about through persuasion. It is too late to undo that harm, but not yet too late for the rest of us to ensure that we keep the Republic.

But for that to happen, there must be some serious soul-searching. Jews intent on climbing the ladder of what they consider success must ask themselves: is it really worth it? And at what price?

Making It: Faustus Agonistes

"*On the one hand, we are commanded to become successful – that is, to acquire more of these worldly goods than we began with, and to do so by our own exertions; on the other hand, it is impressed upon us by means both direct and devious that if we obey the commandment, we shall find ourselves falling victim to the radical corruption of spirit which, given the nature of what is nowadays called the 'system,' the pursuit of success requires and which its attainment always bespeaks.*"
- Norman Podhoretz, *Making It* (1967)

When seeking success requires selling one's soul to "the system," not everyone makes the right choice. But as long as there is an option, redemption is still possible. The "American national character," however, demands accepting both, at once living with the contradiction and suffering its pathological consequences. In his 1967 autobiography, aptly titled *Making It*, Norman Podhoretz sought to describe "how the two warring American attitudes toward the pursuit of success" revealed themselves in his own life up to that point.

Having taken over as editor of the influential magazine of the American Jewish Committee *Commentary* in 1960, Podhoretz had indeed "made it." By 1967, he had become intelligentsia royalty. As the author, critic, and playwright Terry Teachout observes in his preface to the book's fiftieth anniversary edition, "he was so much a part of the liberal scene that Woody Allen joked about it in *Annie Hall*."[54] Though Woody Allen's liberals are (or at least sound like) mostly Jews and/or New Yorkers, the Catholic Teachout attests to the relevance of Podhoretz's experiences to his own quintessentially American story. "I read *Making It* not long before I moved to New York to pursue a literary career," writes Teachout; yet "I recognized at once the common aspects of our superficially different personal experiences." The liberal scene was real and cutthroat not only for Jews, but they seemed to excel at the game.

That pursuing the American dream has often entailed unsavory choices is unsurprising. To be sure, when it came to making compromises, Jews had it down to a science. Centuries of experience had taught them how to survive when other civilizations were swept into history's proverbial dustbin. Podhoretz recounts one event in particular: a lesson taught him by a Brooklyn schoolteacher who urged him to effectively turn his back on the ghettoized life of his émigré parents, working-class Jews from Galicia. In so many words,

> [s]he was saying that because I was a talented boy, a better class of people stood ready to admit me into their ranks. But only on one condition: I had to signify by my general deportment that I acknowledged them as superior to the class of people among whom I happened to have been born.... [W]hat I did not understand, not in the least then and not for a long time afterward, was that in matters having to do with "art" and "culture" (the "life of the mind," as I learned to call it at Columbia), I was being offered the very same brutal bargain and accepting it with the wildest enthusiasm.[55]

By the ripe age of thirty-five, he came to fully appreciate that success was better than failure, and that being rich was better than being poor. (My father used to complete the adage, noting also that being healthy and young was better than being sick and old.) Then, "moving on to higher subtleties," he saw that power was also rather desirable, not to mention fame. There was, however, a downside: he started to notice that these goodies came with price tags – "some obvious, some not very well advertised" - and the final tab eventually proved prohibitive.

Podhoretz can find only one reason why he so readily accepted the bargain he would later call "brutal" with such unmitigated "enthusiasm." The choice had been - indeed "had to be [-] blind; there was a kind of treason in it: treason toward my family, treason toward my friends. In choosing the road I chose, I was pronouncing a judgment upon them, and the fact that they themselves concurred in the judgment makes the whole thing sadder but no less cruel."[56] Podhoretz's word for his serial compromises is startlingly accurate: "conversions." It is, in fact, literal.

Persecuted with hardly any intermission throughout their history of exile, the Jews had usually been given choice to convert to Christianity (and later, to Islam) lest they be banished or even killed. This practice started as early as the thirteenth century in Southern Italy, but results were minimal. The first mass conversion took place in 1391 in the Iberian Peninsula, after bloody pogroms, when over a hundred Spanish Jews were baptized. Soon hundreds of thousands followed. Most of these Spanish and Portuguese Jews, known as *conversos*, did not genuinely embrace Catholicism. They continued practicing Judaism in secrecy, thereby earning the derogatory label of *marranos* (swine). Their conversions had been only nominal.

Other conversions, almost exclusively forced, took place in Eastern Europe during the 17th and 18th centuries. But it was the Enlightenment that precipitated the largest voluntary conversions. These took place mostly in Western Europe, most dramatically in German-speaking territories, notably Prussia and the Austro-Hungarian Empire. It was this latter, in many ways more tragic because frankly shameful, conversion model that Podhoretz adopts to describe his own odyssey. No one had forced him to do as he did. Sure, assimilation is preferable if your goal is blending in and succeeding as a member of a minority, but your life doesn't depend on it. If you are willing to abandon your tradition and beliefs for so little, do they even mean anything to you anymore?

What accounted for such craving for acceptance even absent full-fledged persecution? For over seventeen hundred years, Jews had continued to feel that Israel remained in God's graces, that God is compassionate and would eventually save His people if they obeyed His commandments. Accordingly, they did not succumb to the low self-esteem that psychologist Kurt Lewin found prevalent among other discriminated minorities.

Lewin's research shows that negative stereotypes tend to occur among the victimized, often turning almost to self-hatred. It is accompanied by a desire for the same respect and rewards enjoyed by the higher-status minority.[57] Jews, however, seem to have been relatively unafflicted in their sense of dignity throughout most of their history. Until the Enlightenment. Paradoxically, the relative progress and partial emancipation[58] which made the process of assimilation much easier, led not to greater but reduced self-esteem, to greater insecurity and anxiety. With the erosion of religious and cultural identity, Enlightenment quasi-equality amounted to a watershed in Jewish evolution. Though much was gained, far more was lost.

What happened, explains the eminent scholar of Jewish history Raphael Patai, was that Jews became convinced that

> modern European culture was superior to theirs, and that they must acquire European culture for their own benefit. ... The acquisition of European culture was believed to be the key to the modern world, whose rewards were now desired. Finding themselves barred from full (or even partial) acceptance into European society despite their laboriously acquired European culture, the Jewish Enlighteners felt frustrated, and the Lewinian law began to operate: frustration led to aggression, not toward the Gentile majority whose values were continued to be admired and desired, but toward their own group and themselves. That, in its barest outline, is the genesis of the new post-Enlightenment phenomenon of Jewish self-hatred.[59]

Podhoretz identified the precise time when he personally had succumbed to the cursed disease: “I had to signify by my general deportment that I acknowledged them as superior to the class of people among whom I happened to have been born.” It was not only or even primarily about “deportment” but about “culture,” or what he learned to call “the life of the mind.” It took a few more years before he would realize, to his horror, that what he had sacrificed was something far more precious, almost irretrievable. It was the life not merely of the mind but of the soul.

What makes it especially disconcerting to watch American Jews go far beyond emulating their host country’s culture to disrespecting, even repudiating, their own is the remarkable extent to which they have been accepted here in America. That Jews have been exceptionally successful in the New World does not seem to prevent them from suffering nearly the same trepidations, insecurities, and desire to “fit in” experienced under genuinely threatening circumstances. “One manifestation of this tendency,” writes Patai, “was the New Left movement, in which much Jewish self-hate found expression.”[60]

To Ruth Wisse, the "term [self-hate] made little sense." For her, the self-directed aspect "was less relevant than its manifestation against another member of the tribe. Anti-Jewishness in a Jew hurt because one had lost a potential familiar, and because, as Lewin explains, members of a social minority to be liked by everyone else may respond by trying even harder to repudiate their origins." She prefers calling them Jewish anti-Semites: "I studied this subject in Yiddish literature and once new strains of anti-Jewish politics surfaced among anti-Zionists in the 1970s, I quickly recognized them as an aggravating feature of American Jewish life."[61]

For it is that life, American as well as Jewish, unhyphenated but inextricably linked, to which Wisse devotes her talents and passion. It is in America that authentic, unpoliticized Judaism is most needed. Given that, from the outset, "one of the ways Judaism differed from imperial religions was its intrinsic acceptance of co-existence, living among the nations," it is ideally suited for an interconnected global reality.

Not that she sees Judaism as a purely spiritual matter: like every other community, Jews have their own history and a variety of traditions. She agrees with her friend Hillel Halkin's assessment of American Jews who presume to define themselves as "a spiritual people" yet turn their backs on both tradition and faith. The brilliant translator and essayist "had little use for those who wanted to turn Judaism into a new religion of social justice, pointing out that on every contemporary issue that arose – environment, transgenderism and sex change, health care, abortion rights, labor unions, U.S. foreign policy – the *tikkun olam* crowd claims that Judaism's position 'just happened' to coincide with that of the American liberal left."

She cites his words with approval: "Judaism has value to such Jews to the extent that it is useful, and it is useful to the extent that it can be made to conform to whatever beliefs and opinions they have even if Judaism had never existed." The phrase prompts the highest compliment any author can pay to another: she admits wondering "whether there was any point writing if he did it so much better."[62] For once, she was wrong: there is very much a point. Few if any public intellectuals writing today have clarified more eloquently why Jews and America must defend the liberal idea.

But there is one stance of the American liberal left that renders Halkin's accusation especially poignant: an ideologically entrenched form of antisemitism parading as universalism. While teaching at Harvard, Wisse witnessed with alarm how "the Soviet Union was about to collapse, but rather than demolish the reputation of Marxism – as the defeat of Hitler had done to Fascism – the dissolution of the USSR gave the Left free rein to promote leftism without the devastating evidence of how it worked in practice. Political correctness was back in fashion, including the Left's opposition to the Jewishness of Jews."[63] The response from the vast majority, particularly in academia, was silence or - far worse - acquiescence.

But as invariably happens with servile collaborators who imagine they will bypass the firing squad if they can demonstrate more-devout-than-thou credentials, it catches up with them when they must pull the trigger against their own skull. "The *tikkun olam* crowd," as Halkin calls American liberal-left Jews, many of whom agree with the increasingly influential Democratic Socialists of America (DSA), may no longer abstain on the question of "Zionism" as the DSA defines it. They must positively oppose it. Writes Ronald Radosh: "[I]t's not simply that opposition to Israel has been added to a laundry list of intersectional causes that range from the abolition of prisons to the use of gender-neutral pronouns. Israel has become a litmus test to distinguish true believers from fellow travelers."[64]

An apt description indeed. Though originally meant as a compliment, suggesting companions who affably travel together, it refers specifically to communists and their friends, whether in pre-Bolshevik Russia or afterward. Later, it came to apply primarily to Western sympathizers who stopped short of joining the Communist Party in their home countries.[65]

Though not fully trusted by "true believers," however, fellow travelers a century ago in Soviet Russia were as useful then as their ideologically similar counterparts are now to the hardcore radicals in our own age. And just as anti-Semites did not have to join the SS to share and advance the Nazi goal of liquidating the Jews, so today's anti-liberals need not be card-carrying members of anything even as amorphous as Antifa to demonize so-called Zionists. Radosh, who is Jewish, notes the similarity:

> Much as anti-Semites of the past turned Jews into a symbol of everything they thought wrong with the world, today's socialists take anti-Zionism as a symbol of all that is good and holy. With a few minor exceptions, the once pro-Israel socialist movement has joined the frontlines of the far left's long-standing ideological anti-Semitic crusade, masquerading its anti-Semitism, as it always has, as "anti-Zionism."[66]

Rather than liberalism prevailing over hard-core, totalitarian leftism, it seems to be receding. And not only in America but even, albeit to a lesser degree, in the Jews' own homeland. As Hoover Institute scholar Peter Berkowitz points out, "[d]ifferent as they are, Israel and the United States suffer from similar forms of political discord, social fracture, cultural dislocation, and ideological distortion." [67]

The so-called "post-modern" distortion of liberalism is perhaps the most sweeping ideological overhaul in Western thought, being at once cynical and nihilistic. As French theorist Michel Foucault, a must-read for college students across America's campuses, declared in a commendable moment of lucidity and candor, "we are subjected to the production of truth through power, and we cannot exercise power except through the production of truth." To which Berkowitz adds the caveat: "But only when it is convenient. In theory, it follows, as Nietzsche recognized, that if nothing is true, then everything is permitted." Actually, if nothing is true, nothing can even be **said**!

But theory aside, Berkowitz gets to the heart of the matter. Remember Dumpty?

> In practice, Foucault's reduction of truth to power means for multiculturalists and proponents of identity politics that only that which advances their interests and aims is permitted. So they insist that inherited traditions and established claims are arbitrary and devoid of authority. ... [Thus] they have employed to great effect the equation of truth with power to undermine traditional and common-sense claims about morality and politics.

The palpable backlash from ordinary people who are trying to make a living in peaceful and civilized surroundings is heartening. But it may be too little too late, for the elite repudiation of classical liberalism and truth itself is more definitive now than it has been for nearly a century.

Chapter IX:

Global Anti-Liberalism and Antisemitism

Targeting the Twin Towers of the Liberal Idea: The Two Satans

"For radical Islamists, it is a cultural axiom to vilify the crusaders (led by America) and the Zionists as twin brothers."
– Robert Wistrich, *The Lethal Obsession* (2010)

Wherever one found anti-Americanism, observed Herbert Marcuse's friend and colleague Max Horkheimer, the German-Jewish head of the Frankfurt School, "anti-Semitism is also present."[1] But as Robert Wistrich amply demonstrates, this was hardly new. For "since the early nineteenth century, critics as well as admirers often labeled America as the most Jewish nation in the Christian world – with only Great Britain in its imperial heyday rivaling it for that title."[2] When the cleric Ayatollah Khomeini, who took over the dictatorship of Iran's Islamic Republic in 1979, designated America as the "Great Satan"[3] and dubbed Israel "Little Satan," he was but one of many. Whether the big and bad United States was itself a puppet of the "Little Satan," as Osama bin Laden reportedly told his son, or the other way around, was but a geographic, not conceptual, technicality.

Radical Islamism sees the two democracies as the bicephalous dragon spewing secularism and materialism in order to obliterate the spiritual essence of the human race. "Many Muslims tend to regard Americanism and Zionism as the embodiment of a global, transnational, and cosmopolitan world view that remains alien to them,"[4] writes Wistrich. He thus agrees with Israeli writer Yossi Klein Halevi that "Islamism warns against a global culture 'controlled by Hollywood Jews and a borderless world of finance controlled by Wall Street Jews.'"[5] Unfortunately, the

Mullahs' double-demonization of America and Israel has spread with unprecedented rapidity and scope by means of disinformation, realpolitik calculations, weaponized hatred, and just plain weapons.

Its origins, however, predate the Islamist republic, observes Halevi:

> The old Soviet *Pravda* routinely invoked the "Tel Aviv-Washington axis," imagining a Nazi Israel and an all-devouring America. That perspective has now become mainstream in much of the European media. At least so far as the attitudes of many Western Europeans toward the United States and Israel are concerned, the Soviet Union has posthumously won the Cold War.[6]

Surprising as this may sound, facts support it unequivocally. The USSR has masterfully marketed the conflation of anti-capitalism - ergo anti-Americanism - and antisemitism, euphemistically peddled as anti-Zionism. Today's Jew-haters come from both extremist camps. Sometimes they are combined in the same person, as in former member of the radical Marxist Baader-Meinhof gang, now a leader of the neo-Nazis in Germany, Horst Mahler. Call it Left or Right, Cain's brood is hate-filled.

Celebrating the 9/11 attacks for marking "the end of the American century, the end of global capitalism, and also the end of the Jehovah cult and of Mammonism," Mahler spoke for a strange collection of venom-spewing utopianists. With Nazism defeated in war and Russian-style Communism having been dealt a blow by the failed Soviet experiment, who else to denounce if not capitalist America, in cahoots with the Jews - specifically, but not exclusively, Israelis – as the root of all evil?

Neo-Nazis and neo-Marxists howled in unison. As Barry and Judith Rubin explain, "For the extreme left, as well as Arab nationalists or Islamists, this new approach revitalized their failed ideologies and broadened their appeal." It was tailor-made for boosting numbers and impact. "'Progressive' human rights activists could march in defense of Third World dictators; Islamists and pan-Arab nationalists could join hands."[7]

Prominent among those activists were many Jews whose leftist affiliation seemed part of their self-image, regardless (or was it because?) of the ideology's entrenched antisemitism. Ruth Wisse sees it as the latest manifestation of JPTSD (Jewish Post-Traumatic Stress Disorder) characterized by a dysfunctional reaction to age-long persecution and stateless status. To her, it seemed symptomatic of the same lack of self-confidence resulting from the age-long aversion to wielding power, which Wisse describes in great detail in her seminal book *Jews and Power*.

First published in 2007 and reissued in 2020, the book explains specifically how that aversion accounted for the Jews' original infatuation with the Left, specifically in the USSR:

> The secret appeal of Communism to the Jews was its offer of hard power in non-Jewish form.... Many thousands were prepared to sacrifice their Jewish morality to the necessary violence if they could do it under the Red flag. The Jewish left idealized Leon Trotsky for unleashing the Red Terror as well as shaping the Red Army, and then used his 'martyrdom' at the hands of Stalin to absolve him and themselves of responsibility for a murderous regime that he had helped to design and would gladly have ruled if he had not been outmaneuvered.[8]

Jews seemed intent on ignoring the similarities between Communism and fascism, despite the fact that "both movements aspired to the same one-party rule," merely because the former "claimed that right in the name of the disenfranchised." And what group did this apply to most consistently, throughout several millennia? Who else?

But the Jews fell for the ruse. Had they looked more closely at the doctrine they imagined was the mirror image of fascism, they would have discovered it to be merely another version. Thanks in part, though by no means exclusively, to Karl Marx, Communism was congenitally antisemitic. Marx succeeded in making Jews ashamed of their own successes, of having managed to not just survive but thrive whenever permitted to do so, when allowed to use their vast talents. He actually went a step further and vilified them as oppressors, exploiters, greedy money-lovers with no higher aim in life than gathering riches. In brief, scum. No wonder Hitler was inspired by Marxism.[9]

"By putting a Jewish face on the capitalist, Marx shamed Jews in particular for their association with the allegedly exploitative class," writes Wisse. He was completely ignoring the rich tradition of learning, education, and resilience of which they could be rightfully proud. By declaring that capitalism/Jews must disappear, Marx managed to aid both totalitarian impulses, Left and Right, with one fell swoop. She concludes:

"a forced Jews to protect themselves; Communism destroyed their self-confidence."[10]

It had been the ultimate blow – all the more devastating for having been promoted with such verbal dexterity by a descendant of rabbis, then implemented with efficiency and enthusiasm by so many other Jews – in Russia and elsewhere - whose vision had been clouded to near-opaqueness by the cataract of millenarian utopianism.

Bolshevik Antisemitism

"Between 1949 and 1953, the inquisitional spirit reigned supreme.... [and t]he two-pronged campaign against 'bourgeois nationalists' and 'cosmopolites' [another name for Jews] now aimed to annihilate Jewish culture and propagators... [proof of] Stalin's diseased mind, and the widespread belief in an omnipresent American-Zionist threat."

- Robert Wistrich, *The Lethal Obsession* (2010)

It took some time for the full extent of Bolshevik antisemitism to reveal itself. This followed soon after Lenin's passing from the scene in 1924. The first victim was also the most prominent. Indeed, having been designed by Lenin on his deathbed as his successor, he was Stalin's principal rival. The brilliant architect of the February Revolution, charismatic and ruthless, Leon Trotsky was gradually stripped of his positions, and finally expelled from the Party's leadership, the Politburo, in 1929. He spent the rest of his life in exile, until Stalin succeeded to assassinate him in 1940 while hiding in Mexico City. By then, "Trotskyite" had become a synonym for traitor, Jew, and all-around enemy-of-the-people.

Like Cronus, the mythological father of the Greek gods who devoured his own children to prevent being overthrown, so Stalin eliminated fellow-Bolsheviks, most of them Jews. And revolutionary gods they were indeed. Lev Kamenev (Leo Rosenfeld), Grigory Zinoviev (Hirsch Apfelbaum) and Karl Radek (Karol Sobelsohn) had all been intimate Lenin allies. Exiled together, they had all been passengers on the sealed train from Zurich to St. Petersburgh in April 1917. The journey had been arranged by the Germans, who hoped to topple the czarist regime and extract Russia from the war. All of which happened. But also more, much more, beyond anyone's wildest nightmares.

After the collapse of the Nazi-Soviet pact and Germany's invasion of the USSR on June 22, 1941, Stalin desperately needed the help of Western allies. Accordingly, he put his antisemitic crusade temporarily on hold. But his paranoia only increased after the war's end and after FDR's death, partly due to President Harry Truman's much more skeptical attitude toward the Soviet regime. The Jews paid dearly: "Between 1949 and 1953," writes Wistrich, "the inquisitional spirit reigned supreme.... [and t]he two-pronged campaign against 'bourgeois nationalists' and 'cosmopolites' [another name for Jews] now aimed to annihilate Jewish culture and propagators... [proof of] Stalin's diseased mind, and the widespread belief in an omnipresent American-Zionist threat."[11]

By early 1953, "Soviet Jewry was being collectively demonized as 'enemies of the state' by the Ministry of Security and the Soviet government. It was alleged that Jews were anti-Soviet and poisoned by bourgeois nationalism; that they controlled the foreign and domestic policies of the United States; and that they even believed themselves to be 'chosen' to rule the world."[12]

In their seminal book *Stalin's Last Crime: The Plot Against the Jewish Doctors 1948-1952*, Jonathan Brent and Vladimir P. Naumov document a pattern of events which suggest that "Stalin may well have believed that war with the United States might not come until the early or mid 1960s. But he had no doubt it would come."[13] The Jews were to blame above all. And foremost among the culprits was the Jewish Anti-fascist Committee. This despite having been an official Soviet initiative, specifically designed to influence Western public opinion in Russia's favor during World War II.

Once the war was over, Stalin turned against it with full force. "The charge against the committee," write Brent and Naumov, "was that, as Jewish nationalists, they were engaged in undermining the Soviet state at the direction of United States Intelligence largely by spreading American and Zionist propaganda."[14] But in the absence of evidence, the trial was held in secret; the executions of those dedicated and courageous leaders were not revealed until after Stalin's death.[15]

Purging Jews inside the Soviet Union, however, did not suffice. Stalin's regime could not resist recycling *The Protocols of the Elders of*

Zion. The tsarist-era forgery was designed to whip up antisemitic fervor abroad, specifically in the Muslim world. As mentioned earlier, these were purportedly the "minutes" of a secret speech (in some versions, preposterously attributed to Theodore Herzl, the father of Zionism) by the Elders, or Sages, of Zion, the document purports to reveal a two-millennia-old conspiracy. Presumably, a cabal of (anonymous) bloodthirsty Jews, who allegedly already run the world, the Sages are on the cusp of imminent total victory. The Jewish persona that emerges from this travesty embodies Satan, or the Antichrist.[16]

Though widely exposed as a forgery and a hoax by British journalist Phillip Graves in a series of articles, it became one of the greatest propaganda weapons of all time. It even poisoned America. Thanks are due largely to Henry Ford, whose profound antisemitism was deep-rooted. As early as 1915, for example, Ford had blamed "German-Jewish bankers" for causing the Great War.[17] That year, he also funded a Peace Ship to Europe and met with pacifists in Sweden and the Netherlands, and eventually became a strong supporter of the League of Nations and of Woodrow Wilson, who asked Ford to run for Senate as a Democrat in 1918. He lost. But his influence was undiminished.

He was eager to do business, as were the workers. Already in the mid-1920s, "factory workers were seen carrying banners during holiday parades with Henry Ford's name inscribed upon them, along with those of Lenin, Marx, and Stalin."[18] In 1929, he signed a landmark agreement to produce cars in the USSR. (Ford's company later became a major supplier of weapons to the allies.)[19]

Ford once again opposed America's entry into another world war, two decades later. In 1939, he actually claimed that the torpedoing of U.S. merchant ships by German submarines was the result of conspiratorial activities undertaken by financier war-makers ("Jews" in Ford-speak). No wonder Hitler venerated him. In 1998, journalist Michael Dobbs reported in *The Washington Post,* in the context of legal controversies prompted by then-recently declassified documents, that

> [t]he relationship of Ford and GM to the Nazi regime goes back to the 1920s and 1930s, when the American car companies competed against each other for access to the lucrative German market. Hitler was an

> admirer of American mass production techniques and an avid reader of the antisemitic tracts penned by Henry Ford. "I regard Henry Ford as my inspiration," Hitler told a *Detroit News* reporter two years before becoming the German chancellor in 1933, explaining why he kept a "life-size portrait" of the American automaker next to his desk.[20]

Nor was Ford's assistance limited to those early years: as late as 1940, he continued to do business with Germany, including the manufacture of war materiel.

Business aside, it had been mainly Ford's role in promoting antisemitism on a massive scale that earned Hitler's veneration, a sentiment reciprocated by Stalin. Once all three evil geniuses – the psychopathic German painter-manqué, the undereducated American car king, and the Georgian ideological imperialist – decided, however independently, to peddle the *Protocols*, the forgery would become arguably the most potent weapon of all time against the Jews. But while the role of the first two dictators is well known, the latter is only slowly beginning to be understood. This is partly because the KGB, Stalin's secret police, had decided to use a satellite service. It happened to be based in my own native country, Romania.

After defecting to the U.S. in 1978, head of the foreign intelligence arm of Romania's secret police known as the Securitate, General Ion Mihai Pacepa, revealed that Soviet General Aleksandr Sakharovsky had told him and his fellow spies in 1951 that the Soviet Union's principal enemy was America's "Zionist bourgeoisie." Both the U.S. and Israel were in the Kremlin's crosshairs. A few years later, after he become head of the KGB's powerful Foreign Intelligence Directorate, Sakharovsky brought a copy of the *Protocols* to Bucharest and ordered it to be translated, multiplied and surreptitiously disseminated.

> The Securitate's first major *dezinformatsiya* task in the new World War III was to help Moscow reignite antisemitism in Western Europe by spreading thousands of copies of an old Russian forgery, *The Protocols of the Elders of Zion*, in that part of the world. It had to be done secretly, so no one would know that the publications came from the Soviet bloc.[21]

It was not long before "the Securitate was spreading the *Protocols* around the Middle East as well."[22] But after the Six-Day War, the Soviet offensive against the Jewish state escalated. Its official culmination took place at the United Nations, with General Assembly Resolution 3379. A fine specimen of diplomatic travesty, the Resolution proclaims that the august international body "determines that Zionism is a form of racism and racial discrimination."[23] It passed with overwhelming support on November 10, 1975 – ironically, the 37th anniversary of Kristallnacht, when Nazi stormtroopers attacked the Jewish community in Germany. Writes Wistrich: the background "orchestrating campaign [for the resolution] was led behind the scenes by the then mighty Soviet propaganda apparatus, often coordinated with the radical Arab states, the PLO [Palestine Liberation Organization], and the Third World Nonaligned Movement..."[24]

The United Nations was perfectly suited for waging war on "Zionism." First came a proclamation adopted at the World Conference of the International Women's Year in Mexico City on July 2, 1975, demanding "the elimination of colonialism and neo-colonialism, foreign occupation, zionism, apartheid and racial discrimination in all its forms."[611] Not to be outdone, the Organization of African Unity explicitly declared, a month later, that "the racist regime in occupied Palestine and the racist regime in Zimbabwe and South Africa have a common imperialist origin, forming a whole and having the same racist structure and being organically linked in their policy aimed at repression of the dignity and integrity of the human being." On August 30, ministers for foreign affairs of Non-Aligned Countries unable to contain their outrage any longer, decided to "most severely condemn zionism as a threat to world peace and security and call upon all countries to oppose this racist and imperialist ideology."

Imperialism, racism, colonialism, neo-colonialism, the list of isms follows the script. The U.N., after all, was only one small battlefield in a far more extensive war, which targeted not only Israel and the Jews, but liberalism itself, "bourgeois capitalism," and its chief representative, the United States. Hoover Institute distinguished fellow Josef Joffe explains the sinister narrative:

> Indeed, the United States is an anti-Semitic fantasy come true, the *Protocols of the Elders of Zion* in living color. Don't Jews, their first loyalty to Israel, control the Congress, the Pentagon, the banks, the

> universities, and the media? This time the conspirator is not "World Jewry," but Israel. Having captured the "hyperpower," Jews qua Israelis finally do rule the world. It is Israel as the Über-Jew, and America as its slave.[25]

Israel is not a country but a symbol. Nor are Jews just another national group, but proponents of an ideology defined by rapacity and conquest, according to textbooks produced by the Palestinian Authority for the UN Relief and Works Agency (UNRWA), taught throughout its refugee camps but also available worldwide. The bottom line: "colonization constitutes the main point in the idea and a practical implementation of Zionism.... [t]hat is based on the denial and uprooting of the 'other' rather than on co-existence with it or the acceptance of its existence."[26] Colonialism, racism, etc. etc. – the synonyms cascade seamlessly, as if by algorithm ("as if" being a figure of speech).

The textbooks mention neither Israel's vote in favor of the UN General Assembly Resolution 181, on November 29, 1947, calling for the partition of the British-ruled Palestinian Mandate into a Jewish state and an Arab State, nor the Arab states' flat-out rejection of that Resolution, let alone their subsequent denial of Israel's right to exist at all.[27] That "denial and uprooting" describes not Israel but its Islamist foes, is precisely how "Big Lie" tactics work in KGB-style disinformation.

Albeit most often, and with perfect accuracy, applied to the key tactical tool of Soviet active measures, its best-known definition is credited to Hitler. He writes in *Mein Kampf*:

> [I]n the big lie there is always a certain force of credibility; because the broad masses of a nation are always more easily corrupted in the deeper strata of their emotional nature than consciously or voluntarily; and thus in the primitive simplicity of their minds they more readily fall victims to the big lie than the small lie, since they themselves often tell small lies in little matters but would be ashamed to resort to large-scale falsehoods.[28]

The USSR's mastery of the Big Lie put Hitler's to shame.

Anti-Zionism

> "*Anti-Zionism in the 1970s and 1980s increasingly began to look like the leftist functional equivalent of what classical antisemitism had once represented (in the interwar period) for the fascist Right... [thus]*

> *steadily emerging as the lowest common denominator between sections of the Left, the Right, and Islamist circles.*"
>
> **- Robert Wistrich, *From Ambivalence to Betrayal: The Left, the Jews, and Israel* (2012)**

Anti-Zionism is the upgraded version - Antisemitism 2.0.[29] Hardly confined to hatred of Israel – its policies, people, and supporters, Jewish or otherwise - like its cousin anti-Americanism, anti-Zionism is visceral, uncompromising, ideologized hatred. As Warwick University Professor Robert Fine and Kingston University Professor Philip Spencer point out, "in contemporary antizionism… Israel, Zionism and the Jewish state are treated as symbolic representations of all that is illegitimate in the present-day international community."[30] Self-described Marxists, albeit not anti-Zionist, Fine and Spencer explain how this works:

> The Jewish question is not just an attitude of hostility to Jews or to those who invoke the sign of 'the Jews' but a theory designed to explain the winners and losers of capitalist society. It is formulated in terms of dichotomies - the modern and the backward, the people and its enemies, the civic and the ethnic, the postnational and the national, imperialism and anti-imperialism, power and resistance, the West and the rest.[31]

The belief that Jews should have a homeland in Israel, which is what Zionism has traditionally signified, has been hotly debated throughout the two thousand years of Diaspora, various tactics rejected only to be once again reconsidered. Conversely, anti-Zionists have opposed setting up a Jewish state, though often for entirely divergent reasons: some advocated for assimilation, but others, deeply religious Jews, argued that Judaism was primarily if not exclusively a religion, not a state – indeed that statehood would detract from the pious individual principal focus of serving God.

But all that was before Israel declared its independence in May 1948 and recognized by the U.N. a year later. "Contemporary anti-Zionism, whether espoused by Jews or non-Jews, is a very different creature from its pre-state forerunners," notes Wistrich. Although "the emergence of anti-Zionism as a distinctive left-wing mode of post-Auschwitz Judeophobia was already apparent more than thirty years ago," it has metastasized beyond recognition.

The Soviet propaganda effort against Zionism/capitalism/imperialism /racism/etc. shifted into high gear after the 1967 Six-Day War. But that was only the latest stage in the longstanding effort to coopt Muslim, African, Asian, and other Third World populations to join the communist camp. The operation started almost immediately after the Bolshevik take-over in 1917, with the Congress of the People of the East held in Baku in September, 1920. Organized by the Communist International (Comintern) which had been founded a year earlier, in 1919, the conference had been billed as "a congress of...workers and peasants of Persia, Armenia, and Turkey." Attended by nearly two thousand delegates, the Congress released a solution calling for a "holy war for the liberation of all mankind from the yoke of capitalist and imperialist slavery, for the ending of all forms of exploitation of man by man!" In Palestine, it first drove Arabs from their lands "to Jewish settlers; then, … incited them against these same Jewish settlers, sowing discord," the better to control the area."[32] Ironically, the Comintern chairman was none other than Lenin's old friend Grigory Zinoviev/Hirsch Apfelbaum, executed by the KGB in 1936 after being accused of treason on trumped-up charges.

In fact, the Bolsheviks were continuing a policy that had originated in Berlin, masterminded by the Kaiser's advisor Max von Oppenheim, who facilitated Lenin's return to Russia with money from fellow-Bolshevik and friend Alexander Lvovich Parvus, (Israel Lazarevich Gelfand), also known as Helphand. A master geopolitical strategist, Von Oppenheim (a member of the Jewish Oppenheim family of bankers, whose father had converted to Catholicism) was simultaneously working on sparking Muslim jihad through Germany's Turkish allies, a goal he nurtured for over a decade.[33] As it happens, one of Lenin's first Muslim comrades in Zurich had been the same Turkish war minister, Enver Pasha, who had done the Germans' bidding in World War I; they had a common friend in Parvus/Helphand/Gelfand. In the aftermath of its defeat in 1918, a Germany reeling from its wounds temporarily suspended geopolitical intrigue, and the baton reverted to the USSR.

"During the early 1920s," write historians Barry Rubin and Wolfgang Schwanitz, "the leading role in fomenting revolutionary movements in the Muslim world had passed from Germany to the Soviets, who urged

Muslims to overthrow their European rulers."[34] Enver proved eager to cooperate with the Soviet regime, and with Lenin's personal support, he was immediately hired to direct its Asian department. Before long, "Enver would persuade Lenin to support an Islamic religious revolt based on a plan drawn up for the Kaiser."

To compound the irony, and further justifying this strange movie script's low rating, among the principal organizers of the Baku conference designed to rally the "people of the east," besides Grigory Zinoviev, was Karl Radek/Karl Sobelsohn. Another of Radek's meetings with members of the German elite eventually led to the April 1922 Treaty of Rapallo. According to its terms, Germany and the Communist state would renounce all territorial and financial claims to one another's territory. As an additional side benefit, "out of these talks also grew the Bolshevik Jihad."[35] Already Soviet-Muslim cooperation was seen as highly beneficial to both partners, radical differences notwithstanding. Common enemies make for peculiar bedfellows. To be sure, they cannot always be relied upon to wake up on the same side.

Adapting Marxism to Islamism was a remarkable feat of conceptual gymnastics. In their comprehensive 1979 study *Muslim National Communism in the Soviet Union: A Revolutionary Strategy for the Colonial World,* historians Alexandre A. Bennigsen and S. Enders Wimbush document "the complex phenomenon of ideological adaptation and change, of the propensity of some human groups to see in Marxism the answer to their local demands and dilemmas,"[36] all in the name of freedom. And foremost among the groups most intensely targeted by the Communist Party USA were, unsurprisingly, America's Blacks.

First established in 1919, CPUSA counted among its most passionate early members William Patterson, who in 1928 attended the Sixth Comintern[37] Conference in Moscow. One of the leaders of the early civil rights movement, Patterson became national executive secretary of the Civil Rights Congress in 1949. But by then his FBI file had been growing. Believing him to be a potential security threat (not without reason), the State Department denied him a passport, relenting only in 1960. Patterson went on to Leningrad, Peking, and Moscow, where he sought to enroll

African Americans in a newly created school specifically designed for Blacks and other representatives of the Third World.

It would be called the Patrice Lumumba Friendship University. Patterson arranged for five African Americans to be included in the first class, although only one – his daughter, Mary Louise – was to attend. She would later continue her studies elsewhere in the Soviet bloc, namely Cuba. Soon Lumumba U would become a Kremlin grooming school, the third largest university in the USSR. The list of distinguished alumni included Ayatollah Ruholla Khomeini,[38] author of the "Big Satan/Little Satan" metaphor cited above, and Palestinian leader Mahmud Abbas, whose 1982 dissertation – later published in Arabic in 1984, and again in 2011, was titled "The Other Side: The Secret Relations between Nazism and the Leadership of the Zionist Movement."[39]

Besides doubting the existence of gas chambers and numbers of Jewish victims, Abbas accuses the Jews of colluding with the Nazis:

> The Zionist movement did not send any assistance, financial or otherwise, for the victims of Nazism and it did not allow any other side to provide any kind of aid. ... It even placed obstacles in the way of efforts made by Christian groups or by non-Zionist Jews or a number of countries that saw fit to find a solution to this humanitarian problem.

Chutzpa is far too mild a word for what comes next: "All of this wasn't enough – the Zionist movement led a broad campaign of incitement against the Jews living under Nazi rule to arouse the government's hatred of them, to fuel vengeance against them and to expand the mass extermination."[40] World leaders shake hands with such a person and send millions of dollars his way. Who is the worse offender?

Claiming that the movement had been aligned with the Nazis fit with the narrative of Zionist racism and advocacy of genocide. If the Zionists conspired in the murder of other Jews, would they hesitate even for a second to eliminate Palestinians? There is a logic to this, if logic be the word. Not that it matters, since ideology and logic belong to two parallel universes – the kind that don't meet.

For some two decades, it was still possible to think of Israel as little David, a dot encircled by Arab Goliath, the horde of hate-filled neighbors ready to erase the barely visible dot from the map. Then came 1967, and upstart David squashed the Soviet-armed Goliath with such speed and devastation that the injury felt by the Arab victims paled compared to the insult. The Six-Day War proved a decisive catalyst for the New Left which, in the words of Berlin-based historian Paul Hockenos, "discovered" the Palestinians.

In the midst of strong anti-Vietnam sentiment, it suddenly dawned on the radicals, perhaps with a little nudge from headquarters, that here was another victim of world-capitalism. How could they have missed it? Didn't the *Protocols* hold the key to the mystery? Since "Israel's staunchest allies just happened to be Washington, Bonn, and the right-wing Springer group," Israel belonged to the vast antichrist/capitalist/imperialist conspiracy after all. Continues Hockenos: "The Palestinians' liberation struggle fit squarely into the students' Third World paradigms and critiques of colonialism.... The Palestinians were heralded as valiant freedom fighters."[41]

The disinformation virus against the Jews and their state, engineered inside Kremlin's labs decades earlier, spread with stunning rapidity. A radicalized leftist audience hungry for ideological fodder and a murderously resentful Arab-Muslim constituency together provided a highly receptive audience, with results surpassing even its own high standards. A "massive Soviet anti-Zionist campaign that entered a particularly active stage in 1967," writes Kennan Institute scholar Izabella Tabarovsky, "designed by the KGB and overseen by chief Communist Party ideologues, ... succeeded at emptying Zionism of its meaning as a national liberation movement of the Jewish people and associating it instead with racism, fascism, Nazism, genocide, imperialism, colonialism, militarism, and apartheid."[42] The campaign intensified, notes Tabarovsky, and of course "relied heavily on antisemitic tropes borrowed directly from the *Protocols*." Its effect on Western left-liberals was to cement an antizionist attitude.

This mentality was aptly described by Paul Berman, a former leftist who, like Horowitz and Collier, later had "second thoughts," in a celebrated article published by *The New Republic* just a few months before 9/11:

> [T]he New Left's vision of a lingering Nazism of modern life was suddenly re-configured, with Israel in a leading role. Israel became the crypto-Nazi site par excellence, the purest of all examples of how Nazism had never been defeated but had instead lingered into the present in ever more cagey forms. What better disguise could Nazism assume than a Jewish state? [43]

The conflation of anti-Zionism with antisemitism is no longer in doubt. Explains Wistrich:

> Anti-Zionism in the 1970s and 1980s increasingly began to look like the leftist functional equivalent of what classical antisemitism had once represented (in the interwar period) for the fascist Right… [thus] steadily emerging as the lowest common denominator between sections of the Left, the Right, and Islamist circles.[44]

Not even as astute an observer as Raphael Patai could have imagined left-wing anti-Jewish Judaism in America, indeed throughout the world, as anything more than a passing phase. Surely it couldn't last, especially after the U.N.'s infamous 1975 Zionism resolution, when that thoroughly politicized "global debating society of nations rammed [it] through by the unholy triple alliance of Communist, Arab, and Third World countries." How could any reasonable person fail to see the truth? Patai was convinced that the relentless campaign against Israel that had culminated in that preposterous resolution necessarily "reinforced Jewish solidarity all over the world and at the same time effectively reduced to insignificance the last vestiges of Jewish self-hate." By the mid- to late-1970s, thought Patai, "the New Left as a whole, both in America and in Western Europe, was largely a thing of the past."[45]

He had written these words in 1977. But by the time he died some two decades later, in 1996, Patai must have realized how wrong he had been. He would be even more astonished today at the incredible proportion of Jews, preeminently educated, upper and upper-middle-class, veering ever more leftward and more hostile to Israel. This attitude is mirrored also in the sharp increase in antisemitic incidents in the United States, particularly on college campuses.

Nor is the corporate world immune. Kamau Bobb, the head of so-called Diversity, Equity, and Inclusion (DEI) at Google, for example, on June 1, 2021, wrote that Jews have an "insatiable appetite for war" and an "insensitivity to the suffering [of] others."[46] His punishment fell far short of capital: the company reassigned him to work on STEM education efforts.[47] Bobb's mistake had been to accuse "Jews" rather than attribute these traits to "Israelis" or "Zionists;" others will henceforth be more careful. But to call his slip Freudian would be an insult, not so much to the venerable psychologist as to common sense.

Not all sense, however, is common – notably what is sometimes called the death drive (in German, *Todestrieb*), often attributed to Freud, who actually adopted (stole) it from his brilliant colleague, the Russian-Jewish Savina Spielrein (who, as it happens, would lose her life in Auschwitz in 1942). A close variant of self-hatred, the death drive seems to be alive (though perhaps not well), so to speak, at the supersized mother of search engines, worth some $1 trillion. Case in point is the Jewish Diaspora in Tech (JDT), organized by a group of Google's Jewish employees.

This is how JDT's website describes their vision: *We are a community of members of the Jewish diaspora working in the tech industry. By mobilizing our access and our resources, we seek to act in solidarity with all peoples at the forefront of the fight against white supremacist violence and the carceral state.*[48] It then lists its values in dualistic fashion. The group says YES to a number of "values," among them "decarceration and demilitarization;" dismantling, boycotting, and divesting from all "colonial" projects (shorthand for BDS); along with reparations and the redistribution of power and wealth. It says NO to others such as, of course "white supremacy," but also "to borders on stolen land" – which seems superfluous, since it is also against "particularism" and "nationalism," and thus, presumably, to borders on *any* land. Similarly implicit is the opposition to imperialism, colonialism, orientalism, and fascism. (Communism is pointedly not included.) That it opposes discrimination, specifically anti-Blackness and anti-indigeneity, and Islamophobia, is also in keeping with its non-particularist, universalist attitude.

Less clear is the meaning of JDT's opposition to "assimilation," given the group's explicitly leftist tilt, a hallmark of assimilationist Judaism. The reason seems to lie in its insistence on "defending our Jewish values" and "celebrating the anti-colonialist traditions of our Jewish ancestors," alongside support for *tikkun olam*: the JDT claims to be the real inheritors of the Judaic liberal creed. Accordingly, it can claim to oppose both antisemitism and Zionism. On its FAQ site, the JDT congratulates its membership for having managed to escape the "environment of propaganda that is deliberately fostered in many American Jewish congregations and communities." The difficulty of that challenge cannot be overstated: "Deprogramming ourselves and learning to unpack and see through that propaganda takes a lot of work." Herculean, really, when you consider that "[m]any have been made to think that in the aftermath of pogroms and genocide, Jews must have a Jewish state in order to be safe." So stupid, those "many."

The JDT is proudly anti-Zionist and pro-Palestinian. It stands with the victims of the fascist, colonialist, racist regime of Israel, namely the Palestinian Arabs. It is the pro-Israeli, Zionist Jews sympathetic to this militaristic state who have abandoned the "true values" of Judaism: "It is antisemitic to hold Israel to a different standard than other political states simply because it is a 'Jewish state.'" Talk about preposterous. Year after year, Israel is condemned by the UN Human Rights Council in at least five annual resolutions and is the subject of at least five critical reports, while oppressive regimes like Iran, North Korea, and Belarus are criticized in only one resolution. Meanwhile, the world's worst regimes are subject to no criticism. The UN human rights expert on Palestine is mandated only to investigate "Israel's violations" of international law, and not violations by the Palestinian Authority or Hamas.[49] Calling this a case of double standards is to assume that standards still exist.

The Oxymoron of "Democratic" Internationalism[50]

"*American nationalism ... [is] difficult if not impossible to trace, for it is only at the highest level of abstraction that its history is the progress of a continuous idea.*"

- Bernard Bailyn, "Review of *American Nationalism*" (1958)

"*Only in the presence of the enemy can such a thing as la nation une et indivisible [one nation, indivisible], the ideal of French and of all other nationalism, come to pass.*"

- Hannah Arendt, *On Revolution* (1963)

"[T]he themes of anti-Americanism and anti-Semitism long preceded the rise of the United States to superpower status, let alone Israel's Six-Day War conquests."

- Robert S. Wistrich, *The Lethal Obsession* (2010)

"Ironically, and contrary to so many professed good intentions, Jews do most to advance the liberal idea when they stand up to their enemies on their own behalf, and least when they assume excessive guilt in the hope of political absolution, or camouflage the defense of Jews as a loftier cosmopolitan cause."[51] So wrote Ruth Wisse in 1992. But her assessment is still valid, applying to Jews and non-Jews alike in modern-day America who engage in the common fallacy known as mirror-imaging, imagining that humility is everywhere admired, and contrition welcomed. Though understandable, the propensity to project one's psychological and cultural reaction-patterns on others, and assume they respond in similar ways, invariably misfires. People who welcome expressions of remorse are often over-eager to engage in goodwill gestures hoping to appease their enemies, expecting reciprocity.

This is wishful thinking on steroids. Most if not all of America's enemies will no more stop hating it than will Israel's, even if the Zionist state were to abide by every United Nations resolution. Maybe they would be impressed if it committed suicide, but probably not. Because at bottom, the enemies of both nations share an antagonism that no amount of kowtowing and breast-beating can erase. Israel and America belong to a liberal order anathema to their opponents. Like Israel, the American republic is based on principles articulated in the Old Testament, the Torah, implicitly challenging the legitimacy of any system that repudiates them. There is no getting around that fact.

The cluster of beliefs that underlie those principles is not easy to describe. The task becomes exponentially harder as ambiguities emerge through time. "The liberal idea," Wisse's wise choice for describing the multi-layered conceptual elements of liberalism, seems to her ideally suited for describing the animating wellspring of an affinity community bound by a covenant it vows to respect, which applies to each individual in the community with equal force. Best captured in America by the Declaration of Independence, such a covenant enfolds its members and their descendants, though others' inclusion is anticipated and welcomed. Predicated on personal responsibility implying reciprocal rights and obligations, it thrives in a culture that fosters empathy.

Though not strictly an ideology, what was first described by Adam Smith as "the system of natural liberty" may well be labeled *liberalism,* if only to underscore the holistic conceptual reach of the liberal idea and its emotional hold, in a way that purely cognitive, rational philosophical categories cannot do. The problem with most political isms is the preponderance of passion over logic, which undermines most attempts at clarity. With fuzzy connotation overwhelming somewhat less ambiguous denotation, they are catnip for sophists.

As ideologies, anti-isms resist refutation. "Americanism" is not a function of any particular set of government policies, for even when those change, which they frequently do, the antagonism against the United States persists. This is not mere loathing: for by contrast, while many people dislike the French in general and even in particular, there is no anti-Frenchism. Nor, for that matter, is there anti-Irishism or anti-Italianism as such, despite the presence of signs a century ago, particularly but not exclusively in Southern states, expressing hostility against both ethnicities.

Antagonism directed against people qua members of a particular group depends on time and place, as do various rationalizations. Call it tribalism, it comes down to this: my own is better than yours, now go away or suffer the consequences. But something else is at stake here. Political theorist James Ceaser has it exactly right when he defines anti-Americanism as "the political religion of our times."[52] In 2004, he found that "[o]n every continent, large contingents of intellectuals, backed by significant numbers in the political class, organize their political thinking on the basis of anti-Americanism."[53] Today, the situation is far worse.

What constitutes the essence of that attitude, or ideology? Paul Hollander deems it "a deep seated, emotional predisposition that perceives the United States as an unmitigated and uniquely evil entity and the source of all, or most, other evils in the world."[54] Intimately related to fear of modernity and expanding economic as well as cultural globalization, continues Hollander, the predisposition of anti-Americanism is also a result of "the belief that big corporations (capitalism) are in the process of extending their influence and power around the world, and that the United States, as the major capitalist country, plays a prime role in this undesirable process."[55]

Anti-Americanism is thus an unmistakable symptom of hostility to "the liberal idea." Like antisemitism, a particularly identifiable, albeit heterogeneous, group is used as a foil to reify and concentrate resentment. The tactic is notoriously effective in forging political alliances, harnessing quasi-religious zeal couched in lofty-sounding ideals that help dispense with any additional justificatory arguments whose disingenuous and flimsy nature may prove overly transparent.

No one understood this maneuver better than did the great George Orwell. In his underappreciated *Notes on Nationalism*, published in October 1945, Orwell seized the opportunity to fill the semantic void created by a habit of mind that "is now so widespread that it affects our thinking on nearly every subject,"[56] to wit, the political ism. The essay is a masterpiece more relevant than ever.

Leery of coining one more neologism that ends up stillborn, he opts for the next closest thing: an existing dictionary entry in more-or-less-good standing, sanctified by common usage, which, however imperfectly suited for the new job at hand, is reasonably new and just vague enough to permit flexible redefinition through caveat and contextualizing. "Nationalism" seemed just right.

Given the minor inconvenience that in Orwell's usage it does not always, perhaps not even primarily, involve feelings about a *nation* in the usual sense of a race or geographical area, denoting instead a religion (or "church") or class, he has to redefine it first:

> By "nationalism" I mean first of all the habit of assuming that human beings can be classified like insects and that whole blocks of millions or tens of millions of people can be confidently labelled "good" or "bad."[57] But secondly – and this is much more important – I mean the habit of identifying oneself with a single nation or other unit, placing it beyond good and evil and recognizing no other duty than that of advancing its interests.

And since any definition will become clearer when contrasted with an apparent but actually false synonym, he specifies that

> [n]ationalism is not to be confused with patriotism. Both words are normally used in so vague a way that any definition is liable to be challenged, but one must draw a distinction between them, since two different and even opposing ideas are involved. By "patriotism" I mean devotion to a particular place and a particular way of life, which one believes to be the best in the world but has no wish to force on other people. Patriotism is of its nature defensive, both militarily and culturally.

The difference is radical. "Nationalism… is inseparable from the desire for power," and thus requires a careful designation of the target group, or "nation," whose unity a nationalist means to use to fill his need to live meaningfully by identifying with something greater than himself. "The abiding purpose of every nationalist is to secure more power and more prestige," adds Orwell – purportedly "not for himself but for the nation or other unit in which he has chosen to sink his own individuality."

If one expected a member of the notoriously egocentric intelligentsia to be among the least inclined to "sink his individuality" into anything, one would be wrong. After clarifying that the elite set includes Communist Party members as well as fellow-travelers and Russophiles generally, Orwell declares that among them, "the dominant form of nationalism is Communism." A former Communist himself, whose Socialist sympathies persisted long after abandoning all faith in the Soviet system, Orwell defines the term not as a slur, nor, McCarthy-style, a false accusation of Party affiliation, but as a general attitude: "A Communist looks upon the U.S.S.R. as his Fatherland and feels it his duty to justify Russian policy and advance Russian interests at all costs. Obviously such people abound in England today, and their direct and indirect influence is very great."

In particular, a Communist thus defined would follow Russian policy regarding America, which had once again turned sour the brief marriage of convenience during World War II. After Joseph Stalin stated publicly, in February 1946, that "the war broke out as the inevitable result of the development of world economic and political forces on the basis of present-day monopolistic capitalism,"[58] it was back to the old Marxist antinomies. Pro-Soviet nationalist/Communists, in Orwell's sense, were thus necessarily anti-American. This held true not only outside the United

States – specifically in England, Orwell's main target audience – but ominously, within.

Trouble starts once omelets are on the revolutionary menu, and the variously guillotined eggs scramble inside the frying pans of nationalism, yielding double standards. For "[t]he nationalist not only does not disapprove of atrocities committed by his own side, but he has a remarkable capacity for not even hearing about them." This is by no means limited to one side. Orwell reminds any fellow countryman prematurely tempted to self-congratulate that "[f]or quite six years the English admirers of Hitler contrived not to learn of the existence of Dachau and Buchenwald." Similarly, "those who are loudest in denouncing the German concentration camps are often quite unaware, or only very dimly aware, that there are also concentration camps in Russia. Huge events like the Ukraine famine of 1933, involving the deaths of millions of people, have actually escaped the attention of the majority of English russophiles." Ideological myopia is an equal opportunity affliction.

Members of both camps, and others, will likely find themselves fellow-nationalists in other respects. Thus "[m]any English people have heard almost nothing about the extermination of German and Polish Jews during the present war. Their own antisemitism has caused this vast crime to bounce off their consciousness. In nationalist thought there are facts which are both true and untrue, known and unknown." And all nationalists "have the power of not seeing resemblances between similar sets of facts." It is a human predilection difficult to overcome.

Closely related to this cognitive deficiency is the practice of moral equivalence, which presumes to set in balance often preposterously disparate iniquities. Notable among them is the practice of "'comparative trivialization,' as in comparing United States' treatment of the prisoners in Guantánamo to the Nazis' treatment of those they detained."[59] Abuses of Holocaust memory, in fact, have become increasingly common on the liberal-left, particularly in the last few years. In May 2019, for example, Congresswoman Rashida Tlaib mused on *Yahoo News* podcast: "There's a kind of a calming feeling, I always tell folks, when I think of the Holocaust and the tragedy of the Holocaust, and the fact that it was my ancestors — Palestinians — who lost their land, and some lost their lives, their livelihood, their human dignity, their existence, in many ways, had been wiped out." To which Aaron David Miller, advisor to both Democratic and Republican presidents, who is Jewish, could say only that the comparison was "highly arguable."[60]

Arguable, quite highly so, to put it mildly, but seldom argued by increasingly many Americans, Jews in particular, who call themselves liberals. As progressivism has taken over larger segments of their community, *tikkun olam* has served as a conceptual bridge, savvily camouflaged in both foreignness and religiosity to facilitate the transition. It fell to Barack Obama to explain how modern liberalism became all but indistinguishable from the Jewish conception of social justice: "Around the world, we can seek to extend the miracles of freedom and peace, prosperity and security, to more of God's creation. And together we can continue the hard but awesome work of *tikkun olam*, and to do our part to repair the world,"[61] declared the president in his Passover greeting issued by the White House on April 15, 2015.

Nice words, but what did he mean? What does "extending the miracles of freedom and peace" mean in actual practice? The president's most important role is to keep the nation safe. Did the decision to assist Europeans in bombing Libya, thus precipitating regime change only to see it descend in chaos and terror, condoning Russia's invasion of Georgia, releasing billions of dollars to Iran's rabidly anti-American and anti-Israeli mullahs, and abandoning "red lines" in Syria, among other foreign policy moves, repair anything? Did any of that end up "extending" any of those fine goals, the "miracles of freedom and peace?" On the contrary.

By no means should America turn its back on the world, were that even possible. The Founders never thought so, even though scholars have been split between those who argued that most Founders sought to stay out of foreign conflicts and others who believed that they embraced a nascent exceptionalism which regarded the New World as a shining city on a hill. It seems perfectly obvious that originally, in the eighteenth century, the one overarching foreign policy issue before the embryonic United States was sheer survival.

It was no time for isms. Once a peaceful resolution of their disagreement with the Mother Country proved illusory and independence was declared, the signatories of the treacherous Declaration knew that defeat on the battlefield meant certain execution. But to win a war against the mighty British empire, allies were indispensable. With their help, defying overwhelming odds, the ragged colonists miraculously did win. The consummate diplomat Benjamin Franklin delivered France; John Adams patiently lobbied the Dutch to secure a heft loan from the Netherlands; and George Washington put his prior military and intelligence experience to good use, demonstrating extraordinary strategic acumen. The Founding Brothers thus all contributed, each doing his best.

Since the Constitution places responsibility for foreign policy decisions in the president and reserves appropriation of funds to Congress, the drafters demonstrated typical pragmatism in reconciling opposites. Though intending that a large a portion of the population should endorse the decision of Congress, the commander-in-chief had the greatest latitude. This allowed progressive Theodore Roosevelt, alongside Wilson, his co-ideologue who later adopted the liberal label, to seek spreading the American vision of democracy. As defined in their day by John Dewey, that meant empowering people like themselves, elites who knew what was best for the people, which they both interpreted in expansionist terms. But if that was "internationalism," neither used the word. It was thus described only retroactively, and most imprecisely.

As often happens with rhetoric, Wilson's famous "Fourteen Points" document was less influential for what it said than for what it precipitated: bringing the United States into a conflict that did not threaten its borders, seemingly for ideological reasons alone. Wilson summarized them as follows:

> What we demand in this war, therefore, is nothing peculiar to ourselves. It is that the world be made fit and safe to live in; and particularly that it be made safe for every peace-loving nation which, like our own, wishes to live its own life, determine its own institutions, be assured of justice and fair dealing by the other peoples of the world as against force and selfish aggression. All the peoples of the world are in effect partners in this interest, and for our own part we see very clearly that unless justice be done to others it will not be done to us. The program of the world's peace, therefore, is our program.[62]

Should this be considered a fair description of what has been called "liberal internationalism?" University of Sussex Professor Beate Jahn explains recent developments: "Under the Bush administration in the early 2000s, the United States seemed to abandon liberal internationalism altogether. It replaced multilateralism with unilateralism, shunned its friends and allies, ignored international institutions, pursued an aggressive and illegal economic policy, and blatantly violated human rights."[63] Princeton University Professor G. John Ikenberry is among those who disagree: "[I]t is not liberal internationalism that is in crisis but rather America's authority as the hegemonic leader of the liberal world order."[64]

In an article Ikenberry co-authored with Johns Hopkins University Professor Daniel Deudney in 1999, the two argued that "the postwar order was created as a response to the earlier failures of both Wilsonian internationalism and the extreme realism of the inter-war period (and its economic blocs, mercantilism, hyper-nationalism, and imperialism)."[65] The implication is clear: the new form of liberal internationalism under American control has become "multilateral." No longer are international institutions to be "ignored" but respected, and the U.S. may no longer "blatantly violate human rights."

The change from pre-Cold War to the new version of liberalism, writes Jahn, amounts to a veritable crisis. "[L]iberal internationalists trace its roots to arrogant American foreign policies and view a reformed democratic internationalism as the solution." In 2012, the Council on Foreign Relations released a Working Paper by Ikenberry and Deudney recommending that "the United States should initiate a new phase of democratic internationalism based on the "pull of success rather than the push of power" that "deepens democracy globally, prevents democratic backsliding, and strengthens and consolidates bonds among democratic states."[66] Then-president Barack Obama would famously call this "leading from behind."

Though he did not give it a name, President Obama proceeded to implement a new foreign policy of the left-liberals,[67] which Elliott Abrams nonetheless identifies as "an ideology." Its essence was conveyed not by words but through his actions, which Senator George McGovern, the Democratic presidential candidate in 1972, would have heartily endorsed. Writes Abrams:

> The ideas espoused by Obama "incubated" decades ago, and were most likely adopted back at Columbia University or in the Chicago kitchen of his friends of Weathermen fame, Bill Ayers and Bernadine Dohrn.... The enduring hold of that ideology is visible not only in his Iran policy but also, most recently, with respect to Cuba. There, too, he has reversed decades of American foreign policy, and has done so, as in the case of Iran, without seeking any deep concessions from the Castro regime. .... In both instances, Obama has acted not to advance American national interests but to make amends for U.S. policies and actions that he views as the immoral and retrograde detritus of the "cold-war mentality."[68]

It is difficult to overstate the stunning nature of this assessment: that a president would ever act in a manner designed "not to advance American national interests," choosing rather to "make amends" for his country's presumed sins, is predictably seen as a form of weakness and decadence. Far from "repairing the world," it is bound to embolden the nation's enemies.

But in what way can internationalism possibly be "democratic?" When the *demos* includes the whole world, what sort of *krasis* (in Greek, "power") can any one person wield? Ikenberry and Deudney attempt to clarify: "[D]emocratic internationalism," as they see it, "would return liberal internationalism to its roots in social democratic ideals, seek to redress imbalances within the democratic world between fundamentalist capitalism and socioeconomic equity, and move toward a posthegemonic system of global governance in which the United States increasingly shares authority with other democracies."[69] Its aims, then, are "democratic" insofar as property would be more equally distributed in a "post-hegemonic" (homogeneous? surely not liberal) world order.

The authors correctly point out that "American liberal internationalism was shaped and enabled by the domestic programs of the Progressives, the New Deal, and the Great Society. These initiatives aimed to address the U.S. economic, social, and racial inequalities, create a free but efficiently regulated capitalism, recast the American state for an industrializing and globalizing world, and adapt the U.S. constitutional order and the pursuit of freedom to modernity." Those were golden days. Unfortunately, at present, "[a]mong democracies, the United States finds itself an outlier, as other democratic states surpass it on various measures of democratic performance like equity, opportunity, and institutional effectiveness."

Above all, it is deficient in equity. But equity *uber alles* is a tall order:

> Tackling the maldistribution of wealth, income, and opportunity that has increasingly marked contemporary democracies requires reversing many of the policies of Reagan-Thatcher fundamentalist capitalism.... More specifically, the equity agenda requires the restoration of progressive income taxation and heavy taxation of large estates, and greater roles for workers and their unions in corporate governance.

Nor is the equity problem restricted to individuals; it also extends to states. The effort must be transnational, for "[c]losing the 'democratic community gap' will require building links between the United States and numerous non-Western democracies, as well as with longstanding democracies strongly committed to robust government promotion of social and economic equity associated with social democracy." This requires a major reconsideration of America's role in the world.

So-called "democratic internationalism" is but the foreign policy side of America's strategy coin, the other being "the progressive domestic program of renewal." In all probability, argue Ikenberry and Deudney, in the foreseeable future "support for a new domestic progressive agenda will grow. However, this domestic political mobilization is necessary but insufficient to tame and regulate capitalism, given the scale and scope of the global capitalist system..." What must happen is for the U.S. to go beyond "the hypercapitalist world, [for] only a wide coalition of democratic states can establish the common frameworks and standards for regulation, taxation, and growth."

Once capitalism is "tamed" at home, the United States will be much more popular. "If progressives can succeed in turning domestic policy in the United States, they will find themselves in a world hospitable to their agenda, an enlarged democratic world with many potentially willing partners."[70] For that to happen, however, the U.S. must turn toward "multilateral problem solving and global governance." Unfortunately, "[i]nternational cooperation seems to have succumbed to gridlock in multiple areas, such as the environment, trade, United Nations (UN) reform, and the global nonproliferation regime," in no small measure due to U.S. recalcitrance.

The new model of global governance differs somewhat from the original version, which relied primarily on international organizations such as the U.N. and its agencies, as well as the World Bank, the International Monetary Fund (IMF), and others whose membership consists of state representatives. By contrast, "[t]he next generation of global governance will employ approaches that combine agendas of formal international institution building with complementary efforts and strategies from nongovernmental organizations [NGOs], networks of research institutions, local governments, and corporations." Together they constituted a coalition of progressive so-called "epistemic communities,"[71] which in plain English refers to elites consisting of academics, diplomats, and international bureaucrats.

As all of them presume to speak "for the interests of the world's poor" and the alleged good of "the people," Hudson Institute Senior Fellow John Fonte concludes that "the global governance project" is essentially "a grand ideological and institutional enterprise that promises to be of world-historical significance – an attempt to create new political forms above and beyond the liberal democratic nation-state."[72] True to form, those empowered to speak for "all" are the infamous vanguard, the intellectual elite, who claim to know the real interests of the "countless thousands."

American University law professor Kenneth Anderson diagnoses this anything-but-democratic internationalism as a secularization, indeed perversion, of medieval utopian millenarianism in modern garb. It is, argues Anderson, "comprehensible only upon the religious worldview that boldly proclaims the good news of international organizations, differing from the view of the Psalmist – the 'earth is the Lord's, and the fullness thereof' the world, and they that shall dwell therein'" as goes the passage from *Isaiah*. Except this time, scoffs Anderson, it is "the UN, that duly noted steward of the Lord, [who will] inherit the earth."[73]

Poverty itself, claim the epistemic elites, proves incontrovertibly that the rich are violating the human rights of the poor whom they mercilessly exploit. Most NGOs, reflexively progressive, are especially prone to this form of reasoning, self-appointed ambassadors-without-portfolio for "the poor" and self-styled champions of the "public" interest. In an unpublished essay titled "After Seattle," written in 2000, Anderson writes that the "elite media," such as the *Economist*, have only exacerbated the problem by implicitly conferring special moral approval to this lofty-sounding "international civil society." Such bombast only reinforces the arrogant self-righteousness of organizations that are in no way accountable to anyone but their funders, whether government agencies or private donors with individual agendas, however well intentioned.

Anderson charges that the "human rights movement is as a kind of secular religion… increasingly assuming the tone of (prosecutorial) authority and taking its international structures as grounds for the reform of recalcitrant nation-states within what might be thought of [as] the Holy Human Rights Empire."[74] According to a 2006 report released by the U.N. itself, the organization became an ideal conduit for progressivism: "[S]ocial justice first appeared in United Nations texts during the second half of the 1960s. At the initiative of the Soviet Union, and with the support of developing countries, the term was used in the "Declaration on Social Progress and Development," adopted in 1969.[75] Of course it was the initiative of the Soviet Union. Who else?

Three decades later, the rhetoric was solidly entrenched. Writes long-time human rights activist Aaron Rhodes in his 2018 book *The Debasement of Human Rights*: "The early 1990s saw a worldwide resurgence of left-wing politics under a range of slogans providing cosmetic dissociation from Communism and state socialism."[76] In the forefront were the self-styled "'human rights' campaigns, promoting social and economic rights and asserting that civil and political rights by themselves are a recipe for exploitative, even racist capitalism. But these were (and are) movements essentially advocating coercion in the name of human rights."

Do words even matter anymore? When internationalism provides disingenuous cover to global authoritarianism, "human rights without freedom" is the new anti-liberalism, and progress a millenarian euphemism for the Apocalypse, we must turn to Ludwig Wittgenstein. Having reminded us that "philosophical problems arise when language *goes on holiday*,"[77] adding that most "questions to be found in philosophical works are not false but nonsensical,"[78] what else can we do but come home from the semantic sabbatical and take a look at a reality that may escape the pseudo-educated woke but not the commoners whose common sense is still mercifully awake.

Conclusion:

"Freedom in the Fullest Sense"

> *[This is t]he deeper paradox out of which [Tocqueville's "tyranny of the Majority"] was destined to appear. Freedom in the fullest sense implies both variety and equality. ... At the bottom of the American experience of freedom, not in antagonism to it but as a constituent element of it, there has always lain the inarticulate premise of conformity.*
>
> **- Louis Hartz, *The Liberal Tradition in America* (1955)**

Paradox was in America's bloodstream - its Founders had been at once revolutionary and conservative. The War of Independence had been fought less to oppose the nation that gave the world the Magna Carta and proclaimed the principle of representative government than to uphold that very same principle, which the colonists had accused it of betraying. It was by invoking the British tradition that the Founders turned the tables on the British King and Parliament, accusing *them* of violating its sacred values. This was no idle posturing. As Harvard Professor Louis Hartz observes in his seminal *The Liberal Tradition in America* (1955), "[a] series of circumstances had conspired to saturate even the revolutionary position of the Americans with the quality of traditionalism – to give them, indeed, the appearance of outraged reactionaries."[1]

As if that weren't enough, "America piled on top of this paradox another one of the opposite kind," namely, the ineffable novelty of its enterprise. "It had been a story of new beginnings, daring enterprises, and explicitly stated principles.... The result was that the traditionalism of the Americans, like a pure freak of logic, often bore amazing marks of antihistorical rationalism." Hartz is referring to the revolutionary constitutions of 1776 "which evoked, as [Benjamin] Franklin reported, the 'rapture' of European liberals everywhere." The concept of a written constitution thus transcended even the British experience with Common

Law liberalism, thereby becoming "the darling of the rationalists – a symbol of the emancipated mind at work."[2]

So then, what best describes the original form of American liberalism? Was it rationalist, traditionalist, conservative, radical, universalist, nationalist, democratic, individualistic? Clearly, or rather unclearly, it was none and all of the above. Eminently practical men, they were convinced by facts that freedom works. At the same time, they believed that freedom was right. The impetus was profoundly moral and spiritual, based on the principle that each of us had been endowed by our Creator with unalienable rights. That we were all equally unequal was to them self-evident.

Over the course of many decades, however, this outlook gradually eroded. The meaning of liberalism changed almost beyond recognition. Then, the World War II apocalypse showed the full horror of its opposite: tototalitarianism. Bi-winged Right/Left, it prompted a group of like-minded economists and philosophers to regroup and recalibrate. What they considered an existential threat to civilization and human survival itself had to be resisted, lest mankind self-destruct. Their deliberations would result in what came to be known as the Mont Pèlerin Society.

Deliberately avoiding ideological labels, the Society declared itself committed to inquiry and discussion "among minds inspired by certain ideals and broad conceptions held in common, to contribute to the preservation and improvement of the free society."[3] Though principally devoted to defending free markets, it also denounced "the historical fatalism which believes in our power to discover laws of historical development which we must obey, and the historical relativism which denies all absolute moral standards and tends to justify any political means by the purposes at which it aims." Put more succinctly, the target was progressivism and its ideological twins, whether situated on History's putative right or left side, up or down, red-hued, black, or green.

Among the most influential of a group that included such luminaries as Henry Hazlitt, William Roepke, Frank H. Knight, Ludwig von Mises, and Lionel Robbins, was the diminutive intellectual giant Milton Friedman, who would become one of the most celebrated economists of his time. Like his wife Rose a child of Orthodox Jews who emigrated to

America from my neck of the Carpathian woods, Milton appreciated paradox and detested simplistic ideological solutions to complex problems. How is one to settle "the tension between providing for the common social values required for a stable society on the one hand, and indoctrination inhibiting freedom of thought and belief on the other?"[4] He could only answer that it was just "another of those vague boundaries that it is easier to mention than to define." Yet twenty years later, he would defend public funding of religious schools, despite believing that as a rule, government had to be strictly limited to allow greater scope for individual initiative. He did not go as far as his more anarchistic friends in opposing all government action.

Yet he adamantly refused, as had Hayek,[5] to adopt the label "conservatism" outright, insisting that for his philosophy, "the rightful and proper label is liberalism." In *Capitalism and Freedom* (1988), Milton identified, as did Rose, with the nineteenth century liberal who "was a radical, both in the etymological sense of going to the root of the matter, and in the political sense of favoring major changes in social institutions. So too must be his modern heir. We do not wish to conserve the state interventions that have interfered so greatly with our freedom, though, of course, we do wish to conserve those that have promoted it."[6] True liberal conservatives were never violent. But neither were they timorous and afraid of change – on the contrary, they embraced change, innovation, and inclusion, provided it was uncoerced. That proviso made all the difference.

In no way was Milton's idealism solipsistic, monadic, atomistic, asocial – quite the contrary, freedom, he insisted, only makes sense in relation to other people. Taking "the individual, or perhaps the family, as our ultimate goal in judging social arrangements," freedom is meaningless on a solitary island. Political democracy, moreover, must not be understood merely as an electoral system, which is impractical except on a small scale – other arrangements require some sort of representation. Thus in many ways, the most democratic of social arrangements is actually the market, which serves as a sort of "system of proportional representation" that allows each person to "vote" for the goods he prefers and can afford. At bottom, "[p]olitical freedom means the absence of coercion of a man by his fellow men. The fundamental threat to freedom is the power to coerce, be it in the hands of a monarch, a dictator, an oligarchy, or a momentary majority."[7] That seems clear enough, no isms required.

Friedman, who died in 2006 at 94, would undoubtedly have had no objection to being included alongside Hayek in an anthology compiled in 2020 by Hannes H. Gussurarson, professor of political science at the University of Iceland, featuring two dozen theoreticians under the label "conservative liberalism." Ranging from St. Thomas Aquinas to David Hume, Frédéric Bastiat to Edmund Burke, William Graham Sumner to Robert Nozick, the singularly motley crew nonetheless share a common vision: "While they may present various kinds of arguments for their positions, from divine command, human reason, social utility, natural evolution, moral intuition, and common consent, these positions are all in the end based on a choice, which is a commitment to, indeed a celebration of, Judeo-Christian Western civilization."[8]

Opposed to the rationalism of the French Revolution, most of those gathered at Mont Pèlerin agreed with Hayek that "true liberalism has no quarrel with religion. I can only deplore," he would write later,[9] "the militant and essentially illiberal antireligionism which animated so much of nineteenth-century Continental liberalism." Rather, "what distinguishes the liberal from the conservative … is that, however profound his own spiritual beliefs, he will never regard himself as entitled to impose them on others and that for him the spiritual and the temporal are different spheres which ought not to be confused."[10] Jefferson, as well as Hamilton, would have cheered.

Perhaps surprisingly, none of the Founders is included in the anthology - perhaps because they were not mere theoreticians, intent on realistically implementing liberal ideas. Everyone knows that they created the longest-living written Constitution, resulting in the most successful political experiment in history, thanks to more than a century of self-governance at the local and state levels. As improbable as the rise of a phoenix, America managed to unite under one overarching document that at once embraced and transcended the ashes of abstraction. But it must be conceded that the Founders, besides a deep understanding of the primacy of individual liberty and experience in self-governance, possessed in addition an abiding faith in their communal enterprise: they were a team.

Louis Hartz describes this extraordinary outlook as Hebraism - which, unlike "Hebraic," is not restricted to a sect or religion - intimating the idea of "the Chosen People." For there is little doubt that Americans had believed themselves unique in a manner similar to the ancient Hebrews, not as recipients of extra largesse so much as being tasked with momentous responsibilities. They understood that treating one another with respect, in conformity with the supreme covenantal premise, was more likely to lead to peace and prosperity than if they did not. Falling so dismally short of that ideal by failing to outlaw slavery from the outset – admittedly a practical impossibility at the time – only confirmed the truth of this suspicion.

Slavery, of course, had been America's greatest sin that could never be truly forgiven. That other communities, then and later, fared far worse is no comfort. But at least the nation's lodestar had been enshrined in the Declaration. And then America was blessed with its very own Abraham.

Having constituted themselves as a people by choice, America's first citizens still believed themselves impelled by a power beyond themselves, feeling neither rudderless nor alone in the universe. Man would have to use all the powers of his soul – both reason and faith, mind and heart – guided by a light that transcended the visible world. Sometimes reason and faith would collide, heart or mind seeking to eviscerate one another. But then the soul would wisely arbitrate, to reflect the exigencies of communal living and the simple clarity of the Golden Rule. Sometimes.

The paradox embraced by the system of natural liberty was bound to reflect the paradox of surviving in society: at once a monumental challenge and a salvation, it would test the limits of empathy. It takes but a modicum of Comm to grasp that loving oneself does not exclude loving others. Though egocentrism comes first, each baby instinctively oblivious to all but its own survival, maturity soon teaches the virtue of transcending oneself. The solipsist, a hapless Narcissus, sooner or later sinks into bottomless nihilism. But while the Greek mythological figure merely drowned himself, the psychopathic solipsist can drown an entire civilization.

Ideally, one should embrace the fact that true self-love is inimical to myopic egoism. The soul is nourished by empathy. Conversely, pretending that evil will be mollified by license and exempted from punishment does not minimize but exacerbates it. Evil and good are part of this world as are night and day, with dawn and dusk partaking of both. Instead of abolishing antinomies, a sophisticated liberal dialectic is meant to sustain and preserve. Enhancing moral clarity is life-giving. And it starts with the experience of each person, extrapolated to the community. Loving one's family, for example, teaches how others love theirs, and devotion to one's own nation can enhance sympathy for others who are similarly patriotic. But it also means protecting it against dangers. The particular and the universal, far from mutually canceling, are complementary.

In the quintessential American epic *Song of Myself,* Walt Whitman captures the paradox of the one *qua* many, prototype as category, individual as people, part as whole:

I am of old and young, of the foolish as much as the wise,
Regardless of others, ever regardful of others,
Maternal as well as paternal, a child as well as a man,
Stuff'd with the stuff that is coarse and stuff'd with the stuff that is fine,
One of the Nation of many nations, the smallest the same and the largest the same.[11]

The apparent inconsistencies may be difficult to grasp by pure reason. But they are familiar fare in non-Western cultures more readily inclined to accept the complexity manifest in nature and oneself. Whitman invites the reader to sing with him a tune that brings together mankind and the world, and both with the beyond:

These are really the thoughts of all men in all ages and lands, they are not original with me,
If they are not yours as much as mine they are nothing, or next to nothing,
If they are not the riddle and the untying of the riddle they are nothing,
If they are not just as close as they are distant they are nothing.
This is the grass that grows wherever the land is and the water is,
This the common air that bathes the globe....

We are all alike yet all irreducibly different, each destined to make our own choices in separate ways even as we learn from one another, assuming we can, and allow ourselves to do so. The renowned Whitman scholar Ed Folsom describes the background and purpose of the epic:

> When Walt Whitman first began making notes toward the poem that would become "Song of Myself," he jotted down "I am the poet of slaves and the masters of slaves." He was trying to assume a voice, in other words, that was capacious enough to speak for the entire range of people in the nation—from the most powerless to the most powerful, from those with no possessions to those who possessed others. If he could imagine such a unifying voice, he believed, he could help Americans begin to speak the language of democracy, because if slaves could begin to see that they contained within themselves the potential to be slavemasters, just as slavemasters contained within themselves the potential to be slaves, then slavery would cease to exist, because people of the nation would begin to understand that everyone is potentially everyone else, that the key to American identity is a vast empathy with all the "others" in the culture.[12]

Whitman bows before himself as before the other, aware that we are all equally unequal in God's Image, each traveling alone, yet alongside all who ever were and will be:

> *Not I, not any one else can travel that road for you,*
> *You must travel it for yourself.*
> *It is not far, it is within reach,*
> *Perhaps you have been on it since you were born and did not know,*
> *Perhaps it is everywhere on water and on land.*
> *Shoulder your duds dear son, and I will mine, and let us hasten forth,*
> *Wonderful cities and free nations we shall fetch as we go....*

Paradox or contradiction? Either way, it need neither perplex nor stupefy.

> *Do I contradict myself?*
> *Very well then I contradict myself,*
> *(I am large, I contain multitudes.)*

Whitman's expansive vision of the new man in the New World was at once pre-modern and post-modern. The road we all must travel, infinitely long in anticipation, is yet over in an instant. Each walks along a separate road but not alone: none of us could do it without others, to lessen the burden by sharing a common fate. The first settlers especially demonstrated enormous courage taking off to face an ocean on flimsy vessels, with few resources and only a fuzzy notion of what lay at the destination. It is almost impossible to fathom how anyone dared to start over in a land most fifteenth century inhabitants hadn't even know existed. Christopher Columbus's successful landing in what he took to be East Asia looked miraculous, seeming to all the world a kind of rebirth.

The pious Columbus, no mere mercenary, actually did expect to encounter descendants of the Lost Tribes of Israel. Assuming they spoke Arabic and Hebrew, he prudently decided to bring along an interpreter fluent in both languages. He settled on Luis de Torres. Born Yosef ben Ha Levy Halvri, de Torres would thus become the first Jew to land in the Americas.[13] Their ship took off on August 3, 1492. Little did he know that the date would fall exactly one day after the Spanish Edict of Expulsion ordered the forced exodus of the country's Jews.

In Jewish history, that exodus, this time involuntary, would mark the beginning of a new era. "Of the many calamities to befall the Jewish people during their arduous passage from the medieval to the modern world," writes Georgetown University Professor Jonathan Ray, "none was more sharply felt or more widely chronicled by its contemporaries."[14] No prelude to utopia, quite the contrary, a new beginning this was nonetheless for all the world – eventually, as it turned out, even (or especially) for the Jews.

When two centuries later John Locke observed that "in the beginning, all the world was America,"[15] he could not avoid sounding biblical. Not that he minded. Most likely, however, the freethinking empiricist (albeit no atheist), a doctor by training, was making a practical observation. The newly discovered continent presented a unique opportunity to illustrate and test his own "state of nature" theory, as outlined in the *Second Treatise on Government*. And so it was. It would take genius, courage, and Herculean effort, but yes, it worked. The colonists came as close to implementing Locke's theory as he could have hoped, and took it seriously.

The *Treatise* was music to the ears of colonists who wanted security but were reluctant to abandon their considerable degree of personal freedom. Locke had asked: "If Man in the State of Nature be so free, as has been said; If he be absolute Lord of his own Person and Possessions, equal to the greatest, and subject to no Body, why will he part with his Freedom?" The answer was glaringly obvious: he has no choice. For despite "being Kings as much as he, every Man his Equal, and the greater part no strict Observers of Equity and Justice, the enjoyment of the property he has in this state is very unsafe, very unsecure." Members of a community must agree "to unite for the mutual *Preservation* of their Lives, Liberties and Estates, which I call by the general Name, *Property*."[16]

But in their new settlements, as in Locke's model, there were no aristocrats. Each man "an absolute Lord of his own Person and Possessions, equal to the greatest." This Lockeian conception of human liberty is consistent with Hartz's idea of "Hebraism." The presumption of equality among God's children created in His Image would in time lead to the unprecedented religious diversity of colonial America. Mercifully lacking the anti-clerical fury that suffused the radical European revolutionary spirit, observes Hartz, "American liberals, instead of being forced to pull the Christian heaven down to earth, were glad to let it remain where it was."[17]

Spared the murderous fury that had spawned the Jacobin volcano, the American *revolution* reflected that word's etymology as "a cyclical recurrence, a revolving" which occurs in nature as if providentially. The cyclical "return" characteristic of primitive religions, which the renowned Romanian historian of religion Mircea Eliade calls "sacred time," refers to a pre-modern, pre-biblical conception of history as a recurring ritual. It was gradually replaced by a linear view of time, which Eliade calls "profane"[18] because it introduced a secular, non-sacred element: the notion of progress. The pejorative implication of irreverence is not incidental. It was not long before progress would replace the gods themselves as the new idol.

The French Revolution had been the first to apply both the original sense of recurrence and the new focus on progress. On one hand, it sought to reverse the course of history and purify mankind (or at least the French nation) to recapture a pristine utopian virginity. Yet at the same time, it enshrined the state as the instrument of history and nature. Understood by some to replace the biblical deity altogether, it came admittedly close to the dangerous slope leading to pantheism - the idea that God is everywhere, tempting too many to conclude that He is nowhere. Inevitably, the dilemma spilled over into politics. What was the locus of legitimacy? Who had the right to rule? The clergy's role in government, the relationship between church and state, were being reexamined after the Renaissance throughout Europe and beyond. The Reformation had been a direct outgrowth of this new thinking.

The Founders, whatever their personal theological views, emphatically adopted the entire biblical tradition, the Old alongside the New Testament. So too did Isaac Newton and the Scottish philosophers (David Hume being among the best-known exceptions[19]) for a variety of reasons, including concern for public opinion. Benjamin Franklin, for example, wrote to Thomas Paine on December 1757, advising him against publishing his militantly secularist *Age of Reason*: "[T]hink how great a portion of mankind consists of weak and ignorant men and women, and of inexperienced, inconsiderate youth of both sexes, who have the need of the motives of religion to restrain them from vice, to support their virtue, and retain them in the practice of it till it becomes habitual, which is the great point for its security."[20]

That said, the practical Franklin embraced the biblical tradition lovingly and in earnest. When asked to propose a design for America's Seal, he drew on the covenant delivered at Sinai: it depicted Pharaoh drowning at the Red Sea and included the motto "Rebellion to Tyrants Is Obedience to God." A few decades later, in 1852, President Lincoln in his eulogy for Henry Clay used the same imagery: "Pharaoh's country was cursed with plagues," pronounced Lincoln, "and his hosts were drowned in the Red Sea for striving to retain a captive people, who already served them more than four hundred years. May like disasters never befall us!"[21] Nine years later, the disaster would curse America as well. Fortunately, the man whom history and providence placed at its head, who coincidentally shared a name with the first Jew, would see it through.

American history is replete with biblical symbolism. As Rabbi Meir Soloveitchik points out, Abraham Lincoln's repeated references to *Exodus* throughout the Civil War had "underscored the eternal link between Lincoln's life and Passover - the fact that Lincoln's death, marked in the

Hebrew calendar, coincides with Passover every year - [which] is certainly fitting, and perhaps even part of the providence that Lincoln began to see in his own life, and the life of his nation."[22] Like Moses, Lincoln would die after having completed only the first part of the still very long journey ahead, but the nation had finally been set on the right course, away from the curse of slavery.

The Declaration's author was equally devoted to the biblical spirit, notwithstanding his non-sectarian deism. Thomas Jefferson's Seal design similarly invoked the Exodus story, albeit focusing on the journey that followed the Jews' flight from Egypt after Pharaoh's defeat. Rabbi Soloveitchik sees the two designs by the great Founders as perfectly complementary: "Taken together, they give us a political theology of freedom."[23] Escape from tyranny could not have been accomplished without divine assistance, but the ensuing journey would not be guaranteed without human effort. God's protection would still be needed, as always, but it alone was insufficient. That is why man had free will. Fate was a Greek, not a Hebrew concept.

This does not deny the profoundly rational basis of America's founding creed. In no way is the notion of a covenantal deity inconsistent with a libertarian view that individual freedom is the foundation of political action. On the contrary, the assumption of a Higher Power is tantamount to recognizing that all knowledge, all morality, all human discourse is based on premises that must, ultimately, be accepted on faith. Without any assumptions, rationality itself is incoherent.

Too narrow a concept of knowledge, moreover, has no place for what Adam Smith has called "moral sentiments." Rabbi Eliezer Zobin, for example, writes that "like inducive and deductive logic, morality too seems to be a basic axiom of human life.... [W]e humans find morals axiomatic; we see that the suffering of a child, an innocent being suffering, for no purpose is sheer evil. In which case there is no coherence we can bring to the world, unless the world has meaning. Indeed, the scientific endeavor itself is premised upon the assumption we live in a world that can be made sense of, that has a coherence to it."[24] That axiom is a reflection of God's Image.

What ensures human freedom is a covenant implemented through *hesed*, often mistranslated as *grace*. *Hesed,* writes Daniel Elazar, "prevents the covenant from becoming a mere contract, narrowly interpreted by each partner for his benefit alone, by adding a dynamic dimension requiring the parties to act toward each other in such a way as to demonstrate their covenant love; that is, beyond the letter of the law." Since the One who created us in His Image meant us to be free, this can only be thought cruel if freedom is deemed cruel.

But what about atheists? Although the founding generation considered it a requirement for holding state office to swear on the to, in a context of constant territorial expansion. The Declaration is predicated on rights endowed by the Creator. But that means everyone, whatever his or her beliefs. So long as people behave in conformity with this truth, no one asks for philosophical or theological rationale. Even morons have rights. The more thoughtful among the skeptics might consider that "reason" itself is a word, and words describe a reality whose existence is accepted on some sort of faith. That faith inevitably suggests the possibility that some Higher Power may have something to do with our infinitely unfathomable world. This need not imply adherence to any particular sect; just ask any member of Alcoholics Anonymous.

The American liberal experiment was not the work of visionaries. Their concern was to minimize the turmoil and discontent that afflicts any society. Although they considered themselves British subjects, they didn't especially care for elites an ocean away taxing their hard-won earnings and making decisions for them. Having proved they could effectively regulate their own affairs, they saw no reason to have to defer to London. But Americans were not keen on apocalyptic revolutions. They saw little purpose in armed protest, let alone insurrection, except in cases of tyranny. They had not asked for the Revolutionary War; it was hard to fight, and harder to win - its success was anything but foreordained. We are immeasurably lucky to be the beneficiaries of a generation that managed to institute a new system of government without resorting to guillotines.

As Alexis de Tocqueville observed: "The great advantage of the Americans is that they have arrived at a state of democracy without having to endure a democratic revolution; and that they are born equal, instead of becoming so."[25] The Founders' liberalism was mercifully not the result of cataclysmic change of regime "upon the ruins of an aristocracy," as had been the case in France after 1789, where "men who, having entered but yesterday upon their independent condition, are intoxicated with their new power." A bloody overthrow is bound to poison the aftermath of victory. Paradoxically, notes Tocqueville, "democratic revolutions lead [the victors] to shun each other and perpetuate in a state of equality the animosities that the state of inequality created." It is the equality of all against all, perpetual revolution as perpetual revulsion, dystopia as anti-Eden, no matter how passionately its authors insist on the purity of their ideals.

Instead of shunning paradox, why not embrace it, provided it is done wisely and prudently, with maximum of respect for each other? Why not celebrate the complexity of choice, the messiness of compromise and oscillation of uncertainty, the trial-and-error zig-zag of daily life. Security vs. freedom is a false choice; we need both. Seeking to bypass the paradox in one or the other direction risks losing both. Without security, humans cannot live; without freedom, life cannot be human.

One particular cliché holds the key to many a paradox: beware of good intentions. First Friedrich Hayek and later Milton Friedman spelled out how self-righteousness paves the road to serfdom. Call it fairness, or tread on the ambiguity of equality if you must; ultimately, reality kicks in, revealing the consequences of leveling. Write Milton and Rose Friedman in *Free to Choose: A Personal Statement:* "[E]very attempt to make equality of outcome the overriding principle of social organization" has ended in a state of terror. "And even terror has not equalized outcomes. In every case, wide inequality persists by any criterion; inequality between the rulers and the ruled, not only in power but also in material standards of life."[26]

The case of the Jews was particularly puzzling to Milton. I remember traipsing through the snow to the splendidly neo-medieval Mandel Hall, together with my new husband Roger Pilon, to listen to the great man (who served on the committee overseeing Roger's dissertation, "A Theory of Rights," currently being turned into a book destined to become a classic, and soon became a good family friend). The place was packed to overflowing. Friedman's topic that day was "Capitalism and the Jews," a lecture he also delivered that year before the Mont Pèlerin Society.

Calling it a particular case of paradox, he gave his audience fair warning: "My aim here is not to give a ready answer – for I have none." Then he spelled it out:

> Two propositions can be readily demonstrated: first, the Jews owe an enormous debt to free enterprise and competitive capitalism; second, for at least the past century the Jews have been consistently opposed to capitalism and have done much on an ideological level to undermine it. How can these propositions be reconciled? I was led to examine this paradox partly for obvious personal reasons. Some of us are accustomed to being members of an intellectual minority, to being accused by fellow intellectuals of being reactionaries or apologists or just plain nuts. But those of us who are also Jewish are even more embattled, being regarded not only as intellectual deviants but also as traitors to a supposed cultural and national tradition.[27]

He disagrees with Lawrence Fuchs, author of *The Political Behavior of American Jews*, whom he calls "a liberal in the American sense ... [and accordingly] is quick to regard such liberalism as a legitimate offspring of the Jewish values of learning, charity, and concern with the pleasures of this world. He never even recognizes, let alone discusses, the key question whether the ethical end of 'genero through social action' is consistent with the political means of centralized government."

He finds a far more perceptive analysis in sociologist Werner Cohn's unpublished doctoral dissertation "Sources of American Jewish Liberalism," which traces the origins of the European political spectrum along an axis that involved the issues of secularism.

> Beginning with the era of the French revolution, the European political spectrum became divided into a "Left" and a "Right" along an axis that involved the issue of secularism. The Right (conservative, Monarchical, "clerical" [sic]) maintained that there must be a place for the church in the public order; the Left (Democratic, Liberal, Radical [sic]) held that there can be no (public) Church at all.... It was the Left, with its new secular concept of citizenship, that had accomplished the Emancipation, and it was only the Left that could see a place for the Jews in public life.[28]

This impression, according to Cohn, accounts for the Jews' deep-seated distrust of the conservative Right. Friedman agrees with Nathan

Glazer's comment: "I do not think anyone has come closer to the heart of the matter than has the author of these paragraphs." And it is true, as Friedman points out, that the only major leaders of Conservative parties of Jewish origin - Benjamin Disraeli in England, Friedrich Julius Stahl in Germany - were both professing Christians (Disraeli's father had converted, Stahl was baptized at age 19). But that still doesn't answer what happened in America, where "the elite Puritan element was, if anything, pro-Semitic."

Friedman ultimately attributes the affinity of Jews to anticapitalism and the left to "their historical and cultural heritage, which made them specially sensitive to injustice and specially committed to charity. They were reinforced also by whatever the forces are that predispose intellectuals towards the Left." He maintains "that the ideology of the Jews has been and still is opposed to their self-interest," and for decades "could enjoy the luxury of reacting against the anti-Semitic stereotype, yet benefit from the characteristics that that stereotype caricatured."

But possessing the keen eye of a prophet, Friedman catches a glimpse of the future, reflected in the past and, increasingly, "[o]n a much more subtle and sophisticated level, they were in the position of the rich parlor socialists—of all ethnic and religious backgrounds—who bask in self-righteous virtue by condemning capitalism while enjoying the luxuries paid for by their capitalist inheritance." By no means is this attitude the province of Jews. But it is particularly irksome when it is championed by those of us who should – and frankly, do – know better.

Fast forward half a century: same problem, only worse. Ruth Wisse pulls no punches:

> It is no mystery: the American left not only supports the grievance of those others—blacks, women, gays, etc.—but also unites them in a movement *against* the Jews, using the identification of Zionism with racism as its lever. ... In its current bid for power, the progressive American left follows the Soviet example of embracing the Islamist-Arab war against the Jews in Israel as part of the fight against Western imperialism and capitalism—now repackaged to focus on an America that is "systemically racist." And just as in the 1930s, these Jews fall in with their assailants. See how dutifully many of today's Jews, liberals as well as leftists, have marched with B Matter while that organization has embedded anti-Zionism at the heart of its activist vision.[29]

She refers to "liberals as well as leftist," but what difference is there anymore between the two other than one of degree? In her book *If I Am Not for Myself,* she concedes that the motives of many Jews in embracing collectivist ideas reflect a "belief in the better-world-to-come [are] often selfless and genuine. But" – you guessed it - "the road to hell is paved with good intentions."[30]

And evidently, old habits die hard. According to a new study released on September 7, 2022, by the Foundation for Individual Rights and Expression (FIRE), of almost 45,000 currently enrolled students at over 200 colleges and universities around the nation, Jewish students are front and center in promoting progressive cancel culture. This just as their Jewish interests and lives are under attack. Sarah Lawrence College Professor Samuel J. Abrams reflects:

> In pre-war Europe, many Jews felt intense disdain and pressure against them; rather than speak up and push back, many took an appeasement approach thinking that by looking like they are part of an illiberal and dangerous group or ideas, the antisemitism could be held in check. Similarly, the tendency for 20th-century American Jews to align with liberal and progressive causes may be seen as partially motivated by a selective reading of the Jewish tradition, and the motivation to align with the forces most unsympathetic to Jewish group vitality and survival.[31]

It has been long in coming. It is tragic that the very people whose tradition gave us the liberal idea should be reluctant to defend it. As I have sought to demonstrate in this book, surely one of the contributing factors is that language itself has been distorted to make it seem that "liberal" and "progressive" are essentially synonymous. They are in fact opposites.

Ruth Wisse is leery of labels, which is why she prefers conversation and the vibrancy of the *agora,* the marketplace in ideas to isms and jargon. In her poignant recent autobiography, *Free as a Jew*, she recalls her disappointment when teaching at Harvard: "The absence of conservative views, most of which were classical liberal views when I was an undergraduate, meant that students were being shortchanged and poorly served by teachers who lacked the moral confidence to transmit the foundational texts and ideas of America and Western civilization."[32]

The liberal idea is predicated on balancing contrasting forces, on blending interests and embracing the elasticity of change. That progress can never be linear is manifest to anyone who cares to notice: "Sunrise, sunset,/ Sunrise, sunset,/ Swiftly fly the years,/ One season following another,/ Laden with happiness and tears," chant Tevye and Golde. During the transition from one to another, there is miracle and wonder. And what keeps hope alive in us all is the love we bear for one another. The Sixties song that declared "all you need is love" was at least half right. Love is not sufficient; but it is necessary.

Yet here is a gaping abyss between genuine, human compassion for the suffering individual and a very different abstract, pseudo-compassion that thinly veils raw cruelty and deep, unquenchable resentment. The Jewish-German philosopher Hannah Arendt explains:

> Compassion, by its very nature, cannot be touched off by the suffering of a whole class or a people, or, least of all, mankind as a whole. It cannot reach out farther than what is suffered by one person and still remain what it is supposed to be, co-suffering. Its strength hinges on the strength of passion itself, which, in contrast to reason, can comprehend only the particular, but has no notion of the general and no capacity for generalization.[33]

It is a beautiful word, compassion, רַחֲמִים (*rachamin*), whose Hebrew root is shared by "womb" (*rechem*). This has led some scholars to propose that its original meaning was brotherhood or brotherly feeling, Cain notwithstanding. The related concepts are beautifully appropriate together, to indicate the essential relation between God and the people He created, reflected in the covenant that identifies Him as "being full of compassion, forgives iniquity, and does not destroy." (*Psalm* 78:38; see *Exodus* 33:19; *Deuteronomy* 8:18; and *Isaiah* 9:16, among others.) This did not prevent the flood, to be sure; but mankind as such was saved.

And no, it does not apply only to Jews – in fact, it should be extended even to one's enemies. For one reads in *Exodus* 23:5: "When you see the ass of your enemy lying under its burden and would refrain from raising it, you must nevertheless raise it with him." Rabbinic literature considered compassion, sometimes used synonymously with mercy, as an indispensable trait of a good person. (To their credit, they included compassion toward animals as no less significant. Just because they lack human reason, they need greater help and kindness. And anyone who hasn't felt the boundless devotion of an animal has missed an unfathomable blessing.)

But above all, be good to one another. Zechariah, in the book that bears his name, cites God's words: "Execute true justice; deal loyally and compassionately with one another. Do not defraud the widow, the orphan, the stranger, and the poor; and do not plot evil against one another." (*Zechariah* 7: 9-10)

Humans cannot love mankind as such but must love individually; we empathize with another who feels as we do – hence "com-passion," a shared passion or feeling. One of the most common arguments against liberalism is that it lacks compassion, being predicated merely on self-interest, indeed of a crude, materialist variety. And yes, true compassion is predicated on individual freedom, which alone is compatible with personal dignity. That feeling seems to be innate.

Tocqueville admits having interrogated even himself on that score: "I have often asked myself what was the source of that passion for political liberty which has inspired the greatest deeds of which mankind can boast. In what feelings does it take root? From whence does it derive nourishment?" Upon reflection, he concludes that he cannot "believe that a true **love** for liberty can ever be inspired by the sight of the material advantages it procures, for they are not always clearly visible. It is very true that, in the long run, liberty always yields to those who know how to preserve it in comfort, independence, and often wealth; but there are times when it disturbs these blessings for a while, and there are times when their immediate enjoyment can only be secured by a despotism."[34]

Unfortunately, the only way that liberty can be appreciated is exactly like everything else that is truly loved: for its own sake. "It is the intrinsic attractions of freedom, its own peculiar charm—quite independently of its incidental benefits—which have seized so strong a hold on the great champions of liberty throughout history; they loved it because they loved the pleasure of being able to speak, to act, to breathe unrestrained, under the sole government of God and the laws. He who seeks freedom for anything but freedom's self is made to be a slave."

One of America's greatest challenges is how to recapture that passion for liberty that inspired its founding, and so impressed Tocqueville. Jews in particular have a special responsibility, not only to themselves but to the one nation that has embraced them more generously than any other in history. In the first place, they must defend themselves against the ever-growing antisemitism that comes not only from its supremacist enemies but from the so-called "woke left." Ruth Wisse has urged "my Jewish neighbors who are feeling the full brunt of the general rot in the particular form of attacks against them and the Jewish homeland must warn against the self-destruction that accompanies anti-Jewish behavior. But," she continues, "they and the rest of us must also do everything possible to preserve the exceptionalism that is America. In the fateful parable that continues to sound through the ages, we are both Daniel and, here, part of Babylon. It, too, is our responsibility." [35]

To a former inmate of a Communist country, watching the American cultural landscape succumb to groupthink ideology brings back old nightmares. Reruns of a ludicrous script: the double-speak and double-think; the sycophancy; ostracizing and demonizing anyone who dares to dissent; preaching love while practicing hate. Only this time, the setting is America - still land of the free, but here the brave no longer feel quite at home.

It is deeply disturbing to Natan Sharansky, survivor of unimaginable torture in the Gulag: "I am concerned about the ideological environment in the U.S., a global superpower, a beacon of hope for all humanity," he writes in a foreword to David L. Bernstein's excellent new book, *Woke Antisemitism: How a Progressive Ideology Harms Jews*. Sharansky is alarmed by "the emergence of a dogma – some call it 'woke' ideology – not unlike the totalizing ideology I grew up with in the Soviet Union, which has taken the American left by storm and with it many American cultural institutions."[36]

Antisemitism is but one aspect of this totalizing ideology, the same dangerous narrative that has brought misery to millions. As always, it threatens not only Jews but liberalism itself. "In woke ideology," Sharansky explains, "if you substitute the word race for class, you will get almost the exact same Marxist-Leninist dogma in which we were indoctrinated in schools that became the basis of the hatred against dissidents and anyone who dared question the party line." He commends David Bernstein, whose career has been devoted to Jewish activism, for exposing the truth: behind the faux-compassionate clothing obscured by academic jargon lurks the same emperor, no less ruthless for being buck-naked.

But it was not philosophical argument that convinced Bernstein of the dogma's exceptional virulence so much as its absolute intolerance of argument itself. Having always lived among liberal people who were not especially ideological, but simply assumed that helping the less fortunate of every color and creed was nonnegotiable, Bernstein had grown up debating. Used to arguing "both sides of more arguments" than he could remember, with friends who similarly cherished disagreements that only "cemented their friendship," he believed in "free expression and civil liberties operating under the rule of law."[37] A self-described classical liberal,[38] he needed no conversion. He had stayed put; it was the culture that moved left.

Unwilling to keep "squirming in doublethink," he decided he would devote his professional life to helping others like him, disillusioned doublethinkers, find the courage of their convictions. Far more people than dared to admit it, he came to realize, were tired of being forced to agree with outright falsehoods and double standards. Worst still was being cowed into submission by members of a Jewish elite who fawned upon vapid celebrities, mainstream media, and well-heeled nonprofits, seemingly oblivious to their open hostility to Israel and Jews in general and contempt for the Big Satan America. Convinced that American Jews and the country itself were at a crossroads, Bernstein founded the Jewish Institute for Jewish Values (JIWV), seeking a return to the very essence of both Judaism and the Declaration of Independence.

Jews are finding themselves increasingly shunned by their traditional allies. Woke ideology "has become so pernicious and so widespread," observes Bernstein, "that mainstream Jewish leaders have little chance to move the needle on Progressive attitudes on Jews and Israel."[39] For years, these leaders and their members "had to pay lip service, at least, to woke dogma or, in effect, be cancelled by a philosophy that leads inevitably to more antisemitism and undermines liberal principles." And to what end? "In the long run," he concludes, "Jews will be far more damned if they support the dogma." That the damnation is self-inflicted makes it particularly egregious.

Today, the community is deeply divided. *Tablet* magazine editor Liel Leibovitz, who describes himself, like Bernstein, as a devout liberal, recalls a time when "the Jewish tent was wide open." Leibovitz mourns for its demise. He is repelled by the "new cosmology" of intersectional politics.

> Political victories are achieved by draining the landscape of nuance, which allows for the kind of clap-back social media messaging at which their standard bearers excel. To make this work, there must be only two answers to any question: one that is right and commands the allegiance of the entire coalition, and one that is wrong, and which deserves only universal condemnation and scorn. There is only racism or "anti-racism;" "white supremacy" or "restorative racial justice;" nationalism or socialism; and, for Jews, Zionism or anti-Zionism.[40]

This is bad not just for Jews. It is deadly for America and civilization as we know it. It signifies "the end of the mosaic of differing and diverse opinions that, when allowed to sparkle, made America a great and good nation—one whose loss I mourn." What supreme irony, that the mosaic of ideas should be repudiated by members of the Mosaic community itself.

On the eve of Rosh Hashanah 2022, at the beginning of the Jewish New Year 5783, Ruth Wisse penned another eloquent message to her fellow American Jews, reminding them that they "owe America what they owe themselves: to live and flourish as a people within the republic, enriching its diversity, enshrining its pluralism, substantiating its exceptional ability to encourage the individual freedom of citizens and Jewish distinctiveness within the greater whole. That is the base we need to build if we are to join with others who are already actively dedicated to undoing the intersectional campaign that is degrading America."[41]

Amen.

Notes

Introduction: "*Not like the brazen giant*"

[1] Meir Soloveichik, "Observation," *Mosaic*, July 18, 2022.

[2] Cited in the Oral Law, known as *Pirkeit Avot* (in Hebrew, פִּרְקֵי אָבוֹת), first recorded in the second century.

[3] Ruth Wisse, *If I am Not for Myself...: The Liberal Betrayal of the Jews* (New York, NY: The Free Press, 1992), 19.

Chapter I: The Liberal Idea in America

[1] Walter Pincus, "Transcript Confirms Kennedy Linked Removal of Missiles in Cuba, Turkey," *Washington Post,* October 22, 1987.

[2] *Ibid.,* 11-12.

[3] Jaroslav Piekalkiewicz and Alfred Wayne Penn, *Politics of Ideocracy* (Albany, NY: State University of New York Press, 1995), 21.

[4] Sidney and Beatrice Webb, *Soviet Communism: A New Civilization*, 2nd edition, vol. I (New York, NY: Charles Scribner's Sons, 1936), 450. Cited in Piekalkiewicz and Penn, *ibid.,* 20.

[5] Coined to allude to the KKK, which presumably captures America's true identity. According to the Oxford English Dictionary, its first use was in July 1970, in an African-American magazine called *Black World.*

[6] Alfred North Whitehead quipped in his book *Process and Reality* that "[t]he safest general characterization of the European philosophical tradition is that it consists of a series of footnotes to Plato." There's some truth to that.

[7] Arthur Schlesinger, Jr., "Liberalism in America: A Note for Europeans," *The Politics of Hope* (Princeton, NJ: Princeton University Press, 2008), 83-93.

[8] Allen J. Matusow, *The Unraveling of America: A History of Liberalism in the 1960s* (Athens, GA: University of Georgia Press, 2009), 343.

[9] https://pilgrimhall.org/mayflower_compact_text.htm

[10] https://www.americanyawp.com/reader/colliding-cultures/john-winthrop-dreams-of-a-city-on-a-hill-1630/

[11] Eran Shalev, *American Zion: The Torah as a Political Text from the Revolution to the Civil War* (New Haven, CN: Yale University Press, 2013), 3.

[12] https://www.ushistory.org/documents/charter.htm

[13] Meir Y. Soloveichik, 'Proclaim Liberty Throughout All the Land,' *Commentary,* July/Aug 2022

[14] Joseph Isaac Lifshitz, *Judaism, Law & The Free Market: An Analysis* (Grand Rapids, MI: Acton Institute, 2012), 10-11. (Emphasis added)

[15] The Torah ("the law") usually refers to the first five books of the Old Testament, also known as the books of Moses, or the Pentateuch.

[16] *Deuteronomy* 19:14, 25:13-16, 22:1: *Leviticus* 19:13.

[17] Lifshitz, *op. cit.*, 14.

[18] Mechilta d'Rabbi Ishmael, *Masechta Dechaspa Mishpatim,* ch. 19; *Bava Metzia* 71a. Cited in Lifshitz, *op. cit.*, 27.

[19] Writes Menahem Elon in *Jewish Law: History, Sources, Principles*, trans. Bernard Auerbach and Melvin J. Sykes (Jerusalem: Jewish Publication Society, 1994), 1:122: "Although all parts of the halacha are rooted in the same source, share the same principles and methods of analysis, and provide and receive reciprocal support, nevertheless, study of the halachic sources reveals that the halacha did make very fundamental distinctions between its two major categories, namely, monetary matters (that part of the halacha included in the concept of mamon) and non- monetary matters (that part of the halacha included in the concept of isur)." Cited in Lifshitz, *Ibid.* 27.

[20] Lifshitz, *ibid.*, 20.

[21] *Ibid.*

[22] Helena Rosenblatt, *The Lost History of Liberalism: From Ancient Rome to the Twenty-First Century* (Princeton, NJ: Princeton University Press, 2018), 9.

[23] Carl J. Richard, *Greeks & Romans Bearing Gifts: How the Ancients Inspired the Founding Fathers* (Latham, MD: Rowman & Littlefield Publishers, 2009), 154-5. Richard adds that Benjamin Rush and Thomas Paine also cited Cicero repeatedly, particularly concerning natural law, while Benjamin Franklin cited him often on the importance of hard work and virtue – to which a generous, liberal attitude was essential.

[24] *Cicero De Officiis*, translated with an Introduction and Notes by Andrew P. Peabody (Boston, MA: Little, Brown, and Co., 1887), Bk. I, 7.

[25] *Ibid.*, Bk. I, 14.

[26] Richard, *op. cit.,* 12.

[27] Meyer Reinhold, The influence of Cicero on John Adams*, Ciceroniana On Line*, Vol 8 (1994)

[28] Richard, *ibid.*, 153.

[29] Ruth R. Wisse, *Jews and Power* (New York, NY: Shocken Books, 2007), 11.

[30] *Ibid.*, 32-33.

[31] The literature is too copious to cite, but this is one of my favorites: Naomi Harris Rosenblatt's *After the Apple: Women in the Bible – Timeless Stories of Love, Lust and Longing* (2005).

[32] Bernard Bailyn, *Illuminating History: A Retrospective of Seven Decades* (New York, NY: W.W. Norton & Company, 2020), Introduction.

[33] Bernard Bailyn, "Confessional Thoughts on Re-reading *The Ideological Origins*," *The New England Quarterly,* vol. XCI, no. 1 (March 2018) The source for John Adams is *The Diary and Autobiography of John Adams*, ed.

L.H. Butterfield et al. (Cambridge, MA: Harvard University Press, 1961), 1:282.

[34] *Ibid.*, fn. 11: *Cato's Letters*, no. 73 (April 21, 1722), emphasis added.

[35] Edmund Burke, "Speech on American Taxation" (1774), in *The Writings and Speeches of Edmund Burke*, ed. Paul Langford et al. (Oxford, UK: Oxford University Press, 1981-2015), 4:432.

[36] Bailyn, *ibid.*

[37] Bernard Bailyn, ed., *The Debate on the Constitution* (New York: The Library of America, 1993)

[38] Bailyn, "Confessional Thoughts on Re-reading *The Ideological Origins*," 30. Emphasis added.

[39] *Ibid.*, 34.

[40] *Select Works of Edmund Burke*, Foreword and Biographical Note by Francis Canavan (Indianapolis: Liberty Fund, 1999). Vol. 1. "Speech of Edmund Burke, Esq. on Moving His Resolutions for Conciliation with the Colonies, March 22, 1775.

[41] Jacob Howland, *Plato and the Talmud* (Cambridge, UK: Cambridge University Press, 2011), 11.

[42] *Ibid.*, 114-15.

[43] Bernard Bailyn, *The Ideological Origins of the American Revolution* (Cambridge, MA: Harvard University Press, 1967), 25.

[44] *Ibid.*, 26.

[45] *Ibid.*, 55.

[46] *Ibid.*, 56.

[47] *Ibid.*, 234.

[48] Lord Acton, "The History of Freedom in Antiquity," in *Essays on Freedom and Power* (New York, NY: Meridian, 1964), 53.

[49] *Ibid.*, 56-57.

[50] Ruth Wisse, *Jews and Power*, 105.

[51] *Ibid.*, 106.

[52] Joshua A. Berman, *Created Equal: How the Bible Broke with Ancient Political Thought* (Oxford: Oxford University Press, 2011), Kindle Edition 27.

[53] *Ibid.*, 45.

[54] *Ibid.*, 48. Emphasis added.

[55] *Ibid.*, 51.

[56] *Ibid.*, 62.

[57] Pierre Manent, *An Intellectual History of Liberalism* (Princeton, NJ: Princeton University Press, 1996), xvi-xvii. For an excellent analysis of Manent's writings, see Daniel J. Mahoney's *Recovering Politics, Civilization, and the Soul: Essays on Pierre Manent and Roger Scruton* (South Bend, IN: St. Augustine's Press, 2022).

[58] Elazar, *Covenant & Constitutionalism,* 6.

Chapter II: New Eden across the Atlantic

[1] W. K. Jordan, *The Development of Religious Toleration in England: From the Convention of the Long Parliament to the Restoration (1640-1660)* (Cambridge, MA: Harvard University Press, 1932), Vol. III, 475.

[2] Vernon Parrington, "Roger Williams, Seeker," *Main Currents in American Thought* (New York, NY: Harcourt Brace and Co., 1927), I:34-37.

[3] John M. Barry, *Roger Williams and the Creation of the American Soul: Church, State, and the Birth of Liberty* (New York, NY: Penguin Books, 2012), 393.

[4] Howard Chapin, ed., *Documentary History of Rhode Island* (Providence, RI: Preston and Rounds, 1916), I: 215-217.

[5] Barry, *op. cit.,* 310. Emphasis added.

[6] Roger Williams, *The Complete Writings of Roger Williams* (New York, NY: Russell and Russell, 1963), I:142.

[7] Bernard Bailyn, *The Barbarous Years* (New York, NY: Alfred A. Knopf, 2012), Introduction.

[8] *Ibid.*

[9] Elazar, *Covenant & Constitutionalism*, 12.

[10] Charles M. Andrews, *The Colonial Background of the American Revolution* (New Haven, CT: Yale University Press, 1961), 5.

[11] *Ibid.,* 6.

[12] Bailyn, *op. cit.*, 526.

[13] Andrews, *op. cit.*, 26.

[14] *Ibid.*, 41.

[15] Bailyn, *op. cit.*, 521.

[16] *Ibid.,* 60.

[17] Andrews, op cit., 30.

[18] *Ibid.*, 61-64.

[19] Bailyn, *ibid.*

[20] *Ibid.*, 528.

[21] *Ibid.*, 528-9.

[22] *Ibid.*

[23] The subsequent discussion is based on the author's *The Utopian Conceit and the War on Freedom* (Washington and London: Academica Press, 2019), 232-237.

[24] Arthur Herman, *How the Scots Invented the Modern World* (New York, NY: Three Rivers Press, 2001), 82.

[25] Francis Hutcheson, *A System Of Moral Philosophy: In Three Books: To which is Prefixed Some Account Of The Life, Writings, And Character Of The Author,* Vol. 1 (London: Millar, 1755), 294.

[26] Herman, *op. cit.,* 83.

[27] From Thomas Jefferson to Peter Carr, with Enclosure, 10 August 1787.

[28] *Ibid.*

[29] This led historian Thomas West to observe: "One of the striking things about the leading men [of the American Founding] is how different they were in

their particular preoccupations, and yet how much they agreed on principles." *Ibid.*, 24.

[30] Jefferson had written "inalienable" – it was John Adams who changed it, perhaps inadvertently. See Carl L Becker, *The Declaration of Independence a Study in the History of Political Ideas* (New York, NY: Vintage, 1942), 140.

[31] Thomas Jefferson letter to Henry Lee, May 8, 1825.

[32] Carl Becker observes that "the handwriting of 'self-evident' resembles Franklin's." Carl L Becker, *The Declaration of Independence a Study in the History of Political Ideas* (New York, NY: Vintage, 1942), 142.

[33] Elazar, *Covenant & Constitutionalism*, 10.

[34] Joseph Cropsey, *Polity and Economy: Further Thoughts on the Principles of Adam Smith* (South Bend, IN: St. Augustine Press, 2001), 137.

[35] Adam Smith, *The Wealth of Nations*, Bk. IV, Ch. VII, Pt. III, and Bk. IV, Ch. IX. Cited in Cropsey, *ibid.*, 2.

[36] "Tocqueville on Socialism (1848)" *New Individualist Review*, editor-in-chief Ralph Raico, introduction by Milton Friedman (Indianapolis, IN: Liberty Fund, 1981).

[37] Joel Fishman, "Hidden in Plain Sight: Alexis de Tocqueville's Recognition of the Jewish Origin of the Idea of Equality," *Jewish Political Studies Review* 17:3-4 (Fall 2005).

[38] Sean Wilentz, *No Property in Man: Slavery and Antislavery at the Nation's Founding* (Cambridge, MA: Harvard University Press, 2019), 41.

[39] John Jay to the English Anti-Slavery Society, in Henry P. Johnston, ed., *The Correspondence and Public Papers of John Jay* (New York, 1890), vol. 3 (1782-1793).

[40] Samuel Sewall, "The Selling of Joseph: A Memorial," printed by Bartholomew Green and John Allen, 1700.

[41] Wilenz, *op. cit.*, 44.

[42] The Thirteenth Annual Report of the American & Foreign Anti-Slavery Society, New York: 1853.

[43] Bertram W. Korn, *American Jewry and the Civil War* (Philadelphia, PA: Jewish Publication Society, 1951), 13.

[44] *Ibid.*,16.

[45] M. J. Raphall, *Bible View of Slavery*, in *From Sea to Shining Sea: Three Views on Slavery and Secession,* Jewish Virtual Library.

[46] David Brion Davis, *Inhuman Bondage: The Rise and Fall of Slavery in the New World* (Oxford, UK: Oxford University Press, 2006), 85. I thank Professor Robert Paquette for pointing out this reference.

[47] *The Reverend Doctor M. J. Raphall's Bible View of Slavery,* Reviewed by the Reverend D. Einhorn, New York, 1861. Dr. Einhorn preached this sermon and published it in his German-language periodical *Sinai* in pro-Confederate Baltimore. Jewish Virtual Library, *Ibid.*

[48] Arthur Zilversmit, *First Emancipation: the abolition of slavery in the North* (Chicago, IL: University of Chicago Press, 1967), 146.

[49] Ibid., 199.

[50] Adam Smith, *An Inquiry into the Nature and Causes of the Wealth of Nations*, 5th edition (Methuen and Co., Ltd., 1789), Library of Economics and Liberty, 2000, Book I, Chapter X, Part II.

[51] "Madison Debates," Yale Law School, *The Avalon Project.*

[52] Merrill Jensen et al., *The Documentary history of the ratification of the Constitution*, esp. Volume X: *Ratification of the Constitution by the States: Delaware, New Jersey, Georgia, Connecticut* (Madison, WI: 1978).

[53] Willenz, *op. cit.*, 9.

[54] Cited in Robert S. Wistrich, *A Lethal Obsession: Anti-Semitism from Antiquity to the Global Jihad* (New York, NY: Random House, 2009), 12. Wistrich's monumental tome is probably the most incisive and thorough study of this evil phenomenon.

[55] *Cited in Louis Ruchames, "The Abolitionists and the Jews," Publications of the American Jewish Historical Society, December 1952, Vol. 42, No. 2,* 132.

[56] Eli N. Evans, *Judah P. Benjamin: The Jewish Confederate* (New York: The Free Press, 1988), 37.

[57] Maury Wiseman, "Judah P. Benjamin and Slavery," American Jewish Archives Journal, 2007.

[58] *The Congressional Globe*, 35th Congress, 1st Session, March 11, 1858, 1066.

[59] Piekalkiewicz and Penn, *op.cit*, 20.

[60] Jonathan D. Sarna, *American Judaism: A History* (New Haven and London: Yale University Press, 2004), 113.

[61] The documentation surrounding this important incident has been included in several moving exhibitions in New York and Springfield, IL, as well as excellent books on the subject – notably *Lincoln and the Jews* by Jonathan D. Sarna and Benjamin Shapell, published in 2015.

[62] Edward Rothstein, "The Unusual Relationship between Abraham Lincoln and the Jews," *Mosaic*, April 1, 2015.

[63] Meir Y. Soloveichik, "Lincoln's Almost Chosen People," 2020 Erasmus Lecture *First Things*, Feb 2021.

[64] For a superb analysis of Lincoln's use of biblical language, see Fred Kaplan's *Lincoln: Biography of a Writer* (New York, NY: Harper Perennial, 2010).

[65] *Ibid.*

[66] Wilson Carey McWilliams, *Redeeming Democracy in America* (Lawrence, KS: University Press of Kansas, 2011), cited in *ibid.*

[67] *Ibid.*, emphasis added.

[68] David W. Blight adds: "This was no mere hyperbole by one who had so carefully read those prophets and adopted their stories of destruction and rebirth." *Frederick Douglass: Prophet of Freedom* (New York, NY: Simon & Schuster, 2020, 732.

[69]Timothy Sandefur explains the context clearly and succinctly in *Frederick Douglass: Self-Made Man* (Washington, DC: Cato Institute, 2018), 33.

[70]Frederick Douglass, "Oration in Memory of Abraham Lincoln," April 14, 1876, Frederick Douglass Project, *ibid.*,

[71] Gates, *op. cit.*, 804.

[72] Frederick Douglass, "Oration in Memory of Abraham Lincoln," *ibid.*

[73] *Ibid.*

[74] *Ibid.*

[75] *Ibid.*

[76] Frederick Douglass, "The Future of the Negro," *The North American Review*, July 1884, Library of Congress, https://www.loc.gov/item/mfd.24006/

[77] Oscar R. Williams Jr., "Historical Impressions of Black-Jewish Relations Prior to World War II," *Negro History Bulletin*, July/August, 1977, Vol. 40, No. 4 (July/August, 1977), 730.

[78] *Ibid.*

[79] Sandefur, *op. cit.,* 111.

[80] Woodrow Wilson, "States Rights," in Mario R. DiNunzio, ed., *Woodrow Wilson: Essential Writings and Speeches of the Scholar President* (New York, NY: New York University Press, 2006). 201. Sandefur, 113.

[81] Woodrow Wilson, "The Reconstruction of the Southern States," *The Atlantic Monthly*, Vol. 87, 1. Jan. 1901.

Chapter III: Liberalism Gets Hijacked

[1] Sandefur, *ibid.*, 112.

[2] Alan Charles Kors, "The Ethics of Democracy," *The Georgetown Journal of Law & Public Policy* 2020, Vol. 18, 693-703.

[3] Peter Nicholson, "The reception and early reputation of Mill's political thought," *The Cambridge Companion to Mill* (Cambridge, UK: Cambridge University Press, 1998), 464-496.

[4] Cited in Arthur Link, *Wilson: Campaigns for Progressivism and Peace, 1917-1917* (Princeton, NJ: Princeton University Press, 1965), 105-6.

[5] Woodrow Wilson, January 22, 1917: "A World League for Peace" Speech, Miller Center, University of Virginia. Emphasis added.

[6] David Green, *The Language of Politics in America: Shaping Political Consciousness from McKinley to Reagan* (Ithaca, NY: Cornell University Press, 1987), 1-3.

[7] *Ibid.*

[8] *Ibid,* 79.

[9] Woodrow Wilson, "Socialism and Democracy," August 22, 1887. The essay was never published during Wilson's lifetime. Writes Trygve Throntveit: "There is no satisfactory explanation as to why this essay was never published." Throntveit speculates that Wilson had been influenced by his economics instructor at Johns Hopkins University, Richard T. Ely: Wilson's copy of [Ely's] *The Labor Movement in America* (New York: T. Y. Crowell, 1886) is preserved in his personal library at the Library of Congress (hereafter, WL LC), along with a copy of Ely's *French and German Socialism in Modern Times* (New York: Harper & Brothers, 1883). This last Wilson read multiple times, at least once while writing "The State." The book is signed and dated

"Woodrow Wilson, 1883" and inscribed on p. 262: "Oct. 24th, 1883 / November 9th, 1883 / May 29th, 1888." See "'Common Counsel': Woodrow Wilson's Pragmatic Progressivism, 1885–1913," by Trygve Throntveit, in John Milton Cooper, Jr., ed., *Reconsidering Woodrow Wilson: Progressivism, Internationalism, War, and Peace* (Baltimore, MD: Johns Hopkins University Press, 2008), 46.

[10] C. Bradley Thompson, *America's Revolutionary Mind: A Moral History of the American Revolution and the Declaration That Defined It* (New York, NY: Encounter Books, 2019), 363.

[11] *Ibid.*, 364.

[12] *Ibid.,* 371.

[13] See Link, *op. cit.,* 23-30.

[14] Green, *The Language of Politics in America,* 81.

[15] *Ibid.* Emphasis added.

[16] Lord Acton, "History of Freedom in Antiquity," 53.

[17] Louis Menand, *The Metaphysical Club: A Story of Ideas in America* (New York, NY: Farrar, Straus and Giroux, 2002), x.

[18] *Ibid.*, xi-xii.

[19] J. Bradley Thompson, *America's Revolutionary Mind*, 374.

[20] Oliver Wendell Holmes to Alice Stopford Green, October 1, 1901, Harvard Law School Library Digital Suite.

[21] Oliver Wendell Holmes, Jr., "The Gas-Stokers' Strike," *American Law Review*, Vol. VII, April 1873, Harvard Law School Library Digital Suite.

[22] Oliver Wendell Holmes, Jr., *The Common Law* (1881), Harvard Law School Library, Digital Suite. Note*:* *ultima ratio regum* is Latin for "the final argument of kings," which refers to a resort to arms. It is the motto engraved on the cannon of Louis XIV.

[23] Menand, *op. cit.*, 65.

[24] Oliver Wendell Holmes to Frederick Pollock, February 1, 1920, Harvard Law School Library Digital Suite. Also, letter to Oliver Wendell Holmes to Harold Laski, December 9, 1931,

[25] Menand, *op. cit.*, 66.

[26] *Buck v. Bell,* 274 US 200 (1927).

[27] *Ibid.*

[28] Adam Cohen, *Imbeciles: The Supreme Court, Eugenics, and the Sterilization of Carrie Buck* (New York, NY: 2016) offers a heartrending account of this tragic case, as well as a good overview of the eugenics movement.

[29] *Ibid.*, 16.

[30] For bone-chilling details, see *The Nazi Connection: Eugenics, American Racism, and German National Socialism* by Stefan Kuhl (Oxford, UK: Oxford University Press, 2002).

[31] Vladimir Bukovsky documents the practice and theory in his autobiographical masterpiece *To Build a Castle: My Life as a Dissenter* (New York, NY: 1979).

[32]Ian Hutchinson, *Monopolizing Knowledge: A Scientist Refutes Religion-Denying, Reason-Destroying Scientism* (Belmont, MA: Fias Publishing), 2011.

[33] Morton did not hesitate to assert, for example, that the Causasian race was "distinguished by the facility with which it attains the highest intellectual endowments, while the "Ethiopian" (Black) race is "joyous, flexible, and indolent." All of this he gleamed from skull size, but without bothering to differentiate between, say, men and women. And since some Caucasians had been hanged for murder, he flatly assumed that since most of their race were otherwise mostly law-abiding, the total "real" average skull size had to be higher. If only it were a joke. See Samuel George Morton, *Crania Americana; or, A comparative view of the skulls of various aboriginal nations of North and South America* (Philadelphia, PA: J. Dobson, 1839), 5-7.

[34] George R. Gliddon to Samuel George Morton, January 9, 1848, Philadelphia Area Archives Research Portal.

[35]Edward Lurie, *Louis Agassiz: A Life in Science* (Chicago, IL: University of Chicago Press, 1960), 260.

[36] Louis Agassiz to Samuel Gridley Howe, August 9, 1983.

[37] Richard Hofstadter, *Social Darwinism in American Thought* (Philadelphia, PA: University of Pennsylvania Press, 1955), 16.

[38] *Ibid.*

[39] For one thing, Darwin thought that organisms change not because they are somehow forced by their surroundings but – dare one say it? - merely by chance. Moreover, general type, what is usually called species, is nothing fixed: "I look at the term species as one arbitrarily given for the sake of convenience to a set of individuals closely resembling each other," not unlike "variety… [which] is also applied arbitrarily, and for mere convenience [sic] sake." Charles Darwin, *On the Origin of Species*, from John van Wyhe, ed., *The Complete Work of Charles Darwin Online*, http://darwin-online.org.uk/Variorum/1860/1860-52-c-1866.html

[40] Spencer's influence cannot be overstated. Hofstadter, for example, observes that "Oliver Wendell Holmes hardly exaggerated when he expressed his doubt that 'any writer of English except Darwin has done so much to affect our whole way of thinking about the universe." *Ibid.,* 32.

[41] Cited in *ibid.*, 40.

[42]So too, Charles Francis Adams, Lincoln's ambassador to London, although otherwise no follower of James, agreed that evolution provided the perfect rationale for starting a war, for wasting "five or ten thousand million dollars and a million lives, more or less, to enforce unity and uniformity on people who objected to it." Henry Adams, *The Education of Henry Adams* (1907) from *Novels, Mont Saint Michel, The Education* (New York, NY: Library of America, 1983), 925.

[43] Hofstadter, *Social Darwinism*, 91.

[44] *Ibid.*, 114.

[45] Marx to Engels, December 19, 1860, in MEW, Vol. 30, 131.

[46] Hofstadter, *Social Darwinism*, 117.

[47] William James, "Review of Rapport sur le progress de l'anthropologie en France, by Armand de Quatrefages" (1868), Cited in Menand, *op. cit.*, 145.

[48] Cohen, *Imbeciles*, 56.

[49] James W. Trent, Jr., *Inventing the Feeble Mind: A History of Mental Retardation in the United States* (Oxford: Oxford University Press, 2016), 166.

[50] See Richard Schickel, *D. W. Griffith: An American Life* (New York, NY: Simon and Schuster, 1984), 270.

[51] Art Carden and Steven Horwitz, "Eugenics: Progressivism's Ultimate Social Engineering," Foundation for Economic Education, Sept. 21, 2011.

[52] *Ibid.*

[53] David Green, *Language of Politics in America*, 80.

[54] *Ibid.*

[55] Theodore Roosevelt, "What is a Progressive?" Ronald J. Pestritto and William J. Atto, eds., *American Progressivism* (Lanham, MD: Rowman & Littlefield, 2008), 44.

[56] Woodrow Wilson, *Socialism and Democracy*, Essay, August 22, 1887.

[57] John Dewey, *The Ethics of Democracy* (Ann Arbor, MI: Andrews & Co., 1888)

[58] Randolph Bourne, "Twilight of the Idols," *The Seven Arts*, 11 (New York, NY: The Seven Arts Publishing Company, October 1917), 688-702.

[59] Menand, *op. cit.*, 440.

[60] For a succinct analysis of the circumstances surrounding Wilson's decision and its political ramifications, see David Fromkin, *A Peace to End All Peace* (New York, NY: Henry Holt and Company, 1989), 254-262.

[61] Kors, *op. cit.*

[62] Arthur M. Mendel. *Vision and Violence,* in Richard Landes, ed. (Ann Arbor, MI: University of Michigan Press, 1999), 117.

[63] Menand, *op. cit.,* 67.

[64] Woodrow Wilson, "The Study of Administration," *Political Science Quarterly* 2 (July 1887), 197-222.

[65] Frederick Engels, "Anti-Dühring: Herr Eugen Dühring's Revolution in Science," *Vorwärts*, Jan 3, 1877 - July 7, 1878; published as a book Leipzig, 1878.

[66]V. I. Lenin, *State and Revolution*: *The Marxist Theory of the State & the Tasks of the Proletariat in the Revolution,* from *Collected Works*, Vol. 25 (1918), Ch. 1, 3. Lenin Internet Archive (Marxists.org), 1993.

[67] Wilson, "The Study of Administration," *op. cit.*

[68] Herbert Croly, *Progressive Democracy* (1914), from *ibid.*, 267.

[69]Theodore Roosevelt, "Progressive Party Platform, 1912," from *American Progressivism, 274.*

[70] "Wilson and Roosevelt," *New Republic*, November 4, 1916; reprinted on June 24, 2002.

[71] John Dewey, *Liberalism and Social Action* (Amherst, N.Y.: Prometheus Books, 2000), 30.

[72] Edwin L. Godkin, "The Eclipse of Liberalism, Aug. 9, 1900. The article in *The Nation*, however, appears to have been an unsigned editorial. For additional context, see Roger Pilon, "The United States Constitution: From Limited Government to Leviathan," *Economic Education Bulletin*, Vol. XLV No. 12, Dec. 2005, 10.

[73] Bourne, "Twilight of the Idols," *op.cit.*

Chapter IV: National Socialism

[1] John Quincy Adams. "An Address…Celebrating the Declaration of Independence," Speech, July 04, 1821.

[2] Michael McGerr, *A Fierce Discontent: The Rise and Fall of the Progressive Movement in America* (New York, NY: Free Press, 2010), Introduction.

[3] Leonard Rogoff, "Is the Jew White?: The Racial Place of the Southern Jew," *American Jewish History* , September 1997, Vol. 85, No. 3, 195.

[4] I. Arthur T. Abernethy, *The Jew a Negro, Being a Study of the Jewish Ancestry from an Impartial Standpoint* (Moravian Falls, NC, 1910). Cited in Rogoff, ibid.

[5] J. C. Nott, "Ancient and Scriptural Chronology," *Southern Quarterly Review* (1850), 2, cited in Paul A. Erickson, "The Anthropology of Josiah Clark Nott," *KAS Papers*, Nos. 65-66.

[6] Rogoff, *op. cit.*, 201.

[7] Karl Pearson, Life and Letters and Labour of Francis Galton, Vol. II, (Cambridge, UK: Cambridge University Press, 1924), 209.

[8] Lord Acton, "The History of Freedom in Antiquity," in *Essays on Freedom and Power* (New York, NY: Meridian, 1964), 53-56.

[9] For the most comprehensive and brilliant study of this pathology, see Robert S. Wistrich, *From Ambivalence to Betrayal: The Left, the Jews, and Israel* (Lincoln, NE: University of Nebraska Press, 2012)

[10] Sander L. Gilman, *Freud, Race, and Gender* (Princeton, NJ: Princeton University Press, 1995), 20-21.

[11] Rogoff, *op. cit.*, 209.

[12] *Ibid.*, 217. Rogoff cites how "[a] Lithuanian immigrant child in a Southern town recalled how a non-Jewish playmate's mother, fearing contamination, would not let him share a glass with her son. Eugenicists traced social ills to disease, and the Progressive Era was obsessed with campaigns for public health. Not only were Jews allegedly dirty, they were also parasites who finance but do not produce. Eugenicists considered economic parasitism the Jewish racial disease just as they thought the Irishman was susceptible to alcoholism, the Italian to crime, and the African to lust or laziness."

[13] Theodore Roosevelt, "Twisted Eugenics," *The Outlook*, January 3, 1914, 31.

[14] *Ibid.*, 32.

[15] Theodore Roosevelt to Lt. William W. Kimball, Nov. 19, 1897, reel 314, Theodore Roosevelt Papers, Library of Congress, Manuscript Division. See

also Kenneth C. Wenzer, "Theodore Roosevelt and the United States Battleship Maine," *Federal History Journal* 2017.

[16] Cited in "Theodore Roosevelt and the United States Battleship Maine" by Kenneth C. Wenzer, *Federal History* 9, Apr. 2017, 124–28.

[17] Eric Alterman, "How Classical Liberalism Morphed Into New Deal Liberalism," Center for American Progress, April 26, 2012.

[18]Adam Quinn, "The Deal: The Balance of Power, Military Strength, and Liberal Internationalism in the Bush National Security Strategy," *International Studies Perspectives* (2008) 9, 40-49.

[19] TR "had wanted no more than to improve the balance of power… In Roosevelt's conception, America would have been one nation among many…" Henry Kissinger, *Diplomacy* (New York, NY: Simon & Schuster, 1994), 47.

[20]Quinn, *op. cit.*

[21] John Dewey, *The Problems of Men* (New York, NY: Philosophical Library, 1946), 113. Cited in Dmitri N. Shalin, "G. H. Mead, Socialism, and the Progressive Agenda," *American Journal of Sociology*, 93(4), 913-951.

[22] Otis L. Graham, *An Encore for Reform: The Old Progressive and the New Deal* (New York, NY: Oxford University Press, 1967), 5. Cited in Shalin, *ibid.*

[23] John Dewey, *Individualism, Old and New* (New York, NY: Capricorn, 1962), 119. First published in 1929. Cited in Shalin, *ibid.*, 943.

[24] Shalin, *ibid.*, 943-4.

[25] Ludwig von Mises, *Planned Chaos*, (Irvington-on-Hudson, NY: Foundation for Economic Education, 1970), 73.

[26] Interview with James Ledbetter, "Marx the Journalist," *Jacobin*, May 5, 2018.

[27] Iver Bernstein, *The New York City Draft Riots: Their Significance for American Society and Politics in the Age of the Civil War* (Oxford, UK: Oxford University Press, 1991), 169.

[28] *Ibid.*

[29] Established in 1901 in a merger between the Social Democratic Party of America (established in 1898) and some members of the Socialist Labor Party of America.)

[30] For critical additional background, see Ralph de Toledano's *Cry Havoc! The Great American Bring-Down and How it Happened* (New York, NY: Anthem Books, 2006). I am grateful to Jack Dziak for this important reference.

[31] "The Intercollegiate Socialist Society," Alexander Trachtenberg, ed., *The American Labor Year Book* (New York, NY: The Rand School of Social Science, 1916), vol. 1, 156.

[32] "Plan to Win Students to 'New Social Order,'" *New York Times*, Jan. 1, 1922.

[33] Harry W. Laidler, "Socialism in the United States," *Current History*, June 1950, Vol. 18, No. 106, 325.

[34] Richard Hofstadter, *The Age of Reform: From Bryan to F.D.R.* (New York, NY: Random House, 1955), 5.

[35]Theodore Roosevelt Presidency, December 3, 1906: *Sixth Annual Message to Congress*, University of Virginia Miller Center.

[36] Ross L. Finney, *Causes and Cures for the Social Unrest: An Appeal to the Middle Class* (New York, NY: Macmillan Co., 1922), 82-83.

[37] For an excellent succinct analysis, see "Coolidge Prosperity Gave America the Reserve to Weather the Great Depression," by Robert P. Kirby, Significant Papers, Coolidge Foundation, Nov. 13, 2012.

[38] Frank Annunziata, "The Progressive as Conservative: George Creel's Quarrel with New Deal Liberalism," *The Wisconsin Magazine of History*, Vol. 57, No. 3 (Spring, 1974), 224-25.

[39] Ibid. See also Arthur Link, *Woodrow Wilson and the Progressive Era, 1910-1917* (New York, NY: Harper & Row, 1963), 239

[40] For background, see Juliana Geran Pilon's *Why America Is Such a Hard Sell: Beyond Pride and Prejudice* (Latham, MD: Rowman & Littlefield Publishers, 2007), esp. Ch. 11. See also articles by former director of RFE/RL Ted Lipien at usagmwatch.com, for excellent exposes of Voice of America from its inception to today.

[41] Leo P. Ribuffo, "Henry Ford and 'The International Jew,'" *American Jewish History*, Vol. 69, No. 4 (June 1980), 438.

[42] See Kathleen M. Dalton, "Theodore Roosevelt, Knickerbocker Aristocrat," *New York History,* Vol. 67, No. 1, Jan. 1986, 39-65.

[43] Cited in Jeremy Menchik, "Woodrow Wilson and the Spirit of Liberal Internationalism," *Politics, Religion & Ideology*, March 25, 2021, 1-23.

[44] Hans Krabbendam, "'In the interests of all of us…': Theodore Roosevelt and the Launch of Immigration Restriction as an Executive Concern," *European journal of American studies* 10-2, Summer 2015, 1-25.

[45] Adds Krabbendam: "His most important legislative legacy regarding immigration was the Dillingham Commission, which laid the groundwork for the restrictive measures that were implemented in the 1920s. Later in the century, Europe would lose part of its privileged status, but never entirely." *Ibid.* For a comprehensive analysis of the Commission's impact see Robert F. Zeidel, *Immigrants, Progressives, and Exclusion Politics: The Dillingham Commission, 1900–1927* (DeKalb, IL: Northern Illinois University Press, 2004).

[46] Addditional sources: Donna R. Gabaccia, *Foreign Relations: American Immigration in Global Perspective* (Princeton, NJ: Princeton University Press, 2012), 133-39, and John M. Thompson, "Constraint and Opportunity: Theodore Roosevelt, Transatlantic Relations, and Domestic Politics," in Hans Krabbendam and John M. Thompson, eds., *America's Transatlantic Turn: Theodore Roosevelt and the "Discovery" of Europe* (Basingstoke, UK: Palgrave McMillan, 2012), 51-64.

Chapter V: Internationalized "Liberalism"

[1] Jim Powell, *Wilson's War: How Woodrow Wilson's Great Blunder Led to Hitler, Lenin, Stalin, and World War II* (New York, NY: Crown Forum, 2005), 80.

[2] *Ibid.,* 84.

[3] *Ibid.,* 99.
[4] George D. Herron, *Woodrow Wilson and the World's Peace* (New York, NY: M. Kennerley, 1917), 76-7; 142-3.
[5] Cited in Fred Siegel, "1919: Betrayal and the Birth of Modern Liberalism," *City Journal*, Nov. 22, 2009.
[6] Menchik, "Woodrow Wilson and the Spirit of Liberal Internationalism," *op cit.*
[7] Woodrow Wilson, 'The Modern Democratic State,' in Arthur S. Link, ed., *Woodrow Wilson: A Profile* (New York: Hill and Wang, 1968), Vol. 5, 63.
[8] *Ibid.*, 69.
[9] Woodrow Wilson, "An Annual Message on the State of the Union," *ibid.*, Vol. 67, 484-5.
[10] Joseph S. Nye, Jr. "Soft Power," *Foreign Policy*, No. 80, Twentieth Anniversary (Autumn, 1990), 153-171.
[11] See Derek Heater, *National Self-Determination: Woodrow Wilson and His Legacy* (New York, NY: St. Martin's Press, 1994), esp. 15-27. Cited in Allen Lynch, "Woodrow Wilson and the Principle of 'National Self-Determination': A Reconsideration," *Review of International Studies*, Apr., 2002, Vol. 28, No. 2, 424.
[12] Lynch, *ibid.,* 426.
[13] "Woodrow Wilson and the Principle of 'National Self-Determination': A Reconsideration," cited in *ibid.*
[14] *Ibid.*
[15] *Ibid.*, 433.
[16] *Papers Relating to the Foreign Relations of the United States*, 1922, 2 vols. (Washington, DC: Government
Printing Office, 1938), Vol. II, 873-4.
[17] See Richard H. Schultz and Roy Godson, *Dezinformatsia: Active Measures in Soviet Strategy* (McLean, VA: Pergamon-Brassey's Publishers, 1984).
[18] David Green, *Language of Politics in America*, 114-15.
[19] *Ibid.,* 116.
[20] Creel speech, September 22, 1933.
[21] Cited in Frank Annunziata, "The Progressive as Conservative," *op. cit.,* 224.:
[22] *Ibid.,* 226.
[23] *Ibid.*, 229.
[24] *Ibid.,* 120-21. Emphasis added.
[25] Ronald D. Rotunda, *The Politics of Language: Liberalism as Word and Symbol*, (Iowa City, IA: University of Iowa Press, 1986), 56.
[26] *Ibid.*, 59.
[27] Writes Rotunda: "Samuel Beer hypothesizes that to end this semantic problem the New Deal liberals called their opponents 'conservatives.' That [John] Dewey was trying to label the Hoover school of thought as reactionary and that the opponents of FDR complained that Hoover was being unjustly tagged as a conservative does support Beer's reasoning. However, since Hoover did not readily accept the appellation of 'conservative,' and since the United

States did not have a Liberal party that had the right to define "liberal," the confusion continued…" *Ibid.*, 66.

[28] *Ibid.*, 63.

[29] John Dewey, "A Liberal Speaks Out for Liberalism," *New York Times Magazine*, February 3, 1936, 3, 24.

[30] *Public Papers of the Presidents of the United States: F.D. Roosevelt*, 1938, Volume 7, xxix-xx.

[31] Green, *op. cit.,* 124.

[32] *Public Papers, op. cit.,* 586.

[33] See Amity Shlaes's copiously documented *Great Society: A New History* (New York, NY: Harper Books, 2019).

[34] For the State Department's treachery, see Eric Larson's superb bestseller *In the Garden of Beasts: Love, Terror, and an American Family in Hitler's Berlin* (New York, NY: Crown Books, 2011).

[35] Francois Furet, *The Passing of an Illusion: The Idea of Communism in the Twentieth Century,* (Chicago, IL: University of Chicago Press, 1999), 223.

[36] *Ibid.,* 224.

[37] In December 1989, the Congress of People's Deputies of the Soviet Union condemned the pact and its secret protocol as "legally deficient and invalid." Esther B. Fein, "Upheaval in the East: Soviet Congress Condemns '39 Pact That Led to Annexation of Baltics," *The New York Times*, 25 December 1989.

[38] "Max Kampelman, A Hard-Nosed Pacifist," Association for Diplomatic Studies and Training, https://adst.org/oral-history/fascinating-figures/max-kampelman-a-hard-nosed-pacifist/

[39] Cited in James J. Martin, *American Liberalism and World Politics, 1931-1941: Liberalism's Press and Spokesmen on the Road Back to War Between Mukden and Pearl Harbor* (New York, NY: The Devin-Adair Company, 1964), Volume II, 1273.

[40] *Ibid.,* 1274.

[41] *Ibid.*

[42] Green, *op. cit.*, 162-3.

[43] Amity Shlaes, "Herbert Hoover Was Wrong," *The Wall Street Journal*, Nov. 18, 2016.

[44] George H. Nash, "Forgotten Godfathers: Premature Jewish Conservatives and the Rise of National Review," Vol. 87, No. 2/3, 123-157.

[45] *Ibid.*

[46] "Frank S. Meyer," *Religion & Liberty*, Vol. 2, No. 5, July 20, 2010.

[47] Frank S. Meyer, *In Defense of Freedom: A Conservative Credo* (Chicago, IL: Henry Regnery Company, 1962), 1-2. Emphasis added.

[48] Frank Chodorov, *One is a Crowd* (New York, NY: The Devin-Adair Company, 1952), 39-40.

[49] John Earl Haynes and Harvey Klehr, *In Denial: Historians, Communism, and Espionage* (New York, NY: Encounter Books, 2003), 80. In 1992, Klehr became the first American researcher to examine the enormous collection. A year later, Haynes, in his capacity with the Manuscript Division of the Library

of Congress, became the first American expert to examine the treasure trove of CPUSA records included in that collection.

[50] Cited in *Ibid.* See also her *Age of McCarthyism: A Brief History with Documents*, 2nd ed. (New York, NY: St. Martin's Press, 2001; the first edition was published in 1994).

[51] *Ibid.*, 82-3.

[52] See Joshua Muravchik's moving obituary "The Man Who Knew Everything," *Commentary*, July/August 2013.

[53] See Joshua Muravchik's moving obituary "The Man Who Knew Everything," *Commentary*, July/August 2013.

[54] See "The Venona Story," Center for Cryptologic History National Security Agency, National Security Agency.

[55] "The classic cases were [Harry Dexter] White with Henry Morgenthau at the Treasury and Alger Hiss with Stettinius at State, but there were many similar match-ups elsewhere during the course of the Cold War struggle." M. Stanton Evans and Herbert Romerstein, *Stalin's Secret Agents: The Subversion of Roosevelt's Government* (New York, NY: Simon & Schuster, 2012), 255.

[56] Herb Romerstein and Eric Breindel, *The Venona Secrets: The Definitive Exposé of Soviet Espionage in America* (Washington, DC: Regnery Publishers, 2001), 437.

[57] *Ibid.*, 435.

[58] Though mainly a disinformation peddler, a Venona message from December, 1944, reported that Stone was among a group of journalists who provided Pravdin with information about the plans of the U.S. General Staff to cope with the German counteroffensive in the Battle of the Bulge. *Ibid.,* 434-5.

[59] Haynes and Klehr, *op. cit.,* 248-9.

[60] *Ibid.,* 17.

[61] Simon Appleford, "Revealing Political Bias - A Macroanalysis of 8,480 Herblock Cartoons, *Current Research in Digital History*, Vol. 1, 27 August 2018.

[62] "Although Block's cartoons formed just one element of the *Washington Post*'s editorial page, appearing alongside both editorials and readers' letters, they were given special prominence. Johanna Drucker's has argued that 'we *see* before we read…[which] predisposes us to reading according to specific graphic codes before we engage with the language of the text.' … Block's work had the opportunity to influence the reader's understanding of the day's events before other editorial content in the newspaper was read and contemplated." *Ibid.*

[63] Chris Lamb, "Drawing Power," *Journalism Studies*, vol. 8:5, Sept. 11, 2007, 715-729.

[64] Romerstein and Breindel, *op. cit.*, 454.

[65] Norman Podhoretz, *Why Are Jews Liberals?* (New York, NY: Doubleday, 2009), 131-2.

[66] Romerstein and Breindel, *op. cit.*, 451-3.

[67] Podhoretz, *Why are Jews Liberals?*, 138.

[68] *Ibid.*
[69] Furet, *Ibid.,* 283.
[70] *Ibid.*, 381.
[71] *Ibid.*, 384.
[72] *Ibid.*, 347.

Chapter VI: America's Jewish Problem

[1] Seymour Martin Lipset, "The Radical Right: A Problem for American Democracy," *The British Journal of Sociology*, Vol. 6, No. 2 (June 1955), 197-8.

[2] David McCullough, *Truman* (New York, NY: Simon & Schuster, 2003), 742.

[3] Ian J. Bickerton, "Dwight D Eisenhower and Israel: A New Look," *Australasian Journal of American Studies,* July, 1988, Vol. 7, No. 1, 1-12.

[4] Ben Sales and Laura E. Adkins, "'I think it's Israel': How Orthodox Jews became Republicans," JTA, Feb. 4, 2020.

[5] "Trump has strong support among Orthodox Jews, poll shows," *Ami Magazine*, December 19, 2019.

[6] The literature on this topic is gigantic; they include, besides Wistrich's *The Lethal Obsession, Anti-Judaism: The Western Tradition* (2013) by David Nirenberg and *Toward a Definition of Antisemitism* (1990) by Gavin I. Langmuir.

[7] "Semitic" is defined as relating to or denoting a family of languages that includes Hebrew, Arabic, and Aramaic and certain ancient languages such as Phoenician and Akkadian, constituting the main subgroup of the Afro-Asiatic family; it can also be applied to the peoples who speak Semitic languages, especially Hebrew and Arabic. There is no "Semitism" any more than "Indo-Americanism," "Anglo-Saxonism," or any other language-group-ism.

[8] Copiously researched (his sources span 12 languages), *From Ambivalence to Betrayal* is a zenith of the scholar's previous work. It is also deeply personal. Wistrich, who taught at the Hebrew University of Jerusalem and University College London, dedicated his life to documenting the wrong turn taken by his own idealistic co-religionists. He was born in 1945 in Soviet Kazakhstan, where his father, a former "fellow-traveler" of the Polish Communist Party, had been exiled along with his wife, a Socialist sympathizer. He experienced Soviet Communism and, later, Western Socialism, after the family moved to France and then England. After a stint as a college radical, he ended up writing a doctoral thesis at the University of London in the mid-1970s focusing on Karl Marx and Leon Trotsky. A series of superb studies of the Left followed, crowned by *A Lethal Obsession: Antisemitism—From Antiquity to the Global Jihad* (2010), which secured Wistrich's preeminence in this field.

[9] Wistrich, *A Lethal Obsession*, 108. Emphasis added.

[10] For an excellent biography of Marr's life and its context, see Moshe Zimmermann's *Wilhelm Marr: The Patriarch of Anti-Semitism* (Oxford, UK: Oxford University Press, 1987).

[11] Wistrich, *ibid.*

[12] Jerry Z. Muller, *Capitalism and the Jews* (Princeton, NJ: Princeton University Press, 2010), 41.

[13] *Ibid.*

[14] Juliana Geran Pilon, *The Utopian Conceit, op. cit.,* 140.

[15] Cited in Wistrich, *From Ambivalence to Betrayal,* 71.

[16] *Ibid.*

[17] Paul Johnson, "Marxism vs. Antisemitism," *Commentary*, April 1, 1984.

[18] Marx had other famous rabbis among his ancestors, among them Rabbi Judah ben Elaser Halevy Minz. Born in Mayence in 1408, in 1450 he fled persecution to Padua, where he became university professor. Others include the head of the Padua Yashiba, and Rabbi Aaron Lowow, rabbi of Trier, who died in 1712. See "Rabbinical Ancestry of Marx Moulded His Mind, Says Genealogist," *Jewish Telegraphic Agency*, June 19, 1923.

[19] *Karl Marx: Early Writings,* translated and edited by T. B. Bottomore (New York, NY: McGraw-Hill, 1964), esp. 36-40.

[20] Cited in Wistrich, *From Ambivalence to Betrayal,* 85.

[21] Cited in Michele Battini, *Socialism of Fools: Capitalism and Modern Anti-Semitism* (New York, NY: Columbia University Press, 2016), 43.

[22] Battini, *Ibid.*

[23] Michael Barone, *The New Americans: How the Melting Pot Can Work Again* (Washington, DC: Regnery Publishing, 2001), 231.

[24] Steven E. Aschheim, *At the Edges of Liberalism: Junctions of European, German, and Jewish History* (New York, NY: Palgrave Macmillan, 2012), 189.

[25] *Ibid.*

[26] Sarna, *op. cit.*, 195.

[27] Walter Rauschenbusch, "Christianizing the Social Order," Pestrito and Atto, eds., *American Progressivism*, 117.

[28] *Ibid.*

[29] Ronald J. Pestritto, *America Transformed: The Rise and Legacy of American Progressivism* (New York, NY: Encounter, 2021), 142.

[30] *Ibid.,* 135.

[31] *Ibid.,* 27.

[32] Solomon Schechter, *Aspects of Rabbinic Theology* (New York: Schocken Books, 1961). Cited in Feldman, 311. It is interesting to note that Schechter later founded the Conservative Jewish movement.

[33] Egal Feldman, "The Social Gospel and the Jews," *American Jewish Historical Quarterly*, Vol. 58, No. 3, March 1969, 308-322. https://www.jstor.org/stable/23876007

[34] Lyman Abbott, "America's Debt to Israel," *The Outlook*, Vol. LXXXIII, Dec. 9, 1905, 857-58.

[35] *Ibid.*
[36] Sarna, *op. cit.*, 198.
[37] *Ibid.,* 198.
[38] Louis D. Brandeis, "The Jewish Problem: How To Solve It," Speech to the Conference of Eastern Council of reform Rabbis, April 25, 1915.
[39] "Declaration of Principles," Pittsburgh Platform 1885.
[40] Brandeis, "The Jewish Problem," *op. cit.*
[41] William O. Douglass, "Louis Brandeis: Dangerous Because Incorruptible," *New York Times*, July 5, 1964, Section BR, 3.
[42] *Ibid.*, 234.
[43] *Ibid.,* 236. Barone cites Nathan Glazer and Daniel P. Moynihan, *Beyond the Melting Pot: The Negroes, Puerto Ricans, Jews, Italians, and Irish of New York City* (Cambridge, MA: 1963), 167-69.
[44] Many fine novels about the difficult plight of Jewish women are too little known. See for example Francis Booth's article on "Jewish Women in Novels by Early Jewish Female Writers," *Literary Ladies Guide*, Dec. 24, 2021.
[45] Nathan Glazer, *American Judaism* (Chicago, IL: University of Chicago Press, 1989), 46.
[46] Solomon Schindler, "First Steps to Nationalism," *Arena*, XIII (1895), 27-28. For a biographical sketch of Schindler, see Arthur Mann, "Solomon Schindler: Boston Radical," *New England Quarterly*, XXIII (1950), 453-76.
[47] Glazer, 47.
[48] *Ibid.,* 49.
[49] *Ibid.* Edward Bellamy (1850-1898) was a major figure in American socialist circles. As University of Massachusetts historian Howard Quint explains in his seminal history of American socialism, he resembled social reformer Henry George in that he too was "willing to use the government as an instrumentality for achieving social change. Unlike George, he could see no good whatever in the competitive principle."[49] Never having read Marx or Engels, Bellamy's communist views were nonetheless evident from his enormously influential novel Looking Backward: 2000 (1887), which describes a utopian state where private property had been abolished. By the end of the nineteenth century, it had sold more than 200,000 copies, more than almost any other book published in America up to that time.
[50] Glazer, *op.cit.*, 65.
[51] David Horowitz, *Radical Son: A Generational Odyssey* (New York, NY: Simon & Schuster, 1997), 42.
[52] *Ibid.*, 43.
[53] *Ibid.,* 44.
[54] Romerstein and Breindel, *Ibid.,* 398.
[55] *Ibid.*, 427.
[56] Ronald Takaki, *A Different Mirror: A History of Multicultural America* (New York, NY: Little, Brown and Co., 2008), 14.
[57] The most poignant and eloquent depiction of this generation is found in Irving Howe's classic *World of Our Fathers: The Journey of the East European*

Jews to America and the Life They Found and Made (New York, NY: New York University Press, 1977).

[58] Norman Podhoretz, *Why Are Jews Liberals?*, 103.

[59] Paul Johnson, *A History of the Jews* (New York, NY: Harper & Row, 1987), 371.

[60] *Ibid.*, 372.

[61] Cited in Ronald Steel, *Walter Lippmann and the American Century* (New York, NY: Little, Brown & Co., 1980), 194.

[62] Johnson, *op. cit.*, 469-70.

[63] John Earl Haynes, "Hellman and the Hollywood Inquisition: The Triumph of Spin-Control over Candour," *Film History*, vol 10, No. 3, 1998, 412.

[64] Father Charles E. Coughlin, "The National Union for Social Justice," Nov. 11, 1934, Social Security History.

[65] Robert Lacey, *Ford: The Men and the Machine* (New York, NY: Random House, 1986), 217-9. Comments Lacey: "If any one American were to be singled out for his contribution to the evils of Nazism, it would have to be Henry Ford. His republished articles and the currency which he gave to the Protocols… had considerable impact on Germany in the early 1920s – a vulnerable and, as it proved, crucially formative time." *Ibid.*, 229. See also Albert Lee, *Henry Ford and the Jews* (New York, NY: Stein and Day, 1980).

[66] Podhoretz, *Why Are Jews Liberals?,* 121.

[67] *Ibid.,* 122.

[68] *Ibid.*

[69] Franklin Delano Roosevelt, "The Right of the People to Rule," Pestrito and Atto, eds. *American Progressivism*, 251-60.

[70] Stephen Wise to B. A. Hoover, Sept. 8, 1936, cited in Rafael Medoff, *The Jews Should Keep Quiet: Franklin D. Roosevelt, Rabbi Stephen S. Wise, and the Holocaust* (Philadelphia, PA: Jewish Publication Society, 2019), 308.

[71] Medoff, *Ibid.,*301.

[72] *Ibid.,* 313.

[73] In an April 23, 1925, column for the *Daily Telegraph*, Roosevelt wrote that he favored the admission of some Europeans, so long as they had "blood of the right sort." For additional examples of FDR's racial prejudice, see Medoff, *ibid.,* Ch. 8, "Antisemitism in the White House," 283-295.

[74] For an impressively documented exposé of this appalling practice at the NYT, see *The Gray Lady Winked: How the New York Times's Misreporting, Distortions and Fabrications Radically Alter History*, by Ashley Rindsberg (Midnight Oil Publishers, 2021), esp. Ch. I, "Minding the Nazis Less than Most."

[75] Haskel Lowenstein, *Were We Our Brothers' Keepers?: The Public Response of American Jews to the Holocaust, 1938-1944* (New York, NY: Random House, 1988), 206. See also the superb study by David S. Wyman, *The Abandonment of the Jews: America and the Holocaust 1941-1945* (New York, NY: Random House, 1984).

[76] Medoff, *op. cit.*, 308.

[77] Glazer, *American Judaism*, 95.
[78] *Ibid*., 121.
[79] John J. Dziak, *Chekisty: A History of the KGB* (Lanham, MD: Lexington Books, 1988), 7.
[80] https://socialistrevolution.org/our-program/
[81] Dziak, *op.cit.,* 16.
[82] Podhoretz, *Why Are Jews Liberals?,* 122-23.
[83] Earl Browder, "Concerning American Revolutionary Traditions, *The Communist: A Magazine of the Theory and Practice of Marxism-Leninism,* Vol. 17, No. 12, December 1938, 1082. Marxist Revolutionary Archives.
[84] *Ibid*., 1081.
[85] Podhoretz, *ibid.,* 123. Emphasis added.
[86] Elliott Abrams, *Faith or Fear: How Jews Can Survive in a Christian America* (New York, NY: The Free Press, 1997), 128.
[87] *Ibid.,* 146.
[88] Steven M. Cohen, *American Modernity and Jewish Identity* (New York, NY: Tavistock Publications, 1983), 35. Cited in Abrams, *ibid*., 148.
[89] Chodorov, *One is a Crowd*, 32-33.
[90] *Ibid,* 56.
[91] *Ibid.,* 40.
[92] Cited in George H. Nash, *The Conservative Intellectual Movement in America Since 1945* (New York, NY: Basic Books, 1976), 17-18. This is by far one of the most accurate and comprehensive analyses of American conservatism and its relationship to liberalism.
[93] *Ibid.,* 174. Emphasis added.

Chapter VII: Revolutionary "Liberalism" and the Jews

[1] Rosenblatt, *op. cit*., 259.
[2] *Ibid*., 260.
[3]Jo Ann Boydston, ed., *John Dewey: The Later Works, 1925-1953: 1939-1941/Essays, Reviews, and Miscellany*, Vol. 14 (Southern Illinois University Press, 1988), 252.
[4] *Ibid.*
[5] See Juliana Geran Pilon, *The Art of Peace*, ch. 7: "Diplomacy and Commerce."
[6] "Dewey, "Presenting Thomas Jefferson," *ibid*., 219. Emphasis added.
[7] In all fairness, a genuinely sophisticated and highly nuanced explanation of the differences between the radical enlightenment views of Jefferson in contrast to the moderate liberalism of the Federalists may be found in Jonathan I. Israel's monumental study *The Enlightenment that Failed: Ideas, Revolution, and Democratic Defeat, 1748-1830* (Oxford, UK: Oxford University Press, 2020), esp. Ch.22. Dewey's casual analysis falls far short of that high standard.
[8] *Ibid*., 220. Emphasis added.

[9] Ludwig von Mises, *Socialism: An Economic and Sociological Analysis* (New Haven, CN: Yale University Press, 1951), 21.

[10] Richard A. Epstein's magisterial and seminal tome *The Classical Liberal Constitution: The Uncertain Quest for Limited Government* (Cambridge, MA: Harvard University Press, 2014), xi.

[11] Works of Jeremy Bentham, John Bowring, ed., (London, UK: Simpkin, Marshall & Co.,1843), Vol. II.

[12] Samuel Goldman, "Skokie Then and Now," *Mosaic*, April 5, 2021.

[13] *Ibid.*

[14] Hilton Kramer, "The Betrayal of Liberalism: I," *New Criterion*. Sep. 98, Vol. 17 Issue 1,

[15] The intellectuals of the *Partisan Review* are a who's-who of America's premier essayists at the time. They included William Phillips (born William Litvinsky), Philip Rahv (born Ivan Greenbaum) Sidney Hook, Lionel Trilling, Diana Trilling, F.W. Dupee, Mary McCarthy, Meyer Schapiro, Harold Rosenberg, Dwight Macdonald, Clement Greenberg, Lionel Abel, and James T. Farrell, joined later by Saul Bellow, Isaac Rosenfeld, William Barrett, Irving Howe, Elizabeth Hardwick, Delmore Schwartz, Alfred Kazin, Leslie Fiedler, Richard Chase, and Robert Warshow. A "third generation" included Hilton Kramer, Steven Marcus, Susan Sontag, and Norman Podhoretz. Ruth Wisse, "The New York (Jewish) Intellectuals," *Commentary* Nov 1987.

[16] Wisse, *ibid.*

[17] John Stuart Mill, "On Liberty," Project Guttenberg, January 10, 2011 [EBook #34901], 19.

[18] Herbert Marcuse, "Repressive Tolerance," in Robert Paul Wolff, Barrington Moore, Jr., and Herbert Marcuse, *A Critique of Pure Tolerance* (Boston, MA: Beacon Press, 1969), 95-137.

[19] Paul Hollander, *Political Pilgrims: Travels of Western Intellectuals to the Soviet Union, China and Cuba* (Oxford, UK: Oxford University Press, 1981), 206-7.

[20] Alexander Vassiliev Papers, White Notebook No. 3, notes that Neumann's KGB recruitment was approved on Jan. 2, 1943. See Diana West, *American Betrayal: The Secret Assault on Our Nation's Character* (New York, NY: St. Martin's Griffin, 2013), 286. This is the entry in the *Index and Concordance to Alexander Vassiliev's Notebooks and Soviet Cables Deciphered by the National Security Agency's Venona Project*: "Neumann, Franz: Soviet intelligence source/agent. Political scientist, left-wing theoretician, and anti-Nazi German exile in the U.S. After American entered WWII Neumann became an analyst in the German section of OSS. Cover name in After American entered WWII Neumann became an analyst in the German section of OSS. Cover name in Vassiliev's notebooks: "Ruff." Cover name in Venona: RUFF [ERSH]. As Neumann: Vassiliev Black Notebook, 78; Vassiliev White Notebook #1, 58; Vassiliev White Notebook #3, 133. As "Ruff": Vassiliev Black Notebook, 78; *Vassiliev White Notebook #1*, 2, 11,

51, 58; *Vassiliev White Notebook #3*, 131, 133–36. As RUFF [ERSH]: Venona New York KGB 1943, 82–83, 86, 103–4, 127; Venona Special Studies, 26.," 298.

[21] It goes on to list where Marcuse is mentioned: "*Vassiliev White Notebook #1*, 51. *Vassiliev White Notebook #3*, 134–35; *Venona NewYork KGB 1945*, 30–31." *Ibid.*, 264.

[22] See Ralph de Toledano's *Cry Havoc!, op.cit.*

[23] Marcuse, *ibid.*

[24] Marcuse cites J.S. Mill's *Considerations on Representative Government* (Chicago, IL: Regnery Gateway, 1962), 183.

[25] Herbert Marcuse, *Eros and Civilization: A Philosophical Inquiry into Freud* (New York, NY: Vintage Books, 1955), 181.

[26] *Ibid.*

[27] See James A. Rushing, 'The Limitations of the Fencing Bear: Kleist's "Über das Marionettentheater" as Ironic Fiction,' *The German Quarterly* 61:4 (1988), 528-39.

[28] Herbert Marcuse, "Preface to the Vintage Edition," *Eros and Civilization*, viii.

[29] Paul Berman, *A Tale of Two Utopias: The Political Journey of the Generation of 1968* (New York, NY: W.W. Norton & Company, 1996), 228.

[30] Cited in Christopher Swift, "Herbert Marcuse on the New Left: Dialectic and Rhetoric," *Rhetoric Society Quarterly*, 40:2, 2010, 159-60. Swift uses his own translation of Marcuse's speech "On the New Left," and corrects errors in the original transcript.

[31] *Ibid.*, 162-3.

[32] *Ibid.*, 163.

[33] "Herbert Marcuse on the Question of Revolution," *New Left Review*, I/45, Sept/Oct 1967.

[34] Robert Paul Wolff, Barrington Moore, Jr., and Herbert Marcuse, *A Critique of Pure Tolerance* (Boston: Beacon Press, 1969), Includes 1968 Postscript by Herbert Marcuse.

[35] At the time, Avraham Schenker was the head of the Organization and Information Dept. of the Jewish Agency and the World Zionist Organization. In 1947, he had been a Founder of Americans for Progressive Israel, which was to function as a less ideologically-based support organization by the *Hashomer Hatzair*, a socialist-Zionist organization. API's periodical, *Israel Horizons*, was created initially by the Progressive Zionist League in 1952. In 1997, API merged with Education Fund for Israeli Civil Rights and Peace and became Meretz USA. In 2011, Meretz changed its name to Partners for Progressive Israel.

[36] Avraham Schenker, "The New Left, Israel, and the Jewish People,"

[37] Herbert Marcuse, *An Essay on Liberation* (Boston, MA: Beacon Press, 1969), 21.

[38] Oswald Bayer, "Marcuse's Critique of Luther's Concept of Freedom," *Lutheran Quarterly*, Baltimore Vol. 32, Iss. 2 (Summer 2018), 173-204.

[39] Vincent Gheogegan, "Marcuse and 'the Christian Bourgeois Concept of Freedom,'" *Telos* 165 (Winter 2013), 49–67.

[40] Christopher Swift, "Herbert Marcuse on the New Left: Dialectic and Rhetoric," *Rhetoric Society Quarterly*, March 25, 2010, 40:2, 162.

[41] Podhoretz, *Why Are Jews Liberal?*, 148-9.

[42] *Ibid.*, 153.

[43] *Ibid.*, 154.

[44] Peter Collier and David Horowitz, *Destructive Generation: Second Thoughts About the Sixties* (New York, NY: Encounter Books, 2005), 344.

[45] *Ibid.*, 345.

[46] "Leonard Bernstein: Causes and Effecting Change," *The Social Activist*, Sept. 24 – Dec. 13, 2008.

[47] Tom Wolfe, "Radical Chic: That Party at Lenny's," *New York Magazine*, June 8, 1970, 37.

[48] *Ibid.*, 77.

[49] *Ibid.*, 80.

[50] Berman, *op. cit.*, 63.

[51] Tom Hayden, *Writings for a Democratic Society: The Tom Hayden Reader* (San Francisco, CA: City Lights Books, 2008), ch. 2.

[52] See the superb book by Gen. H.R. McMaster, *Dereliction of Duty: Johnson, McNamara, the Joint Chiefs of Staff, and the Lies That Led to Vietnam* (New York, NY: HarperCollins Publishers, 1998).

[53] Roger Kimball, *The Long March: How the Cultural Revolution of the 1960s Changed America* (New York, NY: Encounter Books, 2001), 31-2.

[54] Susan Sontag, *Trip to Hanoi: Journey to a City at War* (New York, NY: HarperCollins, 1969), 87.

[55] Yippies were members of the Youth International Party (YIP), a loosely organized group of radicals founded by Rubin along with activist Abbie Hoffman and satirist Paul Krassner, who specialized in visual stunts designed to bring media attention to anti-Vietnam and other radical protests.

[56] Jerry Rubin, *Do It* (New York, NY: Simon & Schuster, 1970), 105.

[57] Richard J. Barnet and Marcus Raskin, *An American Manifesto* (New York: New American Library, 1970), 23-24.

[58] Susan Sontag, "The Pornographic Imagination" (1967), in *Styles of Radical Will* (New York, NY: Picador, 2002), 35-73.

[59] Kimball, *op. cit.* 91.

[60] *Ibid.*, 93.

[61] Jonathan Cott, "Susan Sontag: The Rolling Stone Interview," *RollingStone*, Oct. 4, 1979.

[62] Marion K. Sanders, *The Professional Radical: Conversations with Saul Alinsky* (New York, NY: Harper and Row, 1970) 27.

[63] *Ibid.*, 28.

[64] Saul Alinsky, *Rules for Radicals: A Practical Primer for Realistic Radicals* (New York, NY: Vintage, 1989), xviii.

[65] *Ibid.*

[66] *Ibid.*, xii.
[67] See the author's *The Art of Peace: Engaging a Complex World* (New York, NY: Routledge, Inc., 2016).
[68] From John Adams to Hezekiah Niles, 13 February 1818.
[69] Alinsky, *op. cit.*, xxiii.
[70] Hillary D. Rodham, "There is only the fight…: An Analysis of the Alinsky Model," Unpublished Thesis, Wellesley College, Wellesley, MA, 2 May, 1969. https://archive.org/details/HillaryClintonThesis/mode/2up
[71] She cites from Dan Dodson, "The Church, POWER, and Saul Alinsky," *Religion in Life* (Spring 1967), 12.
[72] Saul D. Alinsky, "The War on Poverty – Political Pornography," Chaim I. Waxman, ed., *Poverty: Power and Politics* (New York, NY: Grosset & Dunlap, 1968), 173-175.
[73] Hillary D. Rodham, Unpublished Thesis, *op. cit.*

Chapter VIII: Statist "Liberalism"

[1] See Peter Schweizer, *Clinton Cash: The Untold Story of How and Why Foreign Governments and Businesses Helped Make Bill and Hillary Rich* (New York, NY: Harper Books, 2016).
[2] Her citation from Alinsky's 1967 speech, "Is there life after birth?" Rodham, *op. cit.,* 69.
[3] Bryan Burrough, *Days of Rage: America's Radical Underground, the FBI, and the Forgotten Age of Revolutionary Violence* (New York, NY: Penguin Books, 2016).
[4] Dialogue - An Interview with Bill Ayers, *The Point,* Issue 5, Jan. 15, 2012.
[5] Kimball, *The Long March, op. cit.,* 12.
[6] *Ibid.*, 103.
[7] *Ibid.*, 105-6.
[8] Thomas Sowell, *The Quest for Cosmic Justice* (New York, NY: The Free Press, 1999), 12.
[9] *Ibid.*
[10] Ibid., 51.
[11] Ronald Dworkin, *Taking Rights Seriously* (Cambridge, MA: Harvard University Press, 1931), 239.
[12] Chris Edwards and Ryan Bourne, "Exploring Wealth Inequality," Cato Institute, Policy Analysis No. 881, Nov. 5, 2019.
[13] François Furet, *The Passing of an Illusion: The Idea of Communism in the Twentieth Century* (Chicago, IL: University of Chicago Press, 1995), 10.
[14] *Ibid.*, 10-11.
[15] Democratic Socialists of America website, https://www.dsausa.org/about-us/
[16] Nathan Pinkoski, "The Strange Rise of Bourgeois Bolshevism," *Law & Liberty*, May 1, 2020.
[17] Nathan Pinkoski, "Socialism and the Exhaustion of American Liberalism," *Law & Liberty*, May 29, 2020.

[18] Pinkoski, "The Strange Rise of Bourgeois Bolshevism."
[19] Ruth R. Wisse, "A Threat Assessment for American Jewry, Part Two," *Mosaic* 8-4-21.
[20] *Ibid.*
[21] David Horowitz, *The Black Book of the American Left* (New York, NY: Encounter Books, 2012), Vol. 1, "My Life and Times," 155.
[22] *Ibid.*, 157.
[23] *Ibid.*, 159.
[24] *Ibid.*
[25] *Ibid.*, 391.
[26] Isaac Deutscher, *The Non-Jewish Jew and Other Essays* (Oxford, UK: Oxford University Press, 1968), 51.
[27] Proceedings from their NFF conference *Destructive Generation: Second Thoughts About the Sixties*, was published in 1990 by Summit Books, reissued by Encounter Books in 2005.
[28] See Juliana Geran Pilon, *The Bloody Flag: Post-Communist Nationalism in Eastern Europe - Spotlight on Romania* (Piscataway, NJ: Transaction Publishers, 1992).
[29] Wisse, *If I Am Not for Myself*, 189.
[30] Ruth Wisse, "What the Children of American Jewish Communists Needed, and What They Owe," *Mosaic Magazin*e, Feb. 2, 2022.
[31] Podhoretz, *Why Are Jews Liberals?*, 282.
[32] Irving Howe, in Robert Alter, "Liberalism & the Jews: A Symposium," *Commentary*, Jan. 1980.
[33] Podhoretz, *ibid.*
[34] "Rabbi to the rescue," *The Economist*, Aug. 2, 2014.
[35] *Ibid.*
[36] Jonathan Neumann, *To Heal the World? How the Jewish Left Corrupts Judaism and Endangers Israel* (New York, NY: All Points Books, St. Martin's Press, 2018), xii.
[37] *Ibid.*, xv.
[38] Mordecai M. Kaplan, *The Meaning of God in Modern Jewish Religion* (1937) (Detroit, MI: Wayne University Press, 1995), 23-24.
[39] Barnet, Richard J., *Intervention and revolution; the United States in the Third World* (New York: World Pub.Co., 1968).
[40] See Joshua Muravchik's review of *Covert Cadre: Inside the Institute for Policy Studies*, by S. Steven Powell in *Commentary*, October 1988. For the latest research on IPS, see Robert Stilson's "Institute for Policy Studies: The Left's Original Think Tank," Capital Research Center's *Organization Trends*, Aug. 30, 2022, and the entry for IPS at www.InfluenceWatch.
[41] Michael Strassfeld and Sharon Strassfeld, eds, *The Third Jewish Catalog: Creating Community* (New York, NY: Jewish Publication Society of America, 1980), 47.
[42] Kaplan, *op. cit.*, 24-25.

[43]Alan Dershowitz, "Tikkun Magazine Is Trying to Silence Me," *HuffPost*, July 4, 2010.

[44] Joshua A. Berman, *Created Equal, op.cit.*

[45] Daniel Greenfield, "The ADL's new Jewish outreach director hates Jews," *JNS,* January 31, 2022.

[46] *Ibid.*

[47] Daniel Greenfield, "The ADL Convenes a Summit of Anti-Semites to Fight Anti-Semitism," *FrontPage Magazine*, Nov. 10, 2021.

[48] Jonathan Neumann, *op.cit*, 189.

[49] *Ibid.,* 190.

[50] Peter Beinart, "The Failure of the American Jewish Establishment," *Forward*, May 26, 2010. First published in *The New York Review of Books*, May 12, 2010

[51] Cited in Neumann, *op. cit.,* 208.

[52] *Ibid.*, 210-211.

[53] Wisse, "What the Children of American Jewish Communists Needed…," *op. cit.*

[54] Norman Podhoretz, *Making It* (New York, NY: New York Review of Books, 2017), Introduction.

[55] *Ibid.*

[56] *Ibid.*

[57] "Kurt Lewin's explanation of the phenomenon was that in low-status minority groups, the desire arises for the respect and rewards enjoyed by the higher-status minority." Raphael Patai, *The Jewish Mind* (Detroit, MI: Wayne University Press, 1996), 461.

[58] For a splendid comprehensive study of this critical intellectual movement, see Jonathan Israel's magisterial *The Enlightenment that Failed: Ideas, Revolution, and Democratic Defeat, 1748-1830* (Oxford University Press, 2020), *passim*, esp. 850.

[59] Patai, 462-3.

[60] *Ibid.*, 479.

[61] Ruth R. Wisse, *Free as a Jew: A Personal Memoir of National Self-Liberation* (New York, NY: Post Hill Press, 2021), 142.

[62] *Ibid.,* 178-9.

[63] *Ibid.*, 253.

[64] Ronald Radosh, "How America's Largest Socialist Organization Went from Supporting Israel to Boycotting it, Mosaic, Dec. 30, 2021.

[65] See David Caute, *The Fellow-Travellers: A Postcript to the Enlightenment* (New York, NY: Macmillan Company, 1973), ch. 1.

[66] *Ibid.*

[67] Peter Berkowitz, "The Clash Within Liberal Democracy: Israel, the United States, and the West," *Mosaic*, July 21, 2021.

Chapter IX: Global Anti-Liberalism and Antisemitism

[1] Cited in Wistrich, *The Lethal Obsession*, 554.

[2] *Ibid.*, 556.

[3] Ruhollah Khomeini, "American plots against Iran," Iranian Central Insurance Office Staff, 5 November 1979.

[4] Wistrich, *ibid.*, 553.

[5] Yossi Klein Halevi, "Hatreds Entwined," *Azure*, No. 16 (Winter 2004), 25-32.

[6] *Ibid.*

[7] Barry Rubin and Judith Colpin Rubin, *Hating America: A History* (Oxford, UK: Oxford University Press, 2004) 229.

[8] Ruth Wisse, "The Allure of Jewish Power," *Sapir*, Vol. 2, summer 2021.

[9] See Pilon, *The Utopian Conceit*, 140.

[10] Wisse, "The Allure of Jewish Power."

[11] Wistrich, *The Lethal Obsession,* 126.

[12] Wistrich, *From Ambivalence to Betrayal: The Left, the Jews, and Israel* (Lincoln, NE: University of Nebraska Press, 2012), 59. Wistrich cites Jonathan Brent and Vladimir P. Naumov, *Stalin's Last Crime: The Plot Against the Jewish Doctors, 1948-1953* (New York, NY: Harper-Collins, 2003).

[13] Jonathan Brent and Vladimir P. Naumov, *Stalin's Last Crime: The Plot Against the Jewish Doctors, 1948-1953* (New York, NY: Harper Perennial, 2004), 103.

[14] *Ibid.*, 104.

[15] For a powerful description of how that horrible treachery affected their families, see Dora Horn's interview with Ala Zuskin, daughter of Benjamin Zuskin, one of the two founders of the Jewish Antifascist Committee, in *People Love Dead Jews: Reports from a Haunted Present* (New York, NY: W. W. Norton, 2021).

[16] Binjamin W. Segel, in Richard S. Levy, *A Lie and a Libel: The History of the Protocols of the Elders of Zion* (Lincoln, Nebraska: University of Nebraska Press, 1996), 55.

[17] Victoria Saker Woeste, Henry Ford's War on Jews and the Legal Battle Against Hate Speech (Palo Alto, CA: Stanford University Press, 2013), 31.
Stephen Harlan Norwood and Eunice G. Pollack, *Encyclopedia of American Jewish History*, Vol. 1., ABC-CLIO, August 2007, 182.

[18] Less well known is the fate of the 300 workers, many of them Jews, who moved to Russia in the early 30s to build a Ford factory in the city of Gorky. Among them was Victor Herman, whose extraordinary book *Coming Out of the Ice,* described spending 18 years as a Soviet prisoner in Siberia after having been arrested in 1938 for "counter-revolutionary activities." I met Victor in 1979 at my family's home in Detroit, where he had been born; my parents and I became good friends with him. The Ford Motor Company did nothing to help him.

[19] Dana Dalrymple, "The American Tractor Comes to Soviet Agriculture: The Transfer of a Technology," *Technology and Culture*, no. 2 (1964), 191. Cited in Kendalle E. Bailes, "The American Connection: Ideology and the Transfer of American Technology to the Soviet Union, 1917-1941," *Comparative Studies in Society and History*, July 1981, Vol. 23, No. 3, 436.

[20] Michael Dobbs, "Ford and GM Scrutinized for Alleged Nazi Collaboration," *The Washington Post*, November 30, 1998. "Even after the U.S. entered the war, making it illegal for car companies to have any contact with their subsidiaries on German-controlled territory, they did so indirectly, and continued to rely on forced labor."

[21] Ion Mihai Pacepa with Ronald Rychlak, *Disinformation: Former Spy Chief Reveals Secret Strategies for Undermining Freedom, Attacking Religion, and Promoting Terrorism* (Washington, DC: WND Books, 2013), 96.

[22] *Ibid.*, 97.

[23] United Nations A/RES/3379 (XXX) November 10, 1975.

[24] Wistrich, *The Lethal Obsession*, 61.

[25] Josef Joffe, "Nations We Love to Hate: Israel, America and the New Antisemitism," (Jerusalem: Vidal Sassoon International Center for the Study of Antisemitism, 2005), 1.

[26] Dr. Arnon Groiss and Dr. Ronni Shaked, "Schoolbooks of the Palestinian Authority (PA): The Attitude to the Jews, to Israel and to Peace," The Simon Wiesenthal Center and the Middle East Forum, Sept. 2017.

[27] It is worth noting that such textbooks have been funded by the United States ever since UNRWA's establishment in 1949, except for a brief hiatus from 2018 until 2021. When the annual $150 million was reinstated by the Biden administration on April 5, 2021, Voice of America reported that Secretary of State Antony Blinken justified the large check on the ground that it "supports Israeli-Palestinian understanding, security coordination and stability. It also aligns with the values and interests of our allies and partners." That was either false or Israel is neither. For its U.N. ambassador, Gilad Erdan, expressed his "disappointment and objection to the decision to renew UNRWA's funding without first ensuring that certain reforms, including stopping the incitement and removing anti-Semitic content from its educational curriculum, are carried out."[27] Margaret Besheer, "US Resumes Aid to Palestinians With $235 Million," *Voice of America*, Apr. 7, 2021.

[28] See "Joseph Goebbels: On the 'Big Lie,'" in the Jewish Virtual Library, A Project of The American-Israeli Cooperative Enterprise (AICE).

[29] For an excellent demonstration of its use by Western media, specifically *The Washington Post* and *The New York Times*, see Eric Rozenman's *Jews Make the Best Demons: "Palestine" and the Jewish Question* (Nashville, TN: New English Review Press, 2018)

[30] Robert Fine and Philip Spencer, *Antisemitism and the left: On the return of the Jewish question* (Manchester, UK: Manchester University Press, 2017), 116.

[31] *Ibid.*, 124.

[32] Manifesto of the Congress to the Peoples of the East, September 1, 1920. https://lefteast.org/baku-manifesto/

[33] Pilon, *The Utopian Conceit*, 157-164.

[34] Barry Rubin & Wolfgang G. Schwanitz, *Nazis, Islamists, and the Making of the Modern Middle East* (New Haven, CT: Yale University Press, 2014), 71.

[35] Laurent Murawiec, *The Mind of Jihad* (Cambridge, UK: Cambridge University Press, 2008), 203.

[36] Alexandre A. Bennigsen and S. Enders Wimbush, *Muslim National Communism in the Soviet Union: A Revolutionary Strategy for the Colonial World* (Chicago, IL: University of Chicago Press, 1979), xxi. The book is a remarkably detailed analysis of the Bolshevik Communists' evolving tactics, involving national and religious flexibility in an effort to expand Soviet power.

[37] The Communist International (Comintern), also known as the Third International (1919–1943), was an international organization that advocated world communism. It was controlled by the Soviet Union.

[38] See Ilan Berman, *Tehran Rising* (Lanham, MD: Rowman & Littlefield, 2005), 12.

[39] Mahmoud Abbas, in Ronald Cohn and Jesse Russell, eds. *The Other Side: The Secret Relationship Between Nazism and Zionism* (Bookvika Publishing, 2012).

[40] Ronen Bergman, "Abbas' book reveals: The 'Nazi-Zionist plot' of the Holocaust," *Ynetnews.com*, Nov. 26, 2014.

[41] Paul Hockenos, *Joshka Fischer and the Making of the Berlin Republic: An Alternative History of Postwar Germany* (Oxford, UK: Oxford University Press, 2008), 90.

[42] Izabella Tabarovsky, "Soviet Anti-Zionism and Contemporary Left Antisemitism," *Fathom*, May 2019.

[43] Paul Berman, "The Passion of Joschka Fischer," *The New Republic*, Aug. 27, 2001.

[44] Wistrich, *From Ambivalence to Betrayal,* 519.

[45] *Ibid.*

[46] Alana Goodman, "Google Diversity Head Said Jews Have 'Insatiable Appetite for War,'" *Washington Free Beacon*, June 1, 2021.

[47] Will Feuer and Yaron Steinbuch, "Google Reassigns Diversity Chief Who Wrote Jews Have 'an Insatiable Appetite for War,'" *New York Post*, June 3, 2021.

[48] https://jewishdiasporatech.org/

[49] "7 Problems with the Human Rights Council," UN Watch.

[50] A version of this section appeared as "Democratic Internationalism Is Orwellian Newspeak for Illiberal Globalism" in *DocEmetProductions* on April 30, 2022.

[51] Wisse, *If I am Not for Myself*, 90.

[52] James Ceaser, "The Philosophical Origins of Anti-Americanism in Europe," in Paul Hollander, ed., *Understanding Anti-Americanism: Its Origins and Impact at Home and Abroad* (Chicago, IL: Ivan Dee, 2004), 49.

[53] *Ibid.,* 45.

[54] Paul Hollander, *Understanding Anti-Americanism: Its Origins and Impact at Home and Abroad* (Chicago, IL: Ivan Dee, 2004), 12.

[55] *Ibid.*

[56] George Orwell, "Notes on Nationalism," in *England Your England and Other Essays* (London, UK: Secker and Warburg, 1953).

[57] *Ibid.* Here Orwell adds this footnote: "Nations, and even vaguer entities such as the Catholic Church or the proletariat, are commonly thought of as individuals and often referred to as 'she.' Patently absurd remarks such as 'Germany is naturally treacherous' are to be found in any newspaper one opens, and reckless generalizations about national character ('The Spaniard is a natural aristocrat' or 'Every Englishman is a hypocrite') are uttered by almost everyone. Intermittently these generalizations are seen to be unfounded, but the habit of making them persists, and people of professedly international outlook, e.g. Tolstoy or Bernard Shaw, are often guilty of them."

[58] "Speech Delivered by Stalin at a Meeting of Voters of the Stalin Electoral District, Moscow," February 9, 1946, History and Public Policy Program Digital Archive (Moscow: Gospolitizdat, 1946).

[59]Manfred Gerstenfeld, "The Multiple Distortions of Holocaust Memory," Jerusalem Center for Public Affairs, Oct. 28, 2007, Also, Manfred Gerstenfeld, *The Abuse of Holocaust Memory: Distortions and Responses* (Jerusalem, Israel: Jerusalem Center for Public Affairs, 2009).

[60] Sheryl Gay Stolberg, "A 'Calming Feeling,' a Frenzy and a New Front in the War Over Anti-Semitism," *New York Times*, May 13, 2019.

[61] Barack H. Obama, "Statement from the President on Passover," The White House, April 3, 2015.

[62] *President Woodrow Wilson's 14 Points* (1918)

[63] Beate Jahn, "Liberal internationalism: historical trajectory and current prospects," *International Affairs* 94: 1 (2018)

[64] G. John Ikenberry, *Liberal Leviathan: the origins, crisis, and transformation of the American world order* (Princeton: Princeton University Press, 2011), esp. ch. 6.

[65] Daniel Deudney and G. John Ikenberry, "The Nature and Sources of Liberal International Order," *Review of International Studies*, Apr., 1999, Vol. 25, No. 2 (Apr., 1999) 179-196.

[66] Daniel Deudney and G. John Ikenberry, "Democratic Internationalism: An American Grand Strategy for a Post-exceptionalist Era," Council on Foreign Relations Working Paper, November 15, 2012.

[67] For a meticulously documented analysis of Obama's ideological development, see Stanley Kurtz's *Radical-in-Chief: Barack Obama and the Untold Story of American Socialism* (New York, NY: Simon & Schuster, Inc., 2010).

[68] Elliott Abrams, "What the President Thinks He's Doing - The ideological roots of his disastrous Iran strategy," *Mosaic*, Feb. 9, 2015.

[69] Deudney and Ikenberry, *op. cit.,* 1.

[70] *Ibid*., 22.

[71] The term is defined as "a network of professionals with recognised expertise and competence in a particular domain and an authoritative claim to policy relevant knowledge within that domain or issue-area." Peter M. Hass, "Introduction: epistemic communities and international policy coordination." *International Organization*, special issue*: Knowledge, Power, and International Policy Coordination*, Cambridge Journals, Winter 1992, 46 (1): 1–35.

[72] John Fonte, *Sovereignty or Submission: Will Americans Rule Themselves or Be Ruled by Others?* (New York, NY: Encounter Books, 2011), xx.

[73] Kenneth Anderson, "Secular Eschatologies and Class Interests of the Internationalized New Class," in Peter Juviler and Carrie Gustafson, eds., *Religion and Human Rights: Competing Claims* (New York, NY: M.E. Sharpe, 1998), 107-116.

[74] Kenneth Anderson, "After Seattle: Public International Organizations, Non-Governmental Organizations (NGOs), and Democratic Sovereignty in an Era of Globalization - An Essay in Contested Legitimacy" Draft, Aug. 29, 2000, 179. Anderson accuses this group of elite organizations putatively concerned with "human rights" of being served by "liberal internationalism's package deal of liberal global governance and the regulated global market." Ibid., 180.

[75] The International Forum for Social Development, *Social Justice in an Open World - The Role of the United Nations*, UN Department of Economic and Social Affairs, Division for Social Policy and Development, 2006.

[76] Aaron Rhodes, *The Debasement of Human Rights* (New York, NY: Encounter Books, 2018), 99.

[77] Ludwig Wittgenstein, *Philosophical Investigations* (Malden, MA: Blackwell, 2001), § 38.

[78] Ludwig Wittgenstein, *Tractatus Logico-Philosophicus*. Translated by David Pears and Brian McGuinness (London: Routledge, 1961), 4.003.

Conclusion: "Freedom in the Fullest Sense"

[1] Louis Hartz, *The Liberal Tradition in America,* (New York, NY: Harcourt, Brace & World, Inc., 1955), 48.

[2] *Ibid*., 49.

[3] See Bruce Caldwell, ed., *Mont Pèlerin 1947: Transcripts of the Founding Meeting of the Mont Pèlerin Society* (Stanford, CA: Hoover Institution Press, 2022).

[4] Milton Friedman with Rose Friedman, *Capitalism and Freedom* (Chicago: University of Chicago Press, 1962), Ch. 2.

[5] F. A. Hayek, "Why I Am Not a Conservative," *The Constitution of Liberty: The Definitive Edition* (Chicago, IL: University of Chicago Press, 2011), 517-33.

---

[6] Milton and Rose Friedman, *Ibid.*
[7] *Ibid.*
[8] Hannes H. Gissurarson, Twenty-Four Conservative-Liberal Thinkers, Part I, (Brussels, Belgium: New Directions, 2020, 11.
[9] Hayek, "Why I Am Not a Conservative," *op. cit.*
[10] *Ibid.*
[11] https://www.poetryfoundation.org/poems/45477/song-of-myself-1892-version
[12] "Walt Whitman 'more important now than ever," University of Rochester Newscenter, March 22, 2022.
[13] P. J. Grisar, "How Columbus brought America its first Jew," *Forward*, Oct. 11, 2021. See also Maria Rosa Menocal, *The Ornament of the World: How Muslims, Jews and Christians Created a Culture of Tolerance in Medieval Spain* (New York, NY: Back Bay Books, 2003)
[14] Jonathan Ray, *After Expulsion: 1492 and the Making of Sephardic Jewry* (New York, NY: New York University Press, 2013), 11 ff.
[15] John Locke, *Second Treatise of Government* (Indianapolis, IN: Hackett Publishing Co., 1980), ch. V, par. 49, 29.
[16] *Ibid.*, ch. IX, sec. 123, 66.
[17] Hartz, *op. cit.*, 41.
[18] Among his best known are *Patterns In Comparative Religion, Myth And Reality, The Myth Of The Eternal Return,* and *History Of Religious Ideas,* among many others.
[19] See Jonathan Israel, *The Enlightenment that Failed.*
[20] From Benjamin Franklin to Thomas Paine, Dec. 13, 1757, National Archives, Founders Online.
[21] Abraham Lincoln, Eulogy on Henry Clay, July 6, 1852, Springfield, Illinois.
[22] Rabbi Meir Y. Soloveichik, "When Lincoln Died on Passover," *Jewish World Review*, April 15, 2015.
[23] *Ibid.*
[24] Jeffrey Bloom, Alec Goldstein, and Gil Student, eds., *Strauss, Spinoza & Sinai: Orthodox Judaism and Modern Questions of Faith* (New York, NY: Kodesh Press, 2022), 307.
[25] Tocqueville, *Democracy in America*, Book I, ch. III.
[26] Milton and Rose Friedman, *Free to Choose: A Personal Statement* (New York, NY: Harcourt, Brace, Jovanovich, 1980), Ch. V, 135.
[27] Milton Friedman, "Capitalism and the Jews," *Foundation for Economic Education (FEE)*, Oct. 1, 1988.
[28] Werner Cohn, Sources of American Jewish Liberalism: A study of the political alignments of American Jews (New York, NY: New School for Social Research ProQuest Dissertations Publishing, 1956).
[29] Ruth R. Wisse, "Threat Assessment for American Jewry," Part Two, *Mosaic* 8-4-21
[30] Wisse, *If I am Not for Myself*, 83.

---

[31] Samuel J. Abrams, "New Study Shows Jewish Students Are Self-Censoring, but Are They Also Leading the Push to Censor Others?" *Jewish Journal*, Sept. 27, 2022.

[32] Wisse, *Free As a Jew*, 393.

[33] Hannah Arendt, *On Revolution* (New York, NY: Penguin Books, 1963), 85. Irving Louis Horowitz credits Arendt and Tocqueville for truly understanding the distinction between passion and compassion as the great divide of modernity. That divide above all "forms the intellectual background to the American discussions of capitalism in the post-[Second World]war environment," argues Horowitz. "It is a schism between nothing less than the anti-capitalist spirit on one side and the anti-totalitarian spirit on the other." Irving Louis Horowitz, *Behemoth: Main Currents in the History and Theory of Political Sociology* (New York, NY: Routledge, 1999), 349.

[34] Alexis de Tocqueville, *The Old Regime and the Revolution*, transl. by John Bonner (New York, NY: Harper Brothers Publishers, 1856) Book I, Ch. XV.

[35] Ruth R. Wisse, "Is the Writing on the Wall for America's Jews?" *Mosaic*, Aug. 8, 2022

[36] Foreword to *Woke Antisemitism: How a Progressive Ideology Harms Jews*, by David L. Bernstein (New York, NY: Post Hill Books, 2022).

[37] Bernstein, *ibid.*, 23.

[38] He explains: "I use the terms 'liberal,' 'liberalism,' and 'liberal values,' by which I mean classical, small-L liberal values: freedom of expression, free speech, and civil liberties operating under the rule of law." *Ibid.*, 14.

[39] *Ibid.*, 150.

[40] Leil Leibovitz, "Us and Them," *Tablet,* May 25, 2021.

[41] Ruth R. Wisse, "What Can American Jews Do?" *Mosaic*, Sept. 21, 2022

***

Bibliography

Arthur T. Abernethy, *The Jew a Negro, Being a Study of the Jewish Ancestry from an Impartial Standpoint* (Moravian Falls, NC, 1910).

Elliott Abrams, *Faith or Fear: How Jews Can Survive in a Christian America* (New York, NY: The Free Press, 1997)

Henry Adams, *The Education of Henry Adams* (1907) from *Novels, Mont Saint Michel, The Education* (New York, NY: Library of America, 1983)

Saul Alinsky, *Rules for Radicals: A Practical Primer for Realistic Radicals* (New York, NY: Vintage, 1989)

Charles M. Andrews, *The Colonial Background of the American Revolution* (New Haven, CT: Yale University Press, 1961)

Hannah Arendt, *On Revolution* (New York, NY: Penguin Books, 1963)

Bernard Bailyn, *The Ideological Origins of the American Revolution* (Cambridge, MA: Harvard University Press, 1967)

Bernard Bailyn, ed., *The Debate on the Constitution* (New York: The Library of America, 1993)

Bernard Bailyn, *The Barbarous Years* (New York, NY: Alfred A. Knopf, 2012)

John M. Barry, *Roger Williams and the Creation of the American Soul: Church, State, and the Birth of Liberty* (New York, NY: Penguin Books, 2012)

Michele Battini, *Socialism of Fools: Capitalism and Modern Anti-Semitism* (New York, NY: Columbia University Press, 2016)

Carl L Becker, *The Declaration of Independence a Study in the History of Political Ideas* (New York, NY: Vintage, 1942)

Joshua A. Berman, *Created Equal: How the Bible Broke with Ancient Political Thought* (Oxford: Oxford University Press, 2011)

David L. Bernstein, *Woke Antisemitism: How a Progressive Ideology Harms Jews* (New York, NY: Post Hill Books, 2022)

Bryan Burrough, *Days of Rage: America's Radical Underground, the FBI, and the Forgotten Age of Revolutionary Violence* (New York, NY: Penguin Books, 2016)

C. Banc and Alan Dundes, *You Call This Living?: A Collection of East European Political Jokes* (Athens, GA: University of Georgia Press, 1990)

John M. Barry, *Roger Williams and the Creation of the American Soul: Church, State, and the Birth of Liberty* (New York, NY: Penguin Books, 2012)

Carl L Becker, *The Declaration of Independence a Study in the History of Political Ideas* (New York, NY: Vintage, 1942)

Alexandre A. Bennigsen and S. Enders Wimbush, *Muslim National Communism in the Soviet Union: A Revolutionary Strategy for the Colonial World* (Chicago, IL: University of Chicago Press, 1979)

Sacvan Bercovitch, *The Puritan Origins of the American Self* (New Haven, CT: Yale University Press, 1975)

Ilan Berman, *Tehran Rising* (Lanham, MD: Rowman & Littlefield, 2005)

Joshua A. Berman, *Created Equal: How the Bible Broke with Ancient Political Thought* (Oxford: Oxford University Press, 2011)

Paul Berman, *A Tale of Two Utopias: The Political Journey of the Generation of 1968* (New York, NY: W.W. Norton & Company, 1996)

Paolo Bernardini and Norman Fiering, eds., *The Jews and the Expansion of Europe to the West, 1450-1800* (Oxford: Berghahn Books, 2004)

Iver Bernstein, *The New York City Draft Riots: Their Significance for American Society and Politics in the Age of the Civil War* (Oxford, UK: Oxford University Press, 1991)

Stephen Birmingham, *The Grandees: America's Sephardic Elite* (New York, NY: Harper & Row, 1971)

Joseph Blenkinsopp, *Judaism, the First Phase: The Place of Ezra and Nehemiah in the Origins of Judaism* (Grand Rapids, MI: Eerdmans, 2009)

David W. Blight, *Frederick Douglass: Prophet of Freedom* (New York, NY: Simon & Schuester, 2020)

Jo Ann Boydston, ed., *John Dewey: The Later Works, 1925-1953: 1939-1941/Essays, Reviews, and Miscellany*, Vol. 14 (Southern Illinois University Press, 1988)

Theodore Dwight Bozeman, *To Live Ancient Lives: The Primitivist Dimension in Puritanism* (Williamsburg, VA: Institute of Early American History, 1988)

Vladimir Bukovsky, *To Build a Castle: My Life as a Dissenter* (New York, NY: 1979)

Edmund Burke, *The Writings and Speeches of Edmund Burke*, ed. Paul Langford et al. (Oxford, UK: Oxford University Press, 1981-2015)

Bryan Burrough, *Days of Rage: America's Radical Underground, the FBI, and the Forgotten Age of Revolutionary Violence* (New York, NY: Penguin Books, 2016)

Frank Chodorov, *One is a Crowd* (New York, NY: The Devin-Adair Company, 1952)

Adam Cohen, *Imbeciles: The Supreme Court, Eugenics, and the Sterilization of Carrie Buck* (New York, NY: 2016)

Naomi W. Cohen, *Jews in Christian America: The Pursuit of Religious Equality* (Oxford: Oxford University Press, 1992)

Steven M. Cohen, *American Modernity and Jewish Identity* (New York, NY: Tavistock Publications, 1983)

Peter Collier and David Horowitz, *Destructive Generation: Second Thoughts About the Sixties* (New York, NY: Encounter Books, 2005)

Michael Coogan, *God's Favorites: Judaism, Christianity, and the Myth of Divine Chosenness* (Boston, MA: Beacon Press, 2019)

Lewis Coser, *The Functions of Social Conflict* (New York, NY: The Free Press, 1956)

Joseph Cropsey, *Polity and Economy: Further Thoughts on the Principles of Adam Smith* (South Bend, IN: St. Augustine Press, 2001)

Robert Curry, *Common Sense Nation: Unlocking the Forgotten Power of the American Idea* (New York, NY: Encounter Books, 2015)

John Dewey, *Individualism, Old and New* (New York, NY: Capricorn, 1962)

John Dewey, *Liberalism and Social Action* (Amherst, N.Y.: Prometheus Books, 2000)

John Dewey, *The Problems of Men* (New York, NY: Philosophical Library, 1946)

Ronald Dworkin, *Taking Rights Seriously* (Cambridge, MA: Harvard University Press, 1931)

John J. Dziak, *Chekisty: A History of the KGB* (Lanham, MD: Lexington Books, 1988)

Daniel J. Elazar, *Covenant and Constitutionalism: The Covenant Tradition in Politics,* Vol. III (New York, NY: Routledge, 1998)

Elon Menahem, *Jewish Law: History, Sources, Principles*, trans. Bernard Auerbach and Melvin J. Sykes (Jerusalem: Jewish Publication Society, 1994)

Richard A. Epstein, *The Classical Liberal Constitution: The Uncertain Quest for Limited Government* (Cambridge, MA: Harvard University Press, 2014)

Eli N. Evans, *Judah P. Benjamin: The Jewish Confederate* (New York: The Free Press, 1988)

M. Stanton Evans and Herbert Romerstein, *Stalin's Secret Agents: The Subversion of Roosevelt's Government* (New York, NY: Simon & Schuster, 2012)

Robert Fine and Philip Spencer, *Antisemitism and the left: On the return of the Jewish question* (Manchester, UK: Manchester University Press, 2017)

Ross L. Finney, *Causes and Cures for the Social Unrest: An Appeal to the Middle Class* (New York, NY: Macmillan Co., 1922)

John Fonte, *Sovereignty or Submission: Will Americans Rule Themselves or Be Ruled by Others?* (New York, NY: Encounter Books, 2011)

Michael Freeden, *Ideology: A Very Short Introduction* (Oxford: Oxford University Press, 2003)

Milton and Rose Friedman, *Free to Choose: A Personal Statement* (New York, NY: Harcourt, Brace, Jovanovich, 1980)

David Fromkin, *A Peace to End All Peace* (New York, NY: Henry Holt and Company, 1989)

François Furet, *The Passing of an Illusion: The Idea of Communism in the Twentieth Century* (Chicago, IL: University of Chicago Press, 1995)

Henry Louis Gates, Jr., ed., *Douglass: Autobiographies* (New York: Library of America, 1994)

Nathan Glazer, *American Judaism* (Chicago, IL: University of Chicago Press, 1989)

Sander L. Gilman, *Freud, Race, and Gender* (Princeton, NJ: Princeton University Press, 1995)

David Green, *The Language of Politics in America: Shaping Political Consciousness from McKinley to Reagan* (Ithaca, NY: Cornell University Press, 1987)

Samuel Gregg, *Reason, Faith, and the Struggle for Western Civilization* (Washington, DC: Regnery Gateway, 2019)

Alan C. Guelzo, *Reconstruction: A Concise History* (Oxford: Oxford University Press, 2018)

Derek Heater, *National Self-Determination: Woodrow Wilson and His Legacy* (New York, NY: St. Martin's Press, 1994)

Arthur Herman, *How the Scots Invented the Modern World* (New York, NY: Three Rivers Press, 2001)

George D. Herron, *Woodrow Wilson and the World's Peace* (New York, NY: M. Kennerley, 1917)

Michael Hoberman, *New Israel / New England: Jews and Puritans in Early America* (Amherst, MA: University of Massachusetts Press, 2011)

Richard Hofstadter, *The Age of Reform: From Bryan to F.D.R.* (New York, NY: Random House, 1955)

Paul Hollander, *Political Pilgrims: Travels of Western Intellectuals to the Soviet Union, China and Cuba* (Oxford, UK: Oxford University Press, 1981)

Paul Hollander, ed., *Understanding Anti-Americanism: Its Origins and Impact at Home and Abroad* (Chicago, IL: Ivan Dee, 2004)

David Horowitz, *Radical Son: A Generational Odyssey* (New York, NY: Simon & Schuster, 1997)

David Horowitz, *The Black Book of the American Left* (New York, NY: Encounter Books, 2012), Vol. 1, "My Life and Times."

Irving Louis Horowitz, *Behemoth: Main Currents in the History and Theory of Political Sociology* (New York, NY: Routledge, 1999)

Jacob Howland, *Plato and the Talmud* (Cambridge, UK: Cambridge University Press, 2011)

Francis Hutcheson, *A System Of Moral Philosophy: In Three Books: To which is Prefixed Some Account Of The Life, Writings, And Character Of The Author,* Vol. 1 (London: Millar, 1755)

Jonathan I. Israel, *The Enlightenment that Failed: Ideas, Revolution, and Democratic Defeat, 1748-1830* (Oxford, UK: Oxford University Press, 2020)

William James, *The Meaning of Truth* (New York, NY: Longman Green and Co.,1911)

Paul Johnson, *A History of the Jews* (New York, NY: Harper & Row, 1987)

W. K. Jordan, *The Development of Religious Toleration in England: From the Convention of the Long Parliament to the Restoration (1640-1660)* (Cambridge, MA: Harvard University Press, 1932)

Alan S. Kahan, *Mind Vs. Money: The War Between Intellectuals and Capitalism* (New Brunswick, NJ: Transaction Publishers, 2010)

Mordecai M. Kaplan, *The Meaning of God in Modern Jewish Religion* (1937) (Detroit, MI: Wayne University Press, 1995)

Leon Kass, *The Beginning of Wisdom: Reading Genesis* (Chicago, IL: University of Chicago Press, 2003)

Henry Kissinger, *Diplomacy* (New York, NY: Simon and Schuster, 1994)

Julia Kristeva, *Powers of Horror: An Essay on Abjection* (New York, NY: Columbia University Press, 1982)

Emma Lazarus, *An Epistle to the Hebrews* (New York, NY: Federation of American Zionists, 1900)

Joseph Lifshitz, *Judaism, Law & The Free Market: An Analysis* (Grand Rapids, MI: Acton Institute, 2012)

Arthur S. Link, ed., *Woodrow Wilson: A Profile* (New York: Hill and Wang, 1968)

Haskel Lowenstein, *Were We Our Brothers' Keepers?: The Public Response of American Jews to the Holocaust, 1938-1944* (New York, NY: Random House, 1988)

Edward Lurie, *Louis Agassiz: A Life in Science* (Chicago, IL: University of Chicago Press, 1960)

Daniel J. Mahoney, *Recovering Politics, Civilization, and the Soul: Essays on Pierre Manent and Roger Scruton* (South Bend, IN: St. Augustine's Press, 2022)

Pierre Manent, *An Intellectual History of Liberalism* (Princeton, NJ: Princeton University Press, 1996)

Herbert Marcuse, *Eros and Civilization: A Philosophical Inquiry into Freud* (New York, NY: Vintage Books, 1955)

Karl Marx: Early Writings, translated and edited by T. B. Bottomore (New York, NY: McGraw-Hill, 1964)

Allen J. Matusow, *The Unraveling of America: A History of Liberalism in the 1960s* (Athens, GA: University of Georgia Press, 2009)

Michael McGerr, *A Fierce Discontent: The Rise and Fall of the Progressive Movement in America* (New York, NY: Free Press, 2010)

Meredith L. McGill, ed., *The Traffic in Poems: Nineteenth-Century Poetry and Transatlantic Exchange* (New Brunswick, NJ: Rutgers University Press, 2008)

Rafael Medoff, *The Jews Should Keep Quiet: Franklin D. Roosevelt, Rabbi Stephen S. Wise, and the Holocaust* (Philadelphia, PA: Jewish Publication Society, 2019)

Louis Menand, *The Metaphysical Club: A Story of Ideas in America* (New York, NY: Farrar, Straus and Giroux, 2002)

Arthur M. Mendel. *Vision and Violence,* Richard Landes, ed. (Ann Arbor, MI: University of Michigan Press, 1999)

Frank S. Meyer, *In Defense of Freedom: A Conservative Credo* (Chicago, IL: Henry Regnery Company, 1962)

John Stuart Mill, *Utilitarianism* (1863), Project Guttenberg, February 22, 2004

John Stuart Mill, "On Liberty," Project Guttenberg, January 10, 2011 [EBook #34901]

Ludwig von Mises, *Socialism: An Economic and Sociological Analysis* (New Haven, CN: Yale University Press, 1951)

Ludwig von Mises, *Nation, State, and Economy: Contributions to the Politics and History of Our Time* (New York and London: New York University Press, 1983)

Stewart Mitchell, ed., *Winthrop Papers* (Boston, 1931)

Thomas More, *Utopia* (New Haven, CT: Yale University Press, 2001)

Jerry Z. Muller, *Capitalism and the Jews* (Princeton, NJ: Princeton University Press, 2010)

George H. Nash, *The Conservative Intellectual Movement in America Since 1945* (New York, NY: Basic Books, 1976)

Jonathan Neumann, *To Heal the World? How the Jewish Left Corrupts Judaism and Endangers Israel* (New York, NY: All Points Books, St. Martin's Press, 2018)

Daniel Okrent, *Last Call: The Rise and Fall of Prohibition* (New York, NY: Scribner, 2010)

George Orwell, *England Your England and Other Essays* (London, UK: Secker and Warburg, 1953)

Ion Mihai Pacepa with Ronald Rychlak, *Disinformation: Former Spy Chief Reveals Secret Strategies for Undermining Freedom, Attacking Religion, and Promoting Terrorism* (Washington, DC: WND Books, 2013)

Vernon Parrington, "Roger Williams, Seeker," *Main Currents in American Thought* (New York, NY: Harcourt Brace and Co., 1927)

Raphael Patai, *The Jewish Mind* (Detroit, MI: Wayne University Press, 1996)

Ronald J. Pestritto, *America Transformed: The Rise and Legacy of American Progressivism* (New York, NY: Encounter, 2021)

Ronald J. Pestritto and William J. Atto, eds., *American Progressivism* (Lanham, MD: Rowman & Littlefield, 2008)

See Juliana Geran Pilon, *The Bloody Flag: Post-Communist Nationalism in Eastern Europe - Spotlight on Romania* (Piscataway, NJ: Transaction Publishers, 1992)

Juliana Geran Pilon, *Why America Is Such a Hard Sell? Beyond Pride and Prejudice* (Latham, MD: Rowman & Littlefield, Inc., 2007)

Juliana Geran Pilon, *Soulmates: Resurrecting Eve* (New York, NY: Routledge, Inc., 2012)

Juliana Geran Pilon, *The Art of Peace: Engaging a Complex World* (New York, NY: Routledge, Inc., 2016)

Juliana Geran Pilon, *The Utopian Conceit and the War on Freedom* (New York, NY: Routledge, Inc., 2019)

Norman Podhoretz, *Why Are Jews Liberals?* (New York, NY: Doubleday, 2009)

Norman Podhoretz, *Making It* (New York, NY: New York Review of Books, 2017),

Jim Powell, *Wilson's War: How Woodrow Wilson's Great Blunder Led to Hitler, Lenin, Stalin, and World War II* (New York, NY: Crown Forum, 2005)

Carl J. Richard, *Greeks & Romans Bearing Gifts: How the Ancients Inspired the Founding Fathers* (Latham, MD: Rowman & Littlefield Publishers, 2009)

Aaron Rhodes, *The Debasement of Human Rights* (New York, NY: Encounter Books, 2018)

Helena Rosenblatt, *The Lost History of Liberalism: From Ancient Rome to the Twenty-First Century* (Princeton, NJ: Princeton University Press, 2018)

Eric Rozenman, *Jews Make the Best Demons: "Palestine" and the Jewish Question* (Nashville, TN: New English Review Press, 2018)

Ronald D. Rotunda, *The Politics of Language: Liberalism as Word and Symbol*, (Iowa City, IA: University of Iowa Press, 1986)

Barry Rubin and Judith Colpin Rubin, *Hating America: A History* (Oxford, UK: Oxford University Press, 2004)

Barry Rubin & Wolfgang G. Schwanitz, *Nazis, Islamists, and the Making of the Modern Middle East* (New Haven, CT: Yale University Press, 2014)

Rabbi Jonathan Sacks, *The Dignity of Difference: How to Avoid the Clash of Civilizations* (Oxford, UK: Oxford University Press, 2002)

Timothy Sandefur, *Frederick Douglass: Self-Made Man* (Washington, DC: Cato Institute, 2018)

Marion K. Sanders, *The Professional Radical: Conversations with Saul Alinsky* (New York, NY: Harper and Row, 1970)

Jonathan D. Sarna, *American Judaism: A History* (New Haven, CT: Yale University Press, 2004)

Arthur Schlesinger, Jr., *The Politics of Hope* (Princeton, NJ: Princeton University Press, 2008)

Peter Schweizer, *Clinton Cash: The Untold Story of How and Why Foreign Governments and Businesses Helped Make Bill and Hillary Rich* (New York, NY: Harper Books, 2016)

Eran Shalev, *American Zion: The Old Testament as a Political Text from the Revolution to the Civil War* (New Haven, CN: Yale University Press, 2013)

George Bernard Shaw, *An Unsocial Socialist* (New York NY: Brentano's, 1900)

Adam Smith, *An Inquiry into the Nature and Causes of the Wealth of Nations*, 5th edition (Methuen and Co., Ltd., 1789)

Anthony D. Smith, *Chosen Peoples: Sacred Sources of National Identity* (Oxford, UK: Oxford University Press (January 1, 2004)

Susan Sontag, *Styles of Radical Will* (New York, NY: Picador, 2002)

Thomas Sowell, *The Quest for Cosmic Justice* (New York, NY: The Free Press, 1999)

Ronald Steel, *Walter Lippmann and the American Century* (New York, NY: Little, Brown & Co., 1980)

Ronald Takaki, *A Different Mirror: A History of Multicultural America* (New York, NY: Little, Brown and Co., 2008)

C. Bradley Thompson, *America's Revolutionary Mind: A Moral History of the American Revolution and the Declaration That Defined It* (New York, NY: Encounter Books, 2019)

Alexis de Tocqueville, *Democracy in America* (New York, NY: Vintage Books, 1945)

Alexis de Tocqueville, *The Old Regime and the Revolution*, transl. by John Bonner (New York, NY: Harper Brothers Publishers, 1856)

James W. Trent, Jr., *Inventing the Feeble Mind: A History of Mental Retardation in the United States* (Oxford: Oxford University Press, 2016)

Sean Wilentz, *No Property in Man: Slavery and Antislavery at the Nation's Founding* (Cambridge, MA: Harvard University Press, 2019)

Roger Williams, *The Complete Writings of Roger Williams* (New York, NY: Russell and Russell, 1963)

Enoch Cobb Wines, *Commentaries on the Laws of the Ancient Hebrews* (New York, NY: Geo. P. Putnam & Co., 1853)

Ruth R. Wisse, *Jews and Power* (New York, NY: Shocken Books, 2007)

Ruth R. Wisse, *No Joke: Making Jewish Humor* (Princeton, NJ: Princeton University Press, 2013)

Ruth R. Wisse, *Free as a Jew: A Personal Memoir of National Self-Liberation* (New York, NY: Post Hill Press, 2021)

Robert S. Wistrich, ed., *Demonizing the Other: Antisemitism, Racism, and Xenophobia* (Amsterdam: Harwood Academic Publishers, 1999)

Robert S. Wistrich, *A Lethal Obsession: Antisemitism from Antiquity to the Global Jihad* (New York, NY: Random House, 2010)

Robert S. Wistrich, *From Ambivalence to Betrayal: The Left, the Jews, and Israel* (Lincoln, NE: University of Nebraska Press, 2012)

Ludwig Wittgenstein, *Tractatus Logico-Philosophicus* (London: Routledge & Kegan Paul, 1922)

Robert Paul Wolff, Barrington Moore, Jr., and Herbert Marcuse, *A Critique of Pure Tolerance* (Boston, MA: Beacon Press, 1969)

Arthur Zilversmit, *First Emancipation: the abolition of slavery in the North* (Chicago, IL: University of Chicago Press, 1967)

Index

C

X

Y

Z